E STREET SHUFFLE

Also by Clinton Heylin

All The Madmen: A Journey to the Dark Side of English Rock

So Long As Men Can Breathe: The Untold Story of Shakespeare's Sonnets

Still on the Road: The Songs of Bob Dylan vol. 2 (1974–2008)

Revolution In The Air: The Songs of Bob Dylan vol. 1 (1957–73)

The Act You've Known For All These Years:
A Year In The Life of Sgt. Pepper and Friends

Babylon's Burning: From Punk to Grunge

From The Velvets To The Voidoids: The Birth of American Punk

All Yesterdays' Parties: The Velvet Underground in Print 1966–71 [editor]

Despite The System: Orson Welles versus The Hollywood Studios

Bootleg – The Rise & Fall of the Secret Recording Industry

Can You Feel The Silence? – Van Morrison: A New Biography

No More Sad Refrains: The Life & Times of Sandy Denny

Bob Dylan: Behind The Shades

Dylan's Daemon Lover: The Tangled Tale of a 450-Year-Old Pop Ballad

Dylan Day By Day: A Life In Stolen Moments

Never Mind The Bollocks, Here's The Sex Pistols

Bob Dylan: The Recording Sessions 1960–94

The Great White Wonders: A History of Rock Bootlegs

The Penguin Book of Rock & Roll Writing [editor]

Gypsy Love Songs & Sad Refrains:
The Recordings of Sandy Denny & Richard Thompson

Rise/Fall: The Story of Public Image Limited

Joy Division: Form & Substance [with Craig Wood]

E STREET SHUFFLE

The Glory Days of Bruce Springsteen & the E Street Band

CLINTON HEYLIN

Constable • London

For Erik, keeper of the faith
last of the true believers.

Constable & Robinson Ltd
55–56 Russell Square
London WC1B 4HP
www.constablerobinson.com

First published in the UK by Constable,
an imprint of Constable & Robinson Ltd, 2012

A copy of the British Library Cataloguing in
Publication data is available from the British Library

ISBN: 978-1-78033-579-7 (hardback)
978-1-78033-580-3 (ebook)

Printed and bound in the UK

1 3 5 7 9 10 8 6 4 2

Contents

I'm always going to trust the art and be suspicious of the artist because he's generally . . . a stumbling clown like everybody else.
– Bruce Springsteen, 2006

May 2, 2012 – Mama Knows 'Rithmetic

It fell out on a May evening . . .

I find myself in the pit, a green band around my wrist, at the brand-spanking-new Prudential Center in Newark. New York 'muso' Richard has opened the door and I have stepped in for my first E Street show since 2004's Vote For Change, when Springsteen had sounded hoarse from all that hectoring. Tonight, he is saying farewell to the arena leg of the *Wrecking Ball* tour. Stadia beckon – again. But for now, he has a home-state audience in a hyped-up state of mind, iPhones akimbo, ready to greet their returning hero. And suddenly there he is, declaiming to the rafters with the first surprise of the evening, 'No Surrender', the truest anthem on that mountainous multi-million seller, *Born In The USA*.

Alongside me are legionnaires of true believers, one of whom, Larry, had been telling me about seeing him at Joe's Place, a cramped, crumbling Boston bar that had been the E Street Band's home away from home in 1973-74; when 'Rosalita' came out every night and torched the place. A broad grin etches his face when the big boss man announces, half a dozen songs in, that he is gonna do a song he'd never played, well, maybe once: 'Bishop danced with a thumb-screw woman/ Did a double-quick back flip and slid across the floor'.

'Bishop Danced' had been the opening track on a classic seventies Springsteen LP, *Fire On The Fingertips*. Just not one that Bruce himself okayed for release. Rather, it was spawned among the stalls of Camden Lock. A bootleg. But for the hard core, this mattered not. It was a lost Bruce classic, transformed by the band arrangement it never got back in 1973. (He *had* done it more than once – and in Boston – but the last documented version was in Berkeley, March 2 1973.)

And then, as if reading our minds, Springsteen segues into 'Saint In The City' – another blast from the past he rarely takes for a spin these days – and a thought flashes across my mind. May 2. It was forty years ago today that a callow kid from Freehold walked into the office of John Hammond, the legendary A&R man who discovered Billie Holiday, Count Basie, Aretha Franklin and Dylan, and played him a song that knocked his socks off. The self-same 'Saint'.

After this, the show settles into its routine; but in my mind's eye, I am already in rewind, back to the days when he spent his afternoons at WBCN, debuting the likes of 'Bishop Danced' and 'Rosalita' over the radio, and his evenings at Joe's Place. Or Max's. Or The Main Point. And I'm thinking this is a surprisingly good facsimile of those moments and that band; but a facsimile, nonetheless. How he got there – and got from there to here – is the story of the *E Street Shuffle*. And quite a story it is. Because, as he told an expectant audience in Austin this very March:

> 'I had nights and nights of bar-playing behind me to bring my songs home . . . These skills gave me a huge ace up my sleeve. And when we finally went on the road, and we played that ace, we scorched the Earth'.

Prehistory: 1964–72 – Kicked Open A Door To Your Mind

> Till I was thirteen, the body was presumed dead; and that's how I feel about my whole life up till then. I was just reeling through space and bouncing off the walls, and bouncing off people, and I didn't find anything to hold on to or any connection whatsoever; until the rock & roll thing and the guitar. When I found that . . . the other stuff just didn't matter any more. – Bruce Springsteen, 1978

When Jesus gently chastised his wealthy follower, Nicodemus, 'Except a man be born again, he cannot see the kingdom of God,' he presumably did not have in mind the same 'born again' experience which led thirteen-year-old Bruce Springsteen into apostasy. Here was someone who only found 'the Spirit' when he cast aside the teachings of J.C., previously laid down with an iron hand by a series of matriarchal authority figures, from the nuns at the local convent school he attended prior to high school to the mother who presided over the Springsteens' dilapidated leasehold in Freehold, New Jersey.

If Jesus' own take on rebellion failed to lay a seed in Springsteen's mind, the one true religion which by AD 325 garbled records of his pithy sayings had spawned wrapped its talons around the boy from the cradle. But not to the grave. Even if its primary message stayed with him until at least 1981, when he told one Belgian interviewer 'My Catholic education taught me to have fear. This is a religious experience in which you don't look up to heaven, but to the people around you.'

A year later he would write 'My Father's House', the first of several post-therapy compositions to address that time when he lived his whole life in fear. On introducing that song in concert, he struck the same keynote: 'I remember when I was a kid, first thing I can ever remember being afraid of was the devil . . . I guess, my mother was taking me to church and all I heard was about the devil all the time.' As he grew older, that fear turned first to shame and then to anger; because, as he sagely put it in his early thirties, when his replacement religion was no longer fulfilling his deepest needs either, 'That kind of fear is demolishing and shameful . . . It darkens the spirit of religion.'

That resentment had already spewed forth in song: initially, in 1971-72, ones of blasphemous angels and irreverent messiahs. By 1981-82, the themes had become existential terror and endemic faithlessness. For now, it just made him want to vomit: 'There's this smell of religion, this smell that convents have, well, every time I went there I got sick. I just threw up.' What he perhaps failed to appreciate at the time was that his mother's faith probably provided her only solace in a life without hope and a town without pity: Freehold NJ. And it was there that the young Bruce spent his formative years, at first at his maternal grandparents' house, as his parents scrimped and saved to try and raise enough money to strike out on their own. Bruce, meanwhile, was already developing a fascination with the radio – not the music it broadcast, but the thing itself. As he told a Michigan audience in September 1978, prefacing the unsparing 'Factory':

> We all lived at my grandparents'. It was a house that had the first church service and it had the first funeral in town in this house. My grandfather, he was an electrician, and he used to fix second-hand radios. And I remember when I was five years old, before we were to leave [there], he used to take me with him outside of town in the summer. They used to have mining workers, used to come off from the South and work in the fields outside of town, he used to sell 'em radios.

In fact, he had already celebrated his grandfather, Mr Zerilli, in song. One of the first compositions he presented to Mike Appel when signed to a production deal in the spring of 1972 was an autobiographical piece called simply 'Randolph Street'. In it he sought to convey a world through the eyes of a child, one who sees his grandfather as 'a master of the art of electricity' who 'lectured on tubes and circuitry / He was self-employed, but he could never see his way into the light / He had a room full of switches and dials . . . / And a head full of clouds and eyes full of sight'. If a penchant for imbuing ordinary people with magical powers was thus evident this early, songs of autobiography would not prove to be the way he would find himself.

Like many a bright kid living in a cloistered, claustrophobic environment, he retired into the world of imagination when he was barely old enough for school, a form of escape he shared with fellow New Jerseyite Patti Smith, born three years earlier to similar circumstances: an agnostic ex-soldier father, a zealot of a Christian for a Mom, white-trash poor. Not surprisingly, he was quickly labelled a dreamer by his teachers, who failed to provide the intellectual stimulus he sorely needed, and most certainly wasn't receiving at home; especially after the Springsteens finally flew the grandparents' coop to set up home down on South Street.

Barely had they changed homes than the Springsteens had another mouth to feed, and Bruce had a lil' sister. Though it only made tough times still tougher, Springsteen remembered the period after Pamela was born in 1962 as 'one of the best times I can ever remember . . . because it changed the atmosphere of the whole house for quite a while'. (Again an experience he shared with the young Patti, who later wrote the magnificent 'Kimberly' about the night her younger sister was born.) But for the boy from the Jersey shore it seemed Life had already dissuaded Opportunity from making house-calls on the Springsteens. As he later told a St Louis audience, 'I grew up in a house where . . . there wasn't a lot of things that make you aware of the possibilities that you have in life.' Even when it came to the realm of politics, it seemed the adults brooked no discussion – Bruce was informed he was a Democrat, and that was that:

> **Bruce Springsteen**: The only political discussion I ever remember in my house was when I came home from school when I was little . . . It must have been during an election season . . . I was probably . . . eight or nine. And I came home and said, 'Mom, what are we?' And she said, 'Oh, we're Democrats. We're Democrats because they're for the working people.' And that was it – that was the [extent of] political discussion that went on in my house. [2004]

After his pubescent rock 'n' roll epiphany, he would not feel this lack of any intellectual stimulus so keenly. Only in full-blown middle age would he recognize how great the loss had been: 'I didn't grow up in a community of ideas – a place where you can sit down and talk about books, and how you read them, and how they affect you . . . I'm more a product of popular culture.' Fortunately, the popular culture he refers to was enjoying one of its most inspired epochs, which TV and radio ensured seeped into every US household, no matter how close to the breadline. And the Springsteens never managed to do more than make ends meet for their growing family, and sometimes not even that:

> **Bruce Springsteen**: I lived in a household that was caught in the squeeze, endlessly trying to make ends meet. My mother running down to the finance company, borrowing money to have a Christmas, and then paying it back all year until the next Christmas and borrowing some more. So I know what that's like. [2004]

It was Bruce's mother, Adele, who was often the only one who kept hungry wolves at bay. Though his father had once known job security at a plastics factory, in the years before he took his wife to California in 1969 the head of the household bounced from pillar to temporary post in a series of unskilled and unchallenging short-term jobs. The experience left an indelible mark on his son, captured in a couplet he would later cut from 1982's 'Glory Days': 'I was nine years old when he was working at the Metuchen Ford plant assembly line / Now he just sits on a stool down at the Legion Hall, but I can tell what's on his mind'. By then, the not-so-young Bruce could admit, 'There ain't a note I play onstage that can't be traced directly back to my mother and father.'

The two parents themselves were very different in temperament. And of the two there was never any question whom Bruce most resembled, and therefore whose authority he set out to challenge. Like his father Doug, Bruce was a lone wolf who tended to bottle things up, a comparison the *Born To Run* Bruce did not shy away from: 'I'm pretty much by myself out there most of the time. My father was always like that. Lived with my father for twenty years. Never once saw a friend come over to the house. Not one time.' Nor did Doug tend to engage his family in stimulating conversation. Even after Bruce became the subject of press interest, he would describe his father (in the present tense) as someone who 'never has much to say to me. But I know he thinks about a lot of things. I know he's driving himself almost crazy thinking about these things.'

Meanwhile, Doug's stoic wife Adele was the one who bequeathed their only son the work ethic he espoused nightly on stage – 'Her life had an incredible consistency, work, work, work every day, and I admired that greatly' – and when she could afford it, and even when she could not, she would indulge her son's whims. When he was thirteen, his overriding obsession was to own an electric guitar. Forty years later, on the night he was inducted into the Rock and Roll Hall of Fame, Adele's son acknowledged the enormous debt he owed her, specifically and generally:

> **Bruce Springsteen**: I'd like to thank my mother Adele for that slushy Christmas Eve . . . when we stood outside the music store and I pointed to that Sunburst guitar and she had that sixty bucks, and I said, 'I need that one, Ma.' She got me what I needed, and she protected me and provided for me on a thousand other days and nights. As importantly, she gave me a sense of work as something that was joyous and that filled you with pride and self-regard, and that committed you to your world. [1998]

He had wanted a guitar to be his pen and sword ever since he first saw Elvis Presley, the scourge of all American parents who thought they had teenagers on a leash, on *The Ed Sullivan Show*. For him (and his generation), 'It wasn't just the way Elvis looked, it was the way he moved that made people crazy, pissed off, driven to screaming ecstasy, and profane revulsion. That was [the power of] television.' And, as he later recalled, 'I had to get a guitar the next *day*. I stood in front of the mirror with that guitar on . . . and I knew that *that* was what had been missing. But then it was like I crawled back into the grave or something, until I was thirteen.'

Like many a baby-boomer, he discovered that big, cumbersome guitar around his neck looked nothing like it did when nonchalantly slung across his hip by a gyrating Elvis, while forming chords with his puny little fingers wore down his skin and sounded nothing like Elvis did: 'My little six-year-old fingers wrapped themselves around a guitar neck for the first time, rented from Mike Deal's Music in Freehold, New Jersey. They just wouldn't fit. Failure with a capital F. So I just beat on it, and beat on it, and beat on it – in front of the mirror.' He put the guitar aside and went looking for another reason to believe: 'I tried to play football and baseball and all those things. I checked out all the alleys and just didn't fit. I was running through a maze. [But] music gave me something [else]. It was never just a hobby.'

Before he could nail his own manifesto to the doors of perception, though, he had first to reject the faith of his forefathers. By the age of thirteen, he had had enough of the liturgy of lessons he received at the convent school his mother had sent him to. As he put it to Bill Flanagan, recounting this experience, 'That very literal translating of the Bible and the belief that, "This is it, this is all there is, and don't try to step outside this thing!" always seemed a little presumptuous. I [could]n't see how that sort of arrogance – to believe that you've got the inside dope on what the word of God is – would line up with some sort of real spiritual feeling.'

He soon began to show a mile-wide rebellious streak. Initially, when he tried to challenge the authority of the nuns, they demoted him to an infants class and set his fellow pupils on him. So he took off: 'I did a lot of running away. And a lot of being brought back . . . It started when I was in the sixth grade, I was eleven . . . They'd find me and I'd be brought back that afternoon . . . I hated [that] school. I had the big hate. I put up with it for years, but in eighth grade I started to wise off.' He finally announced to his parents that he'd had enough of old-time religious education and insisted on attending the local high school. Their reaction suggested he was, if not quite dead to them, a pariah on long-term probation:

> **Bruce Springsteen**: I quit that [Catholic] stuff when I was in eighth grade. By the time you're older than thirteen, it's too ludicrous to go along with anymore. By the time I was in eighth grade I just lost it all. I decided to go to public high school, and that was a big deal . . . It was like, 'Are you insane??! You are dirt! You are the worst! You're a . . . barbarian!' [1978]

If his parents feared for the soul of the apostate in their midst, worse was to come. At the same time as he lost his faith, Bruce discovered the opposite sex and the true meaning of sin, though it would be some years before he would progress beyond a furtive fumble in the backseat of a borrowed car. After all, we're still talking 1962. Only presidents got to fuck around. Still, he sensed that there was *something* more to girls than sharing a slow smooch at the end of an evening at the local Catholic social club. Placing himself back in just such a moment, one night in February 1975, he described to a female journalist precisely what was at stake:

> 'Okay, I've been staring this girl down for hours and I don't aim my sights too high, if you know what I mean. It's five to ten, five to eleven, whenever the dances used to end, and a song like this [turns up the radio] would come on. So I start walking across the dance floor, and let me tell you, that is a *long* walk. Many a night I never made it across. Y'know, I'd start walking and get halfway, then turn back. 'Cause you weren't asking a girl, "Do you want to dance?" You were asking her, "Do you *wanta*? My life is in your hands! We're not talking about a dance; we're talking about *survival*." If she said, No [he curls up in a ball]; but if she said Yes, you were saved. 'Cause man, dancing is more than just holding a girl in your arms.'

But the walls of Jersey's Jericho did not tumble so easily. As he told a small Boston club crowd one particularly gregarious night in January 1974, 'At the parochial school dances – like the [Catholic Youth Organization] things – they had this one woman that would come around and embarrass you, pull you out of your chair and pull you into the middle of the room . . . And then, when you go back to school on Monday; and the girls would all sit over there, and boys would all sit over here, and you had those little green ties . . . and green pants.' No wonder he wanted out. There was another problem with the dances organized by the likes of the CYO – the music. It was strictly for squares. And by 1963, he was starting to hear music on his mother's preferred morning radio station, WNEW, that didn't sound like it had been recorded in Squaresville, daddy-o:

> **Bruce Springsteen**: We never had a record player in the house, never had records or anything like that, not until I was thirteen or fourteen. But I remember my mother always listened to the radio – she always listened to the AM stations. Elvis was big then, in the early sixties, and the Ronettes, all the Spector stuff, and the girl groups from New York, which is what for me is a big part of my background. The Ronettes, the Shirelles, the Crystals, the Chiffons, who put out a lot of great music at the time. And then the big English thing happened, the Beatles and all that stuff, and the Stones, Manfred Mann . . . So the music that got me was what was on AM from 1959 to 1965 . . . My roots were formed by then: Roy Orbison; the great English singles bands; the girl groups from New York; Chuck Berry, of course. [1975]

No longer a dead man walking, the teenage Bruce had been saved by the blood, sweat and tears of Spector, Leiber and Stoller. Nor is salvation too strong a word for how he came to feel. Indeed, when on his first English tour he described that Damascene radio experience to England's preeminent rock critic, Nick Kent. And his choice of words is telling indeed: 'The music on the radio gave me my first real reason for being alive . . . Whenever I heard a new record – now we're talking about the early to mid-sixties, all that stuff from Elvis to Spector . . . Tamla, Stax, all the British bands – that music sounded so miraculous that it sucked me out of my surroundings and presented me with this sense of . . . wonderment.'

However, if it was Elvis who again provided the parameters for further Pop lessons, it was a very different Elvis from the one he had previously seen on Ed's primetime weekly bulletin. This was the Hollywood Elvis; the one who sang cheesy fare like 'Can't Help Falling In Love', 'Viva Las Vegas' and 'Follow That Dream', not the life-affirming promise of 'Hound Dog', 'Blue Suede Shoes' and 'Jailhouse Rock'. And though Springsteen would cover all three of these post-army soundtrack songs in the post-*River* era, it was hearing 'the British bands' that banished Movie Elvis from his thoughts.

And once again it took that snake-oil salesman Ed Sullivan to show him the way. For it was on February 9 1964 that Ed turned over his show to four boys from Liverpool with tight trousers and even tighter harmonies, The Beatles. Just eleven weeks after an assassin's bullet (or three) snatched away JFK, and seemingly the hopes and dreams of a generation, this fab foursome landed on a distant shore and shook the shifting sands of American youth, for good. Like many a contemporary, a stunned Springsteen had been waiting a lifetime for something like this: 'This was different, shifted the lay of the land. Four guys, playing and singing, writing their own material.' Indeed, he would spend the next twenty years trying to create a similar explosion in someone else's soul:

> **Bruce Springsteen**: The Beatles opened doors . . . If any stuff I do could ever do that for somebody, that's the best . . . Rock 'n' roll motivates. It's the big gigantic motivator, at least it was for me . . . That's the real spirit of the music. You have to click that little trigger, that little mechanism. [1978]

The message had a profound effect on an entire demographic, but in the long run most then-kids got on with living the life their parents had mapped out for them, reserving their little rebellions for their nights out dancing or in relationships with unsuitable suitors (a subject the Jersey devil would explore thoroughly at the sessions for *The River*). But it took the fourteen-year-old Springsteen over, and stayed with him for the next two decades. His reasoning was simple, but profound: 'Rock 'n' roll came to my house where there seemed to be no way out. It just seemed like a dead end street . . . nothing I wanted to do except roll over and go to sleep, or something. And it came into my house – snuck in, ya know – and opened up a whole world of possibilities.'

He had heard the good news, and a connection with some other shadows who passed across his peripheral vision at the public school he now attended; even if many remained immune to the message he heard in the subliminal signals coming through on his mother's radio. As schoolmate Toni Hentz told biographer Christopher Sandford: 'He was dirt-poor, wore britches [to school] and liked what we still called nigger music. You can imagine how it set him apart.' But if such antipathy affected Springsteen, he quickly learnt not to let it show. Because he now had a secret he could call his own: 'Music . . . provided me with a community, filled with people, and brothers and sisters who I didn't know, but who I knew were out there. We had this enormous thing in common, this "thing" that initially felt like a "secret".'

Make no mistake, though, his (and others') post-Sullivan epiphany placed him (and them) in immediate opposition with the town elders. Because, like it or not, he was stuck in 'a real classic little town . . . very intent on maintaining the status quo, [where] everything was looked at as a threat; kids were [certainly] looked as a nuisance and a threat'. And the one immediate authority figure he could not avoid on a daily basis was his father, who had gradually seen his own life go down the drain and now thought he saw the mark of Cain on his increasingly wilful son. What he *actually* saw was a grim determination from his galvanized seed that he would not end up like *that*:

> **Bruce Springsteen**: It wasn't until I started listening to the radio, and I heard something in the singers' voices that said there is more to life than what my old man was doing . . . and they held out a promise – and it was

> a promise that every man has a right to live his life with some decency and some dignity. And it's a promise that gets broken every day in the most violent way. But it's a promise that never ever fuckin' dies, and it's always inside of you. But I watched my old man forget that. [1981]

The corrosive effect of witnessing a father's impersonation of a pressure cooker night after night can only be imagined. In 1995 Springsteen suggested it might have been seeing his younger self staring back at him that actually set his father off: 'Growing up, [it] was difficult for my Dad to accept that I wasn't like him . . . Or maybe [that] I was like him, and he didn't like that part of himself – more likely . . . [But] I was a sensitive kid . . . [and] for me, that lack of acceptance was devastating, really devastating.' The psychological scars were indelible enough to prompt a series of introductions to 'Independence Day' on *The River* tour that were more intense than the performances of the song itself, perhaps because he had something important to communicate that the song merely hinted at:

> 'My father was only a little older than I am right now and he'd come home and just sit in the kitchen at night, like he was waiting for something. He'd send away for all these different books like "How To Be An Engineer" or "How To Be . . ." and try to learn how to do something . . . But for some reason, it seemed like he could never find that one thing that was gonna make him feel like he was living, instead of just dying a little bit every day. And it seems like in school, instead of trying to show you, help you find your place, they were teaching you stuff that was just to keep you in your place. I remember every day when I was young, I'd watch my parents, and it used to scare me so much that I tried to think of some way that I wasn't gonna let it happen to me.'

This evidently wasn't the only thing that scared Springsteen Junior at night. There was also the small matter of his father's temper. In 1976, on the verge of pouring those feelings into his own compositions, he would perform a song at most concerts that he first heard on his mother's radio back in the day, which spoke to him in a way that even The Beatles did not: The Animals' October 1965 single, 'It's My Life'. And he would preface it with a rap that steadily built on a sense of urgency – and implicit violence – layer by layer, line by line, until he would explode into the song itself:

> 'I grew up in this small town, lived in this two-family house on Main Street. My Pop, he was a guard at the jail for a while, sometimes he worked in a plastics' factory [or] in this old rug-mill, until they closed the place down . . .. A lot of times he just stayed home . . . Every night he'd sit in the kitchen, shut out all the lights in the house around nine o'clock, he'd sit there at the kitchen table, used to drink beer all night, smoke cigarettes. I always knew my father'd be sitting there at that kitchen table waiting for me when I came home. Sometimes I'd come in around two in the morning, three in the morning. He'd lock up the front door so we couldn't come in the front, we used to have to come in around the screen door into the kitchen and I'd stand there in the driveway and I could see him, I could see the light of his cigarette butt through the door . . . and I'd slick my hair back real tight and hope I could get through the kitchen before he'd stop me. And he'd always wait till I was just about in the living room and he'd call my name. Then he'd start asking me where I was getting my money from, what I thought I was doing with myself. He wanted to know where I was going all the time, and we'd start screaming at each other, and my mother'd be coming in from the front room to try and keep us from fighting with each other, and pretty soon I'd be running out the back door, telling him how it was my life and I could do what I wanted . . . *It's a hard world to get a break in.*'

That rap was performed at a Red Bank show, when one suspects at least one family member was in the audience and knew whereof he spoke, the long-suffering Virginia, the elder of his sisters. Other nights he could be even more explicit, describing how close he and his father came to exchanging blows. One that Dave Marsh claims he heard began with Bruce talking about how his father 'used to always come home real pissed off, drunk, sit in the kitchen', and built up to Bruce expressing just how this made him feel, 'I just couldn't wait until I was old enough to take him out once.' Not that he ever did. Even at seventeen, he was a writer not a fighter. As to whether his father beat the crap out of his young charge, the fortunate son has kept decidedly schtum, though in recent years he *has* talked about the atmosphere of violence. In 1987, he told *Musician*'s esteemed editor, 'The side of my work that is angry comes from that sense of [a] wasted life; so to a certain degree there's a *revenge* motive going on', a highly curious way of putting it. Later on, he would tend to drop into therapy-speak when suggesting how such experiences infused much of his work, post-*Darkness*:

> **Bruce Springsteen**: I lived in a house where there was a lot of struggle to find work, where the results of not being able to find your place in society manifested themselves with the resulting lack of self-worth, with anger, with violence. And as I grew up, I said, 'Hey, that's my song' . . . I still probably do my best work when I'm working inside of those things, which must be because that's where I'm connected. That's just the lights I go by. [1996]

If feelings of anger and violence took a long time to manifest themselves in song, he learned to feel differently about himself the minute he picked up an instrument: 'When you're young, you feel powerless . . . Your house, no matter how small it is, it seems so big. Your parents seem huge. I don't believe this feeling ever quite leaves you. And I think what happens is, when you get around fifteen or sixteen, a lot of your fantasies are power fantasies . . . You don't know how to channel that powerlessness – how to channel it into either a social concern or creating something for yourself. I was lucky. I was able to deal with it with the guitar.'

After his second Ed Sullivan epiphany, he again picked up that iconic instrument. This time he didn't look half as dumb, while his fingers could now grip the neck. In fact, he held on for dear life as he set about learning the most important lesson, 'Dig yourself'. It was a process that initially led him inward: 'When I got the [first] guitar, I wasn't getting out of myself. I was already out of myself. I knew myself, and I did not dig me. I was getting into myself.' Post-*Darkness*, he went further, venturing to suggest: 'When I started to play, it was like a gift. I started to feel alive. It was like some guy stumbling down a street and finding a key. Rock 'n' roll was the only thing I ever liked about myself.'

If The Beatles represented the vanguard, by the summer of 1964 there were whole battalions of British beat-groups flying the flag, overwhelming America's airwaves. And if he quickly learned to embrace The Beatles *and* the Stones, whose own Ed Sullivan debut in October of that year was equally seismic, he also explored obscurer byways of the British sound. As 1976 covers of 'It's My Life' and 'We Gotta Get Out Of This Place' explicated, he was a huge fan of The Animals long after 'The House of the Rising Sun' closed its doors. In 2004, he was still championing 'the class-conscious music of The Animals . . . I didn't have a political education when I was young . . . It was something that, in truth, I [only] came to through popular music.' In 2012 he devoted a large chunk of a keynote speech at South By Southwest to lauding the Geordie lads:

> **Bruce Springsteen**: To me, The Animals were a revelation. The first records with full blown class consciousness that I had ever heard. 'We Gotta Get Out Of This Place' had that great bass riff, that . . . was just marking time. That's every song I've ever written. That's all of them. I'm not kidding, either . . . It was the first time I felt I heard something come across the radio that mirrored my home life, my childhood. And the other thing that was great about The Animals was there were no good–looking members . . . They put [Burdon] in a suit, but it was like putting a gorilla in a suit . . . Then they had the name . . . unforgiving and final, and irrevocable . . . the most unapologetic group name until the Sex Pistols came along. [2012]

He was also, by his own admission, 'nuts about' Manfred Mann and The Searchers. And, though he only namechecked 'em once in those seventies interviews, he was clearly an early fan of Them, Van Morrison's band of Belfast bruisers who gave American garage bands three of their most essential anthems, 'Gloria', 'Baby Please Don't Go' and 'I Can Only Give You Everything'. Springsteen's initial singing duties in his first proper band, The Castiles, would be on a Them US A-side ('Mystic Eyes'). And at 1978 concerts he managed to namecheck one Them classic ('Lonely Sad Eyes') while parodying the spoken intro of another ('If You and I Could Be As Two'), during the positively Morrisonesque 'Sad Eyes' sequence to 'Backstreets': 'I remember you standing on the corner, with your hair all up, in that pretty new blue dress that your baby bought you . . . Standing there with your sad eyes, your lonely, lonely, lonely, sad eyes . . .'.* For now, though, the young Bruce was content to learn the three chords to 'Gloria', only mimicking the guttural snarl of an Eric Burdon, a Paul Jones or a Van Morrison in the isolation of his own bedroom.

When he did attempt to join his first high-school band, around 1965, it was as a guitarist, pure and simple. Apparently called The Rogues, they gave him a harsh lesson in economics: 'I got thrown out of my first band because they told me my guitar was too cheap.' But it was all he – or, more

* The spoken intro to 'If You And I Could Be As Two' is as follows: 'Twas on a Sunday and the autumn leaves were on the ground. It kicked my heart when I saw you standing there in your dress of blue. The storm was over, my ship sailed through.'

accurately, his mother – could afford. He certainly couldn't afford to smash up a guitar at the end of a gig. Imagine then his shock when he saw his first British rock band in the flesh, if it really was The Who at Asbury Park. He later claimed how sometimes onstage he would 'remember being at a Who concert at Convention Hall in Asbury Park in '65 . . . Maybe there's a fifteen year-old kid who's [also] thinking of playing the guitar . . . I want to inspire that guy.'

Actually, the first documented time The Who played the Convention Hall was in the summer of 1967, by which time Springsteen had found an all-American hero to replace Elvis in his pantheon of inspiration, and had embraced all three electric albums with which Bob Dylan revolutionized popular music and turned lightweight pop into solid rock. Bruce famously recalled his introduction to the nasal tones of Electric Bob when personally inducting the great man into the Rock & Roll Hall of Fame in January 1988:

> **Bruce Springsteen**: The first time that I heard Bob Dylan, I was in the car with my mother and we were listening to WMCA, and on came that snare shot that sounded like somebody'd kicked open the door to your mind . . . 'Like a Rolling Stone'. And my mother, she was no stiff with rock 'n 'roll, she used to like the music, she listened, she sat there for a minute and she looked at me and she said, 'That guy can't sing'. But I knew she was wrong. I sat there and I didn't say nothin', but I knew that I was listening to the toughest voice that I had ever heard. It was lean and it sounded somehow simultaneously young and adult. And I ran out and I bought the single and I ran home and I put it on, the 45, and they must have made a mistake in the factory because a Lenny Welch song came on. The label was wrong. So I ran back, got it and I came back and I played it. Then I went out and I got *Highway 61 [Revisited*] and that was all I played for weeks; looked at the cover with Bob in that satin blue jacket and the Triumph motorcycle shirt. And when I was a kid, Bob's voice somehow thrilled and scared me, it made me feel kind of irresponsibly innocent, and it still does, when it reached down and touched what little worldliness a fifteen-year-old kid in high school in New Jersey had in him at the time. [1988]

This vivid account of that day is slightly at odds with versions previously given on *The River* tour. At a November 1980 show he claimed that, because all he had in the car was 'this junky speaker, I couldn't hear what all the verses were. I couldn't hear all the words. But I remember when he got to the chorus, I always remember that line that just asked, "How does it feel to be on your own?"' It articulated in one cogent phrase the rebellious spirit of the music he'd been listening to since he turned into his teens:

> **Bruce Springsteen**: If you were young in the sixties and fifties, everything felt false everywhere you turned. But you didn't know how to say it . . . Bob came along and gave us those words . . . Man, 'How does it feel to be on your own?' And if you were a kid in 1965, you *were* on your own. Because your parents – God bless them – they could not understand the incredible changes that were taking place. You were on your own, without a home. [2012]

'Like a Rolling Stone' (and the album it introduced, *Highway 61 Revisited*) certainly had as pronounced an effect on American popular song, and culture, as had Elvis and The Beatles on Ed Sullivan. For one, as Bruce went on to explain at Dylan's induction, it demonstrated someone who 'was a revolutionary. The way that Elvis freed your body, Bob freed your mind and showed us that just because the music was innately physical, did not mean that it was anti-intellect. He had the vision and the talent to make a pop song so that it contained the whole world. He invented a new way a pop singer could sound, broke through the limitations of what a recording artist could achieve, and . . . changed the face of rock 'n' roll forever and ever.'

For the next year and a half Bruce immersed himself in All Things Dylan. He also undoubtedly soaked up the various Byrds cover versions that AM disc jockeys generally found easier to stomach; and presumably Them's stunning recasting of 'It's All Over Now Baby Blue', to which he later tipped a hat with the Bruce Springsteen Band's February 1972 rendition. But, as he fully admitted to *Crawdaddy* founder and Dylan authority Paul Williams, he never felt the slightest inclination to venture back into Dylan's pre-electric phase. His reneging from folk music was the point at which *this* apostate tuned in:

> **Bruce Springsteen**: I listened to *Bringing it All Back Home, Highway 61, Blonde on Blonde*. That's it. I never had his early albums and to this day I don't have them, and I never had his later albums. I might have heard

> them once, though. There was only a short period of time when I related; there was only that period when he was important to me, where he was giving me what I needed . . . I was never really into the folk or acoustic music thing. The one thing I dug about those [electric] albums was . . . the sound. Before I listened to what was happening in the song, you had the chorus and you had the band and it had incredible sound, and that was what got me. [1974]

By the time he was picking up the likes of *Blonde On Blonde*, an expensive double-album in a fold-out sleeve, Bruce finally had a little money of his own, which he'd earned from playing locally as the rhythm guitarist in The Castiles, named after a dodgy brand of cigarillos. He had apparently reached at least some kind of rapprochement with his bemused parents, one that enabled him 'to play weekends somewhere and make a little extra dough . . . which is what my parents used to say that I could do. That was allowed.' At the same time he had started doing some intensive homework, though not the kind his parents still hoped for: 'I remember going to see bands when I was a kid, watching the musicians from real close up, studying the way they moved their hands, then going home and trying to copy them.' He had got himself into The Castiles after he spent an intensive forty-eight hours learning how to replicate the guitar on 'The Last Time', the Rolling Stones' breakthrough single – which was in itself quite a trick, because the guitar had been double-tracked.

The Castiles were the quintessential high-school band, with Springsteen the junior member content (for now) to stay in the background. But that diffident demeanour was revealed to be largely a front the minute they stepped out to perform. As bassist Curt Fluhr has recalled, 'Put him onstage with a guitar and he lit it up. It was like somebody had plugged him in.' They provided him with his first band of brothers; though the Castiles' frontman, George Theiss, was more interested in impressing Bruce's elder sister than becoming *his* blood brother.

Remarkably, given how such bands rarely retained their shape for very long when cars and girls entered the frame, The Castiles lasted from 1965 right through August 1968. In May 1966 they even cut a record; albeit just for themselves. The two-sided single, 'Baby I' b/w 'That's What You Get', meant to demonstrate the something they'd got, was a curiously half-assed affair. Both songs, according to their indulgent manager Tex Vinyard, were 'written in the back seat of a car . . . on the way to the studio . . . at the Bricktown Mall shopping centre. George and Bruce wrote those. It was a rainy Sunday. [And] we had no extra strings, so through two-thirds of the songs there's no E string.' Further compromises were required when they got there, as Springsteen himself recently revealed:

> **Bruce Springsteen**: It was a tiny little room . . . and they couldn't stand any volume whatsoever going into the microphones. We had to turn all our amps to the wall and literally put covers over them . . . The recording studio was not set up in those days for any kind of overdrive; they just simply weren't ready to record rock bands in Bricktown, New Jersey in 1965 [sic]. But it was a big deal. [2010]

It has to be said that even in the unprepossessing pantheon of first formative efforts by later legends, The Castiles' offering is particularly wretched. And if it convinced a young Springsteen that maybe they should get more serious, he was always fighting an uphill battle. He did at least convince the others to let him sing some songs: 'Everybody in the band felt that I couldn't sing at all. I think I got to sing one Dylan song. Over the years I started to sing a little bit more, [until] eventually . . . we ended up splitting . . . the vocals.' It proved a wise move, because as Vinyard notes, 'Soon, we let Bruce sing "Mystic Eyes" and The Who's "My Generation". That's how we got the booking in New York.' He is referring to a brief residency at the fabled Cafe Wha? in Greenwich Village, which was probably the full extent of the others' musical ambitions. For Bruce, though, it was just a beginning:

> **Bruce Springsteen**: When I started I wanted to play rhythm guitar in a local band. Just sit back there, play rhythm guitar . . . I didn't wanna sing, just get a nice band and play rhythm. But I found out . . . that I just knew more about it than other guys that were in the band. So I slowly just became the leader. [1975]

The Castiles had run their natural course by the spring of 1967, as the prospect of graduation loomed and real life could begin. But still they persevered. By now, it was clear that Springsteen had no intention of giving up on his dream, even when he became a target for conformists to rag on, verbally *or* physically. As he informed *The Advocate* in 1995, 'I was brought up in a small town [where] anybody who was different in any fashion was castigated and ostracised, if not physically threatened . . . Me and a few other guys were the town freaks – and there were many occasions where we were dodging getting beaten up ourselves.'

Unfortunately, he was ill-equipped to defend himself, something he had learnt at the tender age of ten, as he revealed to a Berkeley crowd one night in June 1978: 'You usually stop fighting by the time you're 18 or 19, I stopped when I was about 10 'cause I got beat all the time, these hands just were not dangerous weapons, you know. I remember I got in a fight with this guy, I beat the hell out of his hood with my forehead, you know (chuckles). Put dents into the thing.'

The troubled teenager was increasingly drawn to the bright neon lights of the Big City – where this boy could be free – and after those nights at the Wha (and possibly before) he began to bunk off school, hopping a bus to midtown. As he told one audience in January 1985, 'I grew up in this small town. When I was sixteen, man, I hated that town; it seemed so narrow-minded and small-minded. I used to get on the bus, take Lincoln Transit to New York City. It used to feel so great when I got out at Port Authority. It was like, "Oh, man, nobody owns me up here."' He was invisible. No secrets to conceal.

To preserve that new-found sense of autonomy he would sometimes stay out all night, even after he took the bus back from the city: 'I used to have a sleeping bag stashed out in these woods, under these rocks . . . and sometimes if it got too late, I'd go out there and just unroll it and sleep in my friend's car, sleep out there under the trees. That spot, sometimes it felt more like my home did than my house did. I guess, everybody needs someplace to go when they can't go home.'*

If he was ill-prepared for a father's fury, or fisticuffs with one of Jersey's more conformist thugs, he was even less ready for military service. Unfortunately for smalltown America, the battle outside a-ragin' was not only in their homeland, but also in the badlands of Vietnam. The spectre of war loomed over all of his generation, and for him a college education, the one cast-iron way to beat the draft, seemed unlikely. Yet beating the draft was something he knew he had to do – 'When I was seventeen or

* Sydney 23/3/85.

eighteen, I didn't even know where Vietnam was. [I] just knew [I] didn't wanna go and die!'

The first thing he needed to do was graduate high-school, which he did. His band even played the Seniors Farewell Dance ten days before graduation. But then he began the actual day, 19 June 1967, by skipping the graduation ceremony altogether, only for it to end with his father making one last, futile attempt to bring his son under his command:

> **Bruce Springsteen**: By the end of high school I didn't have much to do with anybody. I almost didn't graduate because the kids in my class wouldn't let me . . . They weren't gonna let me graduate unless I cut my hair. So on the day of graduation, I left the house and didn't come back. I went to New York and stayed with a friend in the Village, a guy who dealt drugs . . . So the phone rings and it's my mother. Don't ask me how she found out where I was. She's saying there's a graduation party over at my house, which I had totally forgotten about, and she wants me to come home. I say, 'No way. I'm only coming home if there's gonna be no big fight; I don't want to come back and go at it all over again with my father. If he'll promise no big fight, I'll come home.' So, she says OK, no fight. Now, I show up with a girl. I don't know what I could've been thinking of, but I show up with this girl and my father opens the screen door. He pulls me inside by the collar with one hand, leaves her outside . . . drags me up to the [bed]room, and *takes out all the light bulbs* so I've got to sit there in the dark by myself. [1978]

Though he had shown absolutely no aptitude for formal education – perhaps because he never quite saw the point, once churlishly complaining 'they always talked to your head, they could never figure out how to talk to your heart' – by September 1968 he had enrolled himself at the Ocean County Community College 'in a liberal arts course', a situation of which the Jersey Selective Service Board were promptly advised. He was off the hook for now, but as he related in his first-ever interview as a CBS artist, he no more fit in at Ocean County than he did in Freehold:

> **Bruce Springsteen**: I was gonna get drafted and my parents wanted me to go to college. I got there and tried to take psychology, and I kept opening a book and seeing myself in all these different -isms. I thought, I can't get into that. I realized you go into class and everyone would start

> talking about what the norm was, and I figured out I didn't fit into that. So I said, 'Well, I'll try something else' . . . It's not like it is today, where everyone has long hair. This was long ago. [So] I got sent down to the psychiatrist's office. He [had] said, 'I wanna see ya,' and he said, 'I gotta tell ya the students been complaining about ya. Tell me what's the matter.' 'Nothing's the matter.' He didn't believe me, so I quit. [1972]

He preferred to castigate his fellow students and their conformist outlook rather than address his own failure to knuckle down and learn. He was still blaming them in 1984 with the world at his feet, 'I didn't really fit in. I went to a real narrow-minded school where people gave me a lot of trouble and I was hounded off the campus – I just looked different and acted different, so I left school.' His parents must have despaired. His father, who had served in World War II, knew only too well that his son was not cut out for 'fighting off the Vietcong'. And once the Jersey Selective Service Board were notified of his absence from college, he was summoned to a conscription exam in Trenton. Fortunately for him, the reckless side of his character had recently resulted in a 'roadside jam' between his motorbike and another vehicle, and he had come off worse. He was judged 4-F, a physical wreck, unfit to serve. He returned home to give his parents the bad news. All his father said was, 'Good.'

The summer before he arrived at Ocean College the other members of The Castiles finally accepted the inevitable. They had always seen the band as an enjoyable hobby, while their now-leader increasingly viewed music as his Mission in life. They also seemed slightly uncomfortable with the type of material he had started introducing into the set after they all, save the younger Bobby Alfano, graduated from high-school. Covers of Moby Grape's 'Omaha' and The Blues Magoos' 'One By One' sat uneasily with the likes of 'See My Friends' and 'Eleanor Rigby', two of a handful of songs George Theiss now sang at their shows. In August 1968, the band played two farewell shows in Red Bank and Shrewsbury, and that was that. As George Theiss informed *Backstreets*, by that time 'a couple of the guys were going to go to college. I didn't know what I was going to do. Bruce was already working on his next thing. He was already jamming with the guys he would form Earth with. So . . . he just took on what bookings we had and went on.'

As of the summer of sixty-eight, Bruce Springsteen considered himself a working musician. Which meant, one, he hung out with other musicians and, two, he stopped absorbing influences from the radio and began experiencing them directly, sometimes from seeing successful acts in person (when The Doors came to the Convention Hall in August 1968, Bruce made sure he was there); other times, by sitting and watching the competition at the local afterhours clubs where time did not hang so heavy on his hands. He would later claim his infatuation with Dylan also stopped right about then, telling Paul Williams 'I was into *John Wesley Harding*. [But] I never listened to anything after *John Wesley Harding*.' (He was not alone.)

At around the same time he tuned out the AM radio station/s that had served as mentor and muse for his entire time as a teenager: 'AM radio was fine right up until about 1967, when FM came in and started to play long cuts, without any commercials, and you could see the disappearance of the really good three-minute single.' Springsteen did not immediately mourn this loss. In fact, he seems to have embraced the new gestalt, making his new combo, Earth, the FM equivalent of the strictly-AM Castiles. Modelled along the lines of great British three-piece bands like The Who (sic), Cream and the Jimi Hendrix Experience, Earth may have been devised to make Springsteen its all-singing, all-playing focal point, but the songs of Cream, Hendrix and the Yardbirds would be its credo. (The one surviving set-list contains three Hendrix songs and no less than seven drawn from Cream's repertoire.)

That he was not quite ready to take on such a heavy burden of musical responsibility was evidenced by the rapid recruitment of a keyboard player, none other than former Castile Bob Alfano. Unfortunately for Bruce, the summary dissolution of that band had led Alfano to make other arrangements, forming Sunny Jim with fellow Castile, Vinny Manniello, so Springsteen could not always rely on Alfano being available. Sometimes he had to make do with a three-piece point of view.

If this arrangement was an unsatisfactory one, so was having to stick to songs Asbury Park audiences knew if he wanted to maintain a live presence on the Jersey shore. And Asbury Park audiences remained an identifiable type, as this homeboy knew only too well. His 1978 description of it as 'the only beach-greaser town . . . it was like Newark by the sea,' just about summed it up. (As he often joked, 'If you got enough gas in your car you carry on to Atlantic City, if not then Asbury will just have to do.') The loner's own priorities, though, had not greatly changed: 'I wanted to play the guitar, wanted to have a good band, and I devoted most of my energy to that. I had a few friends.'

At this point the one and only thing that set him apart was his dedication. Even the idea of getting a job and settling down gave him the jitters. (When his friend George Theiss got married in 1969, Bruce apparently told him straight out 'You'll never make it now.') Boadwalk habitué Ken Viola told Marc Eliott 'He was . . . the first person from that scene who never really worked a "day" job. Everybody else did, but not him. He never ate much, he'd crash at people's places, he'd sleep on the beach. He was always saying he was going to make it as a musician, that was his big thing, "I'm going to make it, I'm going to make it."' Springsteen subsequently insisted he did have 'a few small jobs before I started playing, but when I picked up that guitar, that was when I could walk down my own path.' [DTR]

All he needed now was some fellow travellers who wanted to share the journey. And, much to his surprise, it turned out there were many like-minded people along the shore. They just needed a place to mingle, and to call their own. That place was The Upstage. It was founded by a local couple with an interest in music themselves, Margaret and Tom Potter (she was the Margaret in Margaret & The Distractions). When they ran into drummer Vini 'Mad Dog' Lopez at The Pixies Inn in Farthingdale, one evening in the winter of 1969, they told him straight out, 'We're gonna start this club in Asbury, it's for jamming.' It was a remarkably visionary ambition. To make the place even less lucrative, they didn't serve booze, and so had no need of a licence:

> **Vini Lopez**: The Upstage had two segments: it had an eight to twelve thing, for kids; and then, the one to five segment: you had to be 21 to get in, but there was still no alcohol. It was just a coffeehouse . . . It was just downstairs, then they put the upstairs in which was more of a rock-oriented room. Downstairs was more acousticy. It just evolved. It was a place for all the guitar players to knock each other off. When Bruce was there, there wasn't anything else like that going on. [But] he just commanded the audience. In them days he was a guitar slinger. He just wanted to play music.

> **Bruce Springsteen**: The Upstage Club was an anomaly . . . They served no booze. It was open from eight until *five in the morning*. I'm not sure

> how they did it! . . . [But] it was a place where bands came from Long Island, from Pennsylvania, all over, in the summertime – at the end of their gigs, they would go to the Upstage . . . So you saw everybody get up and play, just people from all over. And everyone [wondered] who was gonna be the next gunslinger . . . There were no amps; the amplifiers were *in the walls* . . . You would plug in, basically, to the wall, and this huge sound would come roaring out . . . No one had to bring any equipment. That was the point . . . You picked up whoever was there and played, and demonstrated your wares for whoever was around . . . I met most of the E Street Band there; and Southside Johnny. So it was a very pivotal place . . . / . . . When I walked in the first night Vini Lopez was on drums, Danny was on organ and it was a revelation because we had good musicians and there were people playing some original music. [2010/1999]

Up until the moment he found The Upstage, Springsteen had been just another lost soul looking for a scene. As he put it in 1975, 'Straight . . . was all there was at the time. There were groups like the Rah Rahs and the Greasers, and I jumped back and forth, trying to figure out where I fit in, 'till I found out I didn't fit in. I didn't dig the scene that either [band] had happening. So consequently I didn't do anything. I just kinda was.' Hence the covers bands. It took The Upstage to convince him he could get away with playing his own material; that he would be allowed to stretch out and show everyone his self-loading pistol; and that there were musicians on tap who could play follow the leader.

As Springsteen suggests, the first night there he met Vini Lopez and Danny Federici, two key components in every band he formed between 1969 and 1974. According to Lopez, he had already introduced himself to the Earth frontman at a local Italian-American club, IAMA, when Springsteen enthused about the drummer's spell in Sonny & The Starfires, a much-vaunted local covers band who regularly triumphed in those ubiquitous battles of the bands. (As Springsteen fondly recalled in a 2012 speech, these comprised 'twenty bands at the Keyport Matawan Roller Dome in a battle to the death – so many styles . . . overlapping . . . You would have a doo wop singing group with full pompadours and matching suits, set up next to our band, playing a garage version of Them's "Mystic Eyes," . . . next to a full thirteen-piece soul show band.')

Lopez told the young Bruce about this new club, 'and 'bout a month later me and Danny walk in and there he is playing, and we got up and jammed and we made a band.' It would seem Springsteen probably went to The Upstage looking to make a specific connection. But even he can't have imagined that pretty much every musician of consequence he would work with between then and 1975, Clarence Clemons excepted, would be found congregating at this altar to extemporization. Everyone in the place seemed to be in a band, or playing musical chairs between bands.

David Sancious, a local whizz-kid at the keys, captured the flavour of the place describing the night he went there with his friend, Carl Hughes, who already knew Springsteen. As Sancious remembers it, Bruce asked Carl 'if he wanted to jam. Bruce had been going there to jam for a while . . . Carl told him I played keyboards, could I play too? Bruce said, Sure. So we ended up there for hours . . . After that night, Garry [Tallent] came up to me and asked me if I was in a band. I had just quit school . . . He had a band together with Bill Chinook, so I played with them . . . [Then] Steve Van Zandt, [Southside] Johnny Lyon and I had a blues band for a while . . . Just the three of us.' (Ironically, the one band Sancious and Van Zandt would never play in at the same time was the E Street Band.)

'Southside' Johnny was another character with whom Springsteen liked to swap notes. Though they rigorously maintained separate destinies, each would happily bitch to the other about how hard it was to find regular paying gigs. And it was a struggle. As Johnny recalls, 'You'd go into one bar and the people would really like you and treat you fairly. You'd go to another bar four miles away, the next night, and the crowd would hate you, the guy wouldn't pay you, and they'd threaten your life . . . [But] you always had the Upstage Club to go to when you finished the bar work.'

Springsteen had chanced upon a galaxy of musical possibilities, all orbiting around this one club where drugs and drink played no part. Which suited Springsteen just fine. He was a one-man drug-free zone. Not even 'weed'. As he stated in 1996, 'I didn't trust myself . . . putting myself that far out of control. I had a fear of my own internal life.' And so, while other key players in later musical configurations formed less abstemious musical gangs, Springsteen set about riveting components to Steel Mill into place. Only later would he realize what a unique place The Upstage had been, eulogizing its spirit in his 1976 sleeve-notes to Southside Johnny's *I Don't Wanna Go Home*; which followed *Born To Run* into the shops, though not the charts:

> 'You will never see most of these names on another record besides this one, but nonetheless, they're names that should be spoken in reverence at least once, not 'cause they were great musicians (truth is, some of them couldn't play nothin' at all) but because they were each in their own way a living spirit of what to me rock 'n' roll is all about. It was music as survival and they lived it down in their souls, night after night. These guys were their own heroes.'

The Indian summer of 1976 woulda seemed a long way off in the winter of 1969, when Springsteen first visited the surf factory that would serve as communal home, rehearsal space and management office for the longest lasting and most fondly remembered of his pre-E Street bands, first called Child, and then Steel Mill. The factory in question was owned by Tinker West, who fancied managing a band that played the kinda music he liked, Heavy. Originally from California, he had been putting out feelers ever since he saw Vini Lopez and Garry Tallent in a band called The Moment of Truth early in 1968. According to Lopez, Tinker approached him to say, 'You guys are great. If you ever do anything original, look me up.' And so, when Lopez first sat down with Bruce, almost the first question he asked was, 'Do you write any music?' 'Yeah, I've got a few things written.' Another Upstage regular, bassist Vini Roslin (known to everyone as 'Little Vini'), was also of one mind: 'I wanted to play in a band that was going to do original songs in a style that was close to what Cream and Jimi Hendrix were doing at the time. And that's what Bruce was about back then.'

But Lopez, Federici and Roslin were all amazed when their frontman turned up with so many songs already written. Federici later complained: 'Bruce was writing a song a day. It was crazy. It got so I was dreading going to rehearsals, knowing that there was going to be a bunch of songs to be learned every time. And all that material is gone now. Bruce is the kind of guy who just says, "Oh – that was yesterday," and throws it all away.'

Springsteen would unconvincingly claim: 'The main reason I started doing my own arrangements and writing my own songs was because I hated to pick them up off the records. I didn't have the patience to sit down and listen to them and figure out the notes and stuff.' Yet he displayed extraordinary patience crafting his own stuff. As Roslin recalled 'No one [in Child] worked outside jobs, so basically all we did was practice. We spent a lot of hours in a surfboard factory; it was there we'd rehearse all day long.' Which isn't to say that they didn't play *any* covers. That would be a recipe for extinction. And Child *did* wanna play. In fact, Springsteen suggests they 'played for the Fireman's Ball . . . We'd get there and just blow everybody's mind . . . played for the Boy Scouts once, did every kind of gig. High school dances, clubs, anything, we did it. Played in the mental institutions for the patients.' They even 'did a benefit to bus protesters to Washington to protest against the Vietnam War'.

They also played a free gig at Monmouth College, one of their first gigs as Child. It was there that guitarist Lenny Kaye first caught them: 'All I remember about the set was that the lead-singer was a really great guitar-player, he played a black Les Paul and he took command of the stage. They finished their set with a ten-minute version of [Donovan's] "Season of the Witch", which was pretty much *all* solo. And I thought, this guy's great! I found out his name was Bruce Springsteen.' Their paths would cross again just before Kaye became Patti Smith's long-term guitarist and sidekick in the fall of 1973.

Even after the band changed its name to Steel Mill (someone else claimed dibs on the Child moniker), the ethos remained the same. Lopez articulates it thus: 'It was a jam session when we played a lot of times. Never did the songs go twice the same way. Bruce would start it, you pick it up. It was coming from that Upstage [vibe].' Steel Mill became life, the universe and everything to the young colt; especially after his parents snipped the straggling remains of any metaphorical umbilical cord by moving to California that spring. Lopez even thinks the band 'moved into the house on South Street for a little while, but that didn't last because we didn't have any money. So we went back to the surf factory.'

In an early account of his parents' transcontinental relocation, Springsteen blamed the decision to head there on his then-girlfriend, who had 'been to Sausalito, and suggested they go there . . . So they got to Sausalito and realised this wasn't it. My mother [told me] they went to a gas station and she asked there, "Where do people like us live?" . . . and the guy told her . . . the peninsular. And that was what they did. They drove down south of San Francisco and they've been there ever since. My father was forty-two at the time.' Looking back in 2010, Springsteen couldn't help wondering what the hell Doug and Adele had been thinking: 'My parents did a strange thing . . . they moved away from *me* in 1969. Usually you leave home – my parents left home! My sister and I remained in Freehold . . . I was financially independent at that time, to the tune of twenty or thirty bucks a week . . . [But] my parents had nothing. When they left for California, they had $3,000.'

For the next nine months Springsteen harnessed the band's energy and steadily developed a reputation that stretched as far as Richmond, Virginia, but no further. If he had plenty of songs, there was lotsa room in each of them. Most nudged the ten-minute mark. One particularly relentless version of 'The Wind and The Rain' clocked in just shy of nineteen minutes. Thankfully, this was the era when prog-rock stalked the land, and no-one called time on a song or a set. But anyone looking for a direct lineage to the E Street Band sound in Steel Mill would search in vain. A humbler Humble Pie, with a touch of Ten Years After two years too late, the four-piece might have been a shoreline sensation but in middle America they would have been stoned alive. Even the guys in the band were convinced they were plying their wares on the wrong coast, and when Tinker revealed that he still had a few good contacts out west, a plan was cooked up to hit the other Asbury, Haight-Ashbury:

> **Vini Lopez:** We went out to California . . . Christmastime 1969, Tinker knew some people. 'Course, when we went, we visited Bruce's parents . . . Tinker was friends with Quicksilver [Messenger Service], so we stayed at their house, and then we met girls, and stayed at their house[s]. We were out there for like two months. Tinker just said, 'Let's go to California and play this stuff.' Bill Graham [had this regular audition gig. He] called it Hootenanny night. Every Tuesday night. It was like a jam session. It was the Carousel Ballroom. Here we are, we're in Oakland, somehow Bill Graham got the phone number of where Steel Mill was, and I answer the phone, it's Bill Graham. It's like four-fifteen. He says, 'Can you be here for seven and be the first band on?' The place has got like two thousand people in it, over here is regular people, over here is Hell's Angels and their girlfriends. So [after the set] Danny and I have to go to the bathroom, and we have to go through the Hell's Angels to get there, and in walks the guy who was in *Life* magazine beating people with a pool cue at Altamont, and he goes, 'Hey, you're that band from New Jersey, aren't you? New Jersey soul sounds good out here in California!' He liked it, so they had to like it. Then Bill Graham invited us back next week, then . . . he wanted to sign us to some record contract. Johnny Winter had just been signed to

a $300,000 contract and Bill Graham offers us a thousand. And then he wanted all the publishing. That wasn't gonna happen. Tinker said, 'What are you, nuts?' . . . [But] when that happened it caused a little schism between Tinker and certain guys in the band. I didn't care. I didn't write the songs.

Equally surprisingly, rebel-child Springsteen seemed more interested in catching up with his parents than establishing Steel Mill as San Francisco's latest successful import. He was learning something he only articulated a decade later, 'Your family's a funny thing, they will never go away . . . [so] you gotta deal with 'em sometime.' If he was sharing some of his growing pangs with Doug and Adele, he kept a separate set of concerns from his travelling companions. If the three-song demo they cut for Graham one day in February sounded like a band hitching its gear to the nearest bandwagon, it took a 1976 deposition for Bruce to confirm that he 'didn't have the confidence in the band that other people seemed to have'. This was the real reason he didn't take Graham up on his chiselling offer. (He has consistently refused to release any Steel Mill material, and when asked why by Vini Lopez – whilst compiling a 4-CD career retrospective! – claimed it was because, 'I don't look back.') One of the other bands on that audition night was Grin, and the minute Springsteen saw child-prodigy Nils Lofgren wield his axe, he knew he still had a way to go:

Bruce Springsteen: We auditioned at the Family Dogg, which was a well-known ballroom in San Francisco at the time. There was three bands, another band got the job and we thought we were robbed, blah blah, but we really weren't. They were just better than us. I'd played a lot locally, and for a long time hadn't seen anybody better than I was, and I walked into that ballroom that afternoon, there was somebody better than we were. We played a few more shows but I knew that I was going to do something else. [1999]

In fact, Springsteen stuck with Steel Mill for a whole year more, uncertain of direction and unwilling to broach his concerns to Tinker, the band's cheerleader-manager. When Springsteen finally revealed his doubts, the following Christmas, Tinker agreed to accompany him to California a second time. Again, the loner felt in need of a mother and child reunion.

This seems to have been the occasion Springsteen described at a gig in December 1980, ten years later to the day:

> 'Me and this friend of mine decided we were gonna drive across the country, it was right around the Christmastime . . . and we got into this little station wagon and in about three days we drove out to California . . . We were, like, in Arizona on Christmas night . . . and there's nothing as lonely as if you're ever out on an interstate highway on Christmas night . . . We got there the day after and had Christmas dinner with my folks. You always gotta go back, even if it's just to see that it ain't there no more for you.'

This trip represented the first time Springsteen tried to sell himself as a solo artist. But, as he told Paul Nelson two year later, 'Everything was [all] flowers, [as] if something was happening to your mind . . . [So] that fell apart.' He soon realized he was just another ten-a-penny troubadour: 'I was worthless in California, because I had no reputation. But in New Jersey I could make that twenty dollars down at The Upstage on a Friday night.'

Though the trip proved a bust musically, something happened in San Francisco that convinced him to change tack. However, no-one knows what. He certainly would have found the FM airwaves of San Francisco full of the latest Belfast-cowboy songs from the pen of George Ivan Morrison. Perhaps he caught one of Van the Man's rare performances at the Fillmore West that December. Lopez, for one, is sure 'he saw Van Morrison. Maybe in San Francisco . . . Bruce [decided], "We're gonna do that." He came to me and he said, "Vin, I'm gonna stop Steel Mill. But I want you to play drums in this new thing I'm gonna get together. Gonna get Garry [Tallent] on bass, we're gonna have horn players, I'm gonna audition girl singers." It just took on this different feel, Motownish, soul. Tinker didn't like it - he believed in Steel Mill.'

Barely twenty-one, Springsteen realized he was already running out of time. It was high time he found himself a place in modern rock by making music rooted in the previous decade. Though he once again initially insisted the new band would play only originals, this time he had dissenters in the ranks. As Garry Tallent told *Musician*, 'When I started playing with him the idea was, "Strictly originals." And we didn't work . . . We were together nine months, rehearsing in the garage, working just once in a while. Then we decided to . . . learn some Rolling Stones songs and some Chuck Berry songs.'

The (initially unnamed) band still needed a place to play in order to build a new audience, the old Steel Mill audience having taken their ball and gone home. Springsteen was learning a valuable lesson: '[Having] moved from hard rock to rhythm & blues-influenced music . . . I began to write differently. We'd built a very large audience . . . [But] a lot of that audience disappeared and I couldn't keep it going.' He was saved by a change of owners at a bar across the way from The Upstage, called The Student Prince:

> **Bruce Springsteen**: We started to play clubs in Jersey – no club would book us [initially]. I had to go [find] this club. I went to a club on a Saturday night and this place was empty, so this guy had nothing to lose. There was maybe ten people sleeping on the bar. We said, 'Listen, we'll come in, charge a dollar and play for the door.' It got to be a really nice scene, but still when you're in a club which holds 150 people, if it's packed you make $150, we had seven pieces. [1972]

It's a lovely little story, one Springsteen has liberally embellished over the years. However, it would appear he was not the first Shoreline scenester to see the potential of 'the Prince'. The version Southside Johnny told Springsteen-zine *Thunder Road* had 'Bruce . . . putting together what is known today as his Big Band, with two horns and two girl singers, and no money was coming in and nobody had any money. [Meanwhile,] Steve and I had put together the Sundance Blues Band, while Bruce went to California for a couple of weeks. It was a real good band and we played at the Student Prince and did fairly well there. And then when Bruce came back he played in the band for a while to make a little extra bread. He played rhythm guitar and we let him sing one song a night . . . But he dug it, and [finally] he said, "Let's put together a band of everybody who doesn't have any money and play a few dates."'

That short-lived ensemble was the legendary Dr Zoom and the Sonic Boom, whose claim to at least local fame was two shows in mid-May, one at the Sunshine Inn, the other an open-air affair in Union, that served as open auditions for the still not fully conceived Bruce

Springsteen Band. As Springsteen now says, 'We had a big chorus, people's wives and girlfriends sang . . . it was just an outgrowth of the little local scene.' It certainly reflected a musical grandiosity on Springsteen's part that was never going to be economically viable. Even after the Bruce Springsteen Band itself was unveiled, it was always on a crash diet at the expense of either a horn player or a backing singer. As he later put in, mid-song, 'We had a seven-piece band at the time, we had a big band and we brought the band in the first week and we played and . . . we split $13.75 between us, and a few guys quit, you know. The next week I was there with a six-piece band, threw some cat out, next week a five-piece band, this went on for a few weeks.'

The winnowing process actually occupied about three and a half months, by which point the Bruce Springsteen Band essentially comprised the nucleus of the E Street Band for the next half-decade – Vini Lopez, Garry Tallent, Danny Federici, David Sancious, Steve Van Zandt – plus two girl singers, Delores Holmes and Barbara Dinkins who, according to Lopez, 'came right out of the church'. In the interim, Springsteen renounced his prog-rock recidivism, to rediscover the delights of those sixties starlights that had lit his way in high school, thanks largely to his new girlfriend Diane and her Dansette:

> **Bruce Springsteen**: From when I was seventeen until I was twenty-four I never had a record-player. So it was like I never heard any albums that came out after '67 . . . I lived with Diane [Lozito] and she had an old beat-up one that only old records sounded good on. So that's all I played. Those old Fats Domino records, they sounded great on it . . . I listened to the Yardbirds' first two albums. And the Zombies, all those groups. And Them. [1974]

He thus found himself in the summer of 1971 rediscovering the excitement of that first epiphany: 'I had to go back . . . I started really getting into it, go[ing] back, dig[ging] out all the old singles and stuff and see[ing] what I'd missed.' (A similar, contemporary experience prompted Tom Verlaine to form a prototypical Television.) One thing he seemingly missed on its first appearance, January 26, 1967, was Stax singer Eddie Floyd's defining LP *Knock On Wood*, with its drip-feed of soul classics: the title track, 'Something You Got', 'Raise Your Hand' &c. But now he got it.

As he told Paul Nelson the following year: 'Ever since I got that Eddie Floyd record, 'Raise Your Hand', there ain't nothing like it. I really got involved with [soul] after that. That feel. To where I [was inspired to] put together a big band.'

A big band meant not only girls, but also saxophone. If he was going to succeed in blending those Memphis and Caledonia soul strains and bring them to the Shore he was going to need someone who could make the four winds blow out of his sax. A big man. In keeping with the mythic nature of the Big Man's contribution to the E Street story, Springsteen by 1975 had a regular spiel about the first time he met the mighty Clemons, 'There I was in Asbury Park on a dark, rainy night. A hurricane just came in, I'm walking down the street at three in the morning . . . had my jacket bundled up around me . . . walking through the monsoon, I seen this big figure dressed in white, walking with a cane, walking like there was no rain and the wind wasn't blowing; just walking like it was a beautiful summer day.'

Lopez remembers it a bit differently: 'Tinker's girlfriend, Carey, was in the Joyful Noise. She says to me, "You gotta hear this sax player, Clarence." So one night me and Tinker and Danny and Bruce pack up in the car, go down to Bayville and see him in The Spirits . . . Said hello . . . I don't know about all those stories 'bout the door blew open, all that stuff. It was at a Spirits Gin Mill down in Bayville.' Nor did Clarence leap at Bruce's offer of mutual penury. As he said in his autobiography, 'I [already] had a gig, and Bruce didn't hear horns in his music yet.'

It might be nearer the truth to say that Clarence couldn't hear any place for himself in the Bruce Springsteen Band. Springsteen was still indulging in lengthy guitar workouts on originals like 'You Mean So Much To Me', 'She's Leaving' and 'The Band's Just Boppin' The Blues', all songs which survived into the E Street era in modified form. 'She's Leaving', which got the full stretch-out-and-busk treatment, was a rare exercise in autobiography. When he sang lines like, 'Yes I'm bitter, oh how I'm bitter/ And it feels good to say it out loud'. he presumably knew their target would hear the message loud and clear but was too inflamed to care. But then, you can't start a fire without a spark. Indeed, according to Lopez, he also 'wrote "Fire" so Delores had something to sing. "Driving in my car . . ." came from them days. [But] Tinker didn't exactly get behind it. We didn't get any gigs, we were starving. There was no clubs. There was nothing.'

Not surprisingly, the bandleader was growing increasingly frustrated by the parochial nature of Asbury Park's music scene: 'One hour out of New York City and you were in the nether world. Nobody came to New Jersey looking for bands to sign. That didn't happen . . . I did shows in my late teens and early twenties when I was playing to thousands of kids, but nobody really knew about that . . . They were just local events.'

By this time it was December again, the traditional time for Bruce to break up a band and go visit the folks. He still harboured some half-assed idea he might make it as a solo singer-songwriter in northern California, even though he had just been told that he simply did not have the sorta material to make it in that notoriously cut-throat area of the industry. The observation had come from none other than Mike Appel, a successful songwriter-producer who was looking to extricate himself from the Wes Farrell organization and strike out on his own. Appel knew Tinker, or vice-versa, and through Tinker's auspices a meeting was arranged at which Springsteen told Appel, 'I'm tired of being a big fish in a little pond.' He then played him what he presumably thought were his two best songs, one of which was certainly 'Baby Doll', a song he later demoed for Laurel Canyon:

> **Mike Appel:** I was so unimpressed. They didn't seem to have any hooks, they weren't cohesive songs really, in the true sense of trying to craft a pop song; I just remember the intensity. It almost seemed like it was too intense for what the results were. [But] he was very humble and very polite. I told him, 'You want an album deal?' 'Well, yes, I would.' 'Well, you're gonna have to have a lot more songs than two songs.' So he said, 'Well, I'm going to San Mateo to see my parents for the Christmas holidays and I'll write.' I said, 'Alright, the door's always open.' That's the way we left it.

In his introduction to the highly-selective 1999 collection, *Songs*, Springsteen suggests, 'I always had a notebook full of acoustic songs. I'd do the occasional coffeehouse, but mostly that material went unused. The songs required too much attention for a crowded bar on a Saturday night.' The evidence that he had started to write in this new vein came just before he met Appel that first time in late November 1971. He apparently performed 'If I Was The Priest' first at The Student Prince some time that fall.

Perversely, he elected not to play this important cut to Appel, a fellow

Catholic. Yet here was a song which would have shown a potential surrogate father that this son had a whole new bag. Rarely has there been a more heartfelt cri de cœur from a fallen angel, the most telling couplet being: 'Me, I got scabs on my knees from kneeling way too long/ It's about time I played a man and took a stand where I belong.' Indeed, it would be this cut that the young Bruce would reveal when legendary CBS producer John Hammond Snr later asked him if he had any songs he dared not play. But that life-changing moment was still six months and a few dozen songs away. For, true to his word, Springsteen was heading for California on a mission, and he wasn't going to return until he was a singer-songwriter who could make Mr Appel sit up and take notice.

Part I

Born With Nothing

Chapter 1: 1971–72 – Songs About Cars & Girls

> I'd always had a band but I also wrote acoustically on the side quite often, and occasionally I'd play that music in local coffee houses. But [in 1972] I focused on it and committed to it in a way that I hadn't before. – Bruce Springsteen, 1999

If the 22-year-old Springsteen had a stock of coffeehouse songs to take with him to California in December 1971 – which I somehow doubt – then very few survived the trip. He returned a fully-fledged singer-songwriter, with a gift for wordplay and a notebook full of songs. But they were all songs that followed the template of 'She's Leaving' and 'If I Was The Priest', the two scraps he did transfer from his Bruce Springsteen Band songbook. Nothing in the original songs he played with Steel Mill, and almost none of those he played with the BSB, lead on to this landslide. Inspiration came fast, and it came hard. And it came from nowhere. Ain't that always the way!

Not in the rock world. Precious few seventies rock artists spent seven years scuffling around the vortex of creative fusion, barely dipping a toe in the void, only to dive in head first. The one obvious comparison from an artist of comparable stature would have to be the young David Bowie, né Jones, who a year later would respond to the songs that now flowed from Springsteen's pen with barely contained zeal. Bowie himself had been a recording artist for six years, in styles anachronistic and uncharacteristic, when in 1969 he wrote 'Space Oddity', a song that was a quantum leap on everything which came before.

So it was with Springsteen. And in his case, the breakthrough song was probably 'For You', which he almost certainly wrote 'for' Diane Lozito. As one witness to their relationship put it, 'Diane was very feisty, very wild, and pretty as hell.'[DTR] If 'She's Leaving' was Springsteen's first post-breakup song to strike the right note, then 'For You' was his 'Don't Think Twice, It's Alright', a fare-thee-well disguised as a return. In this case he had seemingly walked in on an on-off girlfriend's attempted suicide – 'It's not that nursery mouth I came back for/ It's not the way you're stretched out on the floor'. This summons up a kaleidoscope of memories of the woman in question and their frenzied relationship, good and mad; along with the realization that this ain't gonna work out because, 'Your life was one long emergency'. The final words, 'My electric surges free', make it clear that the singer has, or is about to, split; in Springsteen's case, to California. (He would tell counsel in 1976, 'I was having personal problems at the time with girls and things. It was just a good time to get away.')

He would later tell an enquiring English journalist, 'Some songs, I'm down in them more . . . It varies, I guess, depending on how close I was to that particular situation at the time. [But] a song like "For You", I'm right down in it.' And anyone who questions the autobiographical nature of this song should check out his spoken preface to one of the first full-blown E Street versions, in Uniondale NY on June 3, 1978:

> 'This is a song I wrote back in, I guess, 1971. I was living on top of this drugstore in Asbury Park and I didn't have a band, I was playing by myself. I was doing some gigs . . . at the old Gaslight Cafe and Max's Kansas City by myself, and I remember I was breaking up with this girlfriend and I went away for a week; and I came back and she'd painted all the walls to my room black. That's not true, actually she'd painted 'em all blue.'

By the time of that *Darkness* tour, such a starkly personal song was the exception. But in those first few months of 1972, songs of this kind were the rule. And it was probably these lyrical looks in the mirror that broke the dam, releasing a torrent of word-tripping songs. He had also evidently been disinterring old Dylan records, because 'For You' very obviously copied one of Dylan's most regular lyrical tricks in those amphetamine years, using a noun as an adjective: 'Princess cards', 'barroom eyes' (a close cousin to 'warehouse eyes' in 'Sad Eyed Lady of the Lowlands'), 'Cheshire smile', 'Chelsea suicide', 'nursery mouth'* &c. It was presumably the recent

* 'Sad Eyed Lady' begins 'With your mercury mouth'

publication of the first Dylan biography, by Anthony Scaduto, that had prompted such a reimmersion. After all, he needed some reading matter for that long drive to San Mateo. Maybe he hoped to pick up some tips on how going from manic rocker to solo folkie could be a route to fame.

'For You' was not the only song of this period to dissect the same relationship, or awfully similar ones, but it was one of only two Californian self-examinations to survive the first-album cull. There was 'Marie', another song in this vein about 'another' masochistic relationship. Full of violent images, one of which provides its burden – 'Marie, she skins me alive / Burns her initials in my hide, and then leaves me all alone / Branded to the bone' – this was one instance where the scars were not merely mental. One doubts it is mere coincidence that this 'queen of all the stallions' took her name from the Mother of God (via another pre-Diane girlfriend). Another song transferred to the so-called 'London demo-tape'* was 'No Need', which took this confessional tone to new heights, admitting, 'I'm one of those people who measure love in pain', a realization it would take him fifteen years to relocate. There are yet further Dylanisms – 'She's my queen and I'm her tramp'; 'She's a broken winged angel refugee' – as he fumbles for a voice he could call his own.

One imagines he took a great deal of time honing and toning these wordy lyrics as he drove to and from the west coast. This time he was travelling that lonely road alone, his only companion a sense of obligation: '[My parents] didn't have any money to buy me a bus ticket, much less an airplane ticket. So I'd drive out to the West Coast maybe once a year to see them.'

Later, he would describe spending 'several months trying to make a living as a musician in the Bay Area. It didn't work out. There were too many good musicians, and I'd left my rep as "bar band king" in Jersey. So . . . I drove back to New Jersey and did some bar gigs and I started to think that I needed to approach the thing somewhat differently. I began to write music that would not have worked in a club, really. It required too much attention . . . But I felt . . . I was going to have to do something very distinctive and original. I wanted the independence, the individuality of a solo career.' Which rather sounds like a conflation of two separate trips to

* The track-listing of the so-called 'London demo-tape' is as follows: Street Queen. Southern Son. Henry Boy. If I Was The Priest. Vibes Man. Song To The Orphans. She's Leaving. The Song. Arabian Night. Cowboys Of The Sea. Four other songs were also lodged with Intersong, including 'No Need'.

San Mateo, the Christmases of 1970 and 1971. Or maybe it took him a year, and a confirmatory trip, to see his original plan through.

He certainly could not have spent 'several months' there in 1971-72 as he was still in New Jersey in mid-December, and was back east by late January. And it was a week's drive either way. But in the *weeks* he was there he did finally decide – after much toing and froing – to go down the solo route. Initially at least he seemed to think such a change of tack required he bare his soul. As he put it in 1974, 'I had to write about me all the time, every song, 'cause in a way you're trying to find out what that "me" is . . . [But] y'know, you [also] have to be self-contained. That way you don't get pushed around.' He would later testify, during a 1998 UK court-case designed to bury once and for all these very songs (after a UK company threatened to release them in quasi-official guise), 'The music that you come up with when you are sitting in your room alone with your guitar late at night is one of the most personal things in your life.' These certainly were.

Among the songs he wanted kept out of the official canon were 'Randolph Street' (see previous chapter), the sacrilegious 'If I Was The Priest' and a song known as 'Family Song' aka 'California, You're A Woman'. The last of these ostensibly addressed the coastal state itself, but was really directed at his still-demanding parents, verbalizing for the first time the inner hurt he felt growing up: 'Ya know how when you're young, there's such a distance between you and your family/ You can't ever see things from the same point of view/ Papa wants a lawyer and mama she wants an author/ And all you want is for them to want you'. Another line positively drips with the blood of Cain, 'My papa turned away when I needed him the most'. Finally, the singer expresses the hope, 'When I grow up and have my own kids/ I'll love them all I can and let 'em make their own minds'.

Demoed for Laurel Canyon on his return east, this song was hastily buried with trowel and shovel, never even being copyrighted at the time. Yet its overarching theme would continue to infuse the songs he felt possessed to pen in the next six months, though by the time he began crafting the likes of 'Lost In The Flood' – a song he fully admits was a case of him 'trying to get a feeling for . . . the forces that affected my parents' lives . . . the whole thing of the wasted life, [which] was very powerful to me' – the meaning was sometimes lost in the obfuscatory imagery of a New Dylan. Which is what, for a while, he seemed to want to be (later protestations notwithstanding). In *Songs*, he would insist, 'I wrote impressionistically and changed names to protect the guilty . . . to find something that was identifiably mine.'

If so, the process was decidedly hit and miss. The opening couplet of a song like 'Arabian Nights', 'Shrieks of sheiks as they run across the movie screen/ A thousand sand-dune soldiers led by an Arabian queen' almost begs to be parodied. At the same time, there are hints of later widescreen epics which would bear the Springsteen imprimatur: 'Outside my window I hear another gang fight/ It's Duke and the boys against the Devil's best men/ And both sides have drawn their knives'.

Wholly enthralled by the process, quality control was not his primary concern. As he told *Crawdaddy*'s Peter Knobler the following January: 'About a year ago, I started to play by myself . . . [and] just started writing lyrics, which I never did before. I would just get a good riff, and as long as it wasn't too obtuse I'd sing it. So I started to go by myself and started to write these songs.' For now, a fair number retained some attempt at self-analysis. Lines like, 'The lady feels it's enough to just be good/ But the doctor has this need to be understood', or the not-so-assured, 'The lady feels the doctor's made of stone/ But the doctor's heart, it just ain't fond of home' – both from 'Lady and the Doctor', once shortlisted for *Greetings from Asbury Park* – seem like candid descriptions of Doctor Zoom. Disconcertingly, he also described 'the Doctor' visiting 'the animals in their stalls, shoot[ing] them full of juice'. Not quite ready to lie on a couch and spill the beans, he preferred to let songs do the talkin', even as his days as a guitar-totin' gunslinger drew to a close:

> **Bruce Springsteen**: On the guitar I never felt I had enough of a personal style where I could pursue being a guitarist. When I started to write songs I seemed to have [found] something where I was communicating better . . . / . . . I think I'd [finally] decided that if I was going to create my own point of view, my own vision, it wasn't going to be instrumentally – it was going to be . . . through songwriting . . . I had no band for a while, [so] I just wrote a group of songs that felt unique to me. [1978/1992]

Excited by all he had achieved in the six weeks he'd been away, he couldn't wait to play his new songs to the men who, back in November, told him they needed work. And so it was that on February 14, 1972, he returned to the offices of Mike Appel and Jim Cretecos and played them and their go-fer office boy Bob Spitz, 'If I Was The Priest' and six songs he had penned in the last few weeks: 'Cowboys of the Sea', 'The Angel', 'It's Hard To Be A Saint In The City', 'Hollywood Kids', 'Arabian Nights' and 'For You'. But it was not the still-unfinished 'For You' that hit the stunned trio square between the eyes. It was 'Saint In The City'. Appel asked the nervous songsmith to sing it again, so he could catch all the words:

> **Mike Appel:** 'Saint In The City' was the song that devastated me. I made him repeat the lyrics, 'cause I wasn't sure he'd said what he said. 'Cause I'd never heard anybody sing these kind of lyrics before. He went right through it again. I [just] went, 'Jesus, I thought that's what you said!' I didn't expect that, especially from where I left off with the guy [two months ago] . . . What God anointed him in the interim?

What he didn't tell the two producer-publishers was that he was still hedging his bets. The Bruce Springsteen Band had just returned from a residency at The Back Door in Richmond, Virginia, where he had debuted an eleven-minute *electric* 'Cowboys of the Sea'. Only after a similar short residency, later the same month, when he and/or another band member got into a contretemps with some other musician/s, did he finally decide to formally call time on this prototype for a big band.

The version of events as he related them to Paul Nelson sounded like the idea for another song: 'We were doing this benefit in Virginia and they took the girls to some drug rehabilitation centre [to crash for the night], and then someone comes up to them and says, "The confederate angels are coming down tonight and we're all gonna fight together." Needless to say, it all erupted the next day, so I got rid of the horn section after that, 'cause I figured I was gonna have to start playing clubs. It was the only way to make it.'

Ken Viola suggested that what actually happened was 'Mad Dog' Lopez got into a fight with one of the trumpet players, a not-uncommon occurrence. The band limped through March, even as Springsteen secretly signed on the dotted line, tying himself to Appel and Cretecos as producers and publishers for the next five albums. He had seemingly now committed himself to the idea of being a songwriter, not a Jersey bandleader. But if later comments can be believed, he never intended to stay in this solo wilderness for long:

> **Bruce Springsteen**: It got to the point where I couldn't afford a band any more, and [so] I split up the band I had. I wrote a mess of songs by myself, on acoustic guitar and I went up and I auditioned for CBS, so everybody thought I was an acoustic folk singer. I put my band back together when I got a record deal. [1975]

Appel, for now, remained wholly in the dark about Bruce's band-plans. Not that it mattered a great deal at this stage. His first concern was getting Springsteen to sign that production deal, and then to secure him a record deal. Simple. As Spitz told music-biz historian Fred Goodman, his boss was a true believer: 'He never thought he was rolling the dice: he knew what he had.'

Springsteen, though, was innately suspicious. Intimidated by any business matter, he initially played dumb. Not everyone was taken in. Spitz, for one, knew a front when he saw one: 'He was nothing in a social situation . . . He had a mousy girlfriend who did all his talking for him, and he had a different one every week. But they were all the same variety: very mousy, very New Jersey, very Gentile, very uneducated.'[MOTH]

Finally Appel called him out on all his stalling, forcing a response. As Springsteen later told Appel's counsel: 'It was a basic deal, [Appel] said. I took it, looked at it once, and brought it back. I told him I didn't know. He said, like, "Come on".' What was he holding out for? Other alternatives were less than zero, and both parties knew it. In the end, Springsteen signed his name – and not in an unlit parking lot, as legend suggests – to a contract that was, in Appel's own words, 'boilerplate. It was always 12% of retail, the producer gets 3%, the artist gets nine.' At the very time Marty Thau was trying to get the New York Dolls to sign a fifty-fifty deal with him and his business partners, Appel was the one risking the shirt from his back, not the kid from Freehold.

In order to try and recoup some of the upfront costs they were about to incur, Appel and Cretecos were looking to demo some of the better songs they had heard their protégé play with a view to placing them with artists who let others write their material, a dying practice ever since Dylan plugged in at Newport but for now the only viable way to get Springsteen's songs out into the world. It was also already apparent that Springsteen had way too many songs for a single record. And the pile was growing bigger by the day. As Appel fondly recalls, 'He would come up from Asbury Park in the morning, and say, "Hey, I've got some new songs I want to play you." He'd come up, pour his heart out. We loved everything . . . He was fully formed. It was so original; we were all just thunderstruck.' Their prodigal surrogate-son was equally amazed, but showed no interest in locating the source of all this analysis-in-song:

> **Bruce Springsteen**: Last winter I got so hyped up, almost getting a guilt complex if I didn't write. A lot of these songs came out all at once – like 'The Angel' . . . Because people had more or less requested I play acoustic, I wrote [like that]. The words come out rhythmically . . . / . . . My songs are very mysterious to me . . . I'll sing a line and I'll know exactly what I mean . . . for that one line! But then I'll go on to things where I'm not quite sure what I meant . . . [Sometimes] you got the universe to think about, but you [also] need something that rhymes with night . . . / . . . I don't dig going into the songs or why I write them, or what I'm trying to do, because I want people to find out for themselves. They should search out the songs. That's what I'm doing. [1972-74]

As he recalled in 1974, the songs at this stage generally came quick, or not at all: 'I got a lot of things out in that first album [period] . . . They were written in half-hour, fifteen-minute blasts. I don't know where they came from. A few of them I worked on for a week or so, but most of them were just jets.' His writing technique, such as it was, lent itself to this grapeshot of images: 'I would sit there with a rhyming dictionary . . . and just pour forth with whatever the images were in my head.' For the first time, he was starting with the words and adding the music later, 'because I imagined myself as being some sort of a poet at the time'. Again, he could have taken his cue from Dylan, who wrote the whole of *John Wesley Harding* that way.

If the new songs came in a flash, they generally told the same story in different settings: 'To me a song is a vision . . . and what I see is characters in situations.' What set Springsteen's songs apart at this point were the familiar characters he put in situations often so incongruous they seemed to be misplaced in space and time. The most wildly ambitious of these, 'Visitation at Fort Horn', appeared on every provisional track-listing for that debut album, but in the end made way for 'Spirit In The Night' and 'Blinded By The Light'. The story of The Captain, The Magician, The Sergeant and an angel, the visitation in the song title is the result of the

Captain hanging Merlin the Magician because 'his magic . . . must be broken', which invokes a storm of epic proportions ('the lightning cracked and the sky was hacked/ By dagger rain it was torn'). Another Madonnaesque captive, who 'commands the light ships that patrol the sea around the rainbow tips,' disappears from the song before the storm rips the fort apart, to reappear elsewhere in similar angelic disguise. On a song like this, he was trying a little too hard to 'present something that was a fully realized world with just myself and the acoustic guitar'.

Another song shot through with similar ambition (and concomitant lyrical lapses) was 'Prodigal Son', a seven-minute epic with a touch of 'Desolation Row' about it: 'And the mercury men with hydraulic joints/ They bribe with a smile and hold you up in the alley at pinpoint/ And ask you to bend over that they may anoint/ You with the holy water of your profession'. With a Zane Grey element from the outset, 'In a place where outlaws are banned from the range', the father patiently awaits the return of the prodigal son. However, it would never make it beyond demo status, washed away by an inspired flood of superior songs with a similar love of wordplay.

Perhaps surprisingly, songs about cars and girls were in short supply at this juncture, though two of the tracks he demoed for John Hammond in May showed he retained the ability to switch gears. There was 'The Angel', a song about a fallen angel with a fetish for cars redeemed by a girl 'in a trainer bra with eyes like rain'. And then there was 'Street Queen', Springsteen's 'Terraplane Blues', where he successfully fused Dylan, Chuck Berry and (unconsciously) Robert Johnson for the very first time: 'Cadillac hips, she's the best on the strip/ She knows how to use a clutch'. But the two songs that really tickled John Hammond's talent-scout bones that day in May when they first met were the one that made Appel sit up and take notice: 'Saint In The City', and the one which shook a metaphorical stick at every nun who'd ever tried to get this novice apostate to toe the line, 'If I Was The Priest'.

Springsteen had not been idle in the six weeks since he finally signed on the dotted line, but neither had Appel. Having talked strategy with Appel, the singer was astonished when 'about three weeks later' Appel told him, 'We'll start at the top. I got you an appointment with John Hammond.' As Bruce later described it, 'It was amazing to me, reading [Scaduto's] book, and then . . . find myself sitting there in *that* office.' But rather than speak for himself, he again allowed a third party to do the talking, almost with catastrophic results.

He described the scene to Nelson a few months later: 'In we go, and Mike, who is a funny guy, he gets into it, he jumps up and here we are with John Hammond and Mike starts hyping John Hammond, "I want you to know, John, this guy's heavy."' Hammond subsequently informed Springsteen 'that he was ready to hate me'. From that moment forth, Hammond viewed his relationship with Appel as essentially combative. Appel, though, insists Hammond never lost his cool:

> **Mike Appel**: When we went in, he had his sunglasses set on top of his flattop crew cut. He was very cordial. We walked in and Bruce sits down with his guitar, and I feel it's incumbent upon me to say something. I say to him, 'I've grappled with lyrics myself. This guy makes it seem like it's nothing to write reams and reams of poetry.' And [Hammond is] nodding, you know, okay, okay. Then I said, 'I can't believe he's written as many things as he has in such a short period of time, at such a high degree of quality.' He started to look at me like he thought I was starting to hype [him]. But he didn't say anything, he was just looking. And I said to him, 'In short, you're the guy who discovered Bob Dylan for the right reasons. You won't miss this.' He said to me, 'Please sit down.'

By the time Springsteen was ushered into the plush offices of the A&R man with the Vanderbilt bloodline coursing through his veins, he was left with precious little time to make his mark. Appel, though, knew what worked and had prepped him to start with 'Saint In The City'. From that opening couplet they had Hammond on board: 'I had skin like leather and the diamond-hard look of a cobra/ I was born blue and weathered but I burst just like a supernova'. It was now Springsteen's turn to nearly blow it. The next song he played Hammond was a new one, the turgid 'Mary Queen of Arkansas', for which Springsteen continued to maintain a mystifying admiration. As Hammond later related, 'I thought that was a little pretentious, and that's when I asked him if he had anything that was outrageous . . . and then he played me "If I Was The Priest". [It was] then I knew that he had that whole natural gift that you can't learn.' He also knew for sure that 'he could only be a Catholic'.

According to Hammond, 'I [then] arranged for him to come down to the studio . . . the next day, but my stipulation was that I didn't want Appel there. Bruce and I worked about two hours together. Alone.' Appel and

Springsteen did a victory jig outside the old CBS building on 57th Street, and spent the rest of the day deciding what other songs they should spring on the CBS scout. However, this was 1972, and the word of John Hammond had long stopped being law at the label. He would need the okay from above to sign anyone, let alone a kid with a guitar, a pushy manager and no track record (unlike in September 1961, when he signed Dylan without any demo lest *that* voice scared the suits off!). On May 3 Springsteen arrived promptly at two, and was ushered into the in-house demo studio, the very one that had served CBS, and Columbia before it, for the past quarter of a century. But, whatever Hammond's wishes, Springsteen and Appel were still joined at the hip:

> **Bruce Springsteen**: Columbia was very old-fashioned: everybody in ties and shirts; the engineer was in a white shirt and a tie and was probably fifty, fifty-five years old. It was just him and John and Mike Appel there, and he just hits the button and gives you your serial number, and off you go. I was excited . . . This was my shot, I had nothing to lose. [1999]

Four of the twelve songs demoed that day would eventually be released on 1998's *Tracks*, including the still-turgid 'Mary, Queen', with which he opened the afternoon session. He also had the steel-cold nerve to play Hammond two songs on which the ink was still wet, 'Growin' Up' (a superior spin-off from the earlier 'Eloise') and 'Does This Bus Stop At 82nd Street?'. Among the seven songs which never made the passage from demo to debut LP (or *Tracks*) were some that shone a brighter light into the recesses of this recidivist's mind. Notably, 'Two Hearts In True Waltz Time', which concerned itself with an illicit affair between a cop and a frustrated wife, 'the ultimate crime/ two hearts locked in true waltz time'. Among forty-plus lines were two that exposed an unvarnished inner reality: 'She needs to be real/ He needs to conceal', though the rhyming dictionary was again overused ('She swings on a vine across the state line' – oh dear). 'If I Was The Priest' also received its definitive rendering, though it would not even make it to the first-album sessions, a month hence. Hammond knew he had found a diamond in the rough. In fact, over the years he would come to insist that their demo was 'better than any tape Bruce has made since, because Bruce is [now] so uptight about perhaps overshadowing somebody else in the band'. (In 1981, he would send Springsteen a copy of the tape as a reminder of what might have been. Springsteen's 'response' was *Nebraska*.)

For now, Hammond had a more important recipient in mind, Clive Davis, head of the label and a persistent champion of Dylan in the days when he had needed label support, and not the other way round. Five days later, he sent Davis the dub and a memo: 'Here is a copy of a couple of the reels of Bruce Springsteen, a very talented kid who recorded these twelve songs in a period of around two hours last Wednesday . . . I think we better act quickly because many people heard the boy at The Gaslight so that his fame is beginning to spread.' Davis responded the next day, 'I love Bruce Springsteen! He's an original in every respect. I'd like to meet him if you can arrange it.' The meeting evidently transpired. Davis told Frederic Dannen, 'Springsteen came to my office for a *final audition* [my italics]. I heard his material, I believed in him. *I* signed him.' For now, Springsteen (and Appel) had the most powerful man at the label on their side. So much so that the singer would later send up this surreal situation in his intro to assorted 1976 performances of 'Growin' Up':

> 'I get to the CBS building with my manager. We get in the audition elevator, a special elevator marked "X". We shoot up to the clouds, passing the stars, passing all the planets. We finally get up [there], the doors open up, they frisk me a few times, and there at this big, solid gold desk, in a long, white robe, with a little wreath around his head was Clive Davis. I said, "Mr Davis . . . I wanna be a rock 'n' roll star." But first he heard my confession. And [then] he said, "Sign here".'

Unfortunately for Hammond, he quickly discovered he was going to have to go through Mike Appel. He nobly proclaimed some years later, 'I didn't want to deal with Mike Appel at all, but I have a sort of loyalty – if someone brings me an artist I feel I *have* to deal with them. It's not right to go behind the guy's back.' In fact, he did everything he could to extract Springsteen from his prior legal arrangement with Appel: 'I asked [Appel] what kind of agreement he had [with Springsteen], and he said, "Oh, don't worry. I've got him signed." . . . I said, "Mike, would you do me a favour? There's a lawyer I'd like you to talk to. He's a lawyer I trust and . . . I'd like him to see the contract." Mike replied, "Well, if you say so." Reluctantly, he went to see this lawyer and the lawyer said, "Mike, this is a slave contract. If you're smart, you won't go through with it, because your artist – if he makes it – is going to hate you."'

The lawyer Hammond had referred Appel to was William Krasilovsky, someone familiar with the music business and copyright law but not affiliated with Columbia. Nevertheless, it was a highly dangerous thing to do. Appel would have been well within his rights to refer the matter to Davis. Krasilovsky would later claim, three decades on and with hindsight to spare, that 'he knew right away . . . Springsteen would one day be sorry he had agreed to Appel's terms'.

In fact, Appel had done Springsteen a huge favour, one that would reap Springsteen (as opposed to Appel) millions in the fullness of time. He had signed Springsteen to a production deal which meant that CBS would have to *license* the recordings from Laurel Canyon, rather than signing Springsteen directly to the label. He thus retained control of all unreleased masters. The standard 'slave-contract' that CBS required of its new artists still talked in terms of 'delivered masters', as if this were the days of the 78 rpm record; and in many ways it still was.

Even the contract Appel and Springsteen signed in early June required two albums a year, a patently absurd demand that was still there because it could then be invoked when artists (inevitably) fell behind on their delivery dates to either a) drop them from the label or b) extend the term of the contract, depending on how they were doing commercially. Hammond, of course, had no problem with this contract. It was pretty much the same one he had cajoled Dylan into signing without independent counsel when he was still a legal minor, a ruse which nearly backfired disastrously when six months later Dylan got himself a manager in a mould Mike Appel could only aspire to: Al Grossman, to whom Hammond also took an immediate dislike. Hammond also seemed to think that Springsteen might be better off on the altogether less prestigious Epic subsidiary. Appel, again, interceded:

> **Mike Appel:** [Hammond] decided that Bruce should be with those younger people up at Epic and not with the stodgier, older people at Columbia – and he got this in his head. I always felt that Columbia was the classiest label on the planet. I just always saw [Bruce's] record going round on that red label, just like Dylan's did, and I couldn't get that out of my head. I had it out with Hammond . . . Hammond was a stubborn,

arrogant, enthusiastic guy. But he was like everybody that was great at what they do – he thought he was right on everything.

Appel and Hammond did not, however, disagree always. On one issue, they were as one. That was their belief that Bruce Springsteen should be marketed as a solo artist, and that the first album should be as close to the demo tape Hammond had made back in May as possible. Springsteen was left in no doubt that this was their preference. But he was less convinced, and once he realized Clive Davis and Jim Cretecos had their doubts too, he quickly aligned himself with their camp:

Mike Appel: Hammond and I were on the same side [of the acoustic argument]. And Clive Davis and Jim Cretecos were not. And Bruce was the arbiter in the middle. I said, 'Your songs are so great. You don't need a band.' Hammond was like, 'Mike, did he buy it?' 'No, he did not buy it.' [The album] was a hodgepodge. There was no order in advance. It wasn't like all *these* songs are going to be acoustic, and all *these* are going to be electric. In the end, what he decided is what we did. Davis is pushing for the band all along . . . I was a purist and Hammond was a purist. We were outvoted . . . I was so impressed by Bruce's lyrics I said, 'Who needs a band when you can write lyrics like that?'

Bruce Springsteen: The record John Hammond would have liked would have been one that the first four or five cuts from *Tracks* sound like . . . And, listening back, he may have been right . . . The music [on that first record] was an abstract expression of my direct experience where I lived in Asbury Park at the time and the kinds of characters that were around; they call them twisted autobiographies. Basically, it was street music . . . Mike and his partner Jimmy [Cretecos] were always very production-oriented; . . . [so] everything was . . . compressed for a slightly hyped sound. And that's the direction *Greetings* . . . went in. [But] I wanted a rhythm section . . . So what we ended up doing was an acoustic record with a rhythm section, which was the compromise reached between the record company, everybody else and me. [1999]

If the battle lines were drawn early, the result was not a foregone conclusion. Springsteen in later years has suggested he had to work hard in order to firmly tilt the album off its acoustic axis. Initially, as he has said, 'You listen to people whose ideas and direction may not be what you want. But you don't know that. [After all,] you just stepped off the street and walked into the studio . . . / . . . I wasn't in the position where I was going to say, "No, I want to do it like this." I was just saying, "Let me do it."' Though compromise – aka fudge – would eventually become the order of the day, the first studio session on June 7 was a strictly acoustic affair, Springsteen cutting 'Lady and the Doctor', 'Arabian Night', 'Growin' Up' and 'Street Queen', the best thing he cut that day, with him playing a Fender-Rhodes, a nod to the Stax sound of the late sixties. It never even figured in early handwritten song-sequences for the album. As it was in the beginning . . .

Even when sessions resumed on June 26, the emphasis still seemed to be on Springsteen the solo artist as he cut acoustic renditions of 'Does This Bus Stop', 'Mary Queen of Arkansas', 'Saint In The City' and 'The Angel', all songs demoed in similar form with Hammond. But the following day it was all change. For the first time, Springsteen brought along some friends from the Jersey shore; specifically, Vini Lopez, David Sancious and Garry Tallent. And the trio had already been prepped. According to Lopez, 'One day I get a call from Bruce, "You wanna make a record?" . . . A couple of weeks rehearsing with the fellas, then we did the album. [But] Danny was on the outs. He had problems with "stuff". There were [also] other keyboard players on the album.' (Specifically, Harold Wheeler.) Tallent wisely didn't have the nerve to challenge Hammond when he suggested bringing in stand-up jazz bassist Richard Davis, of *Astral Weeks* fame, to play on a couple of tracks: probably 'Two Hearts In Waltz Time', certainly 'The Angel'.

At this juncture, the intention seems to have been to make an album divided equally between all-acoustic and semi-electric excursions; five apiece – a presumably-conscious replication of *Bringing It All Back Home*'s half-electric, half-acoustic format. Of the partially plugged-in songs, three were also recorded acoustically – 'Does This Bus Stop', 'Growin' Up' and 'Saint In The City' – whereas 'Lost In The Flood' and 'For You' seemingly exist only in electric configurations.

The latter pair also happened to be the two most realized tracks on this original album, lyrically and musically. (Even if, for the next five years, Springsteen regularly encored with a *solo* piano version of 'For You' that sent chills through those lucky enough to catch it.) 'Lost in the Flood', in particular, raised the bar on his songwriting to date. When he claimed that, in this period, 'I let out an incredible amount of things at once – a million things in each song,' the paradigm of this approach is 'Lost In The Flood', where 'nuns run bald through Vatican halls, pregnant, pleadin' Immaculate Conception/ And everybody's wrecked on Main Street from drinking unholy blood', leaving 'the whiz-bang gang from uptown . . . shooting up the street'. No one this time was gonna be saved. In fact, there is so much going on it would take Bruce until 1975 to truly get to grips with the song.

The sound recording copyrights (i.e. the 'mechanicals') for a ten-song album were transferred from Laurel Canyon to CBS on August 10, suggesting it had got the green light and was geared up and ready to go. Something, though, stopped the presses from rolling. Instead, Springsteen and friends returned to the studio on September 11 to cut three more songs: 'Blinded By The Light', 'Spirit In The Night' and 'The Chosen'; taking the knife to three songs where a thesaurus vied with the rhyming dictionary for dominion: 'Jazz Musician', 'Arabian Nights' and 'Visitation at Fort Horn'.

The change of heart was partly due to Clive Davis sticking his oar in, convinced that the album needed a more contemporary sound. According to Springsteen, in *Songs*, they gave Davis a copy of the August 10 'album', 'Clive handed it back and said there was nothing that could be played on the radio . . . I went home and wrote "Blinded By The Light" and "Spirit In The Night".' Appel, too, was left in no doubt what Davis thought, after he phoned the producer up to tell him, 'I firmly believe [the album] should be with a band. We're not going to get radio play without it.'

There may also have been other factors at work. For one, Springsteen had barely played some of the songs he'd just recorded to a paying audience, and therefore lacked any real sense of which songs might hold a crowd and which might not. A short residency at The Gaslight Au Go Go in May had by his own admission been a bust: 'At the time there was no presentation. I played there two nights and [there was] no response at all.' He also subsequently claimed to have played his old haunt the Cafe Wha, when he 'was on the verge of having a record deal, and . . . was scrubbing away to make some kind of living'. But a six-night residency at the fabled Max's, beginning August 9, was a step up. Upstairs at Max's was the hip joint for all jive-ass songwriters from the Village. Suddenly, Springsteen felt like he was part of a *scene*:

> **Bruce Springsteen**: It was a funny time, '72. I used to come down to Max's Kansas City and play by myself. Paul Nelson would bring some people down. I used to open for Dave Van Ronk, Odetta, all those people were still around. David Blue came down one night and as I was walking offstage he said, 'Hey man, that was great! Come with me.' We got in a cab and went downtown to The Bitter End where I met Jackson Browne. He had his first album out . . . And then late at night the New York Dolls would play at Max's. They'd play at 2 a.m. Max's was still really thriving at the time, the whole downstairs scene was going on. It was the *cusp* of those two things. [1992]

He couldn't help but be influenced by the *energy* and indeed the slightly 'retro' feel of The New York Dolls, especially after he was obliged to return to Max's to crash late one night after missing his bus back to Jersey, only to find the Dolls 'banging away at two in the morning upstairs'. Nor were they the only ones who knew The Cadets' 'Stranded In The Jungle', a song Springsteen namechecks in 'Jazz Musician'. Paul Nelson, in his precarious A&R position at Mercury Records, would successfully sign The New York Dolls to the label before year's end, having been too late to sign Springsteen himself. Nothing if not generous with his recommendations, he was the very dude who in a former life challenged Dylan to drop protest songs, edited *Sing Out*, and championed Dylan's switch to folk-rock, before becoming chief rock critic at *Hullabaloo* and a regular *Rolling Stone* reviewer. He was in a strong position to champion Springsteen to all and sundry in the enclosed world of east-coast-based rock critics:

> **Bruce Springsteen**: Before I had an album . . . [Nelson] was bringing a lot of people down to see me . . . He would always have somebody with him . . . Then there was a fellow, Paul Williams, who had *Crawdaddy* magazine before it was the magazine, when it was just the mimeographed sheets of paper that you would buy in the Village, which was the first piece of serious rock criticism I'd ever laid my eyes on . . . So there was this small group of people who were sorta at the core of a different kind of writing about rock music . . . Those were the kind of people you

hooked up with at the time. You felt like, this guy *needs* this thing as much as I do. [2007]

One of those critics had been noting Springsteen's progress ever since he caught him in Child, covering Donovan in power chords. Lenny Kaye, though, was underwhelmed by the new Bruce: 'I'd already made the transition into being a rock writer . . . [when] I heard that Bruce was giving a solo performance down at Max's; it was like a residency. Anyway, I went to see him, and he's there playing piano, playing guitar . . . I remember thinking, "What happened to this wild rocker I remember on the steps [of Monmouth College]?" I remember feeling a [sense of] disappointment that this guy who could really turn it up, there he is [now] behind the piano . . . I heard a lot of Van Morrison in it. I never saw any Dylan in him at all, 'cept these run-on sentences, but [even] the way he ran them on . . . was [more] Van Morrison. There was a direct line of influence. But I was moving towards avant-rock and noise, so my attention was more towards the Dolls or The Stooges. By then, I just wanted to hear the amps howl.'

Nelson, too, remembered 'there was a lot of writers down that [first] night; and the [general] reaction was, "Boy, he's been listening a lot to middle[-period] Dylan records." Because it came off a lot like that without the band. [But] by the third song it was [clear] there were a lot of other things going on in there.' If Springsteen himself baulked at the Dylan comparisons, he was equally unhappy to be compared to another fellow east coast song-poet, insisting, 'I'm not Lou Reed. He has some good stuff, and there are some of the same subjects, but we take them at different angles.'

He was already looking to place some distance between his own trash-can characters and those of New York's downtown song-poets. Penning yet more new songs to spring on the attendees at Max's, specifically 'Henry Boy' and 'Song To Orphans', he was starting to think he might want another crack at the album Appel thought he'd completed. 'Song To Orphans' was another long, wordy song, with a great lil' chorus that kept the whole thing together: 'So break me now big mama, as Old Faithful breaks the day / Believe me, my good Linda, let the aurora shine the way'. The orphans – who perhaps doubled as 'The Chosen' – would only appear in the final verse, having been 'abandoned on silver mountains / Or junked in celestial alleyways'. At this point, Springsteen cut a studio version of one song – possibly this very track – which 'came out like nine minutes something. We had a steel player on it and we had Clarence, who played a great solo.' He told Nelson he 'fought like a mother' to get this on the record, but there simply wasn't room. 'Song To Orphans' was never going to cosy up to your average AM listener. But as Springsteen informed Nelson, the transition into street band, minus choir, had begun:

> **Bruce Springsteen**: Immediately John [Hammond] says, 'You're a folksinger, period.' . . . And so I said, 'Alright, I got signed by myself, I'll play by myself.' But I slowly started to push to get a little more band. You can see it on the record – towards the end I finally started to break the light a little bit. I got this sax [player], a really good cat who used to play with James Brown [*sic*]. And I went back to playing a little [lead] guitar. Now the band is starting to come around to . . . some real funky music trip. [1972]

Two other songs were also cut as the album changed tack in September. 'Blinded By The Light' and 'Spirit In The Night' would be the template for what Springsteen was calling 'some real funky music trip'. As he subsequently informed Dunstan Prial, 'I knew that when it came time to present that [music] the best way to do it, I felt, was with a group behind me. I wanted to present it that way because I knew I could be exciting onstage and I could get people excited about the music.' The folks from Jersey certainly expected something like what he had been playing on the shore the past three years: 'The people back home used to bitch all the time because . . . I was a big guitar player around town; for years that was what I did. I didn't sing, I didn't write songs, I played guitar . . . Then I got a record deal and I made a first album with no guitar on it.'

The addition of sax and electric guitar was just what the album needed. As he explained to Nelson, '"Blinded By The Light" wasn't really an acoustic song. Finally, I brought Clarence in, and that kind of opened the way for me to get more of the feeling I wanted to.' As for 'Spirit In The Night', it was his first song 'about' a car and a girl since 'Street Queen', although he later felt moved to insist, 'If you've listened carefully to "Spirit In the Night", you'll know that it's about two people who leave town in their car to go and truly love each other for the first time near a lake. I find it hard to say that [it] is *about* cars.' It provided a perfect segue into 'Saint In The City', Clarence showing himself to be a perfect foil to our newly-galvanized frontman. But although they sounded good on those two tracks, Bruce had a way to go before converting Appel, who still held the purse strings:

> **Mike Appel**: The [band] came down and played, but I thought it was more like for us to hear what they sounded like *as a band* . . . / . . . Miami Steve was there, Clarence Clemons, Garry Tallent, Danny Federici, Vini Lopez. Okay. They play 'Hard To Be A Saint In The City', 'Does This Bus Stop' . . . / . . . and my first impression was that they didn't really add much to the music, to the sound. I don't think Davey Sancious was there . . . [But] that was the most screwed-up audition. Guys didn't know the songs, they weren't together, they weren't adding anything, and I told Bruce [as much]. 'No,' he said, 'I need a band.'

If Appel thought he had been attending an audition, he had been misinformed. According to Danny Federici, now returned to the fold, 'After it was over, I went up to Bruce and said, "Well, what's the story?" He said, "It's not an audition." There was no audition; it was a rehearsal. And we went out on the road seven days later.'[BTR] Bruce, though, had simply not thought it through. In his naivety, he seemed to think a record company advance of $25,000 would be sufficient – after recording costs and Laurel Canyon's cut – to fund a touring band for the time it took to write and record a second album. Nor did the fact that he had neither a manager nor a booking agent seem to faze him. He simply asked Appel to take on the former's duties, and then sent him to the William Morris Agency to find a suitable booking agent; who, like the new sax player, was black. And a life-saver. As Appel said: 'Sam McGee kept us alive'. But he still wasn't sure *he* wanted the added responsibilities. Once again, Springsteen dug in his heels until he said yes. It was a decision he would come to rue:

> **Mike Appel:** We weren't managers. In fact, we signed Bruce to a production/publishing contract in February or March '72, and it wasn't until about six months later that we signed him to a management contract. He wanted it. He said to me, 'I want you to be my manager.' Because people were hitting him up to be his manager. I said, 'That's not really my thing.' [Out came] that stubborn streak. Bruce can be mule-stubborn when he wants to be. He said, 'No, I want you to do it.'

If Springsteen simply disregarded the no-cost lesson in rockonomics he'd gained from running a big band the past eighteen months, David Sancious didn't make the same mistake. He found himself, 'living in Richmond doing sessions when he asked me to record and go on the road. I agreed to play on the album, but I didn't really want to go on the road at that time.' He knew it would be a long, hard slog. And Springsteen was a rather demanding boss. As the frontman recalled in 2002, 'I needed to be able to call the shots, [but] I needed musicians who were very dedicated to me and to the music we were gonna make together.'

Miami Steve, though present at some *Greetings* sessions, would also be absent from the as-yet-unnamed E Street Band when in late October 1972 it took to the road to spread the word on an album that was not really theirs. Like The Attractions, who in 1977 would champion Elvis Costello's debut album *My Aim Is True* live, though he'd actually recorded it with soft-shoe rockers Clover, the E Street Band now perforce became electric evangelists for *Greetings from Asbury Park*. Springsteen's schizophrenic approach, though, initially required an acoustic prelude introducing the singer-songwriter responsible for 'Mary Queen of Arkansas', 'The Angel' and a handful of other angsty excursions.

Meanwhile, the CBS publicity-machine swung into gear. The boss was on board when a marketing budget of $50,000 was approved – maybe not a Moby Grape-like sum, but a testimony of faith nonetheless in the product this prodigal had produced. Even before the album rolled off the presses, Clive Davis had personally got in touch with Jon Landau, the then record editor for *Rolling Stone*. As Landau remembered it in 1977, 'He told me he was particularly interested in . . . this album and would I pay special attention to it . . . I said I would give it to one of our best critics. I gave it to Lester Bangs.' Bangs was not 'one of' *Stone*'s best critics; he was head and shoulders *the best*. Nonetheless, he was an odd choice. An acolyte of everything scuzzy and arch-advocate of bands who tipped their hats to the Velvets and The Stooges, he was hardly Mr Singer-Songwriter. But, as *Crawdaddy*'s Peter Knobler remarked during an October 1975 overview of Springsteen's initial rise to prominence, '[Because] he was Clive Davis' pet project . . . there was knee-jerk antagonism to a product being pushed too hard.' Even from Landau.

As it happens, Bangs saw through the hype to the heart beating within. He also had the smarts to namecheck The Band and Van Morrison as primary influences. (It took Springsteen twenty years to own up to The Band's profound influence at this time, admitting how much he 'liked the way Robbie Robertson was writing at the time with The Band. Sort of colloquial. It sounded like people telling stories . . . as if you were sitting on the couch.') In conclusion, Bangs suggested 'Bruce Springsteen is a bold new talent with more than a mouthful to say . . . Watch for him; he's not the new John Prine', a clever little dig at the last 'New Dylan' to sail on the hype barge.

However, Bangs' medium-length review of *Greetings* didn't run until the July 5 1973 issue, nigh on six months after the album appeared, by which time Springsteen was well along with his next offering. It was all in keeping with *Rolling Stone*'s long tradition of missing the boat with anything happening more than a mile away from Laurel Canyon or Haight-Ashbury, one it never really relinquished. Even with the likes of Landau and Nelson on staff, it would be 1978 before they ran their first cover story on 'The Springsteen Phenomenon'.

As such, Springsteen and his supporters would be primarily reliant on the likes of *Crawdaddy, Creem* and *Circus* to spread the word. Thankfully, *Crawdaddy*'s ex-editor Paul Williams and current editors Peter Knobler and Greg Mitchell were almost in competition to see who could be more effusive about this New Somebody. The latter pair ran a five-page piece in the March 1973 issue, presciently entitled, 'Who Is Bruce Springsteen and Why Are We Saying All These Wonderful Things about Him?' *Creem*, meanwhile, turned Bruce's debut offering over to its one remaining *enfant terrible* of protopunk journalism, Dave Marsh, who spent most of it slamming CBS for 'trying to steal the scene by the usual act of ritual infanticide, i.e. claiming that Bruce is the Baby Bobby Dylan'. He had decided burying Dylan was the best way to praise his bastard son: 'There's one crucial different between him and Dylan, see, Bruce Springsteen's no has-been.' Already, the strategy which CBS had so expensively adopted was having a negative effect on Springsteen's public profile, and doing precious little to generate airplay. As of April 1973, Appel and his artist were left to generate their own hype, one based on word of gaping mouth from those who caught him on stage, alive as live can be.

Chapter 2: 1973 – Hammond's (Other) Folly

> Onstage is about as carefree as I can get, that's where things switch off and you're just *living*, you know. Most of the rest of the time, it was always my nature to [over-] analyse. – Bruce Springsteen, 2006

Thirty years on from the release of *Greetings from Asbury Park*, Springsteen would recall a conversation with Appel in which he asked his new manager, 'How did we do?' Appel replied, 'We didn't do very well. We sold about 20,000 records.' 'Twenty thousand records! That's fabulous! I don't know 20,000 people. Who would buy a record by someone they have no idea about!??' Perhaps recalling the story in Scaduto of how Dylan's eponymous debut had sold a mere five thousand copies in that first year, Bruce decided there ain't no success like relative failure. What he forgot was that the near-disastrous sales of *Bob Dylan* led one cruel wit in the organization to dub the folksinger 'Hammond's Folly'. For a while the name stuck. Thankfully, back then Hammond had the ear of the president, Goddard Lieberson, and when one executive even hinted they were thinking of dropping Dylan, Hammond replied, 'Over my dead body.'

How ironic then, that the next singer-songwriter of note Hammond signed – a decade later! – should be marketed by the same label as a New Dylan. Hammond didn't see it, telling Pete Knobler in January 1973, 'When Bobby came to me, he was Bobby Zimmerman. He said he was Bob Dylan; he had created all this mystique [about himself]. [But] Bruce is Bruce Springsteen. And he's much further along, much more developed than Bobby when he came to me.' Others inside the record company probably wanted to send a message to Bob, who had allowed his five-year

CBS contract to die a natural death the previous August. Appel hinted as much when asked about the whole New Dylan hype in 1975, after CBS found another way to hype his man:

> **Mike Appel**: [Dylan's] lawyer comes in and asks for the world . . . And then when the negotiations fail . . . the whole world was looking at Columbia Records, and everyone was taking potshots at them. They were very nervous. Very uptight at this particular time, trying to prove themselves. [So] they might have said, in the heat of the moment, 'Screw Bob Dylan, we're going to take Bruce Springsteen and use him and show that guy just where it's at.'

By the time Springsteen was ready to return to Max's for a second residency – this time with band in tow – he was itching to shake off such shackles and rock this joint. And, as Appel notes, '[If] there was a [key] difference between Bruce and Bob Dylan lyrically: Bruce's lyrics were more spastic, more emotional, more energized than Bob's . . . [but] once you start dealing with the live show, it's a whole different thing.' That he adopted an approach reminiscent of Dylan's 1965-66 electric tour – starting out solo, before bringing out the band to rip it up – was neither here nor there, though the approach almost cost him one important convert, in town to play two sell-out shows at Radio City Music Hall, who stopped by the club on February 1:

> **David Bowie**: I originally went to Max's to see an artist called Biff Rose, a quirky but interesting writer . . . I stuck around as there was another act on. So this guy is sitting up there with an acoustic guitar doing a complete Dylan thing. My friend and I were about to leave when he started introducing a band who were joining him onstage. The moment they kicked in, he was another performer. All the Dylanesque stuff dropped off him and he rocked.

Being able to play some stuff acoustic did have its advantages. It made it a whole lot easier to do 'in-house' radio sessions, a strategy Appel and Springsteen adopted early on, after both realized a gauche Bruce was possibly the worst interviewee in Rockville. Dick Wingate, who would end up as marketing manager to the man, met him first that summer of

'73, when 'he was brought up to WVRU by the Columbia promotions person and he was dressed exactly like the cover [of *Greetings*]. White t-shirt. It's the middle of the summer . . . we didn't put him on the air because he didn't seem like he wanted to. He was very, very shy. He didn't have a whole lot to say. Then when I see him perform a few months later, it was like, "Holy shit!"'

Here was something else Bruce had in common with Van Morrison (though in Morrison's case, he frequently hid his own inarticulacy behind a torrent of four-letter words), a comparison contemporary critics noted far more than the Dylan one. Indeed, Paul Nelson in their first interview required (and got) a response from Springsteen himself: 'I listen to Van Morrison because he [has always] had a lot of elements of other music that I love – even the latest album, *St Dominic's [Preview]* – and I listen to him a lot because he's a great singer.' Morrison was also a great improviser. By 1972 he would usually do these long mid-song raps that gave audiences raptures, though the first instance of it on record dated back to the earliest days of Them, when on the fade-out to 'Little Girl' he expressed a desire to 'little girl, little girl, little girl, I wanna fuck you', resulting in the fastest recalled LP in Decca's history.

(Springsteen seemed on the verge of replicating this feeling a number of times in 1980 when intersecting 'I Wanna Marry You' with a similar extended reverie: 'Sometimes at night when I lie in bed I still see her face . . . running round my head . . . here she comes . . . walking down the street . . . here she comes . . . walking down the street . . . she's looking so fine, she's looking so sweet . . . she's so fine, she's looking so sweet . . . and someday I'm gonna make her mine . . . she's gonna stop. She ain't just gonna pass me by, she's gonna stop. She ain't just gonna pass me by, she's gonna stop. She ain't gonna just pass me by, she's gonna stop. She ain't gonna pass me by . . . little girl, little girl, little girl . . .')

For now, though, Springsteen's on-stage stories were one way of figuring out which characters might work in song. As Clemons wrote, in one of the few genuinely illuminating sections of a dull autobiography, 'This was how the guy thought . . . in stories. And there was no end to them. He could go on and on and on, and the stories were actually fucking good. He'd throw in little insights and nuances that made the characters come to life. He gave them dimension. They all had secrets.' One wonders what the small audience thought when he went into such a story the night he debuted 'Rosalita' in Richmond, Virginia in February 1973, a year almost to the day after the Bruce Springsteen Band were run out of town:

> 'I was eight years old. I'd been hitchhiking around the country for five years . . . I was something else . . . and I got arrested for loitering, and they put me in the same cell as James Brown. He looked me in the face and he said "Ungh, aah . . . ain't it fun?" The next time he opened his mouth to say something, out came (some James Brown-style music), then he walked away. Just by sheer coincidence, in the very next cell, sitting there with his surfboard was Dennis Wilson of the Beach Boys. I said, "Dennis, what are you doing in that cell with a surfboard?" Said he was looking for the perfect wave. He came up to me, looked me in the face and said (band does "Fun, fun, fun"). Then he split. By sheer coincidence they [then] brought in Wilson Pickett for being, uh, too funky or something. I forget the exact charge but he came up to me and said, "Son, if you're ever in trouble, all you got to do is . . ." and showed me this . . .'

Where did such tall stories spring up from? Indeed, where did that sassy stage-persona come from, period? Recalling those days in a Springsteen feature, Martin Kirkup described how he 'once saw him go into a ten-minute monologue between songs, all about the trouble his band used to have with the mafiosos in Jersey, and then say to an audience of six hundred, "Now, hey, that's in confidence. I wouldn't want that to go outside this room."' And Peter Knobler recollects him introducing one song at this time with, 'This is the songwriter-poet as innocent,' and the next one, 'Now the songwriter-poet as pervert.' Both got a laugh. He also learnt how to play with the very idea of autobiographical revelation onstage. On his first live radio broadcast he came up with a particularly surreal explanation for why he got a 4-F in the army induction exam:

> I lived 18 years of my life next door to a gas station in a small town in New Jersey and it was Ducky Slattery's Sinclair Station. Ducky Slattery had this one line he ripped off the Marx Brothers, anytime anybody'd come into the gas station, he'd always say "You wanna buy a duck?" That was his big line, not too original but it worked, you know . . . [Well,] my father killed a duck for Thanksgiving once. Helped me get out of the draft. I went down to the Army, told 'em ever since I seen my father kill that duck, I

> go crazy every time I see a duck. If I was out there on the battlefield in Vietnam and a duck came walking by, I might go nutty, I might shoot generals or something.

He seemed able to deliver such stories with an innate, comedic sense of timing, acquired from God knows where. A couple of years later, when telling a story about his and Miami Steve's pursuit of one particularly unattainable girl – the preface to the E Street Band's extended reinterpretation of 'Pretty Flamingo' – he sent up the whole idea of such storytelling by stopping mid-rap, having got to where 'it was about quarter to twelve . . . and I said "Steve, Steve, I'm in love, I got to find out what this girl's name is."' He then informed these Philly fans, 'The fact [is], I could go on with this story and tell you that I did find out [her name] and that we broke into the house and knocked everybody down, picked her up and ran down the street, but the real story is we gave up and went home.'

And yet, when you put him on the radio in a sterile studio with just a mike and a DJ for company, he froze up, as he did that day up at WVRU. Which didn't stop the hipper east-coast DJs from putting him on the radio. They, and his manager, just quickly realized that a broadcast of the live act was the way to go. From day one, Appel realized that 'if you could, through a King Biscuit Flower Hour or a WNEW . . . if you could get Bruce to do a two, two-and-a-half-hour show over the air, you're covering those airwaves for [all] those hours!' Springsteen also learnt to appreciate the enduring rewards of such a strategy:

> **Bruce Springsteen**: There were a few cities where we developed strong early audiences . . . The support of the old-school radio stations was enormous and incredibly important. It was where the band's live experience paid off . . . It was a very organic, grassroots growth that you were able to get going in those days. It was a combination of the band's excellence in live performance and a system that could *respond* to that excellence . . . It was a very different day and age. The music business was much smaller, there was no entertainment media . . . there was no coverage of rock music on television . . . The upside was you had quite a bit of room to grow, experiment, and get your act together. [2010]

However, to put this in context, America is a big place, and away from the east coast such a plan was (for now) doomed to failure. As Appel recently noted: 'If you went down to Virginia, he could even play at a theater and damn near sell the whole place out. So it wasn't like he was a nobody everywhere. But you're talking about . . . the Northeast – and that was it, basically. You couldn't take him anywhere else.' For those converts, though, every live broadcast from 1973 to 1975 (and there were at least three a year) provided Affirmation, beginning at Max's on January 31, 1973, when Springsteen made his, and King Biscuit's, radio 'in concert' debut.*

And he did it via a stunning 'Spirit In The Night' with the band, straight after the brand-new 'Bishop Danced' solo, which he had introduced at his first acoustic radio session three weeks earlier as 'a song about this bishop and his woman and this violin-player, and this little girl who lost her mother to mathematics. And it's about pancakes and . . . James Garner, and how he married this woman with one eye, who kicks like a mule. And it's about the sexual patterns of elderly boys, and this little boy who thinks that the Indians are still in the woods, only nobody sees them.' Still in love with quick-fire rhymes ('double-quick back flip . . . fiddlestick fiddled quick') and madcap monikers (Baby Dumpling, Maverick Daddy, Mama Tuck), Springsteen unrepentantly basked in the reflected glory of ever-more rococo rhyme-schemes.

If King Biscuit had no need for more than three or four songs, Appel smartly ensured the whole of one Max's set was recorded. And it was quite a set! It had been four and a half months since *Greetings* was completed, and the faucet remained on full-blast. 'New York City Song', 'Song To Orphans', 'Saga of the Architect Angel' and 'Thundercrack' were now added to the *Greetings* songs, and would all enjoy favour in the months (and years) ahead.

Though none of the four (save the first verse of 'New York City Song') would make the second album, 'Thundercrack' would be a show-stoppin' encore for the next fifteen months. Rhyming for kicks, but no longer gratuitously, he throws out some of his most infectiously memorable lines: 'She moves up, she moves back/ Out on the floor there ain't nobody cleaner/ She does this thing she calls the Jumpback Jack/ She's got the heart of a ballerina', the lyric of someone who has finally discovered

* There has been much dispute about what was played on King Biscuit at the time, but certainly broadcast at some point in 1973 were 'Spirit In The Night', 'Bishop Danced', 'Mary Queen of Arkansas' and 'Song To The Orphans'.

rhyme needs its own internal 'rithmetic. 'Thundercrack' also showed he had adapted well to the demands of writing for a band. As he put it in 1992, 'I became more arrangement-orientated. I got more interested in how the thing was going to function as an ensemble.' 'Thundercrack', a quintessential example of 'function[ing] as an ensemble', was evidently written at the end of 1972, one of a flurry of songs fusing the lyrical grandiosity of *Greetings* with an endlessly inventive musical chutzpah. Songs like 'Rosalita', 'Thundercrack' and 'Kitty's Back' hinted of great(er) things:

> **Bruce Springsteen**: When I went on the road, I took the point of view I developed on my first record and I began to just write with the band in mind, with the idea of mixing those two things . . . [When it came to] the second record . . . I said [to myself], 'Well, I want to hold onto these characters, this point of view and this writing style, but I want to include the physicality of rock music, or band music.' [1999]

And yet, when he entered 914 Sound Studios on January 29 to demo some new songs ahead of his second Max's residency not one of them was a ballbuster. The five songs demoed over the next two days were 'I Met Her In A Tourist Trap in Tiguara' – which sounds more like one of his concert raps, and remains uncirculated – 'Architect Angel', 'Janey Needs A Shooter', 'Ballad of a Self-Loading Pistol' and 'Winter Song'. If none of them were attempted at the *Wild, the Innocent* sessions (though 'Architect Angel' appears on a September 1973 shortlist, presumably in demo guise), he was still working on 'Architect Angel' at the early *Darkness* rehearsal sessions and 'Janey Needs A Shooter' at the *River* rehearsals. So stockpiling songs for future projects began this early.

Of the songs themselves, 'Architect Angel' was another Zane Grey meets Zero in Jungleland epic, a saga which stretched 'from the cellar ways to the attics and all across the plains', thus anticipating future panoramas. But the architecture ain't quite there. 'Ballad of a Self-Loading Pistol', if it anticipates anything, anticipates *Nebraska*, being about a father who teaches his son to shoot and shows him 'the story of the self-loading pistol', only for the boy to end up killing someone in a hold-up. He duly boasts to his father, 'Your son, he's an outlaw/ And this blood feels good on my hands'.

'Winter Song' demonstrates that allusions to prostitution in three other winter 1973 songs ('Janey Needs A Shooter', 'Tokyo' and 'Hey Santa Ana') were no passing whim. This one is specifically about, 'Winter, that old icy whore', who can make one 'drip like honey down soot mama's leg' and works for 'the mademoiselle/ who holds the keys to all these doors around her waist/ And rings the bell'. If 'Winter Song' puts some cracks in that Freehold facade of Catholic coyness, the magnificent 'Janey' breaks the dam. 'With her doors open wide, she begs, come inside', one of Janey's come-ons, is uncharacteristic of the *Greetings*-era songwriter. The song depicts the loose lady in a series of liaisons with every kinda profession – a gynaecologist who 'tears apart her insides'; a mechanic who 'smashed my car with [a] big tow bar'; and a peeping-Tom cop who likes to 'peek in my window every night'. Each of them is haunted by the lady who 'needs a shooter'.

If 'Janey Needs A Shooter' introduces one of Springsteen's great heroines, 'Tokyo', a song demoed three weeks later, again at 914, introduced another. Looking for a recommendation from a Catholic priest for 'a cheap virgin', the padre helpfully suggests, 'You can try Rosalie, around the corner and across the street, word is out that she's fast'. (Anyone who doubts Rosalie and Rosalita are one and the same should note that early versions of the latter song refer to her 'sweet samurai tongue', not her 'soft sweet lil' girl tongue'.) 'Tokyo' was another song which although not attempted at the second-album sessions, survived live into 1974. He already knew it was horses for courses.

In fact, the only song demoed in February 1973 that did make the summer sessions – and album – was something he'd been playing around with for months, but had yet to spring on the band; even on Clarence Clemons, the archetypal vibes man. 'Vibes Man' is often portrayed as the germ of an idea he then added to 'New York City Song', making 'New York City Serenade'. In truth, the released 'Serenade' owes far more to 'Vibes Man' than 'New York City Song', though it was the latter which Springsteen worked up at spring shows, and 'Vibes Man' which stayed secret – until that moment in mid-July when he took the first verse of 'New York City Song', the *whole* of 'Vibes Man' and made a single serenade. Lyrical losses from 'Vibes Man' would be minimal, though he does delete a couplet revealing the fish lady's battered past: 'You were born black and blue/ You didn't have to wait for somebody to hit you', his first reference to domestic violence in song (these lines appear in the first known performance of 'New York City Serenade', at Max's in mid-July, but not on the end-of-month My Father's Place broadcast).

'New York City Song' also lost its own reference to wife beating in the coupling process: 'She got a dirty Big Daddy whose fist pump like gears/ He's kept her in hope, supplied her in fear'. But it is the proto-'Jungleland' ending to 'New York City Song' that is the greater loss, hinting at something ground-breaking to come: 'Some people say he was the holder of the cosmic keys/ Oh, and his throat was choked with lightning from some childhood disease/ And with a tommygun blast he got the people screamin', till he falls helpless in Times Square, just like street scum/ Cryin', New York City kill their young [x2]/ And from a tenement window I heard sighing'. Through the spring of 1973 'New York City Song' regularly opened a set which, even before *Rolling Stone* condescended to review Springsteen's slightly-stilted debut album, was moving at warp speed away from that tentative template.

With 'Thundercrack' the other bookend to every ballroom blitz, a callow Springsteen seemed positively fearless about the type of song he would perform; the newer and obscurer, the better. Probably the most lyrically ambitious of the songs *no one* in the audience knew was 'Hey Santa Ana', using as it did the idea of a town waiting on the appearance of its own personal saviour, in this case Santa Ana, 'he who could romance the dumb into talkin''. While 'the giants of Science' start out fighting for 'control over the wild lands of New Mexico', in the end they 'spend their days and nights . . . searching for the light . . . just to be lost in the dust and the night'.

Chancing again on that newfound lyrical sophistication, the song's narrator-observer describes each character in the song with an eagle eye: Kid Cole, Kansas, Max ('some punk's idea of a teenage nation') and, of course, Contessa, the object of his lust, who runs the Rainbow Saloon. The song ends in classic Springsteen fashion, with a plea to dance the night away ''cause only fools are alone on a night like this!', the perfect coda to a song which ultimately proved too 'Dylanesque' for his liking:

> **Bruce Springsteen**: 'Santa Ana' is just a series of images, but it works, there's a story being told. But later I turned away from that kind of writing because I received Dylan comparisons. If you go back and listen it's really not like Dylan at all, but at the time I was very sensitive about creating my own identity, and so I moved away from that kind of writing. [1999]

He already knew it was one thing to play with audience expectations in a club. It was another thing entirely to attempt the same when you're the no-name support act for someone else's tour, as happened that spring with the likes of Blood, Sweat & Tears, Black Oak Arkansas and Chicago, none of them suitable bed-partners. The show with Black Oak Arkansas was further soured by that band's decidedly southern attitude to Springsteen's saxman. (Lopez recalls, 'We get done playing, me and Clarence are backstage and one of the band guys comes up to Clarence and says, "You can't be back here." We were a bunch of skinny white kids from New Jersey with a big black guy in our band. I guess some people didn't like the black man thing.') Such slots obliged them to promote product. And, indeed, the one extant soundboard tape of these 'support' slots (Berkeley, March 2) shows the E Street Band slowly coming to grips with the *Greetings* songs, with a stunning 'Lost In The Flood' and a knockout 'Blinded By The Light' the highlights of a seven-song, forty-minute set.

Three months later, they found themselves even more at odds with audiences on an east-coast stint with the bombastic Chicago, an arena act if there ever was one. Almost from the opening night in Richmond, Va., a clear line was being drawn. Ironically, that was the night Springsteen got heckled by *former* fans because, as Lopez says, 'They wanted to hear Steel Mill stuff.' On a radio phone-in the previous afternoon, Springsteen had actually been asked to do 'Resurrection', an old Steel Mill song, but preferred to play the brand-new 'New York City Song'. Which was pretty much the case at all the Chicago shows. *Greetings* barely got a look in. Springsteen preferred to spring the likes of 'Tokyo', 'Hey Santa Ana', 'Thundercrack', 'Rosalita' and 'E Street Shuffle' on mystified attendees. At The Spectrum in Philadelphia, they even ran tape on live versions of the last two (and maybe captured the definitive 'Rosalita' into the bargain). But even these soon-to-be concert classics failed to rouse the cataleptic Chicagoans as the band played on. As Lopez sarcastically notes, 'When you're on stage at a Chicago concert and you're looking off the stage, there's nuns, priests, people in wheelchairs for the first ten rows. You're not seeing anything past that.'

Arriving at Madison Square Garden for the last two nights of the tour – knowing CBS execs would be there checking on their investment – Springsteen finally made a concession to promoting his latest fab waxing, performing 'Spirit In the Night', 'Blinded By The Light' and 'Lost In The Flood', the three most dynamic cuts from the album at this point, on night one as part of a full, one-hour set. When the audience demanded an encore, and got a ten-minute 'Thundercrack' for their pains, Appel had to cross swords with the Garden management. Lopez takes up the story: 'We actually got in trouble . . . because we did an encore song – shouldn't have done it. The next night they took us off the [video] screen; half an hour, that's it. 'Cause it was overtime. We went three minutes over time and it cost them [like] $10,000.' Appel suspects it was Chicago who took umbrage: 'Bruce really did great that night. He knocked them dead. So the next night the guys from Chicago wouldn't let us use their video.' Either way, it was both a promising end to the tour, and the start of a solid policy on Springsteen's part that he would not play arenas *ever* again, one he cogently articulated the following year to a nodding Paul Williams:

> **Bruce Springsteen**: I did the Chicago tour. I did that tour because I had never played big places. And I said, I ain't gonna say no, because I don't know what they're like. So we went and played it, about fourteen nights in a row. I went crazy - I went insane during that tour. It was the worst state of mind I've ever been in . . . just because of the playing conditions for our band. I couldn't play those big places. It had nothing to do with anything that had anything to do with me . . . So I won't go to those places again. That was it. Usually we won't play any place over 3,000 - that's the highest we want to do. We don't want to get any bigger. And even that's too big . . . I'm always disappointed in acts that go out and play those [big] places. I don't know how those bands can go out and play like that . . . If you get that big you gotta realize that some people who want to see you, ain't gonna see you. I'm not in that position, and I don't know if I'll ever be in that position. All I know is that those big coliseums ain't where it's supposed to be . . . I don't know what people expect you to do in a place like that. Especially our band - it would be impossible to reach out there the way we try to do. Forget it! [1974]

There was another problem with support slots. They didn't give Springsteen time to build momentum. Hence, his description of these Chicago shows to another long-time supporter the following year: 'We got introduced, walked on stage, blinked and that was it. It's hard to show an audience what the band is about in that little time.' All he could do was hope anyone at CBS who did catch that first MSG show or heard the couple of tracks from Philadelphia was converted. Because by the time he decamped to 914, the third week in June, he needed all the label help he could get.

On May 29, Clive Davis had been summoned to the office of CBS president, Arthur Taylor, and told to clear his desk immediately. At the front door he was 'met by two CBS security men and served with the company's civil complaint against me, alleging $94,000 worth of expense-account violations'. Davis would rise again at his own label, Arista, but Bruce had just lost his one powerful ally at CBS. Hammond, too, was effectively dead in the water, any hands-on relationship he had with his protégé ending the night he caught one of the Max's shows and had a heart attack in mid-set, his third in the past few years. Though, according to a *Rolling Stone* report, Hammond's doctor blamed the heart attack on his 'enthusiasm at the Springsteen' show, he was simply not a well man. And when sessions for a second Springsteen album started in June, again at 914 Sound Studios in Blauvelt NY, a small hamlet near the New Jersey border, Appel decided the night time was the right time. A paranoid Hammond was convinced that 'Mike had the sessions start at midnight so I couldn't come'. In fact, Appel bent over backwards to accommodate Hammond, while also trying to balance the books:

> **Vini Lopez:** We were the graveyard shift, because Melanie was working [at 914] at the time, so we had to work around her. Louis Lahav was there. [Mike] was demanding. I used to go pick up John Hammond – we'd go to CBS, wait for him, drive to Blauvelt, do the session, put him in the car, drive him back, then go home. But . . . somehow, him and Mike never hit it off. So it got to the point where he said, 'I'll come, but only if *he* don't come.' So Mike didn't come.

On the one time Hammond went to 914 and Appel *was* there, the A&R man wasn't shy of offering an opinion: 'I noticed that Bruce was having a beautiful time listening to the band. He'd lock himself up in a sound-proof booth, then sing to the tracks. So I said to Mike, . . . "This is no way for Bruce to record. Bruce has got to be stimulated by live performance. He has to get his kicks from the band . . . When you're doing this thing with the headphones and being locked up in an isolation booth, you've lost the battle."' But Appel wasn't interested in 'having a beautiful time', he was there to make a record.

Thankfully, Hammond soon realized he was a spare wheel, leaving Appel to it, though he couldn't resist a last parting shot in his 1977 autobiography: 'Once Bruce was signed with Columbia, Appel wanted no part of me, or of what Columbia could contribute to the development of his star.' The exact opposite was true. Without Davis, and with Hammond's enmity toward Bruce's business manager/producer plain to see, Appel's only recourse was to blow everyone at the label away with Springsteen's second album. Which would also be the E Street Band's first.

The sessions began in earnest on June 22, a week after their Chicago commitments came to an end – dry runs in mid-May resulting only in the slow-burn 'Fever' and a prototype 'Circus Song' – and would be extremely business-like. Just nine sessions were required to produce *The Wild, the Innocent & the E Street Shuffle*, Springsteen's most realized album of the seventies, along with another album's worth of ambitious cowboy-mouth shuffles. Predictably, he began by recording five songs in a single day, all of which were worthy of release (though none would be till the nineties): 'Thundercrack', 'Phantoms', 'Hey Santa Ana', 'Seaside Bar Song' and 'Evacuation of the West'.

Of these, only 'Evacuation of the West' had yet to receive its live debut. Instead, Springsteen reserved one of his most emotive vocals for the studio version. When he sings that final couplet, 'Good God, I think they're dying/ In the wind you can hear them sighing', it feels like he's saying goodbye to every wild-west figure conceived in the past year and a half, and a bunch of childhood dreams, too. He indubitably was.

If 'Thundercrack' and 'Hey Santa Ana' were both proven crowd-pleasers, 'Seaside Bar Song' and 'Phantoms' had only been road-tested at the end of the Chicago run, and were still unknown quantities. 'Seaside Bar Song', with that 'squeaky little keyboard figure straight from Johnny & The Hurricanes country' (to quote Giovanni Dadomo), for all its innate sense of fun addressed the price paid for trying to 'live a life of love'. When the morning comes, the singer is sure the protagonist's 'papa's gonna beat you, 'cause he knows you're out on the run'. But for now, the main aim was to not 'let that daylight steal your soul''.

The two protagonists in 'Phantoms', Jamie, who 'rides down a broken highway . . . [his head] filled with crazy visions of negroes and white women in evening gowns', and Jessie, who is 'calling to him in the hills', have even more pressing problems. 'Fly[ing] in strict formation over the hills of St

Croix', the Phantoms are looking to save Jamie from 'the Christian army' waiting for him in them thar hills. Neither song lasted the distance as inch by inch, track by track Springsteen edged towards his wildly innocent goal:

> **Bruce Springsteen**: On the second album I started slowly to find out who I am and where I want to be. It was like coming out of the shadow of various influences and trying to be me . . . Songs have to have possibilities. You have to let the audience search it out for themselves. You can't say, 'Here it is. This is exactly what I mean,' and give it to them. You have to let them search. [1974]

Three days later, he returned to work some more on these songs – as well as the already-debuted 'Circus Song' and 'New York City Song', each about to evolve into the more identifiable 'Wild Billy's Circus Story' and 'New York City Serenade'. Meanwhile, 'Phantoms' was *devolving* into 'Zero and Blind Terry', which he set to the self-same backing track. Gone were the Catholic soldiers and the cowboy-outlaws as 'Zero & Blind Terry' announced the second stage of Springsteen the songwriter. From now on, 'There was more of the band . . . and the songs were written more in the way I wanted to write.' 'Zero & Blind Terry' tells the tale of two eloping lovers, Zero and Terry (who is never described as blind in the song), caught in the crossfire of a gangland confrontation: 'The Skulls met the Pythons down at the First Street station/ Alliances had been made in alleyways, all across the nation . . .' Terry seems to share the same Dad as Rosalie. To him, Zero is 'no good/ A tramp, a thief and a liar', so he hires some state troopers 'to kill Terry and bring Terry back home'.

How it ends is left for the listener to decide, or would have been if he hadn't decided to hold the song over for the next album. Appel tried his best to steer Springsteen right, and he had no doubt 'Zero' was a winner, but, as he openly admits, by the time of the second album Springsteen 'was the final arbiter, always, about everything. We never even tried to ride roughshod over Bruce. Bruce was the boss about everything to do with his recordings.' And Bruce had acquired some hard and fast ideas about making each album a Statement:

> **Bruce Springsteen**: I was always concerned with doing albums, instead of collections of songs. I guess I started with *The Wild, the Innocent &*

> *the E Street Shuffle* . . . particularly the second side, which kind of syncs together. I was very concerned about getting a group of characters and following them through their lives a little bit. [1984]

To realize this vision, he still lacked one component. It was one he felt he had been missing all along – David Sancious, 'a man whose notes belong in quotes, whose groove has hung loose, twenty years old, [with] digits of solid gold'. Stalwart of the Bruce Springsteen Band, and habitué of the Upstage, his introduction into the band he always belonged in proved positively painless. As Lopez asserts, 'He was The Dude. The way I play, I just fit right in with him. A couple of nights, we were doing this other stuff, Bruce turned around and said, "That's *it*, that's the stuff."' He was also the reason 'the band' became the E Street Band (The Band having already been taken as the name of another fabled 'backing band'). But it wasn't because of his musical contribution. It was because, to adopt Lopez-lingo, 'When we were on tour, we'd get to his house [on E Street] and we'd wait forty minutes for him to come out of his house. We spent a lot of time waiting for David!'

By the time Sancious punched the clock on June 28, 'Zero and Blind Terry' was already recorded, but he still happily overdubbed a new part that made all the difference: 'I came up with this one organ riff that Bruce really loved. There is one part that's real slow, and I did a cathedral-type voicing.' He was also on hand when it came time to transform 'Vibes Man' and 'New York City Song' into the semi-symphonic 'New York City Serenade'. He already knew Springsteen would give every E Streeter latitude musically, even as the sound in his head overrode all others:

> **David Sancious**: There were a couple of keyboard ideas I came up with [on *The Wild, the Innocent*], but I don't think they constituted the arrangement of the songs. Bruce works in such a way that whenever he writes a song, he knows exactly how he wants it to sound. There's space on there to interpret, but he'll verbally tell you what kind of thing he wants, and then it's up to you.

After that first batch of sessions in late June, remaining sessions had to be slotted around live commitments; with a third landmark residency at Max's in mid-July – this one in tandem with Bob Marley's original Wailers

– providing the perfect opportunity to break in both Sancious and some new songs. These included an exquisite elegy to summer's end on the Jersey boardwalk, 'Fourth of July, Asbury Park', known universally as simply 'Sandy'. At the time of its live debut he was still honing the lyric. The original second line ('Sparkin' an empty light in all those lonely faces, reachin' up like bandits in the sky') would make it to the initial studio recording, but not to the album. Likewise, a final verse finds 'them northside angels . . . parked with their Harleys way south out on the Kokomo'.

Even though he was still working on this so subtle song, he elected to open with it at a private bash in San Francisco just four days after the Max's run came to an end. The shindig in question was the CBS Sales Convention, a three-day affair at which the E Street Band was expected to follow Edgar Winter's White Trash, who restricted their set to fifteen minutes – which was how much good material they had – and let rip with smoke bombs and fireworks to hide the fact. Lopez thinks, 'We were supposed to open the show, and Edgar Winter . . . insisted, "No, we're opening the show", and we didn't have pyrotechnics [like them]. And [then] we had to go on after them. We just did our thing.' John Hammond later suggested, 'Bruce came on with a chip on his shoulder and played way too long.' So much for championing his own signing! But Springsteen made his point *his* way, 'I followed Edgar Winter with his smoke bombs . . . You can't compete with that. So Danny and I did "Sandy", which I had just written, just accordion and acoustic guitar.'

He had actually been in a strange mood all day. West coast promotion man Paul Rappaport remembers: 'He walked into the hotel, looking a little dishevelled, and he said, "Rap, what day is it?" "You mean, what time is it?" "No, what *day* is it?" So something was up . . . [But] in those days not all of Columbia was behind Bruce. There were three or four of us.' Aside from 'Rap', there was Ron Oberman, fresh from Mercury and a music man through and through. And Pete Philbin. Period.

The band would soon need all their support, and then some, as they returned to New Jersey to put the finishing touches to an album whose overarching vision was quite unlike anything the past coupla years had produced in Rockville. At two sessions in August, Springsteen put the finishing touches to the studio 'Sandy', scrapping a children's choir and making engineer Louis Lahav's wife, Suki, multi-track her backing vocals instead. He also persevered with 'Thundercrack' and 'Zero and Blind Terry', both of which fell at the final hurdle, in the former's case because it never came close to the energy it generated in concert. There was another lost song, too, 'Fire On The Wing' (later shortlisted for *Tracks*). It would be late September before they finally had the album in the can, after Springsteen decided he needed something which stamped this new ultra-confident songwriting self on the record. It took till then for Springsteen to pen, arrange and record his most ambitious song to date. Originally called 'Puerto Rican Jane', it would be released as 'Incident on 57th Street'.

Asked in 1975 if he ever felt self-conscious when writing about people and scenes from his own life, he suggested: 'You don't have to put it into words . . . You just write the songs and that's what comes out,' citing 'Incident' as an instance where he felt 'more of an observer'. For the first time, the *auteur* inside was yelling 'Roll 'em'. 'Puerto Rican Jane' seems like a duskier Janey, still in need of a shooter; and in Spanish Johnny, she seems to have found him. Johnny himself is a chancer who can't resist the importunings of the other 'young boys' when they whisper 'You wanna make a little easy money tonight?' He slips from his snug bed and sleeping lover to go off into the night. Though we are spared the bloody denouement, Spanish Johnny is a close cousin of the punk whose dreams will gun him down when the story climaxes in 'Jungleland'.

Now all he had to do was sequence such shuffles. A September shortlist for *The Wild, the Innocent* lists six of its seven eventual songs (the one missing, surprisingly, is 'E Street Shuffle'), as well as 'Thundercrack', 'Santa Ana', 'Zero and Blind Terry' and 'The Architect Angel', which could never have fitted onto a single album. It would have required a double set of *Exile On Main Street* proportions. 'Seaside Bar Song', one of the most spontaneous-sounding tracks from the sessions, had already been set aside, probably because, as Appel observed, 'He never took a relaxed approach to music. He would find some cute little riff, or something, and he'd end up thinking it wasn't important enough to put on the album.' It would, however, make *Tracks* at a time when he proffered an explanation for why such songs got the snip:

> **Bruce Springsteen**: Things didn't get on because there wasn't enough room, or you didn't think you sang that one that well, or the band didn't

> play that one that well, or you wanted to mess around with the writing some more. 'Zero and Blind Terry' was a big song we played live all the time. [1999]

There is almost as much unity among the material that didn't make *The Wild, the Innocent* – including the likes of 'Bishop Danced', 'Fever' and 'You Mean So Much To Me', all played live in the first half of 1973 – as there is to those that made the grade. Springsteen even uncharacteristically expressed a desire to release such a record the night after opening the *Born In The USA* tour: 'I do have an album of outtakes from *The Wild, the Innocent & the E Street Shuffle* that feels just like that record. There may be a whole album's worth of it . . . I'm singing all the crazy words, and it's like those songs. Some time I'd like to get that out.'

It would have made for a very different album from *The Wild, the Innocent,* which had the Sancious imprint in every nook and cranny, from the string arrangement on 'New York City Serenade' to the jazz-funk of 'Kitty's Back' and 'E Street Shuffle'. Of all the band members he was the one who now took Bruce's licence to improvise and ran with it, without ever blundering into a Weather Report-like jazz-fusion. As Sancious asserts, 'Most people don't understand what you're doing when you say improvise. They think you just sit down and start riffing away, but it's really a lot more refined than that.'

And yet, for all its musical advances on *Greetings*, there was a sense in which *The Wild, the Innocent* was a premature bulletin from a band still coming to terms with such grand material. In a letter to a radio executive, John Hammond suggested that there was an air of disappointment at the label: 'Bruce's performances [on the LP] do not have the ease or the joy of his live appearances and have the feeling of material being far too carefully worked over. It's all pretty embarrassing for Columbia, since most of us here have felt that this album doesn't do him justice.'

Sancious and co., though, were just warming up. The period between July 1973 and January 1974 saw this band in their onstage element, wending their way down E Street and straight into the likes of 'Incident on 57th St', 'Kitty's Back' and their namesake shuffle, with something magical happening nightly. It would even prompt a certain nostalgia from the man who broke the spell, Springsteen himself, twenty-five years later: 'We had come out of a band that had jammed a lot, so when I put the band together as an ensemble, they had this tendency to want to play and play and play. [The band's] style was quite beautiful and very responsive and just totally original. [But] it only lasted for a very brief period.'

In that 'brief period', he revived 'Something You Got' and 'Walking The Dog' from the Bruce Springsteen Band repertoire, and 'Let The Four Winds Blow' from Lozito's collection of Fats Domino 45s. A coupla recast originals from that earlier 'jam-band', 'Secret To The Blues' and 'You Mean So Much To Me Baby' also found renewed favour. If the former was quickly dropped, the latter by January 1974 had assumed epic proportions, reflecting 'this tendency to want to play and play and play'. Something unique was happening, and the whole band was instinctively attuned to it. Appel sensed it, too. When they returned to a familiar hunting ground, Joe's Place in Boston, for a three-day residency (January 4-6, 1974), he decided it was high time they were captured on tape. Twenty-three days later, he rolled tape again at another intimate club show in Nashville, hastily arranged because CBS reps were in town for a convention, and Appel wanted to show them what they were missing:

> **David Sancious**: Sometimes you get a bunch of accomplished players together and it sounds stale, but with us it was like every note was tight in place, but with *heart* . . . That band was a real good thing for Bruce, because he was writing things at that time beyond the scope of normal rhythmic things. The songs were real funky, jazzy ballads that I felt achieved more mileage, [using] a different approach.

Yet just a few days later Springsteen pulled the plug, removing the E Street Band's central ballast, and making a mockery of all his talk of loyalty and blood brothers. He fired his oldest musical collaborator, Vini 'Mad Dog' Lopez, supposedly because of an exchange of words and fisticuffs at ten paces with Appel's brother, Steve, after a show. The argument, as per usual, was about money. Lopez believed, 'We were being cheated. Well, Mike Appel's brother and I had a few words. I pushed him and he went down.'

Lopez states that the disagreement dated back to the day David joined the band: 'When they brought Sancious in, we weren't making a lot of money, but instead of giving him what we were getting, they took it out of our money . . . I had a problem with that. That's probably one of the reasons I got fired. When I have I problem, I say something. They branded me a troublemaker . . . I'd be like, "What about the band getting some royalties?" Mike was like, "Whoddya think you are? Chicago? This is Bruce Springsteen." [But] when it came to getting paid, me and Danny were the ones who went to New York to the office to get everyone their money. Bruce said, "You guys do that, you're good at it".' He had no intimation he was treading on thin ice when the boss came a-callin' that early February afternoon:

> **Vini Lopez:** When he came to my house and told me I was out of the band, I was taken aback. Whenever we came off the road, I used to have his guitars, and the next day he'd come over. I said, 'You're kicking me out of the band? I get a second chance, right!' He goes, 'There are no second chances. It's a dog eat dog world. You're done.' He said I was a shitty drummer, said, 'You can't do this and you can't do that.' . . . [In the end,] I said, 'There's the door,' and handed him his fucking guitars . . . We were steam-driven, so I get blamed for being steam-driven.

Appel thinks it was a combination of the two, his temper *and* his time-keeping. But, he insists, 'In Vini's defence, he was more of a drummer in the Keith Moon sense, always trying to make the drums like a lead guitar, not just keep a beat, and what would happen invariably is he would lose the beat . . . [However,] Vini had also got on the wrong side of Bruce a few times: he had punched my brother out, stupid things. He would get feisty with Clarence. So Vini was always problematic on that side of things . . . [In the end,] it was Bruce's decision.' And it was one which threatened the equilibrium of an outstandingly original band.

That possibility, however, was lost on Bruce, and the other lynchpins in the current set-up, Clemons and Sancious. Clemons in his autobiography suggests he had already voiced concerns to Springsteen: 'Vinnie "Mad Dog" Lopez had trouble keeping time. It was fucking everything up, but Bruce is such a loyal guy he couldn't bring himself to fire him. It was becoming a real problem.' Meanwhile, at some point Sancious mentioned a friend who played drums and knew how to walk the dog. He later put a disingenuous spin on the switch: 'Bruce had decided to change drummers, and I told him about Ernest ["Boom" Carter] . . . He auditioned a bunch of kids, and Ernest came and tried out.' But Carter was hardly gonna fly up from Atlanta – as he did – just to 'try out'. Carter's recruitment barely a week after Lopez got the boot rather suggests Sancious began importuning Bruce before that fateful February afternoon.

As it happens, Carter was an inspired choice. Though he didn't have the frenetic style that came part and parcel with the 'Mad Dog' moniker, nor was he quite as busy. And he could keep time on a dime. But he was Sancious's, not Springsteen's man, and the newly-forged alliance made for none of the do-or-die camaraderie of the original E Street Band. Springsteen seemed to sense it, because in an April interview he was already talking about how 'the band's built to be flexible – that way if everybody leaves tomorrow or everybody stays, it'll work out'. He had never talked this way before.

Lopez's limitations seemed less evident to those critics who had just received copies of Springsteen's second long-playing instalment. Just as he was handing Mad Dog his cards, *Rolling Stone*'s Ken Emerson was praising the band, who 'cook with power and precision', in a timely but terse second-album review. *Creem*'s Ed Ward, given more latitude, was unstinting in his praise: 'The rhythm section . . . is able to cope with all the changes nicely, as well as propelling the band along when things are at their most frantic . . . [while] the music has the same kind of freedom as good jazz, and . . . the beat and drive of good rock.' Ward's only concern, in a rave review that compared *The Wild, the Innocent* (favourably) with *Astral Weeks*, was whether 'his band can play anywhere near this good on stage'. He need not have worried.

Indeed, Ward was just about the only major rock critic in America not to have checked out the E Street band in their performing pomp. The British music press were predictably tardier, but *NME*'s Charles Shaar Murray called it right when he did suggest, 'After seeing Springsteen you realize that his records are dumb and irrelevant; forget 'em, they're trash, they're a shadow show in a distorting mirror, and he's not really there at all. It's possible to hear his records and hardly dig him at all; it ain't possible to see his show and walk out quite the same. I mean, the cat is *good* . . . And I was blown over when I saw him live and discovered that the aspect of his work that had impressed me the most [his white r&b voice/musical identity] was, in fact, the deepest and most central core of his work.'

Though CBS had cut the marketing budget for his second album in half, and *Rolling Stone* had relegated him to the also-rans review-section, it mattered not. Word of mouth, by the spring of 1974, was something else. As Springsteen himself asserted, post-*Born To Run*: 'You couldn't get the whole story from the records we did earlier but whenever we played, it was like – instant!' In fact, for all the good press they were getting, Springsteen doubted it was this which turned things around. He told *Street Life* the next year, 'I've had a million good articles but they don't sell records. Why? 'Cause the kids don't care what they read . . . The kid on the street, he heard about you from a friend. So he buys your record. He comes to see you, he likes your band. He tells his friend, who decides to check it out for himself. And that's how you get the circle going.' After the fact, he would suggest it was a strategy of sorts: 'We didn't start selling records till we started playing smaller places. It's a slow process. But I was always certain.'

Unfortunately, as David Bowie could have told him, with the right show things might ultimately work out fine, but it was damn wearing on the wallet (and nerves). If everyone needs a push, Springsteen got two solid shoves the second week in May, both the direct result of articles written by converts who caught the Boom-era E Streeters that spring, and aired their thoughts in forums so far off the beaten track only someone reading the tea-leaves of popular culture could have been led there. That the first of them resulted in a wholesale change in the attitude of his record label was mere happenstance. It came just in time. As Appel recalls, 'We were just about forgotten completely, and it forced us to start thinking about how we were going to survive . . . / . . . When I called up the promotion men, nobody would pick up the phone. There was nothing we could do.' Even advocates like Paul Rappaport at the label were meeting a brick wall: 'We had to fight for money for Bruce. I remember being in a [CBS] convention and I was jumping up and down, "This is rock & roll history. We need money!" And the head of promotions is going, "I don't care about rock & roll history. We have budgets."'

Everyone was playing for their lives. Night after night. On April 26, the boys pulled up at Brown University to play the Alumni Hall. Dick Wingate, already a fan, became an acolyte that night: 'I'd never been so thunderstruck in my life; and I just remember being floored . . . The performance was beyond anything I'd seen. I'd seen the [Who] *Quadrophenia* tour, I'd seen [Floyd do] *Dark Side*, but this was so personal. It didn't feel like a show.' But it was actually one of Wingate's fellow students whose interview with Springsteen put a Persian among the doves:

> **Mike Appel**: Clive Davis and John Hammond are no longer effectively at CBS. We had no champions – we had low-ranking champions. But we had no big guys . . . I said [to the label], 'What do you want me to do? . . . You're not gonna give me permission to do the album. What do you expect me to do? I'm not gonna sit on my hands.' They could care less . . . And Bruce is acutely aware of all this. 'Cause I told him this is what's happening. I said [to Bruce], 'There's a guy named Irwin Siegelstein, from NBC Television, who's now running Columbia Records, and he's definitely not on our team.' As fate would have it, Bruce was doing a concert at Brown University, and I set him up with a little interview with the Brown University paper, and in that interview he mentions how Irwin Siegelstein is stymying his career. Now Bruce never says a bad word about anybody on the planet, but this one particular instance he happens to mention this guy. Irwin Siegelstein's son goes to Brown University, and he's a fan of Bruce Springsteen. So he calls his father immediately, 'Dad, what are you doing? This guy is the greatest . . .' So Irwin Siegelstein calls me up, and says, 'Bruce Springsteen bad-mouthed me [blah blah blah].' I'm thinking, 'Wow, what a lucky break.' I blurted out, 'He's going to do an interview with *Rolling Stone*. He's got a lot of bad things to say. This is the way it is between you and us.' Total lie. He says, 'I want you, Bruce and your attorney at Mercurio's tomorrow at one o'clock. We'll settle this once and for all.' I said, 'Irwin, we'll be there.' We sat down and hammered it out, 'We wanna go in and record the record.' 'Okay, [but] no more interviews where he bad-mouths me.' . . . From then on, they got on board.

In fact, Springsteen kept Siegelstein's name out of his rant at the label's expense; but his exasperation had come through loud and clear: 'Of course I don't know how Clive [Davis] would have turned out as time went on. Anyway, Clive and I got along. He came down – he still came down after he got ousted to see how we were doing. He was interested. Now I'm a pain in the ass to them is all and, you know, they want to make somebody else famous . . . I haven't sold many records yet and we don't see eye to eye on a lot of things.' And if this wasn't enough, he further complained 'They're bugging me for a single. I don't know, maybe they mean well, but I doubt it.'

If it was a highly uncharacteristic outburst, Springsteen had never been a willing interviewee. When Robert Hilburn asked for an interview after a July 1974 Santa Monica gig, 'He asked why I wanted to talk to him and whether it wasn't better to let fans just listen to the music, rather than read about the artist as well.' He went on to gently berate Hilburn, '[Rock] interviews are like questions and answers where there is no answer, so why is there a question?' He had a simple faith in his ability to communicate, and in rock audiences in general, his own in particular. He had already informed Hilburn, his first important west coast advocate, 'You should never be "satisfied" [with your performance]. Once you're satisfied, you're dead. You've got to ruffle people, stir them, make them have wants, make them realise their desires . . . Don't just make them boogie and jump up and down. That's a hoax.' It was a mantra he held onto throughout the most trying year of his career:

> **Bruce Springsteen**: Some people can be stopped and other people can't be stopped . . . I can't stop, they can't make me stop ever, because I can't stop. I don't know what I'd do. If you're dealing with people who say, 'Ah hell, I gotta go back to hanging wallpaper,' or who say, 'I don't know if I want to play or if I want to get married.' If you have to decide, then the answer is don't do it. If you have a choice, then the answer is no. [1974]

So when he ran into the reviews editor from *Rolling Stone* outside Charlie's Place, Cambridge on April 10, 1974, he was relieved to find Jon Landau had come to see the show. Landau's interest had been piqued by the second album and, like Ed Ward, he was curious how they sounded live. If Landau's local review of *The Wild, the Innocent*, posted in the window of Charlie's Place, was essentially positive, he thought Lopez's drumming 'a weak spot', and found the recording to be 'a mite thin or trebly-sounding, especially when the band moves into the breaks'. When Springsteen introduced Landau to his producer inside, Appel rightly called him out, 'So you don't like the album's production, huh!' Coming from the man who had gutted the most abrasive band to ever come out of Detroit's Grande Ballroom (Landau produced the MC5's weak second album, *Back In The USA)*, Landau's comments suggested an expertise he simply did not have.

But Springsteen did not know that. And the critic was saying the things he wanted to hear.

Though he loved it, Landau did not review the show that night. Rather, he checked them out again at the Harvard Square Theatre a month later, when he somewhat memorably 'saw rock & roll future and its name is Bruce Springsteen'. So fast did that night pass before his eyes that he imagined he'd seen a 'two-hour set', initiating that great Rockritic contest to see who could most inflate the length of a live Springsteen set. (For the record, there is no such thing as a four-hour Springsteen show!) For Landau it all boiled down to one question: 'When his . . . set ended I could only think, can anyone really be this good, can anyone say this much to me, can rock & roll still speak with this kind of power and glory?'

To put his epiphanic critique in context, the mid-seventies were the heyday of such bulletins from jaundiced critical claimants. Whether it was then-critic Patti Smith lauding Television, Lester Bangs and Nick Kent testifying to The Stooges, Richard Williams experiencing Roxy Music or Jonh Ingham being blown to kingdom come by the Pistols, everyone was looking for the next big thing; and the ad-men knew it. The issue before *Rolling Stone* ran Bruce's 'rock & roll future' ad, they carried an ad for Weather Report that risibly announced, 'The Future is Here'.

As John Lombardi put it in his 1988 *Esquire* 'roast' of 'Saint Bruce': 'Bruce was a rock critic's dream, a means of rationalizing nostalgic feelings of "rebellion" and blue-collar sympathy with comfortable middle-aged incomes and "life-styles".' Unlike most of the others listed above, he did not represent any kinda threat to The Pantheon. His was a reclamation, not a deconstruction, of Rock's decade-long history. The most telling line in Landau's review is not the oft-quoted one, but the one which preceded it: 'I saw my rock & roll past flash before my eyes.' And if Springsteen was an answer to critics' prayers, the influence Landau still exercised was an answer to his. As he recently observed, 'The power of rock criticism in the seventies would be unrecognizable perhaps to rock writers today . . . It was a powerful forum, particularly for people who were just starting [like me].' Dave Marsh, who edited Landau's review, later claimed on both their behalves that the review was a conscious act of hyperbole:

Dave Marsh: However you wish to view the pros and cons of that whole 'hype' issue, the fact remains that Columbia was on the point of dropping Bruce from the label straight after *E Street Shuffle* had initially bombed. Jon and I knowingly interceded with that article. Clive Davis had been ousted and only the press department really believed in Bruce's worth. You could say that we were aware of our intentions.

Whether Springsteen approved of being hyped a second time was a question neither Landau nor Marsh deigned to ask. He certainly needed their help, as Bruce duly admitted after the review went viral: 'At the time we weren't doing so good, and it helped me out with the record company.' At least Landau's review made no mention of Dylan, not even in passing. For Springsteen, this was important: 'I wanted to get away from the Dylan comparisons at the time . . . At the time I was self-conscious about it and trying to find my own voice.'

When *Rolling Stone* finally ran a non-review piece on the artist in September 1974, he went to great pains to convey those musical influences as one big melting pot: "'I like [Dylan]. The similarities are probably there somewhere. But . . . shit, man, I've been influenced by lots of people. Elvis was one of the first. Otis Redding, Sam Cooke, Wilson Pickett, the Beatles, Fats [Domino], Benny Goodman, a lot of jazz guys. You can hear them all in there if you want.' At this time one could almost check the influences off, such was the sweep of styles the 1974 E Street Band embraced in concert. The show Landau reviewed featured an almost-showband arrangement of the Blue Belles' 'I Sold My Heart To The Junkman', while a segue into Jimmy Reed's 'Bright Lights, Big City' in the middle of 'Kitty's Back' was so seamless it seemed just another part of the unravelling saga of a stripper with a heart of gold.

But just about the time this panorama of *a priori* pop was bubbling to the surface, CBS were dictating in what direction they wanted Springsteen's career to go. Yes, the purse strings had been relaxed enough for his recording career to resume, and there was even a commitment of sorts to 'repromote' *The Wild, the Innocent* (which was now starting to sell steadily despite their worst efforts); but they were still bugging him about *that* single. Such was the state of affairs when Landau received a call shortly after his birthday, May 22. It was Bruce: 'He said he was having problems . . . in his relationship with Columbia Records and . . . his problems in recording. He said there was this fellow Charlie Koppelman who, because of the lack of commercial success [to date], wanted to impose some kind of direction on Bruce's future recordings.'

It seems the deal Springsteen and Appel had reached with Siegelstein came with strings attached. As Springsteen now told a British paper, 'They want me to put out a new single before they let me do the album.' The idea of a non-album single was actually a good one (it was still the norm on the other side of the pond), but Springsteen wanted to get on with building castles in his own conceptual sky. On July 12 1974 he decided to show CBS his vision could not necessarily be contained by seven inches of vinyl. He was back in New York for a three-night residency. This time he had moved up in the downtown world, as far as The Bottom Line. He decided it was high time he debuted his latest spin on *West Side Story*, 'Jungleland'. At the same time he had a new lighting man, Marc Brickman, who could sell his songs like no other lightman could:

> **Mike Appel**: Marc [Brickman] started using a special overhead spot on Bruce, which none of us had ever seen before, and much more dramatic colours . . . Well, this guy . . . transformed this little ratty show we had developed into something we'd never thought about before. Now, suddenly, we could all see new horizons. I mean . . . his performance took on dramatic dimensions that raised the entire show to new visual, musical and emotional heights. He began to literally die at the end of 'Jungleland'. He'd clutch the microphone and go down on the stage and die! [DTR]

'Jungleland' was the apotheosis of everything Springsteen had been working towards since he 'got more interested in how the thing was going to function as an ensemble'. And it was what more critical fans had been anticipating. One of them, *Playback*'s Lorraine O'Grady, had predicted in a February 1974 overview of his career to date that *The Wild, the Innocent*'s successor might be 'a rock opera based on the characters in it, that [is] even more magnificent than *W, I & E.*'. She also noted, 'He's become more actor than singer.' 'Jungleland' soon became this method actor's nightly audition. In fact, the song at this juncture was essentially of a piece with the jazzed-up NYC songs from *The Wild, the Innocent*, with Sancious still playing the role of Bruce's bag-man. The song even resolved itself with an 'extra' verse that, like 'Incident on 57th Street', held out the hope everything could work out fine:

> Beneath the city two hearts beat, soul cool engines tired and brave,
> Them coloured girls cry like violent angels in port authority halls.
> And in the tunnels in a machine you hear the screams
> Drowned out by the roaring trains.
> And layers above are locked in love as he appears on Flamingo Lane.
> And an angel rises from his hand and disappears – down in Jungleland.

Few who witnessed any of the Bottom Line shows left unimpressed. Clive Davis, in the midst of setting up Arista, took time out to check out his former signing; and shook his head at what an opportunity CBS were missing. In fact, just as Springsteen – after nine months of writer's block – had again unlocked his muse, CBS were finally delivering on their promise to give his latest album the big push. That fortnight's issue of *Rolling Stone* carried a full-page ad on page three which reprinted most of Landau's *Real Paper* rave, with the famous 'I saw rock & roll future . . .' line in 36-point type emblazoned across the top of the page, and a photo of the second-album sleeve at the bottom of the page. They had lived up to their part of the bargain. Now all Bruce had to do was produce an album that delivered on the fulsome promise of the shows that spring. It was time to roll tape again. And again.

Chapter 3: 1974–75 – Trading In Wings For Wheels

> People thought [*Born To Run*] was a record about escape. To me . . . I always felt it was more about searching. – Bruce Springsteen, 1984

On August 1 1974 Springsteen, the E Street Band, producer Mike Appel and engineer Louis Lahav returned to 914 to commence work on that difficult third album, a make or break effort for all concerned. Despite all the protestations, Springsteen had dutifully recorded the single CBS said they wanted back in May, and the plan now was to use these sessions to put the finishing touches to the two tracks already recorded, 'Born To Run' and 'So Young And In Love', to maybe lay down the already-debuted 'A Night Like This', and to secure a usable basic track for 'Jungleland', already earmarked as the centrepiece of the album. The August 1 tape box suggests they cut two takes of 'Jungleland', the second complete. A show in Central Park on the third – the infamous Anne Murray show, when most of a five thousand strong crowd came to see 'support act' Springsteen, and many that stayed did so only to heckle the presumptuous Murray – called a temporary halt to the sessions, but when all shows for the next ten days were cancelled to continue recording it seemed they were finally getting down to things in earnest.

In fact, a certain urgency had been injected into these sessions with the news, relayed to Springsteen first, that Sancious and Carter were leaving the band forthwith to form their own jazz-rock combo, Tones, who had their own record deal in the offing. Sancious's departure was a prospect which had never been too far away. Springsteen had talked about the possibility after the Brown gig in April, openly admitting, 'Davey is very jazz-oriented [and] I'm sure he'll have his own band in years to come, whenever he feels he's ready.' But he clearly did not expect it to happen quite so soon and when Sancious did break the news, he took it badly:

> **David Sancious**: I wish I could've done it differently. A lot of the guys in the band were shocked. They didn't know I had [already] told Bruce. There's no easy way to do that kind of thing, leaving people you really dig. [But] I didn't leave for any reason other than I wanted to do what I [ended up] doing . . . There came a point when my desire to do this was so strong that I started to feel that maybe it was taking my attention away from Bruce's thing. It was only fair for me to take off and make room for someone who wanted to do it with Bruce. When I told Bruce, I sensed that he was disappointed.

Any headache Sancious caused Springsteen was compounded by taking Carter, too. The gamble the frontman had taken when replacing the fiercely loyal Lopez with a man who had little investment in the E Street ethos had not paid dividends. As Carter openly admitted to Brucezine *Backstreets*, 'I was closer with David than Bruce. He was someone I grew up with. And when he decided to leave the band, I felt I should go too. Plus, we had this music that we always wanted to do, and [now] we had the chance to do it . . . It was always there that David wanted to leave and that I'd probably go with him.' Clemons, for one, was nonplussed: '"Boom" was living with me, and he didn't tell me he was leaving. I didn't understand [why].'

One immediate result was hot August nights at 914 putting 'finishing touches' to the three tracks they thought they nearly had in usable form. Of these, 'Born To Run' was almost there. Having recorded a basic track live with the band in May, Springsteen had added his vocal (probably on June 26). But now he had all these grandiose ideas for overdubbing instrument on instrument until the whole thing was buried beneath sonic strata. The initial idea was a good one. As he says, he had written 'and conceived [the song] as a studio production. It was connected to the long, live pieces I'd written previously by the twists and turns of the arrangement.' In other words, he was trying to jam all the 'twists and turns' of the ten-minute 'Thundercrack' into a four-minute track. And the song's live 'debut' at The Bottom Line in July suggested he was onto something. The air positively crackled with electricity when the song ended; and then came sustained whoops of affirmation. But he had forgotten that less is sometimes more. As Sancious says on the *Wings For Wheels* DVD, 'Lotsa, lotsa stuff [was overdubbed] – all of which wasn't used; there was synthesizer stuff, horns, all kinds of stuff.'

Driven to distraction by Springsteen's demands, engineer Louis Lahav refused to give up: 'It was more than just cutting a song. It was this *thing* you believed in so much – like a religion . . . It was [done on] a sixteen-track, but it was packed, like a thirty-two track today. You couldn't relax in the mix for a second.' In the process they abandoned several mixes with strings, clearly Springsteen's attempt to emulate one avowed inspiration, the instrumental track 'Because You're Young'. (Recorded by Duane Eddy in 1960, though the song 'was made into a real trashy old movie . . . he had a great sound to his guitar'.) There was also a belief that he could somehow capture a Spectoresque sound appropriate to the seventies:

> **Mike Appel:** [How was] the great 'Born To Run' done? Well, Jeff Barry had told . . . me how [Spector] produced records. And Bruce says, 'I want my records to sound like Phil Spector,' and I said, 'I know how that is.' He said, 'You do? Well, that's the way we're gonna do it.' So I said, 'All we need now is a song.' He writes 'Born To Run' and announces he's gonna do it at this open-air gig at Swarthmore College. And . . . I could just hear the riff. [But] recording it took us six months.

Production values were not all Springsteen was trying to emulate. The other song cut back in May, 'So Young And In Love', seemed like a pastiche of a mid-sixties Philly single, a self-conscious reaction of sorts to that modern rock sound. Here was Springsteen's response to the ever-increasing number of recordable tracks available in a studio yielding ever thinner-sounding records: pressing rewind. Shortly after these August sessions he informed *Melody Maker*'s Michael Watts that 'it was the genuine, horny old stuff he dug. The Beatles were [too] pop, the Stones he stopped buying after *December's Children*. Something to do with the fancy production.' He wanted a sound that was as broad and wide as the songs he had started writing:

> **Bruce Springsteen**: We approached the record the way that some of the early sixties producers like Phil Spector or Brian Wilson would approach their records, which is to create this *sound*. It's sort of an extreme record.

> The only concept that was around was that I wanted to make a *big* record, you know, just like a car, *zoom*, straight ahead; that when that sucker comes on it's like *wide open*. No holds barred! [1975]

Principle and practice, though, would prove reluctant bedfellows. When Appel delivered a rough mix of 'Born To Run' to the record company in early August, they were underwhelmed. (He would tell Springsteen in a typed memo that month, 'CBS has taken the single that we worked on for three months, to be frank, lightly.') The recording of 'Jungleland' was not going any better. Peter Knobler's 1975 *Crawdaddy* profile describes one evening at 914 when 'they spent until 4 a.m. playing "Jungleland" . . . fourteen times straight through. Inevitably, someone would blow a line and the entire take would be shot.' Even after they got it right, Springsteen decided to rewrite the last two verses – determined to prove the maxim that no lyric was ever finished, only abandoned. As the departing Carter concluded, 'Recording was like trial and error. Bruce had so many different ideas about how the songs should sound. I think we tried them all, and then some.' The problem went deeper: he needed the final say, but didn't know what he wanted to say.

> **Mike Appel**: Bruce had a lot of ideas. But he wasn't knowledgeable about the studio. He had definite ideas, so many that he didn't know which one to pursue. He had so many ways of expressing the same song . . . / . . . The truth of the matter is, Bruce had [now] lost his direction, his energy, and to some extent his confidence. [BTR/CH]

In the end, they had to call time on the sessions and return to the road just to keep this whole rickety venture afloat. The departures of Sancious and Carter couldn't have come at a worse time. As Appel spelled out to Bruce in the above memo, 'We've only worked twenty nights out of a possible 123 nights in the last four months . . . [And] the record company is already annoyed for having advanced us the money for an LP that they won't receive for months yet.' In fact, the situation was so bad that Appel's partner, Jim Cretecos, announced he wanted out, allowing himself to be bought out for a bargain-basement $1500:

> **Mike Appel:** When I bought him out, I didn't actually buy him out. Jules [Curz] actually bought his shares in Laurel Canyon. I bought them from

> Jules six or eight months later. Nobody had the fifteen hundred bucks! Jimmy always felt that he was screwed, that he shouldn't have sold his rights. [But] I don't know if it was his idea or his wife's idea . . . I handled most of the business stuff during the day, then go in the studio at night. Jimmy was great in the studio at night, no problem. Well, Bruce always wanted the guy who was in the studio to do the sound console in concert – it's two different skills, but in Bruce's mind, it was one skill. And [Jim] was just getting together with this woman – he wanted to stay home. He didn't want to go out on tours, [so] finally I said I'm gonna go on with Bruce, carry the torch so to speak, and I did. Then Bruce, of course, became successful and . . . [suddenly] you're talking about something that is quantifiable.

The outfit's financial worries even managed to permeate Springsteen's thick hide. When English rock journalist Jerry Gilbert called that summer, he caught him in an uncharacteristically talkative mood: 'We're at the lowest we've ever been right now. It means that if we don't play every week of the year then we don't have money . . . Hopefully I'll be getting some money from Columbia; and maybe with David Bowie doing some of the songs, that'll be good . . . I'd just like to get some income, because in the last two years we've just managed to make ends meet. And sometimes we don't.' Bowie had been threatening to use at least one Springsteen song on his next album. Paul Nelson would tell the full story in the original draft to his 1975 *Village Voice* Springsteen feature, but then cut it at the last minute:

> The [New Jersey] singer was in [Philadelphia] when David Bowie was recording *Young Americans* there, and the two met briefly. Things went very well. Bowie had just finished doing a song, and during the break, asked an engineer to order lunch for him. Various musicians wandered about, smoking and talking. When the food came, Bowie retired to a side room, ate it, then started recording again. Springsteen was both shaken and amazed. "He didn't even ask his band if they wanted anything," he said, "And when the food came, he didn't eat it with them." To a young man from Asbury Park, the power of stardom had been made clear. Not only could he not understand it, he hated it.

Bowie himself was later asked about this session, and recalled 'sitting in the corridor with him, talking about his lifestyle, which was very

Dylanesque – you know, moving from town to town with a guitar on his back . . . Anyway, he didn't like what we were doing, I remember that. At least, he didn't express much enthusiasm.' Springsteen was frankly appalled by what Bowie had perpetrated on 'It's Hard To Be A Saint In The City', which he had turned into ersatz white soul, part of what the Brit-rocker called 'the squashed remains of ethnic music as it survives in the age of muzak rock'.

If the experience shook Springsteen to the core, it made him doubly determined to keep Heart and Soul the twin pillars of the E Street Band's collective sound. But the despairing tenor of Appel's memo had struck home. In October 1974, Springsteen carried his complaint to Paul Williams: 'We have to play, because if we don't, everything falls apart. We don't make any money off records. We have to go out and play every week, as much as we can. If not, nobody gets paid . . . There's no money saved at all. You can't sell 80,000 records and have any money saved. Unless you're totally by yourself.' In fact, as Appel recalled, booking agent Sam McKeith 'had become the most important factor in our lives. He was getting us three or four college dates a week . . . so we wouldn't die.'

Sure enough, they *were* soon back on the road again, booked for shows through the fall; and whatever economies were being made, they were not in the band department. After a series of auditions, Springsteen had replaced the most versatile musician in the band and his jazz/rock beatmeister with a classically trained pianist in the Richard Manuel mould, and a timekeeper, pure and simple. Somehow, he still kept the E Street Band moving forward. Not only had he recruited Roy Bittan and Max Weinberg, on keyboards and drums respectively, via a *Village Voice* ad, but he was now bringing up his engineer's wife Suki Lahav on backing vocals and violin for certain songs; notably a captivating 'Incident on 57th Street', the set-defining 'Jungleland' and a gypsy-caravan rendition of Dylan's 'I Want You' that injected pure mercury into the set.

He had evidently already been thinking about the Dylan song before talking to Michael Watts in September, going into a verbal riff on the power of those three little words, '"I want you" – that's it, the ultimate statement you can make to anybody. What else can you say? And that's the greatest lyric in the song, those three words, in the whole damn song! I put that on, man, and I get blown away, I get blown down the street, 'cause there's no hoax there.' Audiences were awestruck by Bruce's audacious arrangement. So much so that even Springsteen wasn't always sure what to make of their reaction:

> **Bruce Springsteen**: I'm not into people screamin' at me, like Bowie. Once they do that, it's over. I'll go back to playing the small clubs. I'm not there for them anyway. I'm there for me, y'know, that's all. If they can dig it, cool, if not, they don't have to come. I'll still be the same. A lot of times the audience thinks that they are there to scream at you. They think that's what you want, maybe. And that's not it. I can dig silence after a tune. Like we did Dylan's 'I Want You' and the response was exactly, well, it was somewhat confused. Some were digging it and others weren't sure. I can dig that. That got me off. [1975]

In fact, the fall 1974 shows saw the introduction of a steady stream of sixties classics, as if providing a context by displaying musical roots he was not sure had been previously provided. It was a format he retained through the whole *Born To Run* era. Yet, when asked the following year by an English reporter about these 'oldies', he snapped brusquely back, 'We don't play no oldies . . . They may be older songs, but they're not nostalgic. I was never into that at all . . . "Sha La La", "It's Gonna Work Out Fine", "When You Walk In The Room" – they're great, they're great today, right now!' He even mastered elements of rockabilly and doo-wop well enough to debut an E Street version of Johnny Rivers' 'Mountain of Love' that spanned both styles, affirming the appositeness of another contemporary comment: 'I'm not real familiar with the old r&b artists, but whatever I hear, I digest very quickly, and it comes right back out the way I want it to.'

Just as in that other lifetime, 1971, he had been delving into parts of his musical heritage he felt he'd missed, or treated too lightly. As he admitted after a 1978 show, 'What came out of New Jersey in the early sixties was the girl groups . . . [and] I was listening to the radio at that time, but it was only later when I was starting to work that I went back and bought the records.' In 1998 Springsteen described how in that summer of uncertainty he would 'lie back . . . at night . . . and listen to records by Roy Orbison, The Ronettes, The Beach Boys, and other great sixties artists. These were records whose full depth I'd missed the first time around. But now I was appreciating their craft and power.' And then there was Spector, who for a key period in the sixties made every 45 an event: 'Phil's records felt like near chaos, violence covered in sugar and candy, sung by the girls who were sending Roy O. running straight for the antidepressants. If Roy was opera, Phil was symphonies, little three–minute orgasms, followed by oblivion.'

So when Springsteen introduced pop ballads like Sam Cooke's 'Cupid' or Ben E. King's 'Spanish Harlem' onstage, he was both enhancing his audience's musical education and demonstrating the band's versatility and virtuosity. The diffident Lahav was duly impressed by the subtlety of his vision: 'Bruce used the violin only for the romantic side of him. I played only on the slow songs. Bruce was in total control . . . He was willing to accept suggestions; but always, he had the last say.' Reviewers agreed the addition of Lahav was an inspired touch. Susan Ahrens astutely described her as 'not so much a member of the band as . . . Bruce's personal vision . . . Her sweet strains of violin and blonde ethereal presence soften Bruce's tough guy approach to a point of punkish sensitivity.'

Suki might have been surplus to requirements on the more raucous songs, but she served as tangential inspiration for two originals which entered the set that fall, 'A Love So Fine' (aka 'So Young And In Love', with a new punchline) and 'She's The One'. Springsteen later claimed he wrote the latter 'because I wanted to hear Clarence play the sax in that solo', but the spoken intro prior to its live debut suggested it had a more lust-driven inspiration. Someone had the hots for 'The One': 'About 20 years ago somebody discovered this beat, [which] was such that husbands would rape their wives . . . It would turn intellectuals into babbling idiots. Good girls get bad when they hear this beat, and bad girls get worse.'

At this formative stage, 'She's The One' also looked back to the time when Springsteen last got seriously hurt in a relationship, the 'For You' phase of his songwriting ('You were with me in New York the time . . . I got beat/ And you ran and left me wasted, Mama, right there in the heat'). Compounding such feelings is a deep-seated hatred for the place he came from: 'Most of all I hated that town and what they did/ I hated the way they made us live'. This ragbag of conflicting emotions would only resolve itself after the 'betrayal' element transferred to 'Backstreets'.

'She's The One' wasn't the only song in a continual state of flux throughout fall 1974. 'Jungleland' continued to co-opt bits and pieces from other arrangements to its increasingly operatic cause. As Clemons pointed out, 'If you listen to a live recording of "Incident on 57th Street" from that time you can hear the opening violin and piano intro that morphed into the opening of "Jungleland".' Likewise, a guitar part that in the spring had served as an intro to 'Kitty's Back' became a lead break in the Sancious-less symphony of sound. The song grew ever more dramatic, visually and aurally. Appel vividly recalls, 'I would get chills watching Bruce Springsteen die at the end of "Jungleland".'

Performed nightly from October 1974 to February 1975, 'Jungleland' received ongoing lyrical tweaks. More importantly, violin and sax supplanted the jazz abstractions of Sancious, whilst chimes at both ends of the song-cycle signalled the coming and going of Night. By the time of the fabled February 1975 Main Point show the original final verse, largely rewritten, had been shunted before the 'real death waltz' verse. But he was still not quite prepared to shatter the hoodlum's fantasy, so 'in the tunnel of machines, Rat chases his dreams on that forever lasting night'. Surprisingly, given its urban setting, he considered 'Jungleland' one of his most personal songs: 'The subject I sing about is not necessarily *what* I sing about. I'll use situations and probe for the very basic emotions . . . With some of the newer songs I really have to dig deep inside of me to try and understand how I work, so I can put it in the songs. "Jungleland" is like that; it has a lot of little personal things inside it.'

But, however well-crafted the new arrangements, and however easily the new members settled into E Street life, there was a suspicion held by certain critics that the parameters of the band were inexorably contracting, that the spirit of improvisation which drove the Sancious-era combo had been fatally compromised. Lenny Kaye, asked to review a show that October in Boston, sensed that Springsteen and Patti Smith, his new employer, were already heading in wildly disparate directions: 'I remember getting sent up by the *Village Voice* to review his show . . . when he had the girl come out from the wings with the violin. It was in my cross fade of being a writer [and becoming a rock guitarist]; and I began to feel a conflict of interest. I wanted them to be something [else]. I'm into free-form improvisation, finding the noise, and I'm realizing that's not what they're about.' The most expansive band in rock had begun to tighten its belt, even as its frontman planned his next record to have a truly mythic sweep:

> **Bruce Springsteen**: The next album's . . . not actually a concept-type thing, but it's like you get a jigsaw puzzle and you put it down on the floor and it slowly comes together. I've been getting batches of songs, many different melodies and lyrics, and putting them all together . . . Songs around a feeling, a mood. It's going to need a lot more instruments than the other albums to get that feel, but it can be done. [1974]

Actually, Springsteen was struggling to capture *anything* in the studio. And the blame lay squarely at his own brass feet. Instead of working with what he had, he was dreaming of his very own AFM mini-convention. Asked by Jerry Gilbert about his new material in the summer of 1974, he instead talked about how he was 'definitely going to add people, possibly a horn section'. Pressed for specifics, he insisted, 'Lately I've been getting a rush to write new songs and I've got quite a few [done] – some short and some long.' He was finding his previous way of songwriting unfulfilling. Which is presumably why he told Robert Hilburn in early July: 'The writing is more difficult now. On [the last] album, I started slowly to find out who I am and where I wanted to be. It was like coming out of the shadow of various influences and trying to be me.' The songs were only coming through in fits and starts; not as one unified whole, as had been the case for the last two years.

Looking back the following summer, he openly admitted: 'For a while I lost the groove. I lost the spirit of the thing somewhere. It became very confusing to me. I didn't understand what was going on. I was getting caged in all the time – in work and "stuff".' Meanwhile, the label still needed an album, and a definitive mix for 'Born To Run' which could be used to herald the next hopefully-great instalment. Springsteen could no longer even hear its strengths, and in an act of desperation he asked his old(est) friend what he thought. Steve Van Zandt, unversed in production protocol, came from the school that believed, 'Any time you spend six months on [one] song, there's something not going exactly right. A song should take about three hours.' His response surprised Springsteen:

> **Steve Van Zandt**: Bruce had asked me to come in and check out his new song, 'Born To Run'. I thought they were done, so of course me not knowing studio etiquette in those days . . . I pointed out something in the record that I thought was a screw-up and I was right. It changed the

> whole record . . . It was a big moment, because I think people started to realize that I was more than just a friend hanging around, that I also had some insights. Of course, his manager never spoke to me again after this, because I probably cost him another $20,000 to fix it.

In fact, Appel was in full agreement. But Springsteen had stopped listening to him. Finally, in October, 'Born To Run' was mixed, largely by the simple expedient of wiping all the gunk that had been applied since June, and bringing the one guitar figure Steve had heard buried in the mix to the fore. Knowing that the level of anticipation for any new product was growing in Bruceland, Appel decided he would send an advance tape of the song to those radio stations which had proven the most supportive in the last two years. It was something he had done once before, with the seven-minute 'Fever' they demoed at 914 in May 1973. As it happens, the (almost) back-to-mono mix on that November 1974 'Born To Run' would prove cleaner and punchier than the one used on the album. No wonder listeners in Cleveland, Houston, Philadelphia and Boston began to call the stations. Unfortunately, CBS had by now remembered they didn't do non-album singles. As of 1974, singles were promotional items, not product in their own right. And they demanded an explanation:

> **Mike Appel:** CBS was absolutely adamant about not doing anything. They don't release singles without an album! That's why they were so infuriated with me when I sent it to like sixteen FM radio stations. Were they ever angry. ['Cause] when the kids go in the store for the album, there is no such thing. The guys in the stores say to the CBS [reps], 'Where's the album?' 'There is no album.' 'What!! Boy, oh boy.' 'Who gave you that?' 'Mike Appel.'

As is the nature of such things, what seemed like a mistake proved a masterstroke, putting pressure on the label to throw their weight behind Bruce even as work on that third album ground to a halt. A further set of sessions in October had produced only a series of in-house demos. Certainly logged then was 'A Night Like This', a song written at a time when he still wanted the whole record to feel 'like it could all be taking place in the course of one evening, at all these different locations'. The setting of the song, debuted that June in Toledo, was a familiar one – a topless bar at the Coral Inn, from where the stripper and her lover run 'off in the night/ You catch up with her, you take her hand/ You lay your jacket down on the sand/ And she tries to make it alright'. The sleazier aspects of boardwalk life – a constant source of fascination for our one-time altar boy – are never far away. 'The fags come in to drink and dance' at the Shady Bell, while the 'lost boys hide beneath the pier, getting hard, drinking beer'. Finally, the song pans back to reveal this is the night to end all nights: 'Because night after endless night, up and down the boardwalk we search for romance/ But on a night like this, with one last kiss, we die'.

Also recorded at 914 at this time – if not in late October, then later in the fall at an undocumented 914 session – was the still-vengeful 'She's The One'. There was also 'Walking In The Street' aka 'Lovers In The Cold', which Springsteen later claimed he wanted on *Tracks* but could not find the master. And then there was another song, so personal only a solo version would suffice, 'Chrissie's Song' – which should have been released years ago and let 'Walking In The Street' take a hike. All three would appear on the very first bootleg of Springsteen studio outtakes, *E Ticket*, evidently culled from 914 tapes circa 1973-74, compiled for purposes unknown.*

But Bruce didn't think *any* of these songs were ready to be released. 'A Night Like This' would morph into 'Lonely Night In The Park', which would itself become a Record Plant refugee, while parts of the 914 version of 'She's The One' would splinter into the shadier 'Backstreets'. 'Thunder Road' would take its tune – and a single image, 'Babe, I can't lay the stars at your feet/ Oh, but I think we could take it all, just you and me' – from 'Walking In The Street', and its lyrical thrust from 'Chrissie's Song' (at the expense of the line, 'When you're born with nothing in your hands, baby, it's your only chance'). The birth pangs of a new Bruce were proving problematic and painful:

> **Mike Appel:** He was trying to make something great. 'Born To Run' was the kick-off song. That was the song that was taking the band in a whole other direction. That was gigantic. And this is the direction we're going – this is the archetype. So Bruce had to live up to 'Born To Run'. But not instantly – you have to put that kinda time and energy into it if you expect to produce anything *great*. Not [just] good. Portions of the great songs

* Just a single October session – and one song ('A Night Like This') – are listed in the Sony logs. Clearly, their records of fall 1974/winter 1975 sessions at 914 are incomplete.

> come in flashes, but they have to be woven together. Then there's that [inherent] nervousness, not being totally sure that you got it.

Frustrated at himself, Springsteen chose to turn on Appel. Yet Paul Nelson correctly suggested in his 1975 *Village Voice* piece, 'It was Springsteen himself who was responsible for the technical agony and ecstasy.' Nor was Nelson alone in noticing his dissipation of focus in the studio. A CBS rep, on hearing *Born To Run*, remarked, 'It's true that his recordings have been rather poor, but I have yet to meet anyone who knows more about what he's after than Springsteen does . . . The problem is that he's not interested in documenting what he's learned.' [BTR]

Acquiring such a 'rep' in such short shrift, Springsteen was clearly as stubborn as a mule with a bull's head to match. Even his new best buddy Landau told *Newsweek*, after finally getting together in the studio, 'Underneath his shyness is the strongest will I've ever encountered. If there's something he doesn't want to do, he won't.' Like the Orson Welles who made *Citizen Kane* when he was not even twenty-five, the Springsteen who turned twenty-five that September had 'the confidence of ignorance', and he was not about to settle for second best; and he had yet to give up on attempting perfection.

> **Bruce Springsteen**: I wrote ambitiously. From the beginning I wrote wildly big with the idea of taking the whole thing in and being definitive in some fashion. I think the show took on that approach also . . . I was shooting for the moon. And I guess somewhere inside, I felt like I could hit it. [1992]

He was convinced 'writing these mini-epics . . . were meant to make you feel something auspicious was gonna occur.' Central to this conceit was still 'Jungleland'. In fact, as Clemons wrote in *Big Man*, 'In the beginning, I think Bruce was going for a rock opera kind of thing about this character called the Magic Rat. He had lots of songs and themes that were built around this narrative he had in his head. Eventually he let that go, but I know it frustrated him.' A handwritten track-listing for Album #3 dating from spring 1974 devoted a whole side to a four-part 'Jungleland' suite – divided into 'From The Churches To The Jails', 'The Hungry & The Hunted', 'Between Flesh & Fantasy' and 'Jungleland' itself – with 'Zero and Blind Terry' inserted at mid-point.

He was going to have to (re)learn about record-making if they were ever gonna get out of 914 alive. Unfortunately, the man he turned to in his confusion was not Appel, but rather Jon Landau, who later stated (under oath) that in one of their first conversations that spring 'He asked me about the concept of production. He said, "I noticed in your [album] review you mentioned production. I don't really know what *production* means. What is it that producers do?"'

By then, Springsteen had aimed an ill-conceived dig in Appel's direction: 'In the studio I want somebody who can help me where my weaknesses are, rather than anyone ordering me around. That's not where it's at for me. If I didn't know how to play or arrange or do nothing, then it would be different. [But] I know what I want to hear.'

Between October 1974 and February 1975, the third album lay in limbo. What work was done – and it was minimal – failed to discernibly advance the process. Finally, sometime in February – according to Landau's later deposition – Springsteen asked the critic to join them in the studio to see if he could identify the problem. Some of the issues were essentially practical – Weinberg was desperately in need of a little drumming direction. But mainly Springsteen needed to settle on an arrangement and stick with it. Landau told Springsteen he could provide some answers:

> **Bruce Springsteen**: There reached a point where what we knew wasn't enough; it was the third time I'd been in the studio, and I knew the sounds I wanted to hear . . . You're taking something that is not real, it's in the air, and you're trying to make it a physical thing. It's an idea, sounds in your head, and you have to make them exist . . . It reached a point where . . . we were not [even] getting close. Then Jon came in and he was able to say, 'Well, you're not doing it because of *this*, and *this*, and these . . . are blocking what you're doing.' [1977]

Perhaps the real problem was breaking in a band parts of which had minimal studio experience. As Garry Tallent says, 'When we started [*Born To Run*] we were still trying to find out exactly what we did together and how that all worked.' Springsteen, though, did not want 'a strictly professional set-up, because I did not want to contain my talents in that box'. Bringing in session musicians was a non-starter. They would have to work with what they had.

Landau would later suggest there was a fundamental aesthetic difference in approach, telling Michael Watts in 1978, 'I didn't think there was any real point of view, a focus to the sound, on the albums Mike Appel produced. The sound was not integrated into the total aesthetic.' As it presumably was on *Back In The USA*. Yet Appel was as anxious as anyone to break the logjam. If Springsteen wanted Landau to come on board, Appel was prepared to go along with him, even if a producer-critic with nominal studio experience and a high opinion of his musical instincts did not seem like the answer:

> **Mike Appel:** Bruce is a taskmaster. He would get everyone to play everything flawlessly, and we just recorded it. [But] 'Blinded By The Light' was not 'Born To Run' [or] 'Jungleland' – it didn't demand that kind of attention. There was a problem with the piano [on the 914 'Jungleland']; when you put your foot down, it had some kinda squeak. But Landau took umbrage, he said the studio was not up to snuff, 'Look at this pedal.' So I said, 'If everyone is agreed we go elsewhere, we'll go elsewhere. Any suggestions? Record Plant seems okay.' [But] I thought it would go much quicker. Bruce was normally bang-bang-bang, but not this time. He met in match in terms of material, production values, arrangement values. It wasn't gonna be like anything before!

What Appel did not fully appreciate was how high a value Landau would place on what he could bring to the process – demanding 'points' on the finished product, half of which would come from CBS, half from Laurel Canyon. But he had more pressing matters to deal with. The E Street Band was again wracked with division at the end of February as Suki Lahav took leave of the band and, along with husband Louis, of the USA. According to Appel, 'Quite simply, Bruce fell in love with Suki and she with him. She then had to get out to try and save the marriage.' [DTR] This was presumably the fraught situation that prompted Louis to comment in 2010, 'I prefer not to say [why I left the States] . . . [but] I felt a Mack truck might have run me over if I'd stayed one more day.'

The Lahavs departed for Israel, Louis's homeland, just as Springsteen seemed to have got a handle on another song which took his songwriting somewhere potentially exciting. In February 1975 – as 'Born To Run', 'Jungleland' and 'She's The One' continued to live and breathe onstage – 'Wings For Wheels' aka 'Thunder Road', a hybrid of 'Walking In The Streets' and 'Chrissie's Song' he had been working on for months, made its live debut. Initially Lahav's levitating bow vied with Bruce's lovelorn lyrics as they metaphorically lay together on a night like this: 'Now the season's over and I feel it getting cold/ Well, I wish I could take you to some sandy beach, where we'd never grow old/ Ah, but baby, you know that's just jive, tonight's bustin' open and I'm alive/ Oh, do what you can do to make me feel like a man'.

Just as Bruce was looking 'to capture the Cosmos in a [single] note' – as revealed to another lady that month – Suki's gypsy violin was departing E Street, leaving a single hint of what might have been (on the released 'Jungleland', dropped in from an earlier 914 version). On April 18, with Landau's terms having been met, the new regime reassembled at the Record Plant to start again with a keen young engineer in situ, Jimmy Iovine. Iovine had just finished working on John Lennon's *Rock & Roll*, so foolishly believed he already knew the meaning of torturous when it came to making albums with a 'retro' feel. But that experience would be as nothing to this. As he recalled in 1987, by which time he had made a name as a producer in his own right, 'God, it was hard. We worked very slowly, and [Bruce] had a picture in his head of what he wanted. But all of us were very young and inexperienced, so we had to go the long way to do anything.'

Landau's first suggestion was to record the songs as a basic three-piece, and then build from there. He thought 'the sound would be tighter if we cut the record initially as a trio: bass, drums and piano'. But he had picked the least confident and experienced member of the band to lay down its first marker, the not-yet-mighty Max. Van Zandt, who had been brought in to provide Springsteen with another sounding board, and himself some studio experience, was distinctly unimpressed: 'It was all record the drums, record the bass, record fourteen guitar parts, separate everything, layer on layer, everything that's bad for rock & roll.' He was already setting himself in opposition to Landau's studio shtick – a war of attrition that would rage until 1983, culminating in Van Zandt's departure from the E Street Band.

At least he outlasted Appel. In 1992, Springsteen asserted that he and Appel were, in fact, already 'a dead-end street. [When] Jon came in . . . he had a pretty sophisticated point of view, and he had an idea how to solve some very fundamental problems, like how to record and where to record.' In his 1976 deposition, fighting for the right to name Landau his de facto producer, he was rather more specific about Landau's contribution: 'He just made me aware . . . that I could be better than I was . . . He came to rehearsals. He taught my drummer . . . how to play drums in a rock band . . . He changed the tide of the whole thing . . . Things were getting done and things were happening, and we weren't laying in the quicksand anymore. We were coming out of it.'

If Bruce overstates his contribution, even Appel admits Landau brought one trick to the party: 'He was able to analyse each song and break it down into its component parts, and make it seem not such a big thing.' But it was the ever-perceptive Paul Nelson, an old Springsteen supporter and an older friend of Landau, who made the more astute analysis of the Record Plant dynamic, writing after *Born To Run*'s completion: 'If Landau was somewhat in awe of the kind of instinctual genius who could resolve aesthetic problems by compounding them, Bruce had no less respect for someone who invariably got to ten by counting out nine individual numbers, one at a time.' Unfortunately, Landau was not really prepared for the demands placed on him in the psychological battleground to which he had forced entry:

> **Mike Appel:** Any guy who's new to a situation, like Jon Landau, for a while he has the magic, then the drudgery, the everyday commonplace recording grind wears him down. Therefore, whatever magic he has brought to the table has dissipated in short order, and you're left with what Jimmy Iovine would call Bruce Springsteen's drift into darkness. 'Cause Bruce would just sit there and we would talk to him and he wouldn't answer us. He would just sit there. 'Would you like us to bring in another amplifier?' 'You wanna do another guitar part?' Nothing. . . . / . . . [It turned out] Landau's personality wasn't suited to this 'perfect marriage' at all. He was a guy who was always nervous, intense and methodical. Here he was suddenly caught in a situation where he was forced to fight for his position . . . Everything, and everyone, bothered him.

Yet Landau and Springsteen remained united in their primary goal, 'To make the greatest rock & roll record ever made.' All they needed was the know-how. But as Bruce admitted in 1977, 'We [soon] reached a point where what we knew wasn't enough.' It took an outside voice, that of Little Steven, to finally call a spade a spade, and not a long blunt instrument: 'I didn't have the sophistication to be diplomatic . . . [To me], it was [just] like, "This is not working."' Appel gamely admits, 'Miami Steve stepped in and . . . gave the record order. They needed direction and he gave it to them. There was finally a way out. It might not have been the best way, but it was a way out. He didn't bring in tasteful riffs – or at least [not] in my mind . . . – but he got them done.'

When on May 5 Springsteen brought in a sassy new song, 'Tenth Avenue Freeze Out', it was Van Zandt who after multiple incomplete takes told the horn musicians to throw away their charts, and then simply hummed them the part he suggested they play. Bruce loved it. Nor were the horns the only addition to the E Street sound Springsteen was keen to introduce. Suki may have flown the coop, but all his previous talk of strings, horns, violins &c. wasn't just idle chatter. Days were spent working on a string arrangement for 'Jungleland'. Ditto for 'Backstreets', another mini-movie where Springsteen initially equated strings with capturing the cosmos. Yet every layer added seemed to only diminish its impact. How could that be?

> **Bruce Springsteen**: I'd gotten into the idea of production and was interested in doing . . . what Phil Spector did . . . in some fashion. And that took a long time, because no-one really knew how to get the sounds. I liked to put everything on, but then I couldn't understand why the guitar sounds so small. The guitar sounded small, because there were twenty other things on there competing for space. For a really big guitar sound, you just have a guitar with not many other things. It took about ten years to figure this out. [1999]

As a result of Springsteen's inner frustrations and generally darkening mood, what began as an album supposedly about this overwhelmingly joyous feeling, 'I wanted to bring forth – a feeling of enormous exhilaration and aliveness', began to assume a darker side; and it brought along the last few songs that completed the song-cycle. Dredged up from some deep reservoir of betrayal were songs like 'Lonely Night In The Park', 'Backstreets' and 'Meeting Across The River'.

Having, by his own admission, spent an enormous 'amount of time . . . honing the lyrics'. he 'ended up writing most (sic) of the songs in about a three-week period . . . Originally, my mistake was in attempting to write in a particular way I had written before, instead of looking to go a slightly different way . . . In the end, I took a different approach toward some of the lyrics in the songs. If you read them on paper, sometimes they don't look that good, but when you hear them, they've got [just] the right feel. Like some of the sixties songs.'

In the 2005 DVD documentary, he revealed just how self-conscious he decided his earlier songwriting had been: 'I was very aware that I was messing with classic rock & roll images that easily turn into clichés . . . The initial lyric [to some songs] would have been like bad B-picture, whereas the end product was supposed to be . . . imbued with a certain spiritual thing.' This process was rather drawn out. As he told Paul Williams in October 1974, 'I work a lot on the lyrics before we record a song. I get self-conscious about them. So I change them.' Back then he had no idea he would still be working on the lyrics to 'Jungleland' six months later. Only his song-notebook revealed the truth: 'You would take the first page and see a line or two, and fifty pages later you'd get something close to the finished song.' (Thus, only in the studio would he come up with 'Jungleland''s coruscatingly cinematic climax: 'In the tunnels uptown, the Rat's own dream guns him down'.)

Not for the last time, the artistic process took over every waking minute. Despite his best efforts, though, very little was left over which was usable – in his eyes, anyway. He informed *Rolling Stone* in 1984, 'It's the only album where I wrote only one more song than we recorded,' presumably a reference to 'Linda Let Me Be The One', the one Record Plant outtake included on *Tracks*, and a song Landau and Springsteen set surprising store in. An adjunct to 'Janey Needs A Shooter' (which was also apparently considered at one point), the song depicted an array of lost boys waiting for Linda at midnight, 'Talking fast cars and chrome parts, hidden worlds and strange girls/ Empty homes, busted hearts, ending up with Linda in the dark'.

There was at least one other near miss. As Springsteen told Peter Knobler on the album's completion, 'I was going to have a song about back home on there, but I didn't get to it . . . Most of the songs are about being like *nowhere*. Just being out there in the void . . . and trying to make heads and tails out of it, you know, trying to figure it out.' He is referring to 'Lonely Night In The Park', a song included on the first *Born To Run* sequence in early July, then yanked. This song 'about home' also had its shady side, explicated in its final verse, 'And you're thinking of making it home / Oh, but your Mom can't see you like this'. No wonder he informed one journalist: 'All the heavy personal stuff in my songs comes from spending time further up the beach. Up there, they have a boardwalk you can run under.'

But the real deal, and affirmation of a unique vision, was 'Backstreets', a monolithic moment in modern rock that gave the album another perfectly-crafted cornerstone, and Bruce a career-defining cut. Having begun life as 'Hidin' On The River' – listed on a couple of early sequences, but for now confined to those notebooks – Bruce started 'Backstreets' in earnest on April 25 1975. On the earliest known take he is looking to 'blame it on that town', no name necessary, this take also depicting nights spent 'running . . . down the boardwalk, waiting on the corner at the lights'. Boardwalk life writ small. When she takes the only way out, the New Jersey Turnpike, he stays behind to fester in fear: 'I hated you when you went away'. The gung-ho sentiments of 'Thunder Road' and 'Born To Run' are put in reverse. He has closed down every escape route. Originally the album-closer, it indicated the direction his songwriting was now heading in, that darkness on the edge of his hometown.

However, it was not the last song recorded for the album. This appears to have been 'Meeting Across The River', on May 28. Sometimes called 'The Heist', this was another departure for the boardwalk bard. Its characters may have stepped straight out of the grooves of *The Wild, the Innocent*, but they are now trapped in circumstances beyond their control. Perhaps for this reason, Appel loved it and pushed for its inclusion on the album, even if the track ultimately failed to achieve that requisite noirish feel.

Even with every song in the can by the end of May, they were not done, not by a long chalk. Springsteen thought being 'tight, bare, [initially,] allowed us to put stuff on top of it and make it sound big, while still streamlined'. Or not. Unfortunately, he ultimately discovered, 'The sound I heard in my head was not one that was physically reproducible.' Access to a superior studio, and a budget far in excess of anything to date, was having the opposite effect to the one hoped for by those to whom he was contractually bound. Appel, for one, was fast becoming convinced it was an almighty waste of money – *their* money:

Mike Appel: Duke Ellington used to say, 'I don't need more time, I need a deadline,' and I subscribe to that. I don't mean you rush it out; you're not going to create *Sgt Pepper* in two weeks. But you'd be surprised how quick it can go with a gun to your head . . . / . . . Our budget for the first two albums was forty thousand dollars per album. With the third, we got a bump up to maybe fifty thousand dollars. That's the reason I wanted to stay up at 914. We were able to get really good rates up there. However, [as soon as] we moved down to The Record Plant . . . we went over budget in about two seconds; money that . . . ultimately came out of our pockets. [CH/DTR]

By the end of June, everyone was approaching the end of their tethers, and visibly fraying at the edges. The following year Springsteen depicted the resultant ennui, describing one particular moment at the death: 'I was sitting there at the piano in the studio, trying to get down the last cut, "She's The One", and Landau's in the booth and we've been at it for hours and hours. I just lean my head down on the piano. It just won't come. And everybody's tryin' to tell me how to do it . . . The whole thing was like that.'

With a tour booked to start on July 20, things were threatening to get out of hand. He was rehearsing with the band in one studio, overdubbing a vocal to 'She's The One' in another and mixing 'Jungleland' in a third. And at the end of the day he was trudging back to his midtown Holiday Inn room, where his new girlfriend was waiting not-so-patiently for her weary warrior:

Bruce Springsteen: For the whole last part of [*Born To Run*] I was living in this certain inn in New York over west. And the room there had this crooked mirror. And every day, before I'd go over to the studio, I'd straighten out this crooked mirror. And every day when I'd come home, that mirror was crooked again . . . After about a week, the room started to look like Nagasaki anyway. And then . . . this chick I was with one night in Texas calls up and says she's in Jersey, and she doesn't have any place to stay and she's freakin' out! And so finally I say, 'Okay, you can stay here.' So every day I'd go into the studio and there was that [situation]; and then I'd come home and there'd be this crooked mirror and this crazy chick . . . And when I got home around ten in the morning . . . this chick says to me – she says it every night when I come home - 'Is it finished yet?' And I say, 'No.' [1976]

This 'crazy chick' was not just some Texan cowgirl, as the above quote implies. Springsteen was head over heels about the gal, whom *he* invited to New York from the Lone State. Her name was Karen Darvin (later Mrs Todd Rundgren), and although she was initially understanding about the situation, in the end even Springsteen realized, 'She was in this hotel room for hours and she was seeing me only at night . . . She didn't know anybody else. So, of course, she'd get mad at me.'

It only added to the pressure of the situation until, by his own (post-therapy) admission, 'I couldn't separate the things that were frightening me from the things that were beneficial. I was feeling all of a sudden the pull of that loss of self-determination.' For a man who was all about control, such a 'loss of self-determination' was bound to tear him apart. As the sessions themselves reached the pulling-teeth stage, his drive for perfection crossed over into an obsessiveness more commonly found in the local psych ward:

> **Bruce Springsteen**: The [sessions] turned into something I never conceived of a record turning into. It turned into this thing that was wrecking me, just pounding me into the ground. Every time you'd win a little victory over it, accomplish a little something, you'd say, 'Well, the worst is over.' The next day you'd come back in and it would start pounding away at you again. [1975]

It was time for big decisions. Like, what to do about the strings. He wisely decided, 'Once we got the guitars, I think I just wanted the thing more grittier, and the strings kinda took away some of the darkness.' But still he insisted on micro-managing every little overdub, whether it was his own guitar overdub on 'Tenth Avenue Freeze Out' or Clemons' sax solo on 'Jungleland', which the Big Man had been playing nightly for the past year.

Appel, for one, was taken aback: 'Clarence was always capable of doing a solo without Bruce's instructions up to that point, but on "Jungleland", every note, Bruce was going [hand signals], note by note, until the solo was complete.' Clemons recalled this one overdub taking sixteen hours, and all the time 'he was telling me, "More warmth, more movement, I like that note there, let's work around that." We had to find those passages that go to the bone.' Losing control in his private life, Springsteen was over-obsessing at his workplace. By the end of it, he was only going back to the hotel to sleep, further aggravating that psycho-sexual situation.

It finally came time to sequence the record. For once, there was no great surfeit of potential classics he would discard. Yet there remained dissension in the ranks. As Independence Weekend approached, Springsteen ordered Appel from the studio, preferring to construct a sequence of his and Landau's choosing. Of course, he didn't do this in person. He phoned Landau at five in the morning and asked him to break the news to Appel. According to Landau, 'Bruce was very upset' by Appel's intransigence. But on some things, the manager-producer simply refused to back down:

> **Mike Appel:** I would put up with an awful lot of nonsense to get to 'Born To Run', or things like 'Born To Run'. My days were numbered no matter what. Because I think I set a really high standard for material recorded. Bruce was partially responsible for that. Just trying to make songs for pop radio – [songs like] 'Linda', 'Lonely Night In The Park' – they seemed to be pandering a little bit to [that]. I thought they had no place on the album. So I would always be at odds with him on things like that. There *were* times when I said, 'Over my dead body that song's going on the record.'

Appel has long insisted the argument he had with 'Bruce and Jon' at this juncture came about because they 'didn't think that "Meeting Across The River" should be on the album. I did and fought for it like heck. And it is in the album, and two of the songs that they wanted to be in there – "Lonely Night In The Park" and "Linda Let Me Be The One" – I thought that neither . . . was up to his standards, and I fought against [them].' But the sequence they arrived at by July 2 included all three songs. The one song cut was the title track. The album, as of Independence Day, would have run as follows:

> **Side One**: Thunder Road. Tenth Avenue Freeze Out. Lonely Night In The Park. Jungleland. Night.
> **Side Two**: Linda Let Me Be The One. Meeting Across The River. She's The One. Backstreets.

Never happy with how it had come out, Springsteen was seriously planning to leave off 'Born To Run'. Thankfully, wiser counsel prevailed. Sometime during that weekend Appel received a call from Iovine, who told him 'Mike, this is a disaster. Bruce is drifting into darkness. No one can talk to him, and he won't answer me when I try.' Eventually Springsteen realized he needed Appel to give it to him straight, and rein in any last-minute acts of wanton perversity – like preferring the throwaway 'Linda Let Me Be The One' to 'Born To Run'.

The following Monday, when Appel entered his office, Springsteen was waiting for him: 'I want you back to the studio, Mike.' Appel insists, 'I was never like, I told you so . . . He knew I was never lying to him, so when we clashed, he knew deep down [he should] check himself in the mirror.' Getting him to restore 'Born To Run', retain 'Meeting Across The River' and drop the two lesser songs would become Appel's last major contribution to Springsteen's studio canon; and the last time anybody would stand up to the singer in quite that way. It would make for what is probably Springsteen's most perfectly sequenced album, and the one that finally allowed him to achieve the goal he had set himself aged fifteen: 'To play in my own ballpark.'

It still took our man another two weeks to approve the final mix, the artwork and the mastering. But he would not 'let go'. Even engineer Iovine was impressed by his dedication: 'At the end we mixed the album in nine days straight, maybe leaving the studio for a few hours to go home. We even slept there. We had to get it finished, Bruce had shows booked. But he [still] had a picture in his head, and as tired as he was, he wouldn't let go of that picture.' Even at the mastering stage doubts crowded in. As Springsteen recalled in 2005, 'It was the last thing I was gonna have to decide before the record came out and I was simply paralyzed . . . I couldn't let it go . . . but at the same time I was done. I had nothing else to give it.'

It was time to check out of Holiday Inn Room 206, pack his bags and take Karen and the band up to Rhode Island for the weekend. Not for any kinda break, heaven forfend. Rather, their night in Providence represented the start of a tour scheduled to run through the end of the year, and would take in trips to London, Amsterdam and Stockholm and – if all went according to plan – prove Jon Landau to have been a visionary when he saw the future of rock 'n' roll some fourteen months earlier. As it turned out, the question was not, was the world ready for Bruce Springsteen, but was *he* ready for the real world?

Chapter 4: 1975–77 – Cashed In A Few Of My Dreams

> In a concert you reach for something that one can't describe. It's in the air. It's not how much you know, or who the band is, or what notes you're playing. It's something free and intangible. You reach for it the whole time, because it's the most important thing to find . . . Now it's easy for a band to be tight. It's not easy for a band to be loose. To be tight it takes knowledge and work. To be loose . . . takes something else. – Bruce Springsteen, October 1975

In the days of musical theatre, a Broadway-bound show would open out of town, usually upstate, a Poughkeepsie or a Saratoga Springs, or if the wheel-nuts needed more than mere tightening, they'd maybe shuffle off to Buffalo. The fifth incarnation of the E Street Band, after an unprecedented five months off the road, followed this time-honoured example, making its debut at the Palace Theater, Providence RI on 20 July 1975, the first of thirteen shows designed to whip everyone into shape before a five-night, ten-set stint at The Bottom Line announced the new album to an expectant media, and either set the seal on a rosy future or left the latest pretender on the bus back to Jersey.

The band was bound to have some road rust in their bones. They also had precious little time to work up a new set. As Weinberg recalled, 'We went right from the last recording session to a rehearsal room at eight in the morning, we ran through the set and played that night.' They had even less time to teach their latest recruit his parts. Thankfully, soul stylist/guitarist Steve Van Zandt had spent years playing in bar bands, with and without Springsteen. When his buddy called out Manfred Mann's 'Sha La La' as second encore in Providence, it felt just like old times.

This moment excepted, they hedged their bets opening night. Not taking any chance with Lady Luck, Springsteen sang just three songs from the new album, of which only 'Tenth Avenue Freeze Out' was new to the set. For the last time, six of *The Wild, the Innocent*'s seven songs formed its veritable backbone; including all four epics that for the past eighteen months had comprised half of the set and most of the drama. Proceedings opened with a Lahav-less 'Incident On 57th Street', performed with just Bittan's piano accompaniment, followed by 'E Street Shuffle', 'New York City Serenade' (making a fond farewell) and 'Kitty's Back'. By year's end, all four would be trimmed of their sails and – 'Incident' excepted – dry-docked for the duration.

This was no longer the E Street Band of yore, a band built on an extravagant melange of styles as disparate as jazz, soul and r&b, one which allowed everyone to take turns upstaging everyone else just as long as they all remained servant to the song. Little, on the face of it, had changed. A part-time violinist and backing singer had been replaced by a second guitarist and backing vocalist who took on some of Springsteen's parts, freeing the frontman to work on his method-singing. And there were just four new songs to assimilate into the set – two future perennials, 'Tenth Avenue Freeze Out' and 'Backstreets', and the less persuasive 'Night' and 'Meeting Across The River'. But the bandleader had passed through the fire, and come out a changed man:

> **Bruce Springsteen**: When you're leading the band, singing, and writing the songs, eventually you've got to make some choices. I chose to go away from a long jamming sorta style, even though I did it for a long time . . . As I got older I wanted to be more direct, clear, immediate and not waste a lot of time. [1992]

He no longer seemed content to let the band strike up its own rhythm. He wanted a drummer who imposed a beat, and left it at that. When he told a court transcriber in 1976 that Landau 'taught my drummer . . . how to play drums in a rock band', he meant it as a compliment. However, this more metronomic style of playing failed to complement much of the material on which a prodigious live reputation had been forged. In other words, this was not the band Landau recently proclaimed to be 'the future of rock 'n' roll', making any ongoing promotional use of *that* review almost smack of misrepresentation. The reason so many journalists found it hard to equate that review with the *Born To Run* band had nothing to do with how well they played, or how strong the new material was. What surprised many who had already experienced the E Street Band live was just how *orthodox* they sounded now.

The Springsteen who asserted earlier in the year, 'We're a real American band – there are practically no European influences,' could hardly keep a straight face. He was fronting an outfit who were a Jersey boardwalk amalgam of hungry hearts, taking a British Invasion aesthetic and feeding it a steady diet of Memphis stew. Once Miami Steve added some of his own arrangement ideas, and Weinberg stopped trying to emulate Lopez and Carter, the (largely) British sixties sounds and American r&b they grew up on became brushstrokes added repeatedly to the mix, at the expense of any last vestiges of all that jazz.

As the guitar had dominated the two key pre-E Street bands, so it returned to centre stage 1975-77, sometimes in the hands of the ex-gunslinger himself, but much of the time left to Steve Van Zandt. Surprisingly, this significant shift of focus drew very little comment at the time, pro or con; save from *Rolling Stone*'s Dave Marsh, who rather witheringly opined: 'The recent addition of Miami Steve is the [main] difference. Previously, when Springsteen had dropped his guitar to simply sing, the band was left with its focus on the keyboards. No great help since . . . Roy Bittan is inclined to over-embellish everything . . . [whereas] Van Zandt plays perfect Steve Cropper soul licks and great rock leads.'

Of course, Marsh always liked his loud guitars. The trick was recasting the band and still retaining those elements which made them the hottest showband currently playing rock 'n' roll music on the eastern seaboard. Thankfully, they still played like there was no tomorrow, with a no-holds-barred passion that took no prisoners, raising the stakes each and every time. When they rolled into town to play the first of ten sold-out-and-then-some shows back at The Bottom Line, even Bruce knew this was not gonna be like the year before:

> **Bruce Springsteen**: Even the first set we played at the Bottom Line . . . I got real 'in', man. I go 'in' sometimes, instead of going 'out' . . . There was a lot of tension and we were doing a lot of songs live for the first time. And I was really struggling with the material, struggling to get it across.

> A lot of the material on the new album is different. It's a little darker than some of the other things. So that attitude, too, added to the mood. [1975]

He need not have worried. Old and new converts alike championed the main contender come good. Leading from the front was a vindicated Nelson, who suggested in *Village Voice* that his opening show 'makes practically any criticism obsolete . . . Springsteen fashions the kind of seamless, 150-minute performance that most artists can only dream about, never realize . . . Ironically, if he weren't as good as he is – and he is close to being the best we have – no one would be concerned with such minor issues as pace and overreach.'

Marsh chose to focus on the ensemble nature of the performances, feeling that 'the E Street Band has nearly been lost in the shuffle. Which is ridiculous because this group may very well be the great American rock & roll band.' John Rockwell, having forgotten his watch, abandoned all pretence at critical objectivity to begin his *Rolling Stone* pro-Bruce puff-piece proclaiming, 'Nearly three hours into the Friday late show . . .' (none of the shows topped two hours). In fact, Springsteen and the band needed to conserve their energies. Not only were they playing two shows a night, but on the third night there was a live radio broadcast on WNEW of the entire early set.

Appel had smartly revived the practice of live radio broadcasts to spread the word, making the broadcast from The Bottom Line and a similar October coastal bulletin from LA's equally intimate Roxy the twin beacons of a strategy built on the fervent belief that you had not really heard Springsteen till you heard him live. But for now Springsteen's record company resisted – this time because of that great Music-biz bogey, bootlegs. It took Paul Rappaport to spell it out to his fellow reps: 'I told them, "I guarantee you there's gonna be a boot, and I can tell you who's gonna make it. Do you really give a fuck! C'mon, This thing's gonna explode, we're gonna sell millions of records."'

An ever-growing live reputation also smartly sidestepped the issue of whether the album 'Rap' and co. were now promoting was overcooked at the edges and undercooked in the middle. Even *NME*'s Charles Shaar Murray – who suggested in print 'the trouble with Springsteen's new album is that it sounds as if he'd been told too often how *important* he is and as a result has set out to write *important* songs and make an *important* record' – placed such criticism in the context of a two-page rave live review.

Bruce was stoking one set of expectations by quelling another. In the States, reviewers were less concerned with the album's (patent) sonic deficiencies. Greil Marcus in *Rolling Stone* positively celebrated the fact that the lyrics 'are buried, as they should be, hard to hear for the first dozen playings', comparing the E Street Band to Dylan and the Hawks circa sixty-six, which might have been the ultimate compliment if only Dylan hadn't fired the Hawks mid-sessions and made *Blonde on Blonde* with a bunch of Nashville cats instead.

Even the curmudgeonly Lester Bangs, back home at *Creem*, seemed to have been infected by all this Bruceian bonhomie, almost apologising to regular readers of his reviews: 'If I seem to OD on superlatives, it's only because *Born To Run* demands them.' Quoting Kerouac, namechecking Dylan, Morrison and Reed, he celebrates 'an American moment caught at last'. The hubbub even made its presence felt among the starched shirts of the American weeklies, where *Time* and *Newsweek* reigned supreme. When Jay Cocks, an early convert, convinced *Time* to run a cover story on the Bruce 'phenomenon' (a gross overstatement for a man still playing clubs, while the lead single from his album stuttered to a halt just shy of the Top Twenty), *Newsweek* were playing catch-up. Their solution was to send the devoutly unhip Maureen Orth to interview a man for whom hype was Bowie's ex-backing band.

Yet all through the fall this hype had legs, not because *Born To Run* itself was breaking all records or the E Street Band were harbingers of a foretold future, but because the shows just got better and better. The pacing became steadily more pitch-perfect; Springsteen began to grow into his role even as he relinquished the guitar strap; and the band found a way to make the songs from the first two albums, and any A-list covers now substituting for earlier songs he was too embarrassed to perform, fit Springsteen's new-found straitjacket of sound.

Not everyone, though, bought into all this Bruce mania. When Springsteen arrived at Gold Star to meet the great Phil Spector, after a Roxy show that showed every CBS rep just how the west was won, Spector sarcastically shouted, 'Okay fellas, Bruce Springstreet is here . . . Let's show him how to make a record.' Even before *Time* and *Newsweek* joined the bandwagon, the contrary *New York Times* – early champions of the Asbury contender – ran a piece by Henry Edwards which suggested, 'If

Bruce Springsteen didn't exist, rock critics would invent him.' Springsteen later revealed, 'That bothered me a lot.'

And if the American press had its contrary elements, the UK music press, which in 1975 had an influence on its readership that was a mere wet dream to the likes of *Rolling Stone*, was built on contrariness, particularly when it came to uppity colonials claiming, somewhat impertinently, that rock music was *their* music. Not in 1975, it wasn't. When NME editor Nick Logan instructed Andrew Tyler to go see what the fuss was about, it was to the legendary Roxy he was sent. He returned to report that he found 'a frontman for another good rock & roll band, composer of R'n'B-slanted material that tips a little in advance of the mean average', whose lyrics were 'cluttered', and whose melodies and arrangements 'are a patchwork of some of the more dubious R'n'R mannerisms of the sixties'. This was the cover story that ran in the UK's premier music weekly the week before London found out if it was finally ready for this musical magpie. (Bruce shared that cover with Dylan, whose Rolling Thunder Revue he caught in person that month, before venturing backstage to meet the man, whose opening line was a peach: 'I hear you're the new Me!')

The pressure was on even before Springsteen's jet plane landed in London and he strolled onto the Heathrow tarmac. Also at the Roxy mini-residency had been *Old Grey Whistle Test* producer Michael Appleton and its presenter Bob Harris, both there to tie up details of a TV special. The sticking point was the lighting. As Appleton told Tyler, 'The lighting is a very important part of the act, and I can understand his point of view. [So] we're currently investigating the possibility of doing an outside broadcast from the Hammersmith Odeon gig on [November] 24th.'

In fact, the decision was made to shoot opening night (the 18th); *not* Springsteen's return date, six days later (added after shows had already been booked in Stockholm and Amsterdam). While the concert footage they shot was simply too dark to be broadcast, a BBC radio broadcast from Hammersmith, intended to emulate the impact of those from The Bottom Line and The Roxy, was hastily cancelled when Appel saw the mood his charge was in on landing (though he still ran tapes both nights):

> **Bruce Springsteen**: I was in this big shadow, man, right from the start . . . I'm just getting over this [New] Dylan thing: 'Oh, thank God, that seems

> to be fading away,' and . . . 'Phwooeee, I have seen [the future] . . .' No, it can't be . . . So like I'm always ten points down, because not only have you got to play, but you got to blow this bullshit out of people's minds first . . . / . . . I can't be put in a position of having to dig out of somebody's idea of what I am . . . [But] CBS took this [quote], promoted it real heavy, and I was like SENSATIONAL! Cheap thrill time! You know it was a big mistake on their part . . . and I would like to strangle the guy who thought that up, if I ever get hold of him. [1975]

Springsteen wasn't the only one on the warpath the day of his London debut. Appel was equally angry, after 'CBS, unbeknownst to me, decides to take all these arrogant ads, "Is London finally ready . . .?" I was as blindsided as Bruce when I saw those things. Nobody asked my permission for that. I never wanted to be a manager in the first place, and now *I'm* having to deal with everything! And now it's all business.' In the notes to the 2005 official DVD release of that show, Springsteen suggested he overreacted to the situation. Having 'arrived at the theatre [I] created pre-show chaos, stomping through the aisles, pulling promo flyers off the seats in a "The Man can't steal *my* music" frenzy. The record company, of course, was just doing its job, and I was just doing its job, and I was just learning mine . . . real fast . . . Later, all I remember is an awkward record company party, that "what just happened?" feeling, and thinking we hadn't played that well.'

Unlike Dylan and the Hawks in '66, he simply refused to review the tapes to help understand why that night's audience reacted the way they did. As it happens, the audience loved the show both nights. Audience tapes demonstrate them responding to every visual cue, each shift in musical style. Appel, for one, 'loved the fact that the London audience got into him big-time, and the advertisements, all the shit, didn't mean nothing.' But for Springsteen, the curse of Hammersmith would remain in his head long after he returned to the States with tapes of both nights in the hold. Even after returning to London six years later to a media hype that made 1975 look like a roast, he felt some explanation was in order:

> **Bruce Springsteen**: I've always been haunted by the two gigs we played here back in '75 . . . I was a heap of nerves, and because it wasn't working, I kinda went *inside* myself. I saw my whole career collapsing whilst I was playing those songs. It was painful and because I felt guilty 'cause it was

> me, it was my name and my reputation the audience had come to check out. When I left that stage, I . . . just wanted to drop the whole thing, my career as a musician, because my self-confidence was shot. I felt crippled. Everything had gotten too out of control and I felt drained . . . I've got absolutely total recall of those shows because the first one was *so bad* I was ready to blow up fuckin' Big Ben. I stunk that first night, and although the second show was a good show by any standards, at that time the negative aspect of the London trip – and there were a whole number – came to totally exemplify this huge psychic weight on my head. [1981]

He only revised his view of that first show in 2005 after reviewing the tapes: 'I was wrong. With the keys to the kingdom dangling in front of us and the knife at our neck, we'd gone for broke.' Though his abiding memory of the second show as good 'by any standards' was spot on. Two days before the weeklies ran their reviews of the supposed first-night debacle, Springsteen delivered a very different performance, one which represented the way forward for him and his band – if not rock 'n' roll itself.

(Actually, only the agenda-driven *NME* gave a real thumbs-down to 'a gutsy, energetic performer of restricted growth, who plays fair guitar; who makes the very most of his (actually limited) voice; who writes fair if wordy songs; who works tirelessly if not always effectively on stage; whose sense of drama is simultaneously incomplete and overdone; who can't pick musicians; [and] who can't seem to resist the hype put out in his name by Columbia'.)

The E Street Band of yesteryear was laid to rest somewhere over Stockholm. After six days on the road, Springsteen returned to play a set stripped of its wilder, more innocent moments. Out went 'E Street Shuffle' and 'Kitty's Back', the two regular concessions to the Sancious era. In their place came a checklist of Invasion influences any semi-educated Brit could relate to: Manfred Mann's 'Sha La La' and 'Pretty Flamingo', The Searchers' 'When You Walk In The Room'. And wrapping up proceedings in style were three fifties rockers known largely to seventies rock fans from the Beatles' and Stones' recastings, 'Twist and Shout', 'Carol' and 'Little Queenie'.

If much of the second album was sidelined, core first-album songs – 'Saint In The City', 'Lost In The Flood', 'For You' - were stripped bare and, in the former two cases, reconditioned for r&b. 'Lost In The Flood' was almost unrecognisable, with more twists and turns in its new arrangement than 'Born To Run' and 'Thundercrack' combined. Weinberg finally came into his own on these numbers, where subtlety was for squares and the boss preferred the sound of broken foot-pedals.

In March 1977, Springsteen described that second night at Hammersmith as 'one of the best shows we ever played . . . [and yet] when I walked out of that theatre in London, I just wanted to go home . . . back to New Jersey'. How perverse then that he should release the first night – and *only* the first night – on CD in 2006 (both shows were in the vault and the first show had already been released as a DVD). But maybe such perversity was in his DNA. The Hammersmith shows weren't the first *Born To Run* shows Appel had arranged to record. The Roxy radio show had also been taped by Jimmy Iovine, providing a club equivalent for many of the same footstompers (plus the Goffin-King classic, 'Goin' Back', a delicious one-off). Appel was convinced a live record was the smart move now, an affirmation of the past three years of inexorable growth as a combo, a way of clearing the decks and replenishing much-depleted coffers:

> **Mike Appel:** Expenses have gone up, but success hasn't quite caught up with you. There was this great crescendo from the press – writers are falling in love, and they build this and build this, next thing you know he's on the cover of *Time* and *Newsweek*. But in fact the public weren't paying yet, the promoters weren't paying yet. They hadn't caught up with the press. The press was the vanguard. It's just that the money we were able to earn and command wasn't commensurate with the amount of press [we got] . . . [And] we always wanted to do [a live album]. I thought a live album would be good after *Born To Run*. It would give him time to write the kind of material he would need if he was going to compete with *Born To Run*. It would also give him money, and also, 'You never did one of these and you're the greatest live act ever.' [But] I couldn't get him to listen to one tape. He just said, 'I don't want to do it.'

For the first time, Appel and Springsteen were reading different pages. In fact, Springsteen was convinced Appel just wanted him to re-read his back pages. But Appel still insisted on rolling tape at December shows in Toronto, C. W. Post, and Philadelphia, where the band saw out the year with four sell-out shows at one of the great rock venues, the Tower Theater. He thought if he could get Bruce to sit still long enough to check out 'Lost In The Flood' from Toronto, its high tide point; the life-affirming 'Santa Claus Is Coming To Town' from C. W. Post; or that new arrangement of 'Tenth Avenue Freeze Out' set to slow burn, those rap-infused takes of 'It's My Life' and 'Pretty Flamingo', or the final E Street-era outings of 'Mountain of Love' and 'Does This Bus Stop' (all from the New Year's Eve show) then he just might reconsider, baby.

What Appel did not realize was that he had already crossed some ill-defined line in Springsteen's suspicious mind. He did by 1978, by which time he concluded, 'I guess I looked just as guilty to him as CBS. He lumped me in with *Time* and *Newsweek*. [Because] he wanted that fame and glory, but I guess he wanted it on his own terms.' Those terms were as unrealistic and unachievable as the sound in his head, something the singer himself acknowledged when pushing his next LP real hard: 'I [had] worked a year – a year of my life – on [*Born To Run*] and I wasn't aggressively trying to get it out there to people. I was super aggressive in my approach toward the record and toward makin' it happen – you know, non-relenting. And then when it came out, I went, "Oh, I don't wanna *push* it."'

Part of what preyed on his mind was an unnameable fear that *Born To Run* represented the summit of what he had in him. Great as the covers were at the fall 1975 shows, where were the new originals? Back in September, he had actually admitted to Knobler, 'Things've gotten heavier lately . . . Just things starting to weigh in . . . I also haven't written anything in two, three months.' He began to worry the two might be connected, voicing his concerns to Jay Cocks: 'First you write about struggling along. Then you write about making it professionally. Then somebody's nice to you. You write about that. It's a beautiful day, you write about that. That's about twenty songs in all. Then you're out.' And though the good reviews meant nothing, the bad reviews hurt like a bitch. So what exactly was success 'on his own terms'?

> **Bruce Springsteen**: If you see that girl walking down the street and you say, 'Oh my God, life would be ecstasy if she was just my girlfriend,' you're only thinking of the wonderful parts . . . Success is like that girl: If only I had that, I wouldn't have a worry in the world. And then you get it . . . I was cocky enough to think I was something special – along with, of course, thinking you're a fraud and worthless, but that's part of the artistic experience. I had both sides. [2010]

Such self-awareness was reserved for the future. The person he now turned on was *not* the one he saw in the motel mirror. He was sitting across that desk back at the office. The person who had sold his own future to ensure Springsteen had one. In 1978, after successfully extricating himself from the unwavering Appel, Springsteen implied he was the one left spinning: 'At a certain point I realized I wanted to be true to myself, and I had to be tougher than I had been. They always know how to get you – they get you while you're dancing.' As ever, 'they' were attracted by the scent of money. For now, Appel was still the first line of defence. But already the whispering campaign had begun taking steps to remove this impediment:

> **Mike Appel:** We had spoken loosely about [the financial situation] over the years but it was not a pressing concern because there was no money . . . [But] the lawyers were already involved by [Hammersmith]. There is already a problem for the last quarter of '75. Trying to figure a way to get Bruce out of his contract, they would say [to him], 'You can't get out of your contracts just by walking out. You have to have some kind of excuse. We basically have to say that Mike [by] being your producer, your publisher, your manager . . . how could he be all three things, and [still] be trying to get you the best deal with Columbia?' So the attorneys are trying to do everything they can to sour my relationship with Bruce . . . There was a point, maybe January or February [1976], when he got together with me and he played me some songs, 'Rendezvous', some other[s]. I said, 'Gee, they sound great. What are we gonna do?' And he said, 'Well, I just want to get things *worked out*.' I was like, 'Okay, well, how are we going to "work things out"?' He said, 'I'll get back to you.' But he himself never did get back to me.

Things didn't look so clear when waist-high in the black muddy river of commerce. And from now on everything Appel suggested, Landau recommended the opposite. If Appel thought they should issue a live album, Landau thought they should hang fire. If Appel suggested they start work on the next album, Landau felt it was premature. Springsteen himself just wanted to be calling the shots. So when his manager and label began to ask about the next album, he demurred. Only in 1978 would he explain his then-reasoning: 'I didn't want to do another album right away. The whole system is based on the corruption of your ideals, on the watering down of things that are real. If you start worrying about putting out a follow-up album, you get caught up in the machine of the industry.' Nuttin' to do with writer's block, then.

Landau, who had not been there in London, had supposedly 'called Bruce up on the road and told him that Appel's inflexibility toward the press was making Bruce a lot of enemies he didn't need'. There were now two constituencies, the governing party and the loyal opposition, the latter hoping for an election soon. These days, Appel thinks 'Jon was so enamoured with Bruce he just couldn't live without him, and whatever it took to get him "married" to Bruce he would be willing to do.' He certainly didn't play Mr Impartial the day Springsteen called round to his place in LA, when he was working with Jackson Browne on another laborious production, *The Pretender*.

Springsteen told him, '[Mike] wants me to sign this new contract, and he made it clear to me that if I sign these new contracts, he will give me a new deal that will be much better for me, and he will distribute this money according to the new deal. But if I don't sign these new contracts, he is going to hold me to the letter of the old contracts.' He would subsequently claim, 'I was very wary of signing [another contract] with him because of the first one that I signed, y'know, which I had taken around and found was real bad.' Yet he expected Appel to take him at *his* word, the word of a man who had been turned. And Appel knew by whom.

Landau suggested he speak to Myron Mayer, the attorney he used himself. In his own deposition, Appel implied there was some grand plan behind the critic's recommendation: 'Mayer was Bruce's, Landau's, Dave Marsh's, and Atlantic Records' attorney, and he was, I guess, telling them he could get Bruce out of all the contracts, which might then free Bruce from Columbia also, since he was really only signed to Laurel Canyon and not directly to the label. Once free, Bruce could sign for a bundle to Atlantic Records and wholly own all the new songs.' It was a strategy that had almost netted Dylan for Atlantic back in 1972. But Appel's hard-nosed reputation was well deserved, and once he realized that the trust, and therefore the thrill, was gone, there was only ever going to be one way out of this bloody stalemate:

Mike Appel: I hear from his attorneys through my accountant. My [management] contract is 20% of the gross. He says to me, 'Well, I want to give you 10% of the net instead of 20% of the gross. And all the songs

> that I'd published revert back to Bruce Springsteen. And he didn't want me to produce at all.' So I'm saying to myself, 'This guy is definitely not a nice guy.' I was like, 'I have these contracts [already] in place, and you're offering me *this*!' Part of you feels, '[How can] Bruce [be] part of these deliberations?' I was miffed. I went back to my father. I said, 'Hey, Dad, here's what they're offering me.' He said, 'How can you trust these guys?' I was very, very upset. Bruce came in one day and we talked in the office, and I said, 'I can't trust your attorneys. And I don't know how much influence they have over *you*. It's like, we're not the same. It's not the same team. There's been this divisive force here. And, frankly I don't know what to believe anymore.' . . . You say to yourself, 'I've been at this for three and a half years and I finally get it to this point – and this is what you guys are offering??!!' . . . Jules Kurz was our attorney . . . He put me in touch with Leonard Marks. So I went up there. Leonard Marks had said to Jules, 'Have Mike bring the contracts with him.' And he [reads them] and said, 'Okay, it's a divorce. You're never going back.' It was like a knife in my heart: 'You mean this is *it*?' . . . Bruce couldn't stand up to the pressures that were around him at the time. And he gave in. I can understand that. Here he was, coming from nowhere, now he's top of the pops. Not wanting to risk it all. [But] I don't know why Bruce let them build their case on something he knew was not the case. He didn't intercede. He let it go down. When they go through everything, they realize it's like twenty thousand bucks – it's shoeshine money.

Mayer was ill-equipped for such hand-to-hand combat. He was an entertainment lawyer who expected Appel to roll over because he assumed that, like every manager, he would be found to have been dipping his hand in the till. In the end, a thorough examination by a forensic accountant found that he owed Springsteen a few thousand bucks – chicken-feed – and the worst he could say about the Laurel Canyon set-up was that it was 'a very unprofessional way of doing things'.

Appel had another edge. He had previously got CBS to advance them (i.e. him) a quarter of a million dollars against future royalties, to keep the whole thing afloat for as long as it took Springsteen to realize that a live album was the way to go, the occasional arena show was not a betrayal, and the bills would keep coming until he decided it was time to record again. In deposition, Springsteen described their conversation about said advance thus: 'I said, "Michael, how much of that [$250,000] is mine and how much of that is yours? How much do you think I should get?" He said, "Man, you should get at least seventy-five per cent." And I said, "How much, man, am I going to get?" And he said that depended.'

With Springsteen the one holding the gun, it was Appel at the sharp end. He did not blink. As he said in *his* deposition: 'He couldn't [seriously] expect on one hand to throw me out the door, and on the other for me to give him a quarter of a million dollars in advance money from Columbia, recoupable against any and all future royalties, of which, by all right, I had a significant share.' But, of course, he did. Because the one thing the boy from Freehold was not, was reasonable.

Integrity, a word Springsteen bandied around a lot at this time, did not include honouring contracts, or recognizing the key role another had played in his success. Without Appel there would never have been *any* pot of gold, just summer nights on the shore as an oldies act, like his friend Southside Johnny. But every time the manager offered a compromise solution, he was sent away with a flea in his ear: 'I told Mayer that I was still willing to give Bruce half the publishing back, retroactive from the first album, but Mayer . . . said in response, "We want Bruce to have *all* of his publishing."'

Mayer, negotiating from a position of profound weakness, overplayed his hand at every turn, contesting a contract that made it impossible for Springsteen to record for CBS without Appel's say-so, or to nominate a producer without his approval. And it was all there in black and white, if Springsteen had taken the time to read legally-binding documents to which he put his name. But for the bull-headed Bruce it was all a matter of 'integrity', and he expected Appel to take him at his word when he told him that he would see him right.

Meanwhile, he trusted Landau to explain legal matters to him. But if Landau gave Springsteen the impression he understood these contractual nuances, he was blowing smoke. As Marc Elliot noted, after thoroughly examining all the legal paperwork from the suit, 'Landau was obviously telling the truth when he said he didn't know what the contracts really meant. The 50% Landau found so unfair was actually an incentive offer by Appel to reduce his 100% of the publishing to a 50-50 split, which would in effect have given Springsteen 75% to Appel's 25% on all mechanical income, another 50% split of the publisher's share of all performance income, *retroactive* to 1972 (in spite of the fact that the publishing contract had an *automatic* extension clause); [and] half the stock of Laurel Canyon, the production company and the management company.'

Considering the contracts he already had, Appel was being generous to a fault in his attempts to broker a deal. Whereas Landau was focused solely on the prize proffered by Bruce himself, who had already told the ex-critic, 'Look, this is definitely the last record I am doing with Mike.' According to Landau, 'What was on [Springsteen]'s mind was his failure to get his ideas on tape,' for which he blamed the man who had recorded his first album in one week and his second in two; *not* the man whose presence helped turn the Record Plant sessions into a three-month slog.

Fixated on a misdirected sense of betrayal, Springsteen showed himself to be a lousy strategist. The management contract with Appel had a year to run, and the production deal had only two albums to run. And it would have been the easiest thing in the world to OK a live album that counted as one of these. So, all he needed to do to extract himself from Appel's loving grip was record a single studio album with a producer of Appel's choosing – and he had been offered a list of other potential producers, every one of whom had a track record which made Landau's slim credits look risible – while seeing out the management deal. Yes, Appel would continue to get his share of the publishing but, as he had already indicated, that was itself open to negotiation. But Bruce remained the same arrested adolescent his parents once despaired of; and what the suit became about was a truculent teenager getting his way. As his next girlfriend told one biographer, 'Bruce had rules of behaviour and everyone was afraid to cross him.' Appel, though, was not.

The opposition's initial strategy, based on the erroneous belief that Springsteen had been ripped off by Appel, was abandoned the minute he brought in new counsel, in the form of Michael Tannen. As Appel's own counsel, Leonard Marks, informed *Rolling Stone*, 'Springsteen's new lawyers saw that [the accountant's report] was useless because it was so biased and full of holes that you could drive a truck through it.' So Tannen went with 'conflict of interest' instead. Surely, Appel acting as producer-publisher-manager was 'unconscionable', whatever the careers of Andrew Loog Oldham or Joe Boyd might suggest? But, as Appel points out, 'They had forgotten . . . I was not his manager for months after he signed the publishing-production contract. That was a fatal mistake. They didn't look at the dates on the contract.'

In fact, he had only become manager at Springsteen's insistence, and against his better judgement. In his countersuit, Appel also challenged the notion that Springsteen was the only artist here. He rightly resented the painting of himself as a mere businessman. He asked the court to recognize that the 'plaintiff's exclusive right to Springsteen's services as a recording artist, and its right to produce each of Springsteen's albums is of great artistic value, as well as commercial value, to plaintiff.'

But what really did for Springsteen was a particular clause in the original Laurel Canyon contract, signed before he ever 'specifically assented' to the CBS-Laurel Canyon production agreement, or had browbeat Appel into managing him. It read: 'If the fulfilling of this Agreement shall become impossible by reason of "force majore" or any other cause outside the control of the parties hereto, then either party shall be entitled . . . to suspend the operation of this Agreement until such time as such fulfillment shall again be possible . . . During said suspension, Artist shall not be able to record for any other person, firm or corporation in violation of the terms of this Agreement.'

Michael Tannen, who certainly knew how to litigate, still remained confident of ultimate victory, even if the self-assured lawyer felt obliged to inform Springsteen 'I think we should fight this, but it's your life.' His response was never in doubt: 'I'm fighting this to the end. If it takes another ten years, I don't care.'[MOTH] One doubts he'd have given the same answer if he had bothered to ask an older, wiser John Fogerty, who would indeed have to surrender a decade of his career to get away from Fantasy Records. In 2010, Bruce could still believe, 'It wasn't a lawsuit about money, it was about control. Who was going to be in control of my work and my work-life . . . If I don't go in the studio, I don't go in the studio, but I don't go in the studio under somebody else's rules.'

His inability to surrender the slightest element of control – all in the name of art – would ultimately bring his career as an abidingly creative artist to a juddering halt. As for the lawsuit, it merely ensured he paid off one devil he once trusted with the largesse of a devil he never trusted (CBS), all the while forsaking the opportunity to record at a time when he had songs which needed to be caught in the moment. He himself made this point to the court, albeit in an act of craven self-justification: 'I have started countless numbers of songs which I have been unable to develop to their potential for lack of a proper recording opportunity . . . Many of these songs will never be finished.'

And the first of these was 'Frankie', a song he would still be trying to capture at the *Born In The USA* sessions, unwilling to accept he had already caught it in all its transcendent glory at a handful of April 1976 shows. After suffering another nine-month gap waiting on his errant muse, the disillusioned 'future of rock 'n' roll' found a way to move forward that suggested a natural progression from the 'search' songs on *Born To Run*, while taking one step back from the existential angst of *Darkness*. There is still magic in the night, a belief that 'in the darkness there'll be hidden worlds that shine'. In performance that spring he even gave the song its very own Morrisonesque coda, seeking to exorcise the girl's abiding sadness by whispering (to her) over and over the single mantra, 'Walk softly tonight little angel, into the shadows where the lovers go/ Talk softly to me tonight angel, whisper your secrets so soft and low', a couplet that could have walked all the way from Cypress Avenue. When words finally failed him, the Big Man stepped in to lead the song gently into the night. Magnificent.

It had taken Van Morrison a series of bitter disputes with managers who had signed him to far more egregious contracts than anything Appel produced, plus an extended spell away from his hometown, to produce the majestic *Astral Weeks*. And now Springsteen, in the early months of 1976, also began writing songs which looked back in anger *and* regret. Even before he began 'Frankie', he had penned a prototype 'Darkness On The Edge of Town' that addressed lost promises: 'Billy, remember when we were younger, seemed like there was some strange kinda magic out there/ Me and you, we was always runnin', not worrying', didn't care/ You got a good life but Billy I'm still foolin'.' It would eventually become the last piece of the jigsaw-puzzle, a whole album about home ('When I wrote "Racing In The Street", that's like home. And "Darkness On The Edge Of Town". "The Promise", too'):

> **Bruce Springsteen**: Most of the material on *Darkness* is confrontational. It's about somebody that turns the car around and heads back to town . . . That was where I felt there were so many people who had lost that part of themselves . . . and when they did, if they didn't die physically – which many of them did, much younger than they should have . . . they died somewhere inside, [and] that just cut them off from everything and everybody else that meant something. [GD]

These growing pangs had been set in motion by the simple expedient of 'making it'. Already in September 1975 he was describing his hometown thus, 'It's like *desperate faces*. You seen all these guys in Asbury Park and [it's] like, there's *nothing* else.' By May 1976, he was taking time to seriously think about such things: 'I had all that time off, and I spent a lotta time home . . . [and saw] what my old friends were doing, what my relatives were doing. How things were affecting them, and what their lives were like . . . / . . . During the lawsuit, I understood that it's the music that keeps me alive, and my relationships with my friends, and my attachment to the people and the places I've known. That's my lifeblood.'

He had found a subject matter close to his heart. From hereon it would become the central joist to his life's work. In the only interview he gave during the lawsuit, he insisted: 'I can take anything that's thrown in my direction . . . [and] not be abused by it, just take it, channel it, put it in perspective, and then turn it into some kind of thing . . . that'll give me the strength to go the next mile.' That is certainly what he was doing now. The immediate result was some of the most potent songs of his career. One of these, 'The Promise', the highlight of many shows between August 1976 and July 1978, changed everything.

It is the song on which, in a sense, Springsteen's whole songwriting pivots. From his past he drew on the triumphalist 'Thunder Road', but now he turned its central motif to a darker purpose in a repeated refrain ('Thunder Road, we were gonna take it all and throw it all away').* The promise itself was an ideal; the ultimate expression of the integrity he set such store in, which could still be found in the music. As he told a Stockholm audience in 1981, 'In the rock and roll music that I heard [on the radio], there was a promise that there was a meaning in life, a meaning in living . . . but it's a promise that gets easily broken today. There's nobody but yourself, I guess, that can make that promise come true.' The promise was also something greater. As he said at this time, 'The promise as such is connected with human nature, and everyone's longing for redemption. It's about proving your own possibilities.'

There were, however, some who interpreted the song to be 'about' the lawsuit, finding layers of meaning in the sign-off couplet, 'When the promise was broken/ I cashed in a few of my own dreams'. In fact,

* This refrain was not, however, included in the earliest live performance of the song, August 3 1976, where Springsteen sings the line 'It's a loser' instead.

the voicing of this interpretation in print led to wholesale rewrites, which seemed at least partly designed to remove any reference to the psychological scars from the Great Hype: 'I won big once and I hit the coast, oh but somehow I paid the big cost/ Inside I felt like I was carrying the broken spirits of all the other ones who lost.'

'Something In The Night', the other new song Springsteen debuted at a Red Bank August residency, itself referenced the early live versions of 'The Promise' at least twice – 'Sleeping with a stranger in the back seat of a borrowed car' and 'There's something dying on the highway tonight' – confirming they were of a piece. In the original 1976 version he picks up another 'crazy chick' in verse two – probably a cipher for current crazy love, Karen Darvin – trying in a single night, an endlessly rewritten final verse and a single act of copulation, to capture that 'something in the night': 'I pick this chick up hitch-hiking, she just hung her head out the window and she screamed,/ She was looking for someplace to go, to die or be redeemed/ For all the ones caught laughin' in the face of the devil, waitin' 'till the moment is right/ Somewhere we'll surrender to the beauty of something in the night'.

That version, captured in still-life perfection from an August '76 Red Bank show on the 2010 *Thrill Hill Vault* DVD, may be the single most evocative moment of Springsteen onstage on film. The song would even fleetingly acquire an exquisite horn arrangement, for the October '76 New York Palladium shows, along with a lyric rewrite which shattered the lovers' cosy dream – 'When we found the things we loved, they were crushed and dying in the dirt' – leaving the singer alone, contemplating death and redemption.

He'd been thinking a lot about both in the past nine months. And at moments such as these, even his girlfriend couldn't get inside. As he informed Peter Knobler in an unguarded moment the previous fall, 'Karen says, "Sometimes I don't know you," and then other times she knows me real well. There must be times when you say, hey, yeah, that's you, and other times when there's a side of me that, like, you would not know.'

That secretive side had always been there. It was something the observant Michael Watts noted as early as 1974, when fame was a goal, not a reality: 'In pursuing this self-discovery, away from the stage he's grown self-contained, untouched by people in the final analysis. Although easy and friendly, not a bit aloof, he's still a lone star, moving on his own, independent trajectory.' It was a trait the rock-singer now embraced, even as he admitted, 'It gets harder as it goes along. I guess it's because you got to fight your way through more and more of the bullshit. You have to go a little farther than you went the last time. Go a little deeper down into yourself.' He was also discovering that a little distrust of his fellow man might be a healthy thing:

> **Bruce Springsteen**: I was always the kind of guy who liked to walk around and slip back into the shadows . . . Most people are alright, but . . . you gotta keep a certain distance . . . In the end, it's always myself . . . I [just] don't think you can completely trust people . . . There's a point where, when it really comes down, I think everybody will turn. There's just a point where other things become important. [1977]

As he lost control of the things he held to be most precious – his girlfriend, his music, his career – he tightened down that inner lid, allowing any personal confusion to come out only in song. Even the traditional refuge of the working stiff – a local bar and drinking buddies – he denied himself. As he revealed to a journalist on the *Darkness* tour, 'I suppose if I wanted to get drunk I'd go to a bar – on my own – with the precise intention of getting right out of it. But I wouldn't want anybody else to see [me].'

He didn't even seem to relate particularly well to fellow futurists in modern music. When he ended up cruising Cleveland in a rustbucket, the day after a triumphant April 1976 show at the Allen Theatre, with *Creem*'s Robert Duncan and Pere Ubu's Peter Laughner, he only dimly realized that the man at the wheel was as out of control as he was in control; or that the hyper Laughner, who frequented working men's bars with the precise intention of 'getting right out of it', would drink himself to death within fourteen months, age 24. While the lugubrious Laughner drove like a dervish, a frazzled Springsteen regaled the pair with stories of the great Frat-rock bands, a passion he never quite abandoned. It was as close as Springsteen ever got to Cleveland's nascent punk scene.

Another punk scene had also been sprouting wings in New York while he had been at the wheel on E Street. And after his own successful Bottom Line radio broadcast, he and Landau took in Patti Smith's end-of-year Bottom Line gig-cum-broadcast on the back of her own LP triumph, *Horses*. She feigned disinterest: 'He's never really entered my consciousness . . . That night at the Bottom Line all anyone was whispering was that Bruce Springsteen was there. So what? If John Lennon was there I might have a heart attack.' Bruce felt they shared a common bond, even if she didn't. When Patti and her boyfriend, Blue Öyster Cult's Allen Lanier, took in the last two shows at the Palladium in November 1976, Bruce dedicated the highly appropriate Animals anthem 'We Gotta Get Out Of This Place' to the pair. When Patti returned to The Bottom Line for more end-of-the-year shows, he strapped on a guitar and joined in. But Patti remained aloof, and Springsteen gleaned this was another scene to which he was not invited.

The only time he really felt like he belonged to a band of brothers was onstage with the E Street Band. He fully meant it when he said, at this time, 'I play because I don't have a choice. If you have a choice then you should quit. If I wasn't playing at the Palladium I'd be playing at home in Asbury Park. I can't be stopped. I can't stop myself.' This obsession, real and all-consuming, excluded even those nearest and dearest. As he openly admitted the following March, 'Nothing means as much to me . . . I can't tell anyone that they're the most important thing in my life, because nothing in my life could ever be as important as *this*.' It was a realization he had arrived at when just a teenager, and he still felt the exact same way: 'If you're dealing with people who say . . . "I don't know if I want to play, or if I want to get married"; if you have to decide, then the answer is don't do it. If you have a choice, then the answer is no.' It was even dawning on Darvin that he meant these things he was saying; especially after she caught a number of shows in the fall of 1975 when Springsteen prefaced Ike and Tina Turner's 'It's Gonna Work Out Fine' with a telling tale:

> 'I just had a birthday, and I was noticing I was getting old, you know, and I was watching all these friends of mine, realized that almost all the cats that I played with in bands, years back . . . they'd all gotten married and settled down. How many married folks here in the crowd? Who's married here? That's not many, there's a lot of people out there still messing around . . . What started me thinking 'bout it was this guy came to my house, a few weeks ago, knocked on the door, right. I went to the door and this guy dressed in a suit and a briefcase was selling insurance. I knew I recognized the guy right away. He looked real familiar but I couldn't remember where, and I realised I went to high school with him . . . He said he'd got married and had four or five kids and was doing this gig, you know. So it

> started me thinking about all that stuff . . . All you married people can tell me if this is the way it was when you got married.'

After one such show he admitted to one scribe, 'I couldn't bring up kids. I couldn't handle it. I mean, it's too heavy, it's too much . . . I just don't see why people get married.' What had brought him to this place of inner certitude was spending time with his sister Virginia and her husband Micky. Indeed, one night he dedicated the above song to them, 'Ginny, you can tell me if this was the way it was when he proposed to you.' On the penultimate night of the spring 1977 tour, he became more expansive on the subject of relatives as people with not the least idea how to live or when to die:

> '[My] relatives are funny. They're like all these reformed greaser type cats that got married . . . [with] ten kids all running around and screaming and stuff . . . Anyway, this got me thinking about my sister. She married this guy who lived down on Route 9, which was like heavy . . . There was these like Mongolians or something, they had this big gang out on Route 9 – she's with her husband now and I'm an uncle, you know. It started me thinking about this fellow who decides that he's finally through screwing around, messing around, he's gonna settle down. ['Cause] he's found somebody he liked.'

When he started thinking 'bout such things, he set about writing. But these new songs were the exact opposite of 'It's Gonna Work Out Fine' and 'Then She Kissed Me', the two direct nods to Spector in the 1975 set. They were more like those bands like Belfast's Them or Newcastle's The Animals once performed. As he subsequently informed Will Percy, 'The Animals' "We Gotta Get Out Of This Place" or "It's My Life" . . . said something to me about my own experience of exclusion . . . [which is] a theme that runs through much of my writing.' Such songs initially substituted for Springsteen's expositions on his 'own experience of exclusion'. But by the winter of 1977 he was writing songs that made Eric Burdon's gritty Geordie realism seem positively life-affirming. He just wasn't ready to spring them on the faithful fans. The only hint as to the true direction his songwriting was heading in came during a lengthy spoken section he added to 'Backstreets' at the start of the spring 1977 tour:

> 'Till the end, just me and you, baby, just me and you, girl. We could steal away . . . we could steal away – we had it all figured out, I remember we had this plan, you was gonna quit your job . . . and I'd been saving up some money . . . we were gonna slip away . . . and I remember that night 'cause these guys, they had some machines down there and there was this fire that night down by the tracks . . . We were sitting in the backseat of a burned-out old Cadillac . . . I could see fire down on the south-side of the tracks . . . and you promised you was never gonna go anyplace without me . . . I remember you promised that night . . . and the rain came tumbling down . . . and we were sitting there that night . . . / . . . We sat in the backseat of that car, watching it burning . . . and I remember you swore to me . . . I remember you promised . . . I remember you promised . . . I remember you promised . . . and baby, you lied . . . yeah, baby, you lied . . . oh, your pretty li-li-li-li-lies . . . your pretty li-li-li-li-lies . . . I love your li-li-li-li-lies, oh, your pretty lies . . . and tonight I remember wishing that night . . . I wished that God would send some angels to blow this whole town right into the sea . . . I was so sick, I just wished that God would send some angels to blow the whole damn town into the sea . . . made me so sick I just wished God would send some angels to blow that damn town into the sea . . . just wished that God would send some angels to blow us all away, just wished that God would send some angels to blow it all away, blow it all away, just blow it all away, just blow it all away, just blow it all away, just blow it all away, just blow it all away because you promised, because you promised, because you promised, because you promised and you just, you just . . . YOU LIED! . . . YOU LIED! . . . YOU LIED!'

Too late to stop listening to Them now. Standing there onstage in all his revelation, Springsteen remembered how it felt to be on his own, a complete unknown. 'The machines and the fire' had already appeared in 'Frankie' as well as another song rehearsed the summer of 1976, 'Candy's Boy'; while the image of God's angels coming to blow this whole damned town into the sea would spawn a whole song, 'God's Angels'. Yet even as he continued to refrain from playing 'Darkness on The Edge of Town', '32 Ford' (aka 'Racing In The Street'), 'Candy's Room', 'Independence Day', 'The Night Belongs To Lovers' (aka 'Because The Night') in the east-coast heartland of Brucedom, a press release for the spring tour promised fans:

'Bruce and the band will be performing a series of his newly-penned tune[s] which will probably appear on his next album.'

What they mainly got was the frat-rock of 'Rendezvous', already an old song; the call to arms, 'Action In The Streets'; and his anthem to Lot's wife, 'Don't Look Back' – none of which would make the 'next album'. In fact, the emphasis at these shows was more on talismanic songs from his youth like 'Raise Your Hand', 'It's My Life', 'You Can't Sit Down' and 'Higher and Higher' than 'newly-penned tunes'. R&B remained on the welcome table, even as Springsteen was insisting, 'We do some, but it's not where the heart of the thing is . . . That's more Miami's thing, you know . . . working with the horns. But I dig it, it's exciting, it's rock & roll.' He still brought out the appositely named Miami Horns to a few fall 1976 and spring 1977 shows, just to show off his band's adaptability. However, 'Something In The Night', the only song performed in 1976-77 that would *actually* make the next album, got dropped off somewhere in the swamps of Florida.

Four sell-out dates at Boston's Music Hall wrapped things up for another year. The final show, on March 25, ended with the Miami Horns honking away on an exquisite cover of Jackie Wilson's '(Your Love Has Lifted Me) Higher and Higher'. But the Jersey devil was in disguise. He had a wealth of songs which told a quite different tale. And for the first time, it seems he was worried he might be giving bootleggers the heads up on the next album if he played them.

The radio broadcasts also dried up, a reflection perhaps of Appel's lessening influence at a time when Springsteen seemed determined to drop below the radar. Low-key was the order of the day. In fact, prior to the spring tour, a letter from Springsteen's lawyer, Michael Tannen, to CBS's new publicist, Dick Wingate, instructed the label: 'The emphasis in these [press] ads is to be Bruce's scheduled performance and not his albums . . . Bruce wants these ads to be informational; there is no need for "hype".' In his own mind, he was just another anti-rock star plying a trade. A steady stream of bootlegs, the ultimate status symbol for seventies rock stars, suggested otherwise; especially those from the Bottom Line and Roxy radio broadcasts, which duly confirmed he had yet to deliver a studio album that came close to emulating the E Street live experience.

Even his best efforts, though, could not keep his songs off the radio. Throughout the winter of 1977 AM stations blasted out 'Blinded By The

Light' to the housewives of Jersey and beyond, the song steadily rising to number one on the *Billboard* charts while Springsteen hid himself away on the road to somewhere else. A song he last played live in April 1976, the track had been tested on the UK singles market that August, before being released Stateside in January 1977. The new single, though, was not by Springsteen, but by one of his sixties heroes, Manfred Mann, hot on the comeback trail with his Earth Band.

Appel remembers an advance acetate of the Mann version arriving at the office, but neither he nor Springsteen thought it amounted to much: '[Our UK music publisher] Adrian Rudge got Manfred Mann to cover "Blinded By The Light". He says, "Mike, I'm gonna send you the record." It just so happens Bruce is in the office, around eleven in the morning, and says, "Let's put it on." And he goes like this [holds his nose]. Of course, it went right to number one.' In fact, Mann's inspired revamp of the leaden album version showed just how to construct a *pop* song, starting with the chorus and chopping the three wordiest (and weakest) verses, the kind of lesson Springsteen preferred not to take on board. It was everything Mann's previous cover of 'Spirit In The Night' was not. It was surely this earlier botch which caused Springsteen to hold his nose, at a time when he still made occasional calls at the office.

By the summer of 1976 – when 'Blinded' began providing some much needed revenue for the beleaguered music publisher – Springsteen was a stranger at Laurel Canyon. Preparing to take Appel on in court to retrieve his songs and negate their production deal, if Springsteen had known a bit more about litigation and a little less about pop history he might have proven more accommodating. The Who were still paying off Shel Talmy, producer on their debut album and a handful of singles, as late as *Tommy*; David Bowie, who fired manager Tony Defries shortly before recording 'Saint In The City', would pay him a share of everything he earnt through 1980. And in each case the contracts had been considerably less clear-cut than Appel's.

But neither Springsteen nor his record label seemed to treat Appel's claim seriously, at least not initially. As the deposed Appel recalled, 'A few days after the papers were served, Walter Yetnikoff called me up and told me CBS didn't care what the lawsuit said, they were going to go ahead and record the fourth album, produced by Landau. I guess they expected me to roll over and die.' Appel's attorney, Leonard Marks, responded with an interlocutory injunction forbidding Springsteen from entering the studio, and by deposing Yetnikoff, a trained lawyer who was not used to being attached to any such legal leash:

> **Mike Appel:** Walter Yetnikoff was deposed . . . He was irate and crazy and uncontrollable – exactly as you would think. [But] our attorney was relentless. He wouldn't take any nonsense from anyone, whether he be the head of CBS or whoever. He made things difficult for Walter. [Yet] the last time I was with Walter, he said, 'Look, I tried to talk to Springsteen. I tried to get him to come around. I didn't want to see you guys break up.' Cause Walter and I had a good relationship. He knew that I was there for years, and all of a sudden there was this new guy in the situation, and he didn't know what that was. He didn't know whether that had any value. And he interceded, trying to get us back together. [But] when [that] didn't work, he called me up, 'Mike, I talked to Bruce. It's not gonna work. We're gonna have to go with him.' He didn't mince [his] words, 'And it's not gonna be pleasant.' 'Walter, it's not gonna be pleasant for you, either. It's gonna be a knock-down thing.' Injunctions are extremely rarely given. The judge has to say, 'There is an egregious thing happening here to one of the parties. That party is entitled to injunctive relief.' [But] that's when Walter knew there was gonna be problems here, and they were gonna have to solve it some other way. Then, of course, they tried to appeal the case. They lost the appeal five to nothing.

Cast in the blustering image of its then-president, CBS had also overplayed its hand. The simple fact of the matter was, they did not have a legally binding relationship with Bruce Springsteen; they had a *licensing* contract with Appel's production company, Laurel Canyon, to which he was signed directly. Nor was this unheard of. Brian Epstein struck a similar deal with EMI, tying The Beatles to his own company, NEMS, but only indirectly to EMI; and Defries emulated Epstein, licensing RCA each Bowie album for a period of seven years (and eventually making Bowie a very wealthy man). Meanwhile, The Rolling Stones, after finally extracting themselves from the claws of Allen Klein in 1971, only ever licensed product to the labels that distributed their post-Decca catalogue. As for that quick legal victory, Judge Fein, granting the initial injunction, gave a summation that was a damning indictment of Springsteen's team of legal advisers and their whole strategy:

'The papers submitted on the motion are replete with charges and countercharges, for the most part irrelevant to the underlying issue. Defendants deny that Plaintiff played a major role in Springsteen's rise to success . . . [But] the [real] issue is the meaning and effect of the agreements among the parties. There is no showing that the contracts were obtained by fraud or duress, or are unconscionable . . . It is clear that Springsteen's stated refusal to perform for Plaintiff and his intention to perform only for Landau constitute a breach of his contract with Plaintiff, the Springsteen Agreement . . . [because] Landau's rights if any would be founded upon Springsteen's breach of contract.'

As Appel likes to note, 'Even though the contracts that we had were rinky dink, they held up.' In fact, he was in a position to release a wealth of unreleased material without seeking Springsteen's okay or approval. And, as he well knew, they had material – strong material – to spare. A letter from Appel's personal attorney, Jules I. Kurz, to Martin Gold, the day after the injunction was granted, dared to ask, 'Since Mike has all the tapes, should we offer to present CBS with an album pursuant to the terms of our agreement?' Fortunately for Springsteen, Appel was not prepared to remove the gloves. He still hoped against hope that the damage to their relationship might not prove permanent. The artist himself did not waver, 'The moment came when it all could have worked out, [but] I looked around and saw all these people who should have been getting something . . . guys who'd been with me for years now.' Appel was no longer perceived to be one of the deserving poor. Springsteen, though, had found himself in a situation where he was neither judge nor jury:

Mike Appel: Like Leonard Marks said, 'It's a simple story. The guy starts out, he's a nobody. Three and a half years later he's on the cover of *Time* and *Newsweek*. You been managing him and you been producing him all this time. Now he wants out. That's what we gotta sell the judge. It's as simple as that.' We had to show the unreasonableness of the situation. Bruce talks [a lot] about control, but I don't know that it had anything to do with control. 'If you don't want Mike [as producer], what about this other guy, he's done this and this, and you don't want him either.' 'No, no, no, I don't like any of these guys.' That made him seem [more] unreasonable.

If the upholding of the injunction had any effect on Springsteen, it merely made him regress again, throwing the pissy-fits of a put-upon teenager. The first thing he had done was fire Myron Mayer, the man Landau had brought in to advise on the contracts. (Mayer later told Fred Goodman, 'We hadn't prepared Bruce with the realities of litigation that sometimes you win, sometimes you lose . . . We lost that [initial] motion, but litigation goes that way . . . He was upset about that.') Annoyed at not getting his way, he was plainly not used to being asked to explain his own actions under oath. When he was finally deposed by Leonard Marks, the springs came off that inner lid, and a bellicose Bruce blew his stack:

> **Bruce Springsteen**: There was money floating all around the office, all the fucking time, that is. I don't know where it went. I don't know who got it, and I don't know who paid what to who . . . Yes, he gave me any fucking thing that I wanted – that I paid for with my own money. You know, that's exactly what he did, and when the big dollars rolled in, they rolled right into his pocket. So he ain't doing me no favours . . . I have been cheated. I wrote 'Born To Run', every line of that fucking song is me and no line of that fucking song is his. I don't own it . . . I have been cheated . . . My management contract was stolen from me. He told me, 'Trust me, trust me,' and I signed the goddamn thing. And the first thing he did was to go to CBS and he made his deal twice as good, his own personal deal twice as good . . . And it wasn't until I fought to have Jon Landau on *Born To Run* that we had any success recording whatever. On the publishing, he stole my songs . . . Five hundred thousand dollars comes in and Mike slaps it in his pocket, and now he is going to give me half of my own song. Thanks a lot, Bob. I don't live that way . . . It is like this, man, somebody stabs you in the fucking eye and you stab them in the fucking eye . . . You got a lot of fucking balls to sit there [and talk] about my breaking my fucking word when he did [this] to me, he fucking lied to me up and down.

And so on. Every time Marks got him to calm down, he just as quickly steamed up again. Finally, Marks hauled him up in front of Judge Fein, who took Springsteen aside and gave him a short, sharp lesson his own legal team had failed to provide, informing him that a deposition was like being on the stand. Fein later told Marks, 'Springsteen was horrified, and said he had no idea that any of this material was going to be used at the trial in front of the jury . . . He thought it was just an exercise for the lawyers.'[DTR] Marks reported back to Appel that the case was going well, but he couldn't vouch for the mental state of his former friend:

> **Mike Appel:** I think it [was] his [second] deposition, [when] he went absolutely nuts. He jumped on the table. [Leonard told me] he had to make order in the court, 'I had to bring him down in front of the judge in a private session and have the judge read him the riot act.' So uncharacteristic. [But] anybody who can put on a show like he can put on a show, has an energy which can be explosive in other ways also – to lose his temper like that. He is being frustrated. He can't do this, he can't do that, he can't get money, so he's forced to do a lot of things that he doesn't wanna do . . . So he was terribly upset. In fact, Leonard thought it was kinda comical, but I didn't think it was comical. I said, 'This is terrible. I don't find this funny at all. I don't get any kind of kick out of it at all. This is really upsetting. He's killing himself.'

The following year, Springsteen admitted the strain had got to him: 'You know [that] you're gonna fight someone for a year. Every day, toe-to-toe . . . You're gonna wanna kill him and he's gonna wanna kill you. That's what it's all about, depositions. And it takes its toll.' It had certainly taken its toll on him. Appel, though, kept his cool, and although he didn't attend Springsteen's depositions, 'Bruce and Jon came to mine – to put extra pressure on me . . . And I was saying things and pointing at [Bruce] and saying, "He knows it!" And he put the yellow pad up in front of his face. He was [that] embarrassed. I thought I'd die laughing.' By the time Springsteen came off the road at the end of March, it was clear the only way forward was to broach a settlement – to put a price on his loss of faith and breaking of his word. As Appel told Charles Cross, 'It didn't go to trial for a lot of reasons . . . the main reason being . . . they were losing so bad, they didn't dare.'

Springsteen had boxed himself into a corner. Intransigent, ill-versed in the mechanics of litigation, he finally allowed those with more practical heads to cook up a deal which would satisfy both parties. While the terms were thrashed out at the end of May, Springsteen drove to Philadelphia to see Elvis Presley at The Spectrum. The last time he had seen Elvis play, it had been at Madison Square Garden in the company of Mike Appel, a fellow believer. It had been June 1972, a couple of days after they signed to CBS, and Presley was still a magnetic performer with a command of the stage and a band he had made his own. Now, he was a shell of the former shell; a bulbous parody of that once-legendary performer. Springsteen couldn't believe his eyes. Or his ears. Presley could barely hit (or hold) any note higher than middle C. Not surprisingly, he later blamed Presley's long-term manager, Colonel Tom Parker, for the singer's sad decline, claiming in 1981, 'Elvis was destroyed by his manager . . . and damn it, I was almost destroyed by my manager. But fortunately I hit back in time.'

In fact, when he returned to New York on May 30 to sign the legally-binding agreement which would sever his professional relationship with Appel, it seemed like all the fight had gone out of him. He was as sad to see it end this way as his old mate. Appel recalls, 'We were in a lawyer's office. We were at this big conference table. He signed his and initialled every page and then I came in and signed mine. We weren't even in the same room at the time. I had run into him in the lobby . . . Bruce said, "What's the word?" I said, "Not much." . . . It was the end of it.'

Springsteen had gotten what he (thought he) wanted – a new producer, a new contract with CBS which bumped up his royalty rate (which would have happened anyway) and control of his publishing. Appel retained his financial share in the work to date. So what was the financial cost of freedom? Would it prove just another word for nothing left to lose? Well, Appel was to receive around $800,000 over the next five years, paid for by CBS, set against the advances Springsteen would receive directly. Meanwhile, his cut on all future sales of the first three albums was reduced from six to two per cent, while retaining a 50% interest in the twenty-seven songs that Springsteen had recorded and released whilst he had served as his music publisher.

Springsteen had put himself in hock to CBS for the foreseeable. Not only was he again in the red but was likely, at his current work-rate, to stay that way for some time to come. The label had also succeeded in getting him to sign directly to them, making him the first major artist in history to go *from* licensing product *to* the slave contract that still passes for the average record deal; in which the artist pays all his own recording costs yet the label owns all copyrights in perpetuity. In fact, Appel remembers, 'After the lawsuit I was in Mr Chow's in California . . . and I heard these lawyers talking about "The Springsteen Clause". [According to them,] there would be no more production companies to assign the rights.' He at least understood the price someone had to pay:

> **Mike Appel:** The record company must take a position. They can't sit on the sidelines. So they must side with the artist, even if they end up paying off Mike Appel, which they did, because they lost the lawsuit. They still had to take that position. Yetnikoff and I were friends before the lawsuit and after the lawsuit. [But] the artist would then think, 'Well, at least the record company sided with me. They advanced me the money to pay for the lawyers [&c.].' It gave [Bruce] every incentive to kick ass, and get out of debt.

Springsteen stated his own view back in March 1977, 'I feel like you pay and you pay and you pay . . . [then] there's the big payoff.' If Appel's lawyer was claiming 'complete victory', so was Springsteen's, who suggested 'that the press observe who's producing Bruce's next LP; whether or not Laurel Canyon Music or Management has anything to do with it; and who now controls the entire catalogue of previous songs.' But then, as Appel informed Marc Elliot, 'It didn't seem to matter to anybody that the courts had always ruled completely in my favour, and that Bruce Springsteen lost in the Court of Appeals five-nothing. That never fazed anybody. To the general public, and the industry, I was always guilty.'

Finally, Springsteen and Landau could start work in earnest on those 'seventeen clear-cut song ideas' he'd mentioned in a March interview, and any others that had come along in the interim. Surely this time it would be plain sailing, now that Mike Appel was no longer there to constantly remind him of what Duke Ellington always used to say, 'I don't need more time, I need a deadline.'

Chapter 5: 1977–78 – Chasing Something In The Night

> I enter the studio with virtually millions of scattered ideas to which [Jon] Landau, through his unique ability to communicate with me . . . has been able to provide the focus and direction necessary to shape my thoughts into finished musical compositions. – Bruce Springsteen's affidavit, quoted in *Rolling Stone*, 11/8/77

The studio Springsteen entered on June 1, 1977, less than forty-eight hours after the final resolution of his rift with his now former producer-manager, was new to him and his wrecking crew. Atlantic Studios had a history few could match, but this was not the place where Jerry Wexler and Tom Dowd had once weaved their magic. This was a new studio with a nice big recording space. Of the *Born To Run* graduates, just Appel was missing. Iovine, two years older and wiser, was back as recording engineer, and this time Jon Landau was sole producer, though Miami Steve's duties still included co-sounding board. Bruce described this particular dynamic the following year: 'I have an overall idea for the power and stuff that I want to get, and [Jon] has a particular idea for various techniques. Plus there's Steve Van Zandt, my guitar player, and . . . he sorta stands on the raw side of things.'

That first night at Atlantic is the stuff of legends; Marshy legends. On page 207 of his bestselling pop-bio, *Born To Run (1979)*, Dave Marsh described how 'the first evening was spent laying down demos of about twenty songs'. It's an enticing description, but a cassette inlay card (reproduced in the 2010 boxed-set) lists ten songs, only eight of which were cut that night: 'Our Love Will Last Forever', 'Breakaway', 'Don't Look Back', 'Rendezvous', 'Outside Looking In', 'Something In The Night', 'Because

The Night' and 'I Wanna Be With You' – still quite a result for a night's work. But, as Marsh correctly points out, 'laying down demos' was the order of the night. Landau described the session to Paul Nelson the following June, providing background to a *Rolling Stone* cover story, probably revealing more than he meant to about the process: 'The very first thing we did was record all the songs we'd rehearsed in one night, in whatever state they were in. We were all having a great time, real sloppy. "Something In The Night" just really caught fire and sounded great.'

In fact, that first take of 'Something In The Night' would make it all the way to the released album, a year later. Nor was it the only song demoed that first night which 'caught fire and sounded great'. 'I Wanna Be With You' shoulda been a keeper as the band rose to the occasion riding waves of aggression and a lust for life with musical muscle to spare. Springsteen even allowed himself to poke fun at his song-persona in the lyric (a rare lapse), explaining how he lost his job and home because of her: 'Now I lost my job at the Texaco station/ Instead of pumping gas I'd dream of you/ I got thrown out of my house, I got such a bad reputation/ 'Cause all I wanna do is be seen with you'. Sung with a grin, the whole song gave libidos a good name. But already he was self-conscious about what side of him should be represented on this record, after driving himself nuts these past few months obsessing about each and every tiny detail:

> **Bruce Springsteen**: I was living on a farm in Holmdel, New Jersey. I went out and I played in the bars at nights, and we toured a little when we could, to try and keep everything going. And I thought a lot about what kind of record I was gonna make when I had the chance to record again. That is probably why some . . . songs got left off [*Darkness*], because they were a lot of fun, but there was a moment when I said, 'I need to identify myself [in a certain way] at this particular moment.' [1999]

The omission of 'I Wanna Be With You' from even the earliest rough sequences was a portent. The long layoff had changed his whole approach to recording, one he could explicate in 1996, but not in 1977: 'My idea wasn't to get the next ten songs and put out an album and get out on the road. I wrote with purpose in mind, so I edited very intensely the music I was writing. So when I felt there was a collection of songs that had a point of view, *that* was when I released a record.'

Van Zandt, for one, didn't see this coming. As he says in the 2010 documentary on the making of *Darkness*, 'Basically, the first good ten songs you write, you['re supposed to] put them out. Well, that process would end – forever.' The stockpiling of song upon song began on night one, and at no point did Landau intercede in the perfectionist's progress, or explain the economics of what Springsteen was doing to him. His view was that an artist needed licence, and he for one was going to give him enough rope:

> **Jon Landau**: There was no deadline. In fact, it was explained to CBS not to attempt to schedule a release date. My attitude was, 'Why is that a problem?' I knew just from being in there every day, we were working in a very intelligent, meaningful fashion. I had no sense that we were wasting time. [It was] very business-like. Very, very intense. You don't make a record like [*Darkness*] in three, four months. The complete lack of waste on the finished [record], it's a distillation process. He gets all the ideas out there and then it's a constant editing and re-editing, carving away. Other people it's such difficult work to come up with an album's worth of material. [Whereas] Bruce creates so many choices for himself. [1978]

How ironic then that Springsteen should spend much of his downtime that summer listening to a record which was recorded in just three weekends at a cost of £4,000, at what was effectively CBS's London demo studio, and still had more raw anger and attack than what he was producing at Atlantic. *The Clash* would go on to become CBS-US's best-selling import, after they spent eighteen months trying to decide whether they would be sowing the seeds of sedition if it got a domestic release.* As Springsteen recently revealed, 'I always felt a great affinity for not just The Clash, but [all those bands]. When the punk rock movement started, though I was probably technically outside of it here in the States, I felt a deep connection.' And if The Clash had energy to spare, the Sex Pistols had the chops. They, too, made their impact felt across the pond:

* When *The Clash* was finally released in the US, in 1978, it was with a revised track-listing that incorporated non-album singles and deleted punkier paeans – including the contentious 'I'm So Bored With The USA'. Both versions would eventually be released on CD.

> **Bruce Springsteen**: *Darkness* was . . . informed by the punk explosion at the time. I went out and I got all the records, all the early punk records . . . I bought 'Anarchy in the UK' and 'God Save the Queen', and the Sex Pistols were so frightening . . . They made you brave, and a lot of that energy seeped its way into the subtext of *Darkness*. *Darkness* was written in 1977, and all of that music was out there, and if you had ears you could not ignore it. [2012]

How doubly ironic that when The Clash attempted to emulate that debut's impact by recording a proper-sounding album – one their US label *would* release – with their own rock critic turned producer, they merely bored the USA rigid. At least they spent the eighteen months between that eponymous debut and *Give 'Em Enough Rope* issuing some of the best punk anthems ever, on a series of classic non-album 45s that established them as one of the great singles bands of the seventies.

Springsteen, on the other hand, seemed to have developed an aversion to having hits. And yet, he had written some of the decade's best pop songs in the interim, recording the likes of 'Rendezvous', 'Fire', 'Because The Night' and 'Don't Look Back' – all songs he ultimately gave away – at the first dozen Atlantic sessions. At the time Landau had an explanation for this, too: 'He didn't want to have one song that could be taken out of context, and interfere with what he wanted the album to represent . . . Bruce was very suspicious about success . . . / . . . If success was what it was like with *Born To Run*, Bruce didn't want that.' Goddamn those career-defining anthems.

The first song from these sessions he gave away was 'Fire', which he claimed to have written for Elvis, before donating it to a singer on the periphery of the downtown CBGBs scene: 'I sent [Elvis] a demo of it, but he died before it arrived. Then I decided to give the song to Robert Gordon because his voice is a little like Elvis's. When I hear him, I kinda get the impression that Elvis is singing it.' Gordon loved it, and cajoled Springsteen into contributing guitar, even though he had the legendary Link Wray to call on. But Springsteen had to work a tad harder to get a second CBGBs refugee to record another of his cast-offs. In fact, it was only after he stopped trying to write a song 'for her', and just gave her one of those he had lying around, that Patti Smith deigned to deliver him the hit by proxy he refused to allow himself:

Lenny Kaye: He gave us a great song, and Patti made it her own, and we played it like a showband; and Jimmy Iovine saw it and opened the door, which is the thing a great producer [does]. We were offered two songs, at least. We're recording in adjacent studios, and we're friendly, we're both from Jersey, we're both in Record Plant. Jimmy's been in there for months and Bruce, who's very fertile in this period, wrote either one song or two, but he kinda wrote them in *our* style, and I would listen to them on the phone with Patti, and we'd be, 'They're alright, but . . .' They weren't bad, but they were like quirky mongrels. And [then] I remember I was at home and she called me up. She had the cassette Bruce had made of 'Because The Night', and she played it to me and the chorus came on. And we're both lovers of the immortal hit single, and there's no way that chorus could be missed, it was so anthemic. Patti just took them [words] and created the [eventual] verses. Then we brought it into the studio, and Bruce's original demo had a kinda Latin feel, and we just rocked it up. It was bigger. All of a sudden, an unmistakeable, exciting moment in time.

If donating the song was a sop of sorts to Smith, he was responding just as much to a suggestion of Smith's producer Jimmy Iovine, who, in his own words, 'was engineering *Darkness* and producing *Easter* at the same time. Now, Bruce was very understanding and very flexible, because he realized that this was my first real break as a producer. Anyway, one night whilst we were lounging around the Hotel Navarro in New York I told Bruce I desperately wanted a hit with Patti, that she deserved one. He agreed. As he had no immediate plans to put "Because The Night" on an album, I said why not give it to Patti. Bruce replied, "If she can do it, she can have it."'

In the recent *Darkness* documentary, Springsteen claimed 'I [already] knew that I wasn't gonna finish ["Because The Night"], because it was a love song, and I really felt that I didn't know how to write them at the time.' Actually, he had recorded half a dozen terrific love songs at those early Atlantic sessions before deciding this was not the kinda album he was going to make. Early sequences centred around songs like 'The Fast Song', aka 'God's Angels' (in which the capricious candy-girl was characterized as, 'She who is everything/ There's a fever that she brings . . . Sometimes I feel like I'm walking the dead/ The blood rushes through my veins'), 'Candy's Boy', 'Drive All Night', 'Because The Night', 'Talk To Me' and 'Spanish Eyes', songs of desire, frustrated by circumstance. All were worked on in those first six weeks, as were the likes of 'Frankie', 'I Wanna Be With You' and 'Our Love Will Last Forever'.

However, only a hybrid of 'The Fast Song' and 'Candy's Boy' – the composite, 'Candy's Room' – would make *Darkness,* at the expense of all God's chosen, even the 'avenging angels of Eden, with them white horses and flaming swords/ [who] can blow this whole town into the sea'. (Two images from 'Frankie' and/or 'Drive All Night' would also be co-opted to Candy's cause, 'There's machines and there's fire on the outside of town', and, 'In the darkness there'll be hidden worlds that shine'.) Evidently a close cousin of Janey, this Candy still retained her 'mink fur coats and diamond rings' and 'men who'll give her anything she wants/ But . . . what she wants is me'.

But 'Candy's Room', for all its lyrical sophistication, had none of the epic grandeur of a live 'Frankie'. Or the Atlantic 'Drive All Night', which may have emerged out of the long, improvised mid-section to the 1977 live 'Backstreets' – the so-called 'God's Angel' sequence. Slight as the 'Drive All Night' lyrics are, Springsteen (correctly) rated the raw-voiced epic, which appears on a number of provisional sequences for the album, timed at eight minutes (so clearly the 'full' version). Like 'Frankie', though, in the end he decided it was too much of a vehicle for the Big Man: 'The sax is a very warm instrument, and these songs have a little harder, cooler edge.'

As if to prove his point, Springsteen even initially recorded 'Badlands' as a guitar song, at Atlantic, when it was still a conversation between Robert Mitchum and a pulp-fiction cover-girl. At this point its refrain, 'Badlands, tear your little world apart/ You gotta walk it, talk it, man, deep down in your heart', he was singing to another crazy chick who wanted to let rip. Indeed, he initially slipped into a semi-familiar, half-whispered bedside plea when the music dropped on down, later chopped from the song: 'Baby, don't cry now, don't waste your tears/ Baby, don't cry now, we're taking it on the road/ We're taking you on the road, driving till the air turns/ In the evening fields, we'll burn it all and then we'll let go'.

It was only after they actually *mastered* the record that Springsteen decided he 'didn't think we had enough sax on the record, took the guitar out, and Clarence played over that'. It was a belated recognition that Clemons had been almost frozen out of the recording process, not as a sleight to his old friend, but because its *auteur* wanted something very different. As he explained to a number of interrogators on tour, 'The [guitar] leads fit better into the tone of *Darkness* than the saxophone did . . . so consequently there was more [guitar] on the album.' Landau's view was that Springsteen was always 'look[ing] for what [the solo] does for the single cut and for the album as a whole. The sax makes the thing more urban, and I think he wanted to keep more of a small-town ambience.'

When, or if, Bruce explained his reasoning to Clemons at the sessions is unclear, but generally he didn't *explain*. As Landau observed, 'In the studio Bruce tends to do things, and you figure out what he's doing. He doesn't announce, this is what we're going to try.' He demanded much of his co-workers, even if it took hindsight – and happiness – to reveal just how demanding a boss he had been: 'I didn't have a life, [so] it was easy for me [laughs]. But everyone else had to suffer with me . . . It was both self-indulgent and the only way we knew how to do it.' He was right. He 'didn't have a life'. And it showed in the characters who filled these songs:

> **Bruce Springsteen**: [*Darkness*] couldn't be a warm, innocent album . . . because it ain't that way, it wasn't that way for me anymore. That's why a lot of pain had to be there . . . But still, I came out of it . . . I had a big awakening in the past two, three years. Much bigger than people would think . . . Realized a lot of things about my own past. So it's [all] there on the record. [1978]

The onset of an existential dark night of the soul was probably the direct result of the end of his relationship with an emotionally drained Darvin. Although he soon embarked on another fiery relationship with another 'rock 'n' roll chick', photographer Lynn Goldsmith, his inability to hang onto Darvin – the paradigm for every spirited lover to date – and time spent with his sister and her husband, seeing them 'living the lives of my parents', had made him re-evaluate a life which still repeated patterns set in his youth. As he said in 1996 of these years, 'I was locked into a very specific and pretty limited mode of behaviour . . . I had no capability for a home life or an ability to develop anything more than a glancing relationship.' It was a journey's end of sorts for the ex-innocent:

> **Bruce Springsteen**: On *The Wild, the Innocent*, I bought my band in and that had real warm songs and a lot of characters, and . . . a kinda in-society type feeling. Even if it was low-rent. And then, on *Born To Run* . . . it still

> maintains some warmth, but there was a certain element, a certain fear, that started to come in. I don't know why. On this [fourth] record, it's less romantic – it's got a little more isolation . . . / . . . All my albums connect up, but in a particularly conscious way [they] only [do so] on the last two, [where] the characters tend to look towards themselves more . . . Y'see, on the old stuff there's a lot of characters and groups of people; and as it goes along it thins out, people drop by the wayside, until on *Born To Run* it's essentially two: it's a guy and a girl. And here on *Darkness*, there's a lotta times when there's just one. In the end, on the last song, the title song, there's just one . . . just one. [1978]

'Darkness on the Edge of Town', written early in 1976 and attempted at that first week of sessions, was absent from all the early sequences, perhaps because he was still some way from figuring where it fit. On the only circulating alternate take – a slower version with rockabilly undertones, probably from the June 6 session – Springsteen has the first verse but largely bluffs his way through the remaining two. It seems he was still 'laying down demos'.

At this stage, it was 'Racing In The Street' that generally formed the centrepiece of rough sequences. As Landau told Nelson, this potential classic 'was [also] written before the album. We hadn't actually rehearsed "Racing In The Street"; but we knew we were going to do it, and it was from "before". It was written around the time of "The Promise". "Something in the Night", "Candy's Room"(sic), "Racing In The Street" were [all] part of the original concept of the album. And "Darkness" was, too.' 'Racing In The Street' was the song where he did get the girl, but things still turned to shit. It was a point he would embellish on the *Born In The USA* tour when the song was prefaced with a powerful 'walk a mile in my shoes' monologue:

> There was this strip little ways in off this river, and I guess it was like an old junkyard where folks would bring stuff down from town and leave it off there, just to rust out in the rain. There was this little clearing where on weekends we'd get together and that was where I first met her . . . When we first started going out, it was like it always is when you first start going out with somebody, you know, everything is great, you know, laughing at each other's stupid jokes. We had a real good time that summer, but I don´t know

> what happens, I don´t know what changes people. Time. Time passes, and she got to where she didn't talk as much as she used to, didn't like going out at night and started hiding my keys, so I couldn't take the car out. We were good friends for a long time and I know that she understood that when I took the car out, and when I won, that something was happening to me . . . That was the night that we got out of there, we just packed up our bags . . . we´re just gonna keep going . . . and keep searching.

This evocative rap was clearly a way of explicating the song's final couplet, 'Tonight my baby and me we're gonna ride to the sea/ And wash these sins off our hands', lines he apparently inserted to make 'sense of the journey the guy's taking . . . How do you carry your sins? That's what the people in "Racing in the Street" are trying to do.' If the expiry date on residual Catholic guilt was still a way off, these lines were intended to suggest some hope in the darkness:

> **Bruce Springsteen**: At the end of 'Racing In The Street', what I was trying to show is that through all that, and through all the disappointments – in the face of all that, that darkness out there – you still hold on to some element of hope, the belief that somewhere out there, there's some place better than where you are – and if not, [that] at least there's some value in the search. [1978]

It is true that the first take recorded at Atlantic – the so-called 'dying in the street' version – lacks any such redemptive coda. But redemptive codas would generally be in short supply on a final album that lacked a 'Frankie', and turned the once-affirmative 'Something In The Night' into a wreck on the highway. In fact, finding 'some value in the search' became the veritable key to an album that shifted focus with every new song Bruce brought to Atlantic.

Having been inspired for so long in the months leading up to the sessions, Springsteen seemed reluctant to take such largesse at face value. Instead, he worked on songs that took the album somewhere that, for all its hothouse intensity, was monochromatic. At the centre of this whirlpool, there was precious little light and no shade. He would also be guilty of denying fans – at least those without access to bootlegs – evidence that there had been a missing link, a *Basement Tapes* to his very own *John Wesley Harding*, an intermediary 'Album #4':

> **Bruce Springsteen**: Rock 'n' roll has always been this joy, this certain happiness that is, in its way, the most beautiful thing in life. But Rock is also about hardness and coldness and being alone. With *Darkness* it was hard for me to make those things coexist. How could a happy song like 'Sherry Darling' coexist with 'Point Blank' or 'Darkness on the Edge of Town'? I could not face that. [1980]

A song he began at the last Atlantic sessions in August gave the first real inkling that he was finally coming to terms with a difficult upbringing. Sung as one side of a conversation with his Dad ('Papa, go to bed now, it's getting late'), 'Independence Day' was the start of a dialogue-in-song that remained one step removed for some time to come, largely because, as Springsteen said in 1992, '[My Dad] was never a big verbalizer, and [so] I kinda talked to him through my songs. Not the best way to do that . . . but I knew he heard them.' At the same time as he was singing 'Independence Day' – and, indeed, 'Factory' and 'Adam Raised A Cain' for Doug – he seemed to be making the whole album as a statement to his sister, who was struggling to keep her head above water in her Jersey shore home:

> **Bruce Springsteen**: I got a sister and [her and her husband] work two jobs a day, and I go over to their house, and somebody's trying to take their house away . . . and I see them, and they're trying to hold on. It's a fight just to hold on to their beliefs . . . / . . . When I go home, that's what I see. It's no fun. It's no joke. I see my sister and her husband, they're living the lives of my parents . . . That's why my album is the way it is. It's about people that are living the lives of their parents . . . It's also about a certain thing, where they don't give up. [1978]

The sense that he was the one who got away imbued a number of songs written between sessions, of which 'Adam Raised A Cain' – which did not enter the equation until November – was the most angst-ridden. Originally called 'Daddy Raised A Cain', it owed more of a debt to the famous 1956 movie of John Steinbeck's *East of Eden*, starring James Dean, than to the original story in Genesis, to which he seems to have paid very little attention as a child (or as an adult, if his interpretation of original sin was, 'You're born into this life paying for the sins of somebody else's past'). Likewise, his depiction in an early take of his father's ghost 'haunt[ing] these empty rooms rattling his chains' seemed to owe more to Alastair Sim's *A Christmas Carol* than any section of the Old Testament.

According to Springsteen, when he started writing this song he 'went back [to The Bible], trying to get a feeling for it'. But he still expressed dismay after he attended a family funeral at this time, and 'all my relatives were there . . . They're all in their thirties, my sister and all, and they all feel the same way I do. But [still] their kids go to Catholic school and to church every Sunday. They're really under the gun to this Catholic thing.'

'Adam Raised A Cain' finally brought out the gunslinger in the ex-lead guitarist. Landau recalled it being one song where 'we did a lot of takes – every take another fantastic guitar solo . . . [But in the end] we made the right selection . . . Everything that was left out, there was a good reason for leaving it out.' Meanwhile, Landau argued long and hard for the inclusion of 'Independence Day' on *Darkness*. In the end, though, he found Springsteen adamant: 'He didn't want that weight . . . The only problem with the way we work is that it . . . cuts no ice with him, the argument, "Jesus, this deserves to be heard" . . . His attitude is, they become other songs.'

Perhaps surprisingly, at no point did either Landau or Springsteen ever consider making *Darkness* a double album. Bruce certainly would have had enough clout at CBS to demand it, but as Landau stated at the time, 'I never thought we were [working on one]. [Sure,] we have enough material for a double record, but we don't *have* a double record. The reason the material was removed was because it was not a part of the unity of what he was doing.' (Springsteen was terser still: 'It's much easier to centralize on one record.')

Actually, by the time they began to switch from Atlantic Studios to the Record Plant at the end of August, they probably had enough for *three* records.* Yet still he refused to produce a working sequence, or begin mixing this album of strong songs. Even as the sessions stretched into September, Springsteen continued using the two expensive New York studios as his very own private rehearsal room, even allowing superfan Barry Rebo to capture the interminable sessions on open-reel video (for a documentary that would remain forever 'in the works'). Springsteen later described his then-regime thus: 'I can remember working really hard on

* Sony's logs do not indicate the studio (apparently, such information was not deemed 'necessary'), so it is not clear when the switch was made for good, but it does appear that through August and into September some work was still being done at Atlantic (presumably on tracks previously recorded there).

[*Darkness*] . . . I just used to sit in my room eight hours a day and . . . I just worked out each song, verse by verse, real specifically.' Nor was Landau offering the dissenting voice. His view was that, '[Although] we rehearsed for quite a while before we actually started recording the album . . . it makes more sense to be in the studio: to work these things through to their logical conclusion.' So much for providing 'focus and direction':

> **Jon Landau**: It began as a bunch of songs [which had] been around for a while; and we started out by experimenting with different approaches, how much overdubbing we wanted to get involved in, how much live recording. The first period of time was largely spent in evolving what the recording approach was going to be – which . . . evolved into a live type of recording . . . getting that real sense of the band playing together. [1978]

Not only were songs worked on multiple times, but in almost every case they would spend precious studio time (and tape) recording tracks that were really not finished. It was 914 all over again. As an unnamed band member told one biographer, 'Bruce [was] coming in most afternoons with a new first draft . . . It was like painting the fucking George Washington Bridge.' Yes, he had previously 'work[ed] a lot on the lyrics before we record[ed] a song', but he was then recording these rough drafts. Given that he had spent eighteen months preparing for these sessions – and rehearsed the band extensively beforehand – the approach smacked of indulgence, openly encouraged by Springsteen's latest surrogate father figure:

> **Jon Landau**: For Bruce, the easiest thing is getting the idea for the beginning of the song, the hardest thing is finishing. Some songs we'd get 99% of the way through, and he couldn't get that last one per cent that finishes it. Sometimes he'd forge ahead with the same song, [sometimes] he'd circle back to it. A great deal of the time was spent in the evolution of the content, both musically and lyrically. One month it would be a certain set of ten songs, another month it would be half that set, half another set. Songs kept appearing, disappearing and reappearing in different forms . . . circling, circling, circling, getting closer to the centre. [1978]

By the time they had definitively switched the sessions to the Record Plant in mid-September, Springsteen had fully abandoned 'Album #4' and was working on Album #5. When he arrived at work on September 12 he had two new songs: 'Prove It All Night' and 'Ramrod'. The first of these began life by using band arrangement of an old song. On the first take of 'Prove It All Night', he sang the lyrics to 'Something In The Night', save for the refrain, 'Prove it all night, I'll prove it all night for you', and one 'new' element from a draft lyric he'd scrawled in his notebook, 'Well, baby wants a Cadillac, and wants a dress of blue/ And honey, if I can I'd get these things for you/ Girl, I got a hunger, I hunger I can't resist/ There's so much that I want, right now I want one kiss/ To seal our fate tonight'. It would take him four more sessions to really prove it all night.

After another short break, sessions resumed on September 26. Again, though, he spent most of the time working on songs written in the interim, even as he continued to play the likes of 'The Promise', 'Because The Night' and 'Independence Day'. Of the five new songs, 'Someday (We'll Be Together)', 'Breakout', 'Down By The River (Say Sons)' and 'Ain't Good Enough For You' all had the mark of Outtake on them (although he worked on 'Someday' and 'Breakout' for *days*). The one song that suggested real promise was 'The Promised Land', nodding to Chuck Berry in its title, but nowhere else. If Berry used the term ironically, referring to the California he was vainly trying to reach throughout his 1964 classic, Springsteen displayed no such irony. Nowhere in the song was he celebrating '*the* promised land'. Another ditty of defiance, this one literally spat in the face of a portent of biblical proportions – 'I'm heading straight into the storm' – having taken its cue from a single stray line in his lyric notebook, 'Hot rod angels rumblin' through a promised land'. Now that did sound like a Chuck Berry line. (It ended up in 'Racing in the Street'.)

At the end of September another ten-day break was called; but again he returned not with some cogent idea of what to do with the forty-plus songs he already had, but with four more songs – 'City of Night', 'The Ballad', 'English Sons' and 'I'm Going Back', all of which he cut in a single session and then promptly forgot for three decades. A further fortnight sojourn from the studio resulted in still more new songs, one of which he set to the same 'Bo Diddley' riff as 'I'm Going Back' (and, indeed, 'She's The One'), 'Preacher's Daughter'. Then there was the chilling 'Iceman'. Each was an inspired addition to this relentless accruing process.

'Preacher's Daughter', one of the most atmospheric things recorded at the Record Plant, was a five-minute-plus exhortation of love for a preacher's daughter in the teeth of parental disapproval, and as such ticks just about every psychoanalytical box a good Catholic boy could. But rather than being wracked by feelings of fear and loathing, the boy has developed a sense of humour ('It's a long walk to heaven on a road filled with sin/ They'd better open up the freeway to let me in'), and a cinematic gift for visual imagery: 'Well, just as I got the preacher's daughter ready for a light/ There's a V-8 on fire and something ain't right/ And like a she-devil howlin' from the gates of hell/ Goddamn! Here come the preacher in his Coupe De Ville'.

'Iceman' displayed the other side of the coin, a case of Springsteen drawing back the curtain on a troubled psyche only to quietly retire the results. And who can blame him with lines like, 'Once they tried to steal my heart, beat it right outta my head/ But, baby, they didn't know that I was born dead/ I am the iceman, fighting for the right to live'. Maybe the stress from months of sessions was finally getting to him. At least this time he has a girl by his side. It is the 'preacher's girl' again, and the pair are literally hellbent: 'We'll take the midnight road right to the devil's door/ And even the white angels of Eden with their flamin' swords/ Won't be able to stop us'. In the end, though, 'The Iceman' became one more memory he chose to suppress.

These killer cuts – both destined for the scrapheap (where 'Preacher's Daughter' still resides) – were realized in a single inspired October night when the album returned to the main road. At the same time, Springsteen finally got the right coordinates to 'The Promised Land' and attempted something called 'New Fast Song'. He had finally found room for Candy. Now he just needed Adam to raise Cain, which he duly did a fortnight later – after spending equal time on 'I Want To Be Wild' and 'Give The Girl A Kiss', the kinda songs he'd 'bring in . . . to break the tension in the studio' – and he had an album that fit an increasingly bleak worldview:

> **Bruce Springsteen**: My main concern was making an honest record . . . The characters in the songs are people who are inside the system and don't know how to get outside. They're not, like, cerebral. A lot of their thing is based on a certain bluntness, a certain force. I still see a lot of them when I go home. They don't know what to do. They didn't find a guitar; they didn't find anything . . . [And] I wanted a certain intensity. [1978]

'Intensity' became the mantra Springsteen would adhere to even when the wheels fell off on the promotional road – 'I drew from things that I liked on my last album, the drums and the power: I wanted a certain intensity,' – as he set about crafting an album out of solid Rock. For all their repeated discussions about direction, he and Landau kept coming back to a punk-like aesthetic. As Landau told Nelson, 'We [often] used to discuss the sound of the record as it evolved . . . What kind of sound-picture was the record suggesting? We did want an unglamorized sound. There was [to be] no sweetening. We wanted the coffee black.'

Springsteen wanted it to be a double espresso sonic shot, 'to be just relentless . . . a barrage of the particular thing I had in mind', as he explained the following July. What they ultimately got, or so Landau insisted, was something which was 'clear without being too clean – without being too studio, [or] too neat. A real strong middle, real strong bass drum, real good highs . . . What we tried to do this time was get the *Born To Run* excitement, but at the same time [something] a little more concise-sounding.'

That might have been how it sounded in the studio – a notoriously misleading environment, with its state-of-the-art speakers, ideal acoustics and deafening volume – but it was not how the songs came across on tape. And that was a transition for which Landau was ill-equipped. Not that his forte was ever 'producing' the sound. As he informed a European monthly in 1986, 'In the recording studio, I represent the audience. When you read on a record-sleeve "co-producer Jon Landau" it means I helped Bruce to know if the song delivered the wanted effect. I am never involved in the technical side of recording.'

Although Springsteen always listened to Landau, he gave equal credence to Van Zandt, as someone who now had the experience of producing the first two Southside Johnny albums behind him. But Jon and Steve's ideas of how a record should sound were at opposite ends of the spectrum. Springsteen knowingly played the pair off against each other: 'I didn't want any one person to have too much control over what direction the music was taking - so I would yin-yang a little bit. It was the way that I played it.'

He still thought he could get by without the requisite technical input. Just before the sessions commenced, he had insisted in print, 'You can't let the technical side of it get it in the way – you're looking for a complete marriage of structure and spirit.' And he clung to this ideal in the face of all the audio evidence coming out of Atlantic and the Record Plant that the sound on tape was – yet again – *not* the one in his head:

> **Bruce Springsteen**: I fantasized these huge sounds . . . but they were always bigger in my head. And so we constantly were chasing something that was unattainable. The thing that I didn't understand was that if you get big drums, the guitar sounds smaller; if you have big guitars, the drums sound smaller. Something has to give - there's only so much sonic range. But we didn't know this at the time. We just assumed *everything* could sound huge. [2010]

Actually, there was a terrific sounding record being made just across the hall at the Record Plant. The album was called *Easter*, and its producer was on an extended sabbatical from engineering the E Street Band's latest opus. Lenny Kaye, guitarist on those sessions, believes that by the time the Patti Smith Group were building an album around 'Because The Night', Jimmy Iovine 'wasn't working on *Darkness* that much. He was more in our world.' In reality, Iovine had grown increasingly frustrated by the engineering job, perhaps because, as Landau subsequently stated, 'Engineers take a great deal of pride in what they do [technically] . . . [but] Bruce requires an ability to adjust. "It can't be done" . . . never gets said. The only rule.' The final straw came when it became apparent Iovine was not going to be doing the mix on Bruce's record. So he gave Patti the mix he would have given Springsteen – bequeathing her the most AOR-friendly studio sound she ever had.

Before Springsteen himself could produce a statement to match, he would need a final sequence. Through December 1977 he worked on a shortlist of thirteen songs, some lucky, some not. They included Atlantic tracks like 'Come On (Let's Go Tonight)', 'Independence Day', 'Don't Look Back' and 'The Promise'. Also in the mix was 'The Way', a torch ballad he cut back in August, and would still be working on come 12 February 1978 (by which time he was on take sixty-six). Listing the many ways 'you belong to me', 'The Way' culminated in a surprisingly pantheistic version of fidelity, 'The way the river belongs to the sea / That's the way you belong to me'. Also still a candidate for inclusion was 'Streets of Fire', a song which was, as Landau put it, 'something that happened in the studio'.

By January 16, they had a sequence – and a strong one.* But for the second album in a row, this initial sequence was missing its eventual title track. Not only was 'Darkness on the Edge of Town' absent, it had been since June. At no stage had it been a potential title of the album. A number of provisional titles *were* considered that fall; the two favourites, *Badlands* and *American Madness*, both derived from famous film titles. Indeed, throughout the making of *Darkness* Springsteen had been in the grip of the American madness that was film noir.

It had all begun when Landau suggested the two of them watch John Ford's adaptation of Steinbeck's *Grapes of Wrath*. It had a profound effect. Interviewing Bruce the following year, Paul Nelson, by this juncture more film buff than rock critic, commented on the change: 'He talked for the first ten minutes of the interview about how much he'd been influenced by [movies]. And how, like [in] John Ford, the real story [in these songs] is underneath the action.' To another reporter, Springsteen went so far as to describe Ford's *Grapes of Wrath* as 'part of the [album's] production for me. Like, I'm sitting there and I'm watching something that I never watched before . . . and it has an influence, it has an effect on me.'

As it came time to create his own totality, he began to see the album as an audio noir-movie, a reference-point he made repeatedly following *Darkness*'s release: 'There comes a point where the song becomes more and more like a movie. And when that happens you cease to become its creator and assume the role of director . . . My songs have a kinda drive-in quality about them . . . I'm just there, quietly directing . . . / . . . The songs I write [now], they don't have particular beginnings and they don't have endings. The camera focuses in and then out.'

What he now says he got from Ford at that time was 'that elegiac view of history – warmth, fidelity, duty – the good soldier's qualities . . . [because] people [like him] had [an] interest in the undercurrents, the underbelly, an interest in peering behind the veil of what you're shown every day'. It also made him consciously seek 'out forties and fifties film noir such as Jacques Tourneur's *Out of the Past*. It was [this] feeling of men

* The January 16 sequence was as follows:

Side 1: Badlands. Don't Look Back. Candy's Room. Something In The Night. Racing In The Street.

Side 2: The Promised Land. Adam Raised A Cain. The Way. Prove It All Night. The Promise.

and women struggling against a world closing in that drew me to those films. Even the title, *Darkness On The Edge of Town*, owed a lot to American noir . . . [But] I always liked the flash and outlaws of B-pictures – Robert Mitchum in *Thunder Road* and Arthur Ripley's *Gun Crazy.*'

He had already namechecked *Thunder Road* in 'The Promise', though at no point does he ever seem to have considered calling the LP after the song which permanently shifted the parameters of his songwriting; and which, as of January 16, was the designated album-closer, bookending an LP that began with 'Badlands'. But even at this juncture Springsteen had his doubts about the recorded version. Sometime around September, he had rewritten the 'paid the big cost' couplet, after a *Rolling Stone* reporter suggested the song was actually 'about' the lawsuit. The new lines suggested someone a hair's breadth away from *Nebraska*: 'Well, my daddy taught me how to walk quiet and how to make my peace with the past/ I learned real good to tighten up inside and I don't say nothing unless I'm asked'. It was this version, recorded with the full band, which was on the January 16 sequence. Yet eight days later he was back at the Record Plant, recording the song solo at the piano, planning to add strings (according to Landau, a 'string' version *was* cut). But as he would suggest in 1999 – when he had just cut the song solo for a second time, hiding its battered corpse on *18 Tracks* – 'I just didn't have a take of ['The Promise'] I was happy with.'

Even with a sequence that seemed to work, Springsteen allowed doubts to creep in and they centred on three songs, 'The Promise', 'The Way' and 'Candy's Room'. As a result, he expended thirteen sessions over the next seven weeks to applying yet more vocal overdubs and instrumental tweaks to the first two. By March 8, he was ready to throw up his hands and walk away. But he didn't. Instead, at the end of that day's session he went back to a song he last explored the previous June, 'Darkness On The Edge of Town'. He returned the following day and resumed where he left off, though not before running down a take of Them's highly apposite 'I Can Only Give You Everything'.

The day after that, he dug out 'Come On, Come On (Let's Go Tonight)', another song he originally cut that first week at Atlantic – possibly even at the first 'demo' session (Note: there is an undated Sony reel marked 'take one, complete, with Vox [organ]'). As its title indicates, this was originally a guy 'n' girl song and an important benchmark, at least as far as subject matter goes. The implicit threat of violence in earlier songs had been made explicit – not least in its subtitle, 'Let's Go Tonight'. The platitudinous pop opening – 'Hey little girl with the red dress on/ There's a party tonight 'till the early dawn' – is a bum steer belying its true subject matter: getting into a fight. When in the second verse the singer declaims, 'The new world will beat you, on the beach you'll hide', he is not in the land of metaphor, but *On The Waterfront*.

In a number of interviews in 1978 Springsteen talked about the underlying aura of violence he had felt growing up, telling one reporter, 'You go into the bars and you see the guys wandering around in there who got the crazy eyes. They just hate. They're just looking for an immediate expenditure of all this build-up' and another, 'Most of those guys don't go to the bar looking to hit somebody. They go looking to get punched.'

But the song he was ostensibly discussing was one that took 'Come On's last verse as its *starting* point. Called initially 'The Factory Song', later just 'Factory', this new song focused on the build-up of frustration that would inexorably lead to a fistfight ('And you just better believe, boy/ Somebody's gonna get hurt tonight'). Unfortunately, the song itself was a dreary monologue about the drudgery of a daily existence Springsteen himself had never experienced, save second hand. ('I remember my old man was working in this plastics factory [and] my mother, if he forgot his lunch, she used to have to bring it down to him . . . and all I remember, when we used to go in that place, was him standing near 'em loud fucking machines.')

Even if his intention was to suggest he now understood something of the sacrifices his father had made for his family, choosing 'Factory' over 'Independence Day' made some of Dylan's contemporary album choices look positively measured. 'Come On, Come On' wasn't the only song considered from the outset, only to appear on the final album in a form that was a fudge. 'Candy's Room' made it to the January 16 sequence still in a guise more 'Candy's Boy' than 'The Fast Song'. Starting on March 3, he spent three solid days trimming the track and dubbing a new vocal, until he had successfully pruned the song of its avenging angels and at least one naked profession of desire, 'Our love they cannot destroy/ I will forever be Candy's Boy'.

And still they were not done. It would be April 18 before Springsteen approved a second sequence, even though, as Landau says, 'We were working on [just] the eleven [tracks] for the last two months of the record.

We basically mixed twelve songs.' The last-minute casualties were 'The Way' and 'Don't Look Back', both stronger statements than either 'Factory' or 'Streets of Fire', the latter tracks making it to the April 18 sequence, taking the album into fifty-minute territory. That would never do if he was hoping to get the requisite sonic intensity. As for 'The Promise', he still 'felt too close to it'.

With a twelve-song shortlist, no-one in situ seemed entirely sure how to get that barrage-like sound, and with Iovine off making someone else a star it was time to bring in another set of ears. The person they brought in was Landau's suggestion, Chuck Plotkin, currently head of A&R at Elektra and a producer in his own right. When Plotkin heard the tapes that first time, it seemed to him that all 'the players [were] fighting for space inside the music'. As for Springsteen's vocals, he felt they needed to 'keep the voice tucked in, so that you feel like you could understand the words if you wished to try hard enough', while not making them wholly or instantly intelligible (i.e. the Marcusian dialectic). He quickly realized his would be a two-fold task, mixing the record *and* tutoring the artist himself about the art of mixing. Because Bruce not only lacked the technical knowledge to do it himself, he also lacked the self-awareness to relinquish control to someone who did:

> **Chuck Plotkin**: They needed to have somebody who was essentially sympathetic to the artist's role in . . . mixing *and* someone who understood that, among other things, the process for Bruce was learning about how all this stuff worked. I mean Bruce, as accomplished an artist as he was even at that time, had only made four records . . . [But] both of us seemed . . . interested in staying in the saddle until the thing was right.

Even if it meant saddle sores. The combination of levels of paranoia that made Watergate look like a high-school prank, and a relentless, obsessive quest for musical perfection that proved Landau wasn't joking when he told *Rolling Stone* in 1975, 'Bruce is determined before he dies to make the greatest rock & roll record ever made', served to make every 'outsider' who entered the Record Plant the subject of deep suspicion. When record company runner Debbie Gold had a message to convey to Plotkin, she was expected to sit there and wait/rot:

> **Debbie Gold**: Getting into the Record Plant, it probably would have been easier to get into the Pentagon. It was well known during [the making of] *Darkness*, no one got near the place. No record company. No family. Somehow I got in, and I just sat there. There's nobody around. The only people there were Landau, Jimmy, Bruce, Chuck and Tom [Panunzio]. And all I heard for the first week or so was the harmonica on 'Promised Land'. Every time the door [to the studio] opened . . . Then after a week, they say, 'Hey, we wanna play you something.' They sit me down and blast the song, 'Something In The Night' . . . 'So what do you think?' It blew my mind.

What Debbie didn't know was that the basic track she'd just heard had been recorded in a single take on day one – and this was now day one-o-one, and they were still tinkering with it. Nonetheless, Gold was more privileged than anyone who worked for the record company picking up the eye-watering tab for this twelve-month tutorial on the ways of the studio. It was the third week in April when just two invites were extended to CBS staff for a playback session. What they heard had even a Bruce zealot like his marketing manager slightly worried:

> **Dick Wingate:** I had a very strong relationship with Landau, but nobody from Columbia was ever at the sessions. He invited me and [Mickey] Eisher, who was head of A&R, to come to a playback at The Record Plant when it was done. It was just Jon and Jimmy Iovine, and I remember thinking, 'Holy shit! This is a whole new Bruce.' And I knew right away the marketing of the record, which was so much harder and more adult and *dark*, would by necessity have to change dramatically from anything that came before.

Springsteen had made a difficult album, and spent a fortune into the bargain. So it goes without saying that he wanted it released with no publicity, and with a lead single that sounded like, well, one of eight beefy, wordy album tracks (as opposed to one of two clunkers). But 'Prove It All Night' was not a leap-out-and-grab-ya 45. As he almost boasted in *Songs*, 'There was a lot of variation in the material we recorded, but I edited out anything I thought broke the album's tension.' He could equally have said, 'Or might generate AM airplay.' He fervently believed there was this great big audience for the new, serious Springsteen, who would welcome the lack of frivolity and embrace the darkness, and he was prepared to prove it, night after night:

> **Bruce Springsteen**: When I was young, I was a serious young man. I had serious ideas about rock music. I believed it was a serious thing, I believed it should also be fun – dancing, screwing, having a good time, but . . . I also believed it was capable of conveying serious ideas and that the people who listened to it, whatever you want to call them, were looking for something. [1996]

It wasn't like it was *his* money he was laying on the line for his beliefs. It was CBS's bottom line he was endangering, at least until he cleared a million dollars' worth of debt from the Appel suit and eleven months of more or less solid studio time. And still he insisted that *Darkness* should receive the most muted fanfare for any album by an established rock artist since Columbia released Dylan's first post-motorcycle accident effort, *John Wesley Harding*, the week after Christmas 1967:

> **Dick Wingate:** We had this lunch in LA, just him and I, and he said, 'OK, no more sneakers, no more pictures with a beard, no earring. All that stuff, put it away.' I have a letter from his lawyer that was sent to me which specifies, point by point, exactly what has to be approved by Bruce in the way of imaging and packaging. He just wanted to be seen as having grown up. He felt that the whole *Born To Run* thing [had been] so hype driven. He told me, 'I don't want to be hyped. If it was up to me, the album would just appear in the stores one day, with no fanfare, so the music can speak for itself.' So we sat and talked for a while, and we eventually agreed the advertising would have no copy except Bruce Springsteen – *Darkness on the Edge of Town* – The New Album, and the release date.

Back in the day, *John Wesley Harding* had indeed 'just appear[ed] in the stores one day'; and although Bruce might not have remembered this, Landau surely did. His most famous, non-predictive piece of rock journalism was his *Crawdaddy* review of that landmark LP. What he may not have known, or had clean forgotten, was that *JWH* – an unalloyed masterpiece – initially sold less than either its predecessor, an expensive double-album, or its successor, the countrified *Nashville Skyline*, stalling at number three in the album charts. Wingate meanwhile put on a brave face, sending a memo to the rest of CBS's marketing department that in no way sold the album's manifold qualities short:

> Springsteen's 'return' has been a painful and long process in which he trusts only his own instincts . . . He has been involved in approving *everything*, through the packaging, printing, point of sale material and advertising concepts. This will undoubtedly continue until he is confident enough to trust a manager. In the meantime, he has asked that in all the marketing concepts, understatement be the key element. The emphasis will be on his new visual image, without any copy of the 'Future of Rock and Roll' sort that has bothered him in the past. Print, radio and television ads will be simple announcements in the early life of the album, so that the record will take its proper place based on its merits and not hype or superlatives. We have a record that should still be selling well at Christmas by pacing our advertising over the course of the five-month tour (and the various singles) . . . In the end, however, it comes down to the record. *Darkness On The Edge of Town* is truly an outstanding album that requires several listenings to fully comprehend. It's the album we've waited over three years for, and the one to take Springsteen to multi-platinum levels.

The projections made for sales – and marketing budget – certainly suggested the label's faith in their main man was undiminished by the lack of an obvious hit single, or a refusal on his part to do TV appearances or promotional videos.* Their internal unit sales projection as of May 30, 1978, was for domestic sales of *Darkness* to total two and a half million in the next ninety days, rising to three million by year's end. Given that the artist in question had to date sold 1,278,589 copies of *Born To Run*, 534,865 of *The Wild, the Innocent* and 419,764 of *Greetings from Asbury Park*, one wonders on what basis such predictions were made. Or who, this time around, was hyping whom.

CBS were not even sure, right up until the moment the record was mastered in early May, that Springsteen had finally delivered his first

* There were a handful of brief news snippets on local TV stations in 1978, but Springsteen continued to nix any live TV performances, even on the ever-popular *Saturday Night Live*.

album under the new deal. In response to Nelson's question, 'When did you actually know what the ten songs were?' Landau admitted, 'The day we mastered the record.' Even after Bruce chopped 'Don't Look Back' and dubbed on a sax part for 'Badlands', he would not let go. As Wingate recalls, 'The album was brought to LA to master. He was up against the release date, but he [still] decided to go back to New York to put the guitar solo [on 'The Promised Land'] back in.' It left the label pinning its commercial hopes on positive press from the shows keeping the album in the charts; a second (and hopefully third) single surpassing the stilted studio 'Prove It All Night' in airplay and chart action; and, perhaps most important of all, that the rock critics again did their work for them, reviewing a Springsteen record as if it were the Second Coming and Holy Grail wrapped into one.

By assigning the already indentured Dave Marsh to review *Darkness*, *Rolling Stone* were certainly doing their bit. On line two of his rave review, Marsh compared this record to *Are You Experienced, Astral Weeks, Who's Next, The Band* and 'Like A Rolling Stone'. If that wasn't enough to break *any* camel's back, he went on to suggest that 'in the area of production . . . [it] is nothing less than a breakthrough'. A breakthrough no-one reprised or took further, not even Springsteen. But then, here was a man who was determined to hear echoes of Robbie Robertson's apocalyptic 1966 riffs and Yardbirds-era Jeff Beck in Bruce's guitar parts.

He was also prepared to be a voice in the wilderness, celebrating (not lamenting) the fact that 'ideas, characters, and phrases jump from song to song like threads in a tapestry'. Some other US reviewers who agreed with this part of Marsh's critique thought it showed a paucity of imagination. Peter Knobler, a long-term apostle who took on the thankless role of Judas this time, suggested in a two-page *Crawdaddy* review that the album's main flaw was his 'repeated use of scenes and frameworks that [he] pioneered years ago and everyone from Meat Loaf to Billy Falcon has savaged since . . . [He] uses all the same settings – night, cars, driving – [while] quot[ing] liberally from himself – chord changes, guitar riffs, vocal tone'. He even dared to wonder aloud whether '*Born To Run* really had been as far as he could go'. *NME*'s Paul Rambali also found a number of songs 'where he narrowly escapes self-parody'; while an exasperated Mitch Cohen in *Creem* pondered, 'Doesn't this guy ever get in the car just to go get a pack of cigarettes? It's a major production every time he turns the ignition key.'

Such criticisms clearly stung Springsteen. He alluded to them in assorted interviews that summer, insisting, 'The action is not the imagery, you know. The heart of the action is beneath all that stuff. There's a separate thing happening all the time. I sorta always saw it as the way certain people make certain kinds of movies.' Yet even Landau had at one point asked him, mid-session, 'What's all these cars? Why are these people always in these cars?' He found himself required to explicate his underlying aesthetic to his own producer: 'Well, you know, the idea is they're always in a state of movement . . . destination unknown.'

What even the more carping critics couldn't have known was that *Darkness on The Edge of Town*, for all its pugnacious power and V8 vroom, was a muddied melange of Albums #4 and 5. Even Springsteen admitted, the week of its release, that 'most of the new songs were written while we were recording the album. I was formulating a concept in the studio.' The result was neither one thing, nor the other, neither an Atlantic cross-stitch, nor a full record of time spent at the Plant. As Landau broke it down for Nelson, '"Badlands", "Adam Raised A Cain", "Promised Land", "Factory", "Prove It All Night" were all completely conceived and executed after the album began.' Of the others, 'Streets of Fire' was a spontaneous studio combustion, 'Candy's Room' had stripped two superior songs of their spare parts, and 'Darkness on the Edge of Town' and 'Racing In The Street', originally intended for 'Album #4', were recrafted lyrically in order to gain an invite to this beggar's banquet. That left just 'Something In The Night' representing an untainted 'Album #4'.

'Album #4' – the one he sketched out in his notebook, endlessly shuffling the already-engorged deck – was a would-be artefact it would take him thirty-three years to get (back) to. In the meantime, there would be just hints as to what might have been, notably the re-recording of various key songs from the Atlantic period – 'Drive All Night', 'I Wanna Be With You', 'Independence Day', 'Sherry Darling' for *The River*; 'Frankie' and 'Darlington County' for *Born In The USA;* and, even, 'The Promise' for *18 Tracks*. Without this halfway house, *Born To Run*'s successor was always likely to be a shock to the fan system. (Dylan was himself guilty of re-recording inferior versions of three 'basement tape' cuts for a second greatest hits, before realizing these songs were of a piece, and releasing them that way.)

In 1978, Springsteen continued dropping hints about what had prompted this dramatic shift in lieu of that missing album: 'I started with basically the same imagery as before, the same frames of reference, but what's happened to the characters is a little different.' With *Darkness*, he struck a vein he would mine for the remainder of the E Street era. There would be no more seismic stylistic shifts. As he told Marsh the next time around, 'I don't really have a desire to experiment for the sake of experimentation . . . I'm not really that concerned with style.' From now on he intended to create a body of work that was as full of 'warmth, fidelity, duty' as John Ford's:

> **Bruce Springsteen**: I never felt myself to be a revolutionary . . . I'm the kind of guy that's telling this very long story over this long period of time, [knowing that] that craftsmanship and consistency were going to be my friends . . . I think when I connected into some of the filmmakers that I began to really admire at the time, it gave me a template that I didn't find in music somewhere, to explain to myself a little bit of where I was going and what I was interested in doing. [2007]

In a sense, he had only just begun. Meaning, he would have to sell himself to fans all over again. It was high time he started pitching this born-again aesthetic to the heartlands. Even this 'hyper-conscious kid' knew the 'record ain't gonna sprout legs and walk out the door, and jump on people's record players and say listen to me'. The problem was that as soon as he started playing songs from the album – and every show received a near-lethal dose of *Darkness* in the first half, before more familiar fare revived older fans' spirits – he realized what they had needed all along was road-testing, not months in a sterile studio. The immediacy that came with an audience, an amphitheatre and an audio feed was a pattern that had served him well to date. Yet it was one to which he would never now return.

Instead, he pushed the fixed-to-disc *Darkness* like there was no tomorrow, determined to get his message across *after the fact*. Once he delivered the album, the only time he planned to hear those songs again was with the roar of the crowd in his ears. Not surprisingly, their acclaim would stop him from seeing *Darkness* – for all its capital-A Attitude – as falling short of his oft-expressed long-term goal: 'To make the greatest rock & roll record ever made.' By 1981 – when promoting an Album #6 that contained more elements from 'Album #4' than its precursor – he was insisting, 'I simply consider the *Darkness* LP a failure.' He even had some sense of where he had gone wrong, telling Nick Kent, '*Darkness* was the one where we deliberately left off all the fun rock & roll songs. But I don't think a lot of the songs on *Darkness* were fully realized.' By then, all ten songs – even 'Factory' – had been 'fully realized', just not necessarily when the tapes were rolling:

> **Bruce Springsteen**: On *Darkness*, I like the ideas. I'm not crazy about the performances. We play all those songs ten times better live . . . Certain things on [that] record I can listen to: 'Racing in the Street', . . . 'Prove it All Night', 'Darkness on the Edge of Town'. But not a lot, because either the performance doesn't sound right to me, or the ideas sound like a long time ago. [1981]

In 1975, at the end of his tether after *three* months' solid work on *Born To Run*, Springsteen threatened to just scrap the whole record and record the self-same eight songs at The Bottom Line. He never did. It would have been the wrong album, anyway. If ever there was an album that came alive *live* it was *Darkness*; and in a large part, this was because in concert there was also a place for 'all the fun rock & roll songs', the songs he gave away and those he held over to use next time. Context, as this 'hyper-conscious kid' once *instinctively* knew, was all. It was time to let in some light, to allow hope and glory to filter through those drawn Venetian blinds.

Part II

Better Off That Way

Chapter 6: 1978–79 – The Ties That Bind

> I always think I come off sounding like some kind of crazed fanatic . . . but it's the way I am about [playing live] . . . It all ties in with . . . the values, the morality of the records. – Bruce Springsteen, 1978

> I think his live show is so good that his audience will always be big. He hasn't gone any further than *Born To Run*, though . . . Bruce is not surrounded by the best guys. It's the blind leading the blind. – Mike Appel, 1978

With Elvis out for the count, Springsteen set out at the end of May 1978 to claim another crown, that of living legend James Brown. Night after night, over six months of solid, relentless touring, he demonstrated who *really* was the hardest working man in show business. The shows he played at this time – a hundred and ten of them, criss-crossing North America from north-east to south-west, coast to coast and back again – have rightly become the stuff of legends. At a time when his latest album was struggling to pass total sales of *The Wild, the Innocent*, let alone the platinum *Born To Run* – it peaked at five in the *Billboard* chart, two places shy of its predecessor and by the end of 1978 had only sold around 600,000 Stateside – the hype surrounding the shows successfully masked this chastening reality, while serving to reaffirm all the previous hyperbole expended on the E Street Band show that Springsteen had gone to such pains to dampen.

If CBS privately despaired at Springsteen's resolute refusal to do TV, his willingness to donate his most commercial songs to others (the most aired Springsteen song on AM radio that spring was Patti Smith's version of

'Because The Night'), and the austere nature of the only press ads he would approve, they could have no complaints about the way he was promoting the album at the shows, night after night, or talked up the album in press interviews whenever the subject came up. From day one he insisted he always knew *Darkness* 'might be a harder album for people to like than *Born To Run*, because it has less surface warmth or optimism. [But] it's been misinterpreted as being a pessimistic album, which it's not at all meant to be.'

He was determined to drive its defiantly dark message home. On opening night of the tour, with the album still not officially out, he played nine of the ten songs (wisely dispensing with 'Factory'). And he did not stop there. Both 'Fire' and 'The Promise' came up for air, and in the former's case quickly became a nightly rockabilly ritual. If the latter's inclusion merely reaffirmed a belief among fans that he had left off another masterpiece, it proved a less durable inclusion. An early first encore, it passed from the set the gig before his first radio broadcast of the year, July 5. Performed solo at the piano, à la 'For You', here was the definitive rendition. But coming at the end of two and a half hours of rabble-rousing it seemed to take those last ounces of strength and throw them all away, making its mark at the expense of 'Born To Run', 'Tenth Avenue Freeze-Out' and whatever frat-rocker he closed the show with on a given night.

Its inclusion also meant fully half of the 22-song set on opening night was unfamiliar to even the most hard-core fan. Nor did the opening salvo of 'Badlands', 'Night' and 'Something In The Night' make any concessions. Before the audience could catch its breath, they were in the midst of an enveloping darkness. It was an extraordinarily brave strategy, and one to which he adhered unwaveringly, knowing full well that the emphasis on new songs would draw comment even from regular champions of the great contender. When he gave Philadelphia DJ Ed Sciaky – a rabid proselytizer for five years now – an after-show interview in August he made his intentions plain as day:

> **Bruce Springsteen**: I . . . believed in [*Darkness*] a lot. I thought it was more of a difficult record to get into than *Born To Run* was. It was something I spent eleven months doing and I liked it, loved doing it, felt it. I like playing all the songs from it – that's the most fun of the night. So I said to myself, 'Hey, I'm gonna get out there and hustle it' . . . There's a stretch where we go from 'Darkness' to 'Thunder Road', a stretch of songs that

> we do basically in the same order every night because there's a continuity thing that happens. It makes connections, and gives the rest of the show resonance. [1978]

Such self-belief brooked no argument. The *Darkness* songs stayed a part of the shows, and only grew stronger with each nightly workout. As did his belief in them. He even told Peter Knobler, who had already given the LP a lukewarm review, that this 'record meant more [to me] than . . . the other records. So when I made it I wanted to make sure that I was gonna be true to what was real for me now.' The way he did this was to test the songs each night, all night. He expressed delight that fans were starting to 'call out for the new songs . . . it's good to see them going down so well' (actually, none of the dozens of audience tapes of the 1978 shows demonstrate any such groundswell of *Darkness* requests). But there was never any doubt that certain songs which did not leap off the record fast became showstoppers, thanks to the right setting – a stage. 'Badlands' burst from the side speakers every night – raising the roof and the near-dead. 'Racing In The Street' gripped audiences for whom a single viewing of *American Graffiti* was as close as they came to its ostensible subject matter. As for the guitarfest 'Prove It All Night', it made the studio version sound like a demo, and the E Street Band like a revved-up Steel Mill.

The word of mouth, and a crescendo of reviews for those early shows from all corners of the globe (even the home of punk), soon convinced CBS that were they to release (even just for radioplay) live versions of the new songs in real time they might reverse *Darkness*'s downward direction, and send it back up the *Billboard* charts. But Springsteen remained determined to make the record stand on its own two sides. When CBS sent a film crew to a show in Phoenix in mid-June, to capture three songs from *Darkness* and a coupla longstanding concert favourites they could use for promotional purposes, the versions of 'Badlands', 'The Promised Land' and 'Prove It All Night' all burned with a far brighter flame than tamer studio cousins. But as a driven-to-despair Dick Wingate observes, 'The only one he would allow to be released was "Rosalita", which was from an older album. I don't think he thought it was great. He [thought he] was a little stiff.'

It was the 1975 live album argument all over again. When CBS responded by taping an equally great show from Berkeley two weeks later, featuring one of the last meaningful performances of 'The Promise', in order to pull a live version of the nine-minute 'Prove It All Night' as a promotional item for radio stations – a common ploy in the era of 'official bootlegs' – Springsteen nixed the idea. When talk of a live album reared its head, he said he preferred to leave it to the bootleggers to spread the good news:

> **Bruce Springsteen**: If I did a live thing, I would do a double album . . . There'll probably be one coming out pretty soon [anyway], because we've just broadcast on the radio! Most of the time bootleggers are just fans . . . It doesn't really bother me . . . I see where it's coming from. [1978]

The record company doubtless loved reading that kinda comment – and read it they did, because he said it to a whole host of rock journalists backstage at a west coast show a couple of nights after he informed the same purveyors of hot wax, during a live radio broadcast from The Roxy, 'All them bootleggers out there in radioland, roll your tapes.' This is a hot one.' That comment – and a similar one he made on another live broadcast from San Francisco's Winterland Ballroom in December – would come back to haunt him. But at the time, live broadcasts of *five* entire shows – each to different regions of the US – were all part of a deliberate ploy to sell Springsteen's 'live rep' first, and album units second. In fact, a lengthy memo from Landau to CBS's Fred Humphrey that October affirms the strategic significance he and Springsteen placed on these broadcasts:

> 'I think we both agree that the single best promotional tool used during the last four months has been the series of live broadcasts. Of these broadcasts the one done at the Agora, in Cleveland, makes for the best all-around programming. My idea is that a week to ten days in front of selected dates on the tour, we schedule a tape of this three-hour broadcast in that particular market. In addition, we would naturally ask the participating stations to promote this very unique piece of special programming to the hilt . . . The one exception to the use of a pre-recorded tape would be our show at Winterland in San Francisco, on December 15. As you know, a live broadcast has already been scheduled and is in the works. Paul Rappaport has lined up KSAN and appropriate stations in Seattle and Portland . . . The reason for going live in San Francisco is that it continues, despite our best efforts, to be one of our weakest major markets. One of my special objectives in planning this [fall] tour has been to launch a total assault

> on this region. I think the extra excitement that comes from doing a live broadcast . . . as well as the extra promotion we can anticipate from the participating stations, makes this a logical and necessary course of action in this market.'

The Winterland show would be the last of the lot, coming from a tag-on tour at year's end they added in late September, with objectives Landau claimed were 'primarily developmental. Rather than go back to the many markets where Bruce is now a complete superstar, we are concentrating on those markets where we have created a very real excitement, and where, with one more concert coupled with imaginative promotion, we can finish the job.' Making Bruce fulfil his destiny as 'a complete superstar' (aka the future of rock 'n' roll) now required a military-like precision.

The first of the five broadcasts, coming from The Roxy on July 7, was intended to consolidate the success of the 1975 Roxy radio broadcast, which had played such a large part in taking the west coast along with him on that *Born To Run* ride. At the same time, CBS ensured they got their own tapes of the show, which assumed extra importance because he was saying goodbye not just to clubs like the 700-capacity Roxy, but maybe even, in some territories, medium-sized theatres. In fact, the July 7 date had only become available when Springsteen agreed to scrap three nights at the six-thousand-seat Shrine Auditorium and replace them with a single night at the LA Forum, the eighteen-thousand capacity barn the likes of Led Zeppelin, Pink Floyd and The Who had made a home away from home for Brit-rock heavyweights (and audience bootleggers).

Having fought to resist the pull of arenas throughout the whole of the *Born To Run* era – even in territories like Philadelphia, Boston, Cleveland and New York where it had long been a viable option – Springsteen broke his promise to himself just three nights into the *Darkness* tour, playing two shows at Philadelphia's Spectrum, the selfsame venue Appel had struggled to get him to play in 1976 to help clear the backlog of debt, and the very one he had forsworn on behalf of all such arenas after a disastrous support slot five years earlier. His excuse to Ed Sciaky was that 'there were so many people that wanted to come in. After that, it felt good, and it's been [generally] good experiences.' By mid-August he was back at The Spectrum, warming up for three nights at Madison Square Garden, shows he insisted he was playing 'for all the long-term supporters'. He had evidently forgotten his own astute analysis of the drawbacks of these antithetical-to-music mausoleums, expressed to Paul Williams before *Born To Run* raised the stakes:

> **Bruce Springsteen**: There's always something else going on all over the room. You go to the back row, you can't see the stage, [let alone] what's on it. You see a blot of light. You better bring your binocs! What happens [when] you go to those places [is] it turns into something else, that it ain't. It becomes an event. It's hard to play. That's where everybody is playing, though. I don't know how they do it. I don't know what people expect you to do in a place like that. [1978]

For the July 5 Forum show, he went down to just six *Darkness* songs, though he had added 'Because The Night' to the repertoire five days earlier, belatedly reclaiming it for himself – to whoops of approval from the fans. Certain economic issues remained, though, and if Springsteen wasn't hip to the new realities of the road, Landau was. Throughout that whole west coast jaunt in early July, Landau was slowly but surely assuming the helm, rounding up a retinue in case he decided to make the most momentous decision of his career – assuming the reins of management, and taking Bruce to the next commercial plane. He took some persuading:

> **Paul Rappaport**: I got to be part of the planning because he was new at it. Some of the questions he asked me he just didn't know the answer to. I remember being backstage at San Diego Sports Arena, he had this great wrinkled suit – he never had time to get them cleaned – and I remember yanking him, 'The rumour is you're gonna manage Bruce. You really have to do this.' And he was like, 'Rap, I'm not a manager, I'm a writer.' 'Yeah, but you're the only guy he trusts.' We could see Bruce was in trouble and needed [good] people around him. And Jon kept saying, 'I don't know'.

> **Debbie Gold:** By the time they came out to California I knew I had to be . . . a part of this. And Jon said to me, 'If I manage Bruce, you work for me. If not, you work for Bruce.' But still Landau did not make up his mind right away. It was the day of The Roxy show, and I was in Iovine's room, and suddenly I got summoned. That's when Landau finally decided

> [to manage Bruce] . . . Landau learning the ropes took the whole first year I was there. It was fascinating. He got some information from [Michael] Tannen, but I watched him soak up information from all the people around him. He asked the same questions to a lot of different people. I watched what he became, and how he used that information. Don't underestimate that guy!

Lighting man Marc Brickman was one of those who pushed for the man: 'Landau kept saying he didn't want to be manager. But he'd always be around . . . Finally we went out on *Darkness* and it wasn't happening, there were [some] problems monetarily. Suddenly we all said to him, "Why don't you be the manager?"[MOTH] As CBS's Pete Philbin suggests, one immediate result was a switch to arenas where feasible: 'Jon Landau systematically convinced Bruce Springsteen that he was letting his fans down and had to play bigger shows. He provided Bruce with an explanation to change the things he'd said in the past.'[MOTH] If, to Brickman and Philbin, the move in hindsight signalled 'the beginning of the end', initially good vibrations far outweighed the bad. And Springsteen was both the band's biggest hitter and its premier cheerleader, with reserves of energy that left everyone else in the dust:

> **Debbie Gold:** I've never been on a tour like that. He was so excited about playing, every minute of it. And then when the show was over he'd be saying hello to every reporter, every radio station person. It was a dream for me. And then we'd finally get on the bus and be ready to leave, [the rest of us] half asleep, there would be Bruce signing autographs.

As a farewell to how it used to be, the Roxy radio broadcast was certainly a helluva way to go out. The Forum show had been a fairly chanceless affair, and as Paul Rappaport recalls: 'Jon felt we didn't make enough noise. We didn't bust this town open . . . which is why did the Roxy.' The Roxy, though, was the old Bruce going for broke. For the first time, a Springsteen show breached the twenty-five song (and almost the three-hour) mark. Leaving aside the seven songs from *Darkness*, an introductory 'Rave On' (after admitting on local TV the night before that he listened to Buddy Holly every night before going onstage) and a wild-in-the-country 'Heartbreak Hotel', there were spectacular E Street reclamations of 'Fire', 'For You' and 'Because The Night' (from Robert Gordon, Greg Kihn and

Patti Smith respectively). It did what it had to do – it busted the town wide open. His west coast promotion man left the club mid-show just to get some air, and in leaving the epicentre of this media storm caught the zeitgeist in microcosm:

> **Paul Rappaport**: After three days of no sleep . . . I finally go out to the street to try and settle myself down just a bit. Wow, who knew what a scene it was OUTSIDE the Roxy! First, there were at least a couple hundred people with their ears pressed against the walls all the way around the club. On the Sunset Strip, where everyone is nightly cruising and the subsequent traffic jam is legendary, every single car had their windows rolled down and was blaring the show over their radios. People were bopping up and down in their seats and pumping fists outside their windows—whooping and hollering. The whole Strip was rocking out to one giant Bruce show. I am telling you it was extraordinary. It was like the whole town was listening.

The broadcast just got better and better. There was a twelve-minute 'Backstreets' that was part 'Sad Eyes', part 'Cypress Avenue' and part 'Drive All Night'.* (It was in Seattle, a fortnight earlier, that he had started to slip elements of that song into the 'Backstreets' rap: 'I remember then, baby, I′d drive all night. I swore that I′d drive all night, baby, I would drive all night just to taste your tender charms and to have you hold me in your arms, I′d drive all night through the wind and the rain . . . for just one look from your pretty, sad eyes.') And if that was not enough to take the whole of LA's breath away, he debuted two songs that took the essence of *Darkness*'s fatalistic worldview to an even more rarefied level, a fully-realized 'Independence Day' – for his attendant Mom and Pop – and 'Point Blank', a song no one even knew about before that night, being something written after the sessions:

> **Bruce Springsteen**: On *Darkness* I just didn't make room for certain things . . . I couldn't understand how you could feel so good and so bad at the same time . . . The song that I wrote right after *Darkness* . . . was 'Point Blank' – which takes that thing to its furthest. [1981]

---

* The Roxy version of 'Backstreets' on *Live 75-85* unforgivably edited the long spoken section out.

As singular a breakthrough as 'Frankie', 'Point Blank' became a staple of the 1978 shows almost from the minute he debuted it at that all-important Roxy show, addressing what appeared to be new subject matter: an ex-girlfriend's descent into drug addiction on finding the world an unforgiving place. Each live version from July to December included a variant on the verse he sang at the Roxy that first time: 'You hear their voices at night as you lock the door/ There'll be no sleep tonight for baby, she don't believe them lies anymore/ And she stumbles into the morning tryin' for her usual fix/ But, baby, them old distractions, they just ain't got the kicks no more.' The image of being shot point blank by a needle, not a gun, was a rare reflection on the dangers of drugs, addressed to a former girlfriend who went down that poisonous path.

But the song was primarily concerned with the need to escape a world in which 'no-one survives untouched', especially those people with 'hearts full of anger, eyes filled with hate', and was as such a natural development from 'Factory' and 'Badlands'. Hence, the various introductions he gave the song at 1978 shows, which varied from the purely cryptic, 'You wake up one morning and you're left staring . . . point blank'* to the familial, 'This song is for my father. Forty-five years and you wake up to find out you've been shot in the back every day, point blank'.†

Other former (or fanciful) lovers were also on his mind that Roxy night. A frantic 'For You', in its first E Street guise, finally gave the music the same menace as the lyrics, being placed between the definitive 'Candy's Room' and 'Point Blank'. His current girlfriend, though, was back east, which would prove to be a mistake on the photographer's part:

> **Lynn Goldsmith**: *Darkness on the Edge of Town* had just been released and Bruce was in Los Angeles for a week to do shows and press . . . He asked me to be there with him. I refused to come . . . Looking back, I can say I was afraid I'd lose my identity . . . I didn't want to be known as 'Bruce's girlfriend'. I wanted to be 'Lynn Goldsmith, the photographer'. He tempted me, telling me how they were going to climb this billboard on Sunset and paint over it and what a great picture I would get. I knew he felt alone and needed me, but I wouldn't go . . . Miami Steve had a girlfriend, Maureen, who called me and told me about this girl, Joyce,

---

* Passaic 20/9/78.

† Montreal 8/11/78.

> who kept hanging out around the band trying to get to Bruce. I didn't think anything of it. Bruce was the kind of guy who had a hard time even looking girls in the eye. Besides, I believed with all my heart that no one on this planet could be better for him than me. What I didn't take into account was that Bruce wanted to be loved when he needed it, when he asked for it, not just when I felt like it was the right time for me . . . This pretty young thing, Joyce, who looked at him with adoring eyes while I was screaming at him about my career, hooked her fish.

The fish lady's name was Joyce Heiser, and she certainly fit the Bruce bill. A model/actress with wholesome good looks and a willingness to subsume her identity if necessary, she turned up at the Sunset Motel that week often enough for Springsteen's new publicist to nudge Jimmy Iovine, there to record the Roxy, and say, 'She's just the girl for you.' He astutely replied, 'How much d'ya wanna bet she leaves with Bruce?' Heiser, though, was not the only one subsuming her identity for the greater good. Just shy of thirty, Springsteen was still living for the time he spent onstage. For him, every minute offstage was dead time.

Not only was he inspired every night, but he was hoping to inspire every night. As he told Robert Hilburn ahead of the Forum show, 'The greatest thing is going out backstage after the show and seeing some kid there . . . whose face is all lit up. It's like you've done something on stage to get things stirred up inside his head. That's the whole idea – get excited . . . do something.' If *he* had crawled out of Jersey, then others could, too. It was a mantra Patti Smith had adhered to long before she climbed aboard *Horses*; and it made Springsteen an unlikely compadre of punk evangelists on both sides of the pond. In fact, when premier punk journo Tony Parsons caught a show at the New York Palladium in September – and was given the usual 'let's just chat' spiel, designed to ensure such backstage interviews never probed the depths – his *NME* cover-story almost single-handedly gave the boardwalk prophet honorary-punk status.

Not that Bruce was about to brave the British boards. He resolutely stuck to the domestic market for the duration. But if he was unwilling to go toe-to-toe with the dynamic bands of the UK new wave, the best would come to him. Throughout the year, Elvis Costello & The Attractions – who packed almost as much energy into their one-hour set as Springsteen and his cohorts managed across their two-and-a-half-hour marathons

– made regular sorties to the States, building an audience with pell-mell product and dynamite performances. If Costello, in his bug-eyed misanthropic guise, felt obliged to denigrate Springsteen in print (a fact Springsteen gently reminded him of when they recorded a fascinating two-part *Spectacle* in September 2009), he also nagged his CBS rep, Dick Wingate, to let him check out the competition at a rare college gig. That November Princeton show rocked even this jaundiced, ex-Hammersmith '75 attendee's world.

By this point, the shows had begun to nudge the three-hour mark, with twenty-five-song sets the nightly norm. As Springsteen sought to explain, 'We originally started off with a two-hour set. But when the tour got underway, we found it impossible to keep it down to that.' This was in part because he quickly realized he needed to rebalance the set to accommodate more early seventies material. The early shows, where 'Spirit In The Night', 'For You' and 'Rosalita' were token Sancious-era admissions, made too few concessions to fans who had been there from the first. By the time he hit the loyal east coast in August he had begun to slip in the odd 'Incident On 57th Street', an occasional 'Kitty's Back', and even a blue-moon moment like 'Lost In The Flood', sung solo at the piano in Detroit (and fully the equal of former 'For You's). He also introduced, initially just for Texan fans with long memories, a new arrangement of 'The Fever' – only to find it got a response which reminded him his own judgements of a song's merits were hardly infallible. The song intros also began to take on a life of their own, like when he sent up nuns and psychiatrists in a rap that preceded 'Growin' Up':

> I remember I was 12 years old and I was going to this Catholic school and I got sent home for pissing in my desk (cheers) - obviously, a popular pastime - and the Sisters told my mother that I needed psychiatric attention (chuckles). The only people that were more scared of the nuns than the kids was the parents, you know. I remember my old man and my old lady, they were terrified of them Sisters so downtown they take me to this doc and I'm sitting down there on the couch and he says "Son, how did you get this way?" I thought about it and I said, "Doc, I'm glad you asked, because up to now I've kept it a secret, but the fact was I was a teenage werewolf." I said, "Doc, I was out in the street, I remember it was midnight, I looked up, there was a full moon, I felt this hair growing all over my face, I felt

> my fingers get longer and my nails pop out and a guitar pop out of my left side, my pants got tighter and my hair got longer, a man with a cigar come up and stung me on the ass and all of sudden in one moment I looked up and there was this light . . . *I stood stone like at midnight*".

'Growin' Up' also received its own mid-song rap, which only amped up the blasphemy with him and Clarence driving out to the swamplands of Jersey for a conversation with God, whose message was 'just three words, LET IT ROCK!' Meanwhile, 'Backstreets' ventured into the slipstream of *Too Late To Stop Now* again, with its repeated references to the little girl with lonely sad eyes, who cried all night long. Finally he had to break the news to her, 'You've been laughing and lying and now you're back . . . Well, little girl, I've been out too, and I've seen some things and I know all about *you*. We gotta stop . . . if we could only stop . . . it'd be alright, if we could only stop . . . if we could only stop . . . if we could only stop . . . if we could only stop . . . stop, stop, stop, STOP.'

If he wisely refrained from referencing The Man directly onstage, he still found an occasional berth for early Stones ('The Last Time', 'Mona') or The Animals ('It's My Life' in Pittsburgh and Passaic, for the steeltown boys and Jersey girls). But mainly he preferred to remind these all-American audiences of those communal indigenous rock 'n' roll roots. One innovation heralded at the Roxy was retained – opening most shows with a fifties rock 'n' roll cover. 'Good Rockin' Tonight', 'Oh Boy', 'High School Confidential', 'Sweet Little Sixteen', 'Ready Teddy', even 'Summertime Blues' received outings. Asked about this, he insisted, 'I love that early rock & roll. That's what I listen to while I go to sleep: Elvis, Buddy Holly.' But he was also broadening his cultural horizons. Tuning into country stations throughout his American odyssey, he discovered that there was more to the musical landscape than rock 'n' roll. Slowly but surely, a whole wide world of music – and, indeed, literature and film – was opening up to him:

> **Bruce Springsteen**: I went back to Hank Williams and Jimmy Rodgers, to soul and spirituals. Suddenly I found what I had heard back in the old rock & roll records. Or read in that fantastic book, *American Dreams, Lost and Found* by Studs Terkel; or seen in the [John Ford] movie, *The Grapes of Wrath*. [1981]

That August, talking to the trustworthy Ed Sciaky, he admitted, 'What I've been listening to a lot now is Hank Williams.' What he found there would lead to his next stage of development as a songwriter. As he told Kevin Avery, three decades on, 'I liked the toughness of country music and I liked the fact that there was so much of it that was about compromising . . . I was interested in getting that idea into my music.' But this was an epiphany he had to work at – he needed something that would take him further than just the dark end of the street:

> **Bruce Springsteen**: I want[ed] to write music that I can imagine myself singing on stage at the advanced old age, perhaps, of 40? . . . I wanted to twist the form I loved into something that could address my adult concerns. And so I found my way to country music . . . I remember . . . playing *Hank Williams' Greatest Hits* over and over. And I was trying to crack its code, because . . . it just sounded cranky and old–fashioned. But slowly, slowly, my ears became accustomed to it, its beautiful simplicity, and its darkness and depth. [2012]

Initially, he needed to resolve how to incorporate Hank Williams' sensibility in the current shows. He tried the direct approach just once, a guitar/piano arrangement of '(I Heard That) Lonesome Whistle', sandwiched between 'The Promised Land' and 'Prove It All Night' at a show in Pittsburgh at the end of August, gamely assisted by Bittan, the most versatile band member. (In the past couple of years rather than twiddle his thumbs between E Street engagements, Bittan had contributed his musical skills to albums as important as Peter Gabriel's solo debut and Bowie's *Station To Station*, and as shamelessly Springsteenesque as *Bat Out Of Hell*.)

In that moment Springsteen probably knew neither his band nor the bemused audience were quite ready to embrace both kinds of music, country *and* western. But there were still the soundchecks, which could be as epic as the shows themselves, especially if Springsteen was uncertain about an arena's acoustics, or there was some pressing reason he needed the sound to be just right. Such was the case the second night at the Passaic Capitol Theatre in September. Springsteen knew they were taping the next two nights for a possible 'home turf' live album, after a three-night warm-up stint at the equally intimate New York Palladium. He seemed to be gradually reintroducing some older songs into the set for just such an occasion – hence the likes of 'Incident on 57th Street', 'Kitty's Back', 'The Fever', 'It's My Life' and 'Meeting Across The River', all passionately recreated at these last two Passaic shows. Yet he spent much of the soundcheck on the 20th running down Hank Williams songs and Sun-era Johnny Cash covers, every one of which petered out, perhaps because the band refused to join in the fun.

They may have still been wondering when Bruce was gonna get back to the brand-new song they had run through at the start of the soundcheck. His first in months, it went by the name of 'The Ties That Bind', and it was a keeper. But if he *had* performed it at one of these shows, it would have baffled many a fan when a song of the same name appeared on record two years later. Because this was a very different song, and a magnificent one at that, with a great pop hook set to a strong, if undeveloped lyrical idea – 'No-one at my side / There's just a cold dark highway and a thin white line / [Which] will lead me to the ties that bind' – and the whole thing wrapped up by a guitar coda worthy of 'Prove It All Night'. Though already ready to record, it would be stripped bare and rebuilt by November 1, its live debut.

What he wanted was the kinda song which would slot into the record he had already talked to Dave Marsh about: 'I got an album's worth of pop songs like 'Rendezvous' and early English-style stuff. I got an album's worth right now . . . I wanna do an album that's got ten or eleven things like that on it.' Hence, presumably, the reintroduction of 'Rendezvous' – another Atlantic reject – to end-of-year sets, and the version of 'The Ties That Bind' he introduced in November, which made an affirmative pop song out of its Passaic prototype. Two frat-rockers, 'Sherry Darling' and 'Ramrod', also suggested he had in mind a more fun-filled successor; as did a lengthy intro the night he introduced 'Sherry Darling' for the first time, in Charleston, Virginia:

> 'This was a song that we recorded live in the studio about two years ago, the beginning of the summer and it was originally gonna be on *Darkness* but it was too weird, so we left it off . . . There's a whole bracket of music, this is not real well-known, but it was known as Fraternity Rock. It used to be like "Louie Louie", "Farmer John" by the Premiers, uh, what else?, "Double Shot of My Baby's Love" by the Swinging Medallions . . . Oh shit, I'm an old man up here tonight (laughs). No recognition for these songs! It used to be

> anything that was loud, raucous and like, sounded like you'd just had about ten too many beers. So that's what this song was supposed to be, and that's why we gotta start this song off with party noises . . . / . . . and vomiting in your girlfriend's purse is also allowed during this number.'

Was he seriously planning to produce a lightweight pop album – based around some of the lesser songs cut for 'Album #4' – as *Darkness*'s successor? Perhaps the relative failure of *Darkness was* already preying on his mind? But what about 'Point Blank' and 'Independence Day', major works that every night garnered standing ovations, even though they were known only to those who collected 1978 radio broadcasts or caught multiple shows? If, as he later claimed, he wanted to make an album that 'accept[s] the fact that the world is a paradox, and that's [just] the way it is', then there needed to be more of heaven and earth on it than could be contained by the philosophies of 'Rendezvous', 'Ramrod' and 'Sherry Darling'.

He had another problem, of his own making. He had already aired 'Point Blank', 'Independence Day', 'The Ties That Bind' and 'Sherry Darling' in widely-taped live radio broadcasts, which even now were being pressed to bootleg disc: something which, as of July 1978, Springsteen had insisted 'doesn't really bother me'. His introduction to 'Sandy' at the December 15 Winterland show, suggesting the Jersey girls would get to hear this particularly fine version 'through the magic of bootlegging', rather implied he still didn't.

But by 1979 he was no longer so keen on these clandestine copyists. Or more accurately, perhaps, Jon Landau on behalf of Bruce Springsteen was less keen on them. And once Springsteen realized the next studio album was as far away as ever, he was prepared to sign off on the pursuit of the two most redoubtable of these Californian brigands, Vicki Vinyl (née Andrea Waters) and her sidekick, Jim Washburn. They had taken Springsteen at his on-air word and had pressed up the Winterland show in its three-hour entirety. When that three-disc set sold well, they issued the Passaic FM broadcast too, as the memorable *Piece De Resistance*; while CBS held back from issuing either of the two Passaic shows they, and they alone, had.

A Roxy double – pruned of some of its V8 moments – also appeared, prompting Jon Landau's old friend, Greil Marcus, to attempt in a *New West* feature the difficult juggling act of suggesting that the show itself was a must-hear slice of rock history, but that one mustn't buy 'any of the Roxy bootlegs . . . [which] are badly mastered and pressed off-center on second-rate vinyl'. Instead, one should, 'call, write or picket KMET and get them to broadcast the show again, and then, as Springsteen has suggested, roll your own tapes'. Fans simply waited until the bootleg was re-pressed, not off-centre, and bought that. When CBS's lawyers went after Vicki and Jim, the latter was stunned, and attempted to engage with the artist in a futile attempt to get him off his back, based on a misguided idea of the co-relationship between onstage and offstage personae:

Jim Washburn: In 1975, one of our [record] swap meet customers, a Cypress schoolteacher named Lou Cohan, kept pressing Vicki to put out an album by his favourite artist, Bruce Springsteen. She wasn't interested because she didn't like Springsteen's music and few other people had even heard of him then. To get Lou off her back, she showed him how to make a boot himself, and he put out *The Jersey Devil*. [But] I was a fan by the time Springsteen played the Roxy in October that year, and was so blown away by that show that I went with friends to his subsequent show at the UC Santa Barbara gym. After the show, we hung around behind the gym and gave Springsteen a copy of Lou's boot. He seemed delighted, running up to bassist Garry Tallent with it, rasping, 'Hey, lookit this! We've been bootlegged! We've finally made it!' They then pored over the song list together . . . Throughout the course of the [1979] lawsuit, I couldn't believe that Springsteen was behind it. He must be uninformed, this guy who was going onstage and talking . . . about how lawyers shouldn't run the world. I wrote him a letter – wrapped in a rare Ronettes picture sleeve – in which I asked to meet with him, and if he still thought I'd wronged him after I explained our side, I offered to do anything I could to make it up to him. I delivered it to the desk at the Sunset Marquis in Hollywood when he was staying there, and it was promptly turned over to his attorneys, who were not terribly nice about it. Having slept on sidewalks to get Springsteen tickets and all that . . . I still couldn't believe Mr Populist Rocker had gone corporate. As the suit was winding to a close, Springsteen was again in town for a series of concerts. I spent all the money I had getting a room at the Sunset Marquis in hopes of talking to him. Which I did when he showed up poolside, and he made it clear that that's what he had lawyers for, and to leave him alone.

Actually, it was what he had Landau for. It was Landau who, after an LA court awarded Springsteen and CBS $2,150,000 in damages from Vicki and a disillusioned Washburn, gave *Rolling Stone* the requisite quote. It was a master class in how to make the argument an artistic one, while an inner voice screams, 'Where's my *fucking* money?': 'Bruce spends a year of his life conceiving and executing an album so that it will perfectly reflect the musical statement he wants to make. Then these people come along and confiscate material that was never intended for release on an album, sell it, and make a profit on it without paying anyone that's involved.'

There was, of course, no money. Vicki and Jim had already filed for bankruptcy, and anyway Vicki had already ploughed most of the profits into a series of Rolling Stones bootlegs, a band she actually cared for. Springsteen may have ducked Washburn's questions, but he couldn't duck and dive forever, and finally in 1981 he was queried about his *volte face* in attitude to bootlegs by the still zine-like *Creem*:

> **Bruce Springsteen**: I remember when I first started out, a lot of the bootlegs were made by fans, and then there was more of a connection. But it became . . . there was a point where there were just so *many* . . . that it was just big business, ya know? It was made by people who didn't care what the quality was. It just got to the point where I'd see a price tag of $30 on a record of mine that to me just sounded really bad, and I just thought it was a rip[-off]. [1981]

By then, both Landau and Springsteen had learnt the hard way that they were pissing in the wind – and would continue to be soaked just as long as the latter refused to release a live document of the E Street Band, preferably after each tour. They had just spent further futile sums, running to several thousand dollars, pursuing someone who had leaked tapes from the sessions for *Darkness*'s successor. As Gold recalls, 'Some tapes got out. They were playing the rough mixes at like 45th and Broadway. Well, we hired one of the best detectives. It was fascinating. He'd interview [all these] people. There were three or four Bruce fanatics [we suspected]. I take this guy to the Power Station – I learnt more in five minutes than I had learnt in three years [in the studio] . . . It turned out it was a 14-year-old runner, and we had to go tell his mother!' So much for Mr Big.

The premium Springsteen placed on product still played directly into bootleggers' hands. If CBS wasn't going to put out a new studio album in 1979, a bootlegger – this one safe in his European home in Camden Town – was happy to oblige. *Fire On The Fingertip* finally released studio versions of 'Hey Santa Ana', 'Zero and Blind Terry', and 'Seaside Bar Song', and Max's versions of 'Bishop Danced' and 'Thundercrack'. It might have been better called *Tip of the Iceberg*. For that is what it proved to be. Alongside *E Ticket*, an early US bootleg of 914 outtakes which was certainly 'made by fans' – helping to subsidize the first Springsteen fanzine, *Thunder Road*, where production standards far exceeded subscriber numbers – *Fire On The Fingertips* proved that Springsteen's current trouble deciding what tracks to release hardly represented an about-turn in methodology.

By the end of the decade, his indecision in the studio would seem like a full-blown pathology. Yet work on the successor to the anti-commercial *Darkness* started promisingly enough. Determined to be fully prepped before checking in at Power Station, he had been demoing songs on a small cassette-recorder for three months, first in LA, where he had been spending time post-tour getting to know Joyce, and then back in Jersey. Sometime in March 1979, he recalled the band for a series of rehearsals designed to whip the best songs he now had into shape ahead of clock-ticking, money-dripping studio time. He seemed like a man in a hurry, the same person who told Ed Sciaky the previous August, 'Because of the lawsuit, I'm a little behind. I got records I gotta make, a lot of songs I wanna get out . . . I got a lot of catching up to do.'

However, although he seemed to have plenty of song scraps, he didn't have a lot in his locker that could sit comfortably alongside the songs he'd brought to the June 1977 sessions. Of the songs he thought worthy enough to transfer to band rehearsals in mid-to-late March, 'Chain Lightning', 'Night Fire', 'The Man Who Got Away' and 'Under The Gun' all made the transition to sessions (though in 'Chain Lightning's case, not until February 1980). But only 'The Man Who Got Away' made any kind of album shortlist (and that for the aborted 1979 single LP, *The Ties That Bind*). It was time he found a new vein to call his own:

> **Bruce Springsteen**: Your inner world is a mine, and there are many, many different veins. And if you work one vein a lot, it may go dry . . . But then you may, if you turn around and your eyes are open so you can see, you may go, 'Oh, what's that over there?' Chip chip, boom, a vein of a certain

> kind of music may come bursting forth and music will pour out of you – the minute you finish a record, sometimes. [2010]

There was a strong sense that the imagery he was mining that spring had already been thoroughly excavated, and not just in the ephemeral sense of a car, a girl, on the outskirts of town. Thus, on 'Find It Where You Can', a song known only from a solo demo, the girl Bruce is urging to wise up had been addressed this way many times: 'I didn't ask for this conversation/ . . . I'm just another desperate man/ In this world you don't pick and choose, girl,/ You just find it where you can'. Billy also returns, as the whole 'world is tougher than tough' shtick gets another working over in 'Under The Gun', 'Some nights, Billy, I just lie awake/ I pull her a little closer, feel every breath she takes/ I want to go downtown and get me a gun/ You take what you're given when your living, Billy, under the gun'. The best of the new songs initially rehearsed was 'Chain Lightning', another promethean display of pyrotechnics, à la 'Fire'. This time the portents are there for all to hear: 'There's a rumble in the park, there's a thunder in the dark/ A night so quiet – chain lightning'. With a riff lifted clean off Link Wray's 'Pipeline', 'Chain Lightning' suggested his new-found love of rockabilly could have yielded real dividends – if only sessions had proceeded smoothly.

It was not until he sat down at home at the end of March 1979 to read the newspaper that he finally found a thematic starting point for *Darkness*'s successor. For the very first time, Springsteen responded to a public event by immediately writing a song with 'an appropriately paranoid lyric'. 'Roulette' was the riveting result. Directly inspired by the Three Mile Island near-nuclear meltdown on March 28 1979, the song was in the can by April 3 (a partial acoustic home demo exists, showing how quickly he formulated the song's basic components). Faster and fiercer than Dylan's 1971 response to the murder of black militant George Jackson, 'Roulette' would be the neon beacon which would light the way to Springsteen's future as a politicized singer-songwriter.

Never before had he contextualized a first-person narrative inspired by an actual event in real time. This time his narrator was 'a fireman at the reactor' who's treated like he's 'the big expendable'. His faith in the status quo disappears after he loses everything ('I got a house full of things that I can't touch'), until he defiantly roars, 'I left behind the man I used to be/

Everything he believed and all that belonged to me'. All the while the chorus demands answers from the gamesters playing Russian roulette with his life, his wife and his kids. And on this rockin', reelin' ride it is a rejuvenated Weinberg who propels the whole thing to the edge of the precipice. 'Roulette' was an E Street special and, after a year away from the studio, a much-needed reminder of their full arsenal of sound. Only in the final verse does Springsteen's imagination get the better of him, as he constructs a scenario that owes more to *Close Encounters of the Third Kind* than *The China Syndrome*.

A week later, they returned to the studio and captured a song he had been playing since November, 'The Ties That Bind'. Again, it was done in a day, 'with the band playing in a wood-panelled studio with open mikes over the drumkit to get that live resonance.' Maybe this was the way to do things. A song a week. Rehearse it, record it, release it. In *Songs*, he claims this was indeed the intent underlying said methodology: 'I knew I wanted more of the roughness and spontaneity of our live show . . . I was determined to let the band play live and let the music happen.' And in the resultant downtime he could really enjoy the company of girlfriend Joyce, while his ex-marketing manager brought by people he admired to pay their respects:

> **Dick Wingate:** Joyce was a buxom brunette, comely, very attractive. The day I went to Bruce's house with Robin Williams and his then-wife, Vicky, Joyce was there. That day was unforgettable. Robin Williams was in town recording his first album at the Copacabana. My brother introduced me to Robin in Aspen the [previous] winter. He was running a nightclub. We end up skiing together one day – a lot of blow. Now fast forward, Robin gets signed, he's recording three-four nights. I tell him what I'm doing, and he says, I would really like to meet Bruce Springsteen. I talk to Landau, and on a Sunday afternoon Barry Bell and I take Robin and his wife in a limo down to the farmhouse [in New Jersey]. We're pulling up the driveway when we see Bruce is on an [off-road tricycle] with Joyce behind him, with her arms around him, and by the time he comes up to the house, he's limping. I go, 'Are you okay?' He says, 'I'm okay.' Joyce says, 'He kinda sideswiped a tree.' [Maybe] our arrival distracted him, but he'd pinned his leg against the tree. He didn't let on that he was in a lot of pain, and we went on with the day. Robin and Bruce really hit it off, [but] Bruce

> was keeping his leg raised on the coffee table, trying to keep the swelling down, and had taken some Tylenol, or maybe just some aspirin. The day ended and we leave, and the next day Landau calls me and says, 'You know, Bruce was immediately taken to the hospital as soon as you left. He was in a lot of pain.' He just insisted he was fine. [But] he had some internal bleeding and he's [been told] to stay off his feet for [the next] ten days. He was on crutches.

Though not quite as portentous as Dylan's fabled crash fourteen years earlier, Springsteen's motorcycle accident seems to have led him to rethink his whole approach to the forthcoming sessions. And it applied the brakes after a highly promising start to proceedings. When rehearsals resumed in May, he was making Album #4 again, starting with two songs included on scribbled lists for that album but never realized: 'Bring On The Night' and the still alive 'n' kicking 'Janey Needs A Shooter'.

The former made it to Power Station, the latter did not. And yet the May 1979 rehearsal take of 'Janey' – bootlegged on the famous *Son You May Kiss The Bride* LP – remains one of the great unreleased performances of the E Street era. A seven-minute assault on the senses, Springsteen just gets more and more wound up as he ticks off the rivals to Janey's affections; doctor, priest and cop. The cop is no longer a Peeping Tom, but he still uses his badge to try and put the fear of God in the pair of lovers as he 'checks on her every night . . . outside her house his siren roars/ when he knows that I'm inside'. This time, though, the narrator-lover spits the lyrics back with a venom the singer would have been well advised to bottle for the sessions to come. He did not. In fact, before he had even got back to work, he had donated this song to another wilful singer-songwriter, Warren Zevon:

> **Warren Zevon**: During the time that Bruce was prevented from recording by a court injunction, his producer Jon Landau happened to mention to me a whole string of songs Bruce had written but couldn't record. I suddenly latched on to one of the titles mentioned, 'Jeannie Needs A Shooter' (in fact, it was Janie, but I'd misheard). I became obsessed with the line and every time I saw Springsteen . . . I asked him about it and pleaded to hear the song . . . On the one day Springsteen takes off from recording *The River* [sic], [I play] him . . . [my] interpretation of Jeannie

> and her shooter. Bruce loves the arrangement, and likes the first verse . . . [but then] realises the real reason I invited him over. [We] sit down and write the next five verses [together], unfolding a romantic saga of an outlaw pursuing a maiden whilst her father tries to gun him down. Then he played me the original [song], and it was done in completely the opposite way . . . the line wasn't important at all.

Having allowed Zevon to mangle something that fully matched 'Roulette' in intensity, Bruce resumed work at the Station on May 22, concentrating not on any of the songs band-rehearsed that week, but rather ones from dusty old notebooks, the best of which – like 'Janey Needs A Shooter' – he ended up rewriting till they changed from black to blue. By May 29 1979, 'Point Blank' had undergone wholesale lyrical revisions that provided a clearer narrative of loss and regret, but at the expense of its former, noir-ish realism: 'I dreamed I saw you standing on the porch off the house where you grew up . . . You were staring out on the highway like you were waiting for someone . . . And I'll never forget the way you looked when I walked away/ You just stood there waiting, waiting to get blown away'. A rethink was in order if the in-concert classic wasn't to suffer the same fate as 'The Promise'.

Between May 22 and June 13, Springsteen devoted large chunks of time at Power Station to 'Sherry Darling', 'Independence Day', 'I Wanna Be With You', 'Ramrod' and 'Bring On The Night', all songs he'd turned his back on in the summer of 1977. Just two new songs vied with these nostalgic nods to the album *Darkness* could have been. And, although 'Jackson Cage' and 'Be True' would both be released in *The River* era, these original versions were as distinct from their distant *River* cousins as the 1978 prototypes for 'Ties That Bind' and 'Point Blank'. This time songs were getting away from him. The honing process could no longer be relied on to stumble towards some archetypal expression. Sometimes, it just ripped out a song's guts.

'Jackson Cage' was actually the first track recorded on May 22. Originally a song of self-recrimination that demanded change from within, it was some way from the 'trapped by circumstance' lyric it became: 'You take the chances that you've got to take/ You drive hard and you stay awake/ You . . . get used to being bought and sold . . . You learn to cool your temper and collect your rage/ To use it well, down in Jackson Cage.'

'Mary Lou', a song that would become a centrepiece of *The Ties That Bind* in its 'Be True' guise, was an attempt to write both a 'really catchy three-minute pop tune', and something 'that moved lyrically, that linked together in a certain way'. To Springsteen's mind, 'this fellow . . . is trying to say, "Hey, don't sell yourself cheap." It's saying, be true to yourself in some fashion. He's talking to a woman he's interested in, but actually that's a device to address, just how do you find yourself through the falseness of some of those things.' It was a theme he would drive into the ground at these sessions. 'Mary Lou' herself would enjoy three distinct incarnations: 'Mary Lou', 'Little White Lies' and, finally, 'Be True'. Of these, the still-unreleased 'Little White Lies' is closest to that 'English-style stuff', its shameless 'Paint It Black' intro and another dynamic performance from Weinberg driving his boss to the brink of self-actualization.

Slowly, and surprisingly unsurely, Bruce was clearing the decks before unleashing the wave of songs which would send a strong current through the still-projected single LP as well as its more overblown successor, *The River*. It was June 13 before he finally got the backward-looking album he had been working on for the past two months out of his system. That was the day he ran through 'White Town', 'The Man Who Got Away', 'Night Fire' and 'Bring On The Night', songs he had expended a great deal of (cassette) tape demoing that winter.

Through the rest of 1979, he never looked back. The following day he cut 'Hungry Heart'; the day after that, 'The Price You Pay'; and when that was done to his satisfaction, he introduced 'Stolen Car'. The album, after two months spent largely down cul-de-sacs, was back on main street. He would later claim these 'wasted' sessions were all a necessary part of the process: 'It was in struggling to reconcile my previous and present recording approaches that the album found its identity.' But still he clung to the idea of a pop album, albeit one which took as a key point of reference an early seventies Cleveland combo of marginal repute:

> **Bruce Springsteen**: One of my favourite records that summer [of 1979] was *The Raspberries Greatest Hits* . . . I loved the production, and when I went into the studio [initially] a lot of things we did were like that. Two-, three-, four-minute pop songs coming one right after another . . . Steve Van Zandt was [now an important] part of the production team, and we

> finally learned how to capture the kind of dynamics, the explosiveness that we always felt on stage . . . It was the first time that we really caught some of the rawness and excitement of the live show on record. [1999]

'Hungry Heart' was one track whose pop sensibility was set in opposition to the lyrics, with the twin motifs that informed all the key songs recorded that summer – the dead-end relationship ('We took what we had and we ripped it apart') and the river of life leading straight down to death ('Like a river that don't know where it's flowing', a direct reference to The Byrds' death-ridden 'Ballad of Easy Rider'). The river motif cropped up again on 'The Price You Pay', where he tells a young single mother of how he 'could not enter the chosen land/ On the banks of the river he stayed, to face the price you pay'. If he stayed on the banks this time, he went down to the river on 'Stolen Car', the darkest song of his career to date and one which would ultimately lead on to its sister-song, 'The River':

> **Bruce Springsteen**: ['Stolen Car'] was concerned with those [relationship] ideas for the first time: that if you don't connect yourself with your family and to the world, you feel like you're disappearing, fading away. I felt like that for a very, very long time. Growing up, I felt invisible. And that feeling is an enormous source of pain for people. [1999]

'Stolen Car' was another of those songs, like 'Hungry Heart', that he wrote 'in a half hour, or ten minutes, real fast'. In fact, it may have begun as a continuation of that song, initially adopting the self-same phrase to explain why things fell to bits: 'We got married and promised never to part/ Then I fell a victim to a hungry heart'. But this time he took it all *to* heart. In its original guise, 'Stolen Car' was a 'ghost story' told by a spirit in the night, as a spoken intro at the New York December 18 1980 show made abundantly clear, 'Some people make that connection and some people don´t, you know . . . and when you don´t, it´s like you end up like a ghost, it´s like . . . nobody sees you or nobody can feel you. [So] this is a ghost story, this song.'

He even describes the revenant's end: 'There's a river that runs by that little town down into the sea/ It was there in the shade I laid my body down, as she flowed by so effortlessly'. In other words he surrenders to the river, much like the boy in the Flannery O'Connor short story of the same name – which Springsteen had evidently already read, though it would be some years before she got namechecked: 'He intended . . . to Baptize himself and to keep on going this time until he found the Kingdom of Christ in the river. He didn't mean to waste any more time. He put his head under the water at once and pushed forward . . . He plunged under once [more] and this time, the waiting current caught him like a long gentle hand and pulled him swiftly forward and down . . . All his fury and his fear left him.'

The ghost in *this* stolen car is a close cousin of the spirit Robert Johnson invoked at the end of 'Me and the Devil Blues': 'You may bury my body down by the highway side/ So my old evil spirit can catch a Greyhound bus and ride'. It also consciously evoked the classic 'I dreamed a dream' motif of many an Anglo-American ballad for its haunting coda:

> Last night I dreamed I made the call
> I promised to come home forever more
> Once again we stood on the wedding steps at Victory Hall
> And walked arm in arm through the chapel door
> I remember how good I felt inside
> When the preacher said 'Son, you may kiss the bride'.

He knew he had pulled off something special; and wisely took time out to re-evaluate the album's direction. In the next three weeks there would be just two sessions and one finished song (the uncirculated 'Time That Never Was'). But when work resumed in earnest on July 11, with a retake of the newly-composed 'I Wanna Marry You', he had decided his new collection would be a relationship record. And 'I Wanna Marry You', one of his least convincing songs, was to provide a necessary counterbalance to the again-encroaching darkness. Indeed, for a period in 1979 Springsteen seemed very much in love with the *idea* of marriage, while continuing to shy away from the reality (as Joyce was learning), something he admitted only after he found, late in life, a marriage that worked:

> **Bruce Springsteen**: [Marriage] is very different than just living together. First of all, stepping up publicly – which is what you do: you get your licence, you do all the social rituals – is a part of your place in society and in some way of society's acceptance of you. [1997]

Everywhere he looked, friends and family were settling down and he wondered what he was missing out on. As he told a Boston audience, there was one particular speech at his lighting man Mark Brickman's wedding that really got to him: 'The rabbi got up and he started to talk about how [as] long as you're alone, that your dreams, they just remain dreams. It ain't until you reach out . . . [and] you take a chance with somebody . . . that [you take] the first step to making all the things that you're dreaming about a reality.' 'I Wanna Marry You' idealized that very idea: 'A time comes when two people should think of these things/ Having a home and a family/ Facing up to their responsibilities.' But the feeling didn't last and he was soon back at the river's edge:

> **Bruce Springsteen**: I'm in the dark as far as all that [relationship] stuff goes. It took me five albums to even write about it . . . On [this] album the characters are wrestling with those questions – the guy in 'Stolen Car', the guy in 'Wreck On The Highway', 'Drive All Night', the guy in 'Sherry Darling' even. It is a puzzle and a question . . . Everybody seems to hunger for that relationship. [1981]

The songs he completed in the immediate aftermath of 'I Wanna Marry You' rather suggested this was a hunger which slowly ate away at one. In 'Cindy', Springsteen once again portrayed himself as the fool for love, out of his depth, drowning in desire: 'In this world there ain't another like you/ My little candy girl, so hard-hearted and cruel'. At the very same time, the equally terrific 'Loose Ends' laid bare the dreams of some little candy girl on the shore longing to settle down, leaving the narrator literally at the end of his tether: 'It's like we had a noose, and baby without check/ We pulled until it grew tighter around our necks'. He was writing the kinda pop songs that came from the edge of oblivion. And when 'Mary Lou' became 'Be True', he had all but completed the set. Yet it was August 26 before he completed the song needed to round everything out, and it was one inspired by Hank Williams' deliciously mordant 'Long Gone Lonesome Blues':

> **Bruce Springsteen**: 'The River' took a while. I had the verses, I never had any chorus, and I didn't have no title for a long time . . . I had these verses, and I was fooling around with the music. What gave me the idea for the

> title was a Hank Williams song . . . where he goes down to the river to jump in and kill himself, and he can't because it dried up. [1981]

He had certainly taken his time getting to the river's edge. Back in March he had demoed its prototype, 'Oh Angelyne'. Addressing the same failing marriage as 'The River', it was set against the backdrop of a failing economy ('The Man don't need me, so goodbye'), but its burden suggested a possible way out: 'Oh Angelyne, I run to you, I'm running to you . . . you walk the line'. Melodically distinct, 'Oh Angelyne' was a whine before its time. Only in August 1979, when Springsteen gave it another kick-start, did he know where the story needed to lead – 'down to the river'. Initially, this river served as a reminder of good times ('At night on them banks I'd lie awake / And pull her close just to feel each breath she'd take'), but in the end it reminded him of everything he had lost. He heads there again to drown himself, but 'the river is dry'. Even that redemptive baptism has been denied him.

He cut the song in a single session, witnessed by photographer Joel Bernstein who had been shooting Bruce and the band (along with Landau, at Springsteen's insistence) outside Power Station, after informing Landau he thought *Darkness* was a great album but a terrible cover. Given his Neil Young and Joni Mitchell cover credits, Landau knew enough to take him seriously; and after the shoot invited him to the session which began with Springsteen teaching the band 'The River', before they ran through different arrangements. By two a.m., they had the finished song. Bernstein was impressed. So was Springsteen when he saw the contact sheets of the photo-shoot, inviting Bernstein, an accomplished musician in his own right, to spend a few days at his house when the snapper returned to shoot the 'No Nukes' benefits in September.

Bernstein found Springsteen wrestling with the sequence to another album he had invested heart and soul in; a process he had already experienced first-hand with Neil Young. Even before he had written 'The River', Springsteen had constructed a sequence for *The Ties That Bind*, which ran as follows:

> **Side 1**: The Ties That Bind. The Price You Pay. Be True. Ricky Wants A Man of Her Own. Stolen Car.
> **Side 2**: I Want To Marry You. Loose Ends. Hungry Heart. The Man Who Got Away. Ramrod.

But by the time Bernstein arrived, the second week in September, 'Ricky Wants A Man Of Her Own' and 'The Man Who Got Away' had been replaced by 'Cindy' and 'The River'. When Bruce played Bernstein the nine-track album, ending with 'Ramrod' – 'to inform what I was going to shoot' – it was clear 'it wasn't finished'. Nonetheless, Bernstein came away with 'a copy of [that] single album of songs: I [always] preferred it to the released album.' He thus became the first recipient of the legendary *Ties That Bind* LP.

Yet barely had Bernstein returned west before Springsteen pulled 'Ramrod', restored 'Loose Ends' and resurrected the rockabilly 'You Can Look (But You Better Not Touch)'. The result was another 'flawed masterpiece'; one that still shone a light on 'Hungry Heart' and 'I Wanna Marry You' at the expense of 'Roulette' and 'Independence Day'. But even with these lightweight tracks, it developed on *Darkness* without allowing itself to be enveloped by the bleak nightscape. Embracing a gamut of genres from rockabilly ('You Can Look') to prototypical alt-country ('The Price You Pay'), it returned the E Street Band to stage centre, and gave AM stations hooks to hang their programming on. After spending almost a month at the outset reworking songs from 'Album #4', not a single track composed before September 1978 had made it to *The Ties That Bind*. He had moved on. But barely had he delivered the finished album the first week in October than he was sticking his shiny new car in reverse:

> **Bruce Springsteen**: After some recording we prepared a single album and handed it to the record company. When I listened to it later on, I felt that it just wasn't good enough. The songs lacked the kind of unity and conceptual intensity I liked my music to have . . . / . . . It wasn't expansive enough – that was when we decided to go to the two records . . . I wanted a record that balanced the two things that I was doing [at that time], that had a sense of continuity coming out of *Darkness*. [1998/1999]

He was still looking for a bridge that could span Albums #4 and #6. Landau, like the band, was in despair, but knew he'd be wasting his breath trying to change Springsteen's mind. Instead, he found a most unlikely ear to bend. During the fall, for the first time since the lawsuit, he (and Bruce) met up with Mike Appel. They had decided the sums on the latest CBS statement/s simply did not add up and had demanded an audit of their accounts, to which Appel as an interested party and potential beneficiary was invited. Whilst there, Landau confided in Appel, 'Mike, I almost had it. We finished, we had this record done, I walked it in. And [then] Bruce gave me a call and said, "I'm not sure about this and that."' Appel pithily responded, 'Rather you than me, Jon.'

After *The River* ultimately emerged, Springsteen told Robert Hilburn he made his decision not because the original single album wasn't good enough – something Hilburn couldn't have challenged – but rather because 'it wasn't *personal* enough'. Whereas he told Dave Marsh it was scrapped because 'the exuberance of the audience at MUSE had just made the album seem inadequate', a reference to the two shows he gave at Madison Square Garden on September 21-22 to raise awareness of the dangers of nuclear energy – the so-called 'No Nukes' concerts. If the sell-out audiences seemed pleased to see him, and even responded well to the live debut of 'The River', it was not their energy and appreciation but his own mortality that seemed to weigh most on his mind.

On night two, his thirtieth birthday, he again showed that displays of petulance were his default response to anyone who openly defied his *diktats*: in this case an instruction to his ex-paramour Lynn Goldsmith that she not take photos at an event to which she had a photo-pass, and at which he was merely one of a number of headliners. When she continued to snap away even after he gave her 'the look', he dragged her up on stage and publicly humiliated her – and, as it turned out, himself. He then attempted to turn the blame on her, telling the ever-receptive *Rolling Stone*: 'She was doing something she said she wouldn't do. I tried to handle it in other ways, but she avoided them. So I had to do it myself,' thus showing a man who, even in the cold light of day, was incapable of seeing when he was the one blundering in the dark; or who was the likelier to end up shot dead 'on a sunny Florida road . . . [because] she couldn't stand the way he drove', to quote his latest song, 'From Small Things, Big Things One Day Come'.

He remained as far away as ever from making 'the greatest rock 'n' roll record ever made'. So when the EQ'd master of *The Ties That Bind* – the one that turned up at a Pasadena swap-meet in the early nineties, where it was snapped up for $200 – came back from the studio on October 4, Bruce exercised his veto. He decided, mid-life crisis or not, he would return to Power Station and immerse himself in the process all over again. And maybe, this time, he could make a record that would encompass all that the world might allow:

> **Bruce Springsteen**: When I didn't put the album out in 1979 it was because I didn't feel that that [sense of conflicting emotions] was *there*. [In the end,] I felt . . . I just got a bigger picture of what things *are*, of the way things work . . . I wanted that *all* on there. [1981]

Having got over the disappointment of another aborted album, Landau took Bruce's change of mind on the chin, determined to convince himself that Springsteen's 'fear of completion' was not some full-blown pathology; it just reflected someone for whom a perfect plan tomorrow was always better than a good plan today. Perhaps the erudite manager could again help the autodidact Springsteen realize his goal. He informed Nick Kent in 1981 that at this point he gave his friend a play he thought might show him how it was possible to include all things in heaven and on earth in a popular piece of entertainment. No longer was he content to let his charge be the new Dylan. Maybe he could be the new Shakespeare:

> **Jon Landau**: Bruce reached the point where he'd amassed something like forty songs [for *The River*] and was still intent on crafting a single album out of some incredibly diverse musical areas. It became evident to me the only way it could be best resolved for Bruce's artistic benefit was to make the project a double-album package. Initially, he still couldn't quite see it work, he couldn't see a logical sequence in there. So I gave him a copy of *Hamlet*, simply informing Bruce that though the play was a tragedy there was still something quite humorous in a sense, though not light-hearted, on every other page. I think that helped him to open up the overall concept.

A pattern emergeth, methinks. The result would be a lot closer to a comedy of errors than all's well that ends well, the narrator falling between two stools, neither of them solid enough to stand the strain. That outcome, though, was six months and another hundred thousand in studio bills away.

Chapter 7: 1980–81 – Take Me To The River

> I gained a certain freedom, in making the two-record set, because I could let all those people out that usually I'd put away. Most of the time, they'd end up being my favourite songs, and probably some of my best songs, you know . . . I'm the kind of person, I think a lot about everything. Nothing I can do about it. – Bruce Springsteen, 1981

> Bruce had a lot of songs. And he kept doing and doing it . . . But not one song on *The River* matches *Darkness*. He thought too much. He tortured himself thinking about [it]. I think it got to him . . . [But] Bruce thought too much about everything – about writing, about what the critics said, about *everything*! – Debbie Gold

The decision not to release *The Ties That Bind* as-is was nothing new. The one to make a double album was. Initially, he may simply have intended to reconfigure the album (again) to achieve that chimerical 'balance' he was searching for. Four days of sessions the week after the master was made, saw him working again on 'Independence Day' and three new tracks, all of which were in the pop vein: 'Crush On You', 'Where The Bands Are' (which did at least explicate what he was looking for: 'I want something that'll break my chains/ Something to break my heart/ Something to shake my brains') and 'Party Lights' (in which the partner of a girl who married at fifteen sits at home wondering, 'Do you miss the party lights?'). Perhaps he still thought he could find a slot for one of his most important songs if he counter-balanced it with a pastiche Clash or Knack B-side. After all, the album to date was only thirty-nine minutes, and when he told Hilburn in 1980 he scrapped an album the previous September, he suggested it contained *thirteen* songs.*

But if that was the new plan, it didn't last long. Seven weeks later he was back at Power Station, now firmly set on stockpiling more songs. The December sessions – also lasting four days – produced one untitled effort; three with nomenclatures but no fixed abode – 'Dedication', 'Living On The Edge of The World' and 'I'm A Rocker' – and one that was the real deal, 'Take 'Em As They Come'. This rousing call to face down the future was all very affirmative on the surface, but once again it was the singer's way of breaking it to some gal it's over ('All the promises we made/ Lie shattered and broken in the morning light'). At least he was now pastiching New Wave *A*-sides. However, two months down the line, a single worthy addition to *The Ties That Bind* was hardly cause for celebration for either his co-producers or accountant.

It was almost as if he had come to revel in the legend that had formed around his studio excursions, brazenly boasting the following year: 'I stopped feeling bad about . . . spending a long time in the studio . . . I said [to myself], That's me, that's what I do. I work slow, and I work slow for a reason: To get the results that I want.' (The anonymous employee who said of Landau and Bruce, 'Put them in a studio, and they're like two kids in a sandpit', probably came closer to the truth.) His ex-marketing manager Dick Wingate, who came by one day, found plentiful evidence of that pathology: 'I had been at the Record Plant and I had an idea of how many boxes of tape there were [for *Darkness*]; and there were even more boxes for *The River* . . . At one time, one of the tape ops took me in the back room and showed me this mountain of 2" Springsteen tapes. It was literally a mountain.'

Wingate himself had a new act to push, an English band, one of Bruce's favourites. And they had just finished a double album that was already drawing comparisons with *Exile On Main Street*. In mid-November The Clash had finally delivered to a flustered CBS the ultimate twofer, *London Calling*, not in time to make a 1979 US release, but in time to give the import shops of New York a much-needed Christmas present. One suspects that Springsteen, if he did not prise an advance pressing out of Columbia, was one of their first customers. In the New Year, he would set about making his very own *New Jersey Calling*. Again, The Clash had shown him it didn't have to be this

* David Gahr was still taking shots for an album cover on October 16, suggesting a release was still on the cards.

way. In a year when they managed two non-album singles and two U.S. tours, they had found time to cut a double album that retained all the angular attack of punk but gave those amphetamine-rushes a welcome respite.

Springsteen had a message as unpalatable as that of The Clash, but he wanted it wrapped in the audio equivalent of a neat ribbon bow. His own confused state of mind was duly reflected in the music he was now making. As he told *Rolling Stone* in 1987, when everything he had built in the past decade was beginning to crumble and fall, 'From *Darkness* to *The River*, I was attempting to pull myself into what I felt was going to be the adult world, so that when things became disorienting, I would be strong enough to hold my ground. Those were the records where I was trying to forge the foundation and maintain my connections.' But no matter how hard he tried, things still failed to add up and he didn't know why:

> **Bruce Springsteen**: On [*The River*] I just said, 'I don't understand all these things . . . I don't see how all these things can work together.' . . . It was just a situation of living with all those contradictions. And that's what happens. There's never any resolution. You have moments of clarity . . . but there's never any . . . longstanding peace of mind. [1981]

Contradictions abound in the material he was writing. He liked the idea of marriage, but every song he wrote about such folk ended in recrimination, divorce and/or suicide. He wrote longingly about home and the family, but had no proclivity to embrace either. He saw rock as an affirmative, life-enhancing form but all the best songs he had written in the past year were replete with negativity and faithlessness. He wanted to make music that was as commercial as a TV message, but real as a rifle-shot.

And on top of all this he really wanted to get onto record 'the need for community . . . which is what "Out In The Streets" [is] about. Songs like "The Ties That Bind" and "Two Hearts" deal with that, too. But there's also the other side, the need to be alone.' It was 'the need to be alone' which had driven him thus far and provided an impressive private soundtrack; whereas songs of 'community' were not his forte – and never had been. 'The Ties That Bind', good as it was, had been a better song when it was about escape. Whereas 'Out In The Streets' and 'Two Hearts' – two songs written that winter – were greeting-card standard. (In the former's case, he took a perfectly decent rocker, 'I'm Gonna Be There Tonight', and made it about someone who worked 'five days a week . . . loading crates down on the dock' – an experience as divorced from his own life as that of a Thai hooker.)

He was increasingly inclined to idealize the people he grew up around – the self-same folk he once disparaged in interview and lyrics as narrow-minded and uptight. It was like he could no longer delineate the co-relationship between good and bad, hope and despair (themes which imbue everything Flannery O'Connor wrote, and which – with her help – he would locate again). What began as a laudable attempt to write about 'people trying to do that deal with their friends, their lovers and their jobs, trying not to let life drag them down', had become instead an explicit romanticization of the lives of friends and family, obviating 'the need to be alone' as the prime subject-matter for the songs:

> **Bruce Springsteen**: To me, the type of things that people do which make their lives heroic are a lot of times very small, little things. Little things that happen in the kitchen, or between a husband and wife . . . There's plenty of room for those types of victories, and I think the [recent] records have that. [1984]

Where there was a narrator to such 'songs of community', he resembled Springsteen's father refracted through the eyes of an all-seeing son. Yet his real father had moved 3,000 miles away from the godforsaken place Springsteen continued to call home; which in 1984 he admitted was an attempt on his part, 'to maintain connections with the people I'd grown up with, and the sense of the community where I came from. That's why I stayed in New Jersey. The danger of fame is in forgetting or being distracted.' In reality, he remained rootless; a contradiction not always lost on him:

> **Bruce Springsteen**: All my houses seem to have been way stations. That's the kind of person I have been, you know? I don't like feeling too rooted for some reason. Which is funny, because the things that I admire and the things that mean a lot to me all have to do with roots and home. [1984]

The very fact that he continued to rent rather than buy a place rather suggested he still felt like a rolling stone (by now he knew the next line in the Hank Williams song Dylan stole the image from was, 'All alone and lost'). He informed Michael Watts the following spring how he disliked 'dragging too much stuff around. I guess that's . . . why I've avoided buying a house: things just clutter up your life.' He was equally frank to a *Rolling Stone* reporter: 'I don't like to sit at home. I spent years sitting at home. And my family's not there anymore . . . No reason to go home.' If home was where the heart was, it was where the band was (though this may be a sentiment he had yet to share with Joyce).

Having being 'very distant from my family for quite a while in my early twenties', he finally turned the authority-figure with whom he had spent his entire youth locking horns into the hero of a thousand songs. The trait father and son had most in common was that neither was ever 'a big verbalizer' (to use Bruce's own term). Which is why the son spoke to him through his songs. Though he ultimately realized, 'It's probably not the best way to find your way through the woods on those sorts of things, it was part of the way it happened for me and him.' Even in some songs that did not directly address Doug, there was a sense that it was him who was narrating. 'The River', for one. Meanwhile, the raps which prefaced the desultory 'Factory' on *The River* tour would achieve what earlier songs singularly failed to do, they made Doug a sympathetic figure:

> 'My father quit high school when he was 16 years old and the war was on, he went into the army . . . when he'd go to apply for something, they'd tell him the only thing he was qualified for was factory work . . . it wasn't until I got to be about 28 or 29, I started to think . . . 'bout what my folks did with their lives and the dreams that they gave up . . . When I was 16, I couldn't figure out that what my old man was doing, laying on the cold ground at six in the morning, trying to get one of the junk cars to start so he could get to work . . . that he was doing that for me.'

This new-found empathy at least allowed Springsteen to retain his connection to 'Independence Day', the one 1977 composition he didn't do a disservice to in rerecording it for *The River*. He was still putting finishing touches to it in late April 1980, two years and eight months after they first recorded it. (The April 25 tape-box reads 'Take 53'.) At least he wisely resisted rewriting this lyric, though this was not the case with 'Point Blank', which he also returned to that spring, determined to put it right.

He later told Dave Marsh the latter was one of those songs that, 'right up until the very last two weeks, when I rewrote the last two verses . . . didn't exist in the form [it is] on the record'.

At least the song again emulated its 1978 arrangement; as did two more songs from the Atlantic locker he reintroduced to the band at the February 1980 sessions, 'Sherry Darling' and 'Drive All Night'. He had seemingly revived his original plan to make the new record a composite of Albums #4 and #6 ('Ramrod' had already been earmarked for duty). Whether this was because by late February it was plain to him that the new songs he'd written and recorded over the past four months were simply not up to scratch, or because he no longer wrote songs with the same maudlin magnitude as 'Drive All Night', 'Independence Day' and 'Point Blank', he wasn't about to say.

What was certain was that after a promising restart to proceedings in the New Year, things had stalled badly in the past few weeks. The first night back, January 14, they had roared through the best song he had penned since 'The River', 'Restless Nights', and even found time to lay down a terrific cover version of the Cajun classic 'Jole Blon' (to which Gary US Bonds would overdub vocals for his own E Street Band LP, *Dedication*). 'Restless Nights' saw Bruce once again railing at those who think life's a movie, pouring hot verbal oil down on those poor deluded fools locked to 'late-night movie screens [where] young lovers look so sure / Lost in wide-wake dreams that they can't afford'.

But if the finished studio take was another powerful reminder of what made this band tick, it paled in comparison with some of the versions the sextet summoned up on Telegraph Hill three or four days earlier. In that rehearsal space, the song on a number of occasions genuinely entered 'Prove It All Night' territory (and length). Barely contained by the band's undoubted instrumental prowess, it found enough oxygen in that rehearsal room to explode into life. At Power Station, though, Springsteen stuck to his remit – even though containing the whole wide world in three/four-minute pop songs actually meant stopping the band from doing what it did best, stretching the parameters of the American pop song. The rehearsal 'Restless Nights' also confirmed that the earlier version of 'Janey Needs A Shooter' was no fluke, and that the recording equipment should have caught them in rehearsal not record mode if it wanted to capture the 'true' Bruce Springsteen *and* the E Street Band.

Through January and February, this would become their routine. A day or two rehearsing a new song or arrangement. Then (if lucky) into the studio to capture the moment after the fact. Rehearsed the same day as 'Restless Nights' was a fastish, countrabilly arrangement of a new song, 'Wreck On The Highway', that sounded real interesting. But in the three more months it would take him to haul this song's raggedy ass into the studio, it became a near-cataleptic coda to 'Drive All Night'. (On its release, he had the gall to claim it was an example of 'an automatic song . . . that you don't really think about or work on'.)

In some cases, even the drive to the studio rendered a song unrecognisable. In the case of 'Stolen Car', rehearsed five days after 'Restless Nights', Springsteen committed an act of self-sabotage, removing the ghost from his own song, as well as its 'dreamed a dream' reverie, giving it a whole new arrangement to ensure it fit the same notch as other 'downers' he was accumulating. Nor was it the only once-handsome song recorded the previous year given an unnecessary facelift. 'Jackson Cage' was also prepared for a second tour of duty, in the process losing the couplet, 'There is something I must say/ That you've been left to fade away' to another new song, before becoming another case of rattling the Jersey cage.

If some of the latent energy of 'Jackson Cage' still carried over to Power Station, the other song rehearsed the same day, the strident 'Slow Fade', really did fade away. He seemed to have lost the invaluable gift of knowing when to leave something well alone and when to persevere. A promising idea for a song demoed the previous fall, called either 'Mr Outside' or 'Looking After Number One', was recorded mid-March in ersatz reggae form as 'Down In White Town'. By then, he had introduced a helpless dancer from another torch ballad, who 'disappears like the scenery in another man's play/ [Though] at night she dances, oh, to the beat'. The greedy Mr Outside is about to find out, 'Your money and your power . . . won't help you come The Hour/When your kingdom falls to your feet, and you're left like any other thief out on the street'. From somewhere deep in his subconscious he had dredged up this classically Christian conception of the End Times, proving once again that you can take the boy out of the Catholic church, but you can't take the church out of the boy.

'White Town' was at least a welcome thematic departure. But too many of the other songs trod over-familiar ground, swapping lines at will. 'Chevrolet Deluxe' – another song he demoed, rehearsed and then abandoned – not only told us the name of the 'stolen car', but shared its opening scenario: 'I had a wife and kid, and I tried to settle down/ I just wanted to live an honest life on the edge of an honest town/ But in the end they left me dangling in the night'. 'Stockton Boys' revisited 'Come On (Let's Go Tonight)', describing working men who like 'acting tough, making noise/ Man, they just want to get wrecked'. One couplet would make it to record, just not until 1984: 'They wear it in their eyes, they wear it on their shirts/ They come down here looking to get hurt'.

It was only when he took time out to write consciously lightweight material that he rediscovered his gift for combining the deft phrase and the right hook. Thus, on 'Dedication', a song he recorded in December 1979 before donating it to Gary US Bonds, he gave a new slant to the canonical account of the Great Flood, his first humorous reinterpretation of the Book of Genesis, but not his last: 'Well, way back in the Bible time/ A cat named Noah built an ocean liner/ Everybody laughed when they told him why/ But when the rain came, Noah was high and dry'.

The best love song he wrote that winter, 'Your Love', was also given to Bonds, who was keen to play to the E Street Band's strengths. The highlight of his wrought rendition would be that crushing crescendo as realization dawns on the poor misguided fool who has seen 'something new in her eyes' – just as Bonds' voice drops to a despairing whisper, 'Lately you been walking the streets at night/ Like an empty shadow in the morning light'. Another minor classic the bossman gave away.

And yet when Springsteen wrote similar songs for himself, the results put the self in self-conscious. This was perhaps because, as he told *NME* the following June, 'I didn't want to neglect the rock & roll songs, so we put them all on, as well as the slower stuff . . . [But] I don't want to make records like the Fifties or Sixties. There's always got to be some Eighties in there, too.' Some of the results gave Pastiche a bad name. And the worst of the lot was 'Cadillac Ranch'. After six sessions working on this rust-bucket, one wonders how he kept a straight face when singing lines like, 'Hey little girlie, in the blue jeans so tight/ Drivin' alone through the Wisconsin night/ You're my last love baby, you're my last chance/ Don't let 'em take me to the Cadillac Ranch'. If there was ever a Sprucesong that deserved to go straight to the scrapheap, this was it.

Instead, it went straight on the album, which by the middle of April was definitely a double. The shortlist still included 'Cindy', 'Ricki Wants A

Man Of Her Own' – a song recorded in July 1979 that reflected a brother's alarm at the changes in a fast-maturing sister ('She don't care to bring her boyfriends home to pass daddy's inspection') – 'Held Up Without A Gun', 'Be True', 'Restless Nights' and a still-unreleased song called 'Stray Bullet', which he'd been working on since February. But Springsteen would take a degree of flak for omitting 'Roulette', claiming that he 'just didn't like the way it sounded . . . We might redo it and put it out later.' By 1999 he admitted, 'I may have just gotten afraid . . . In truth it should have probably gotten put on. It would have been one of the best things on the record.' So what exactly was his problem?

> **Bruce Springsteen**: I did a lot of rewriting [back then] . . . At the time I was trying to shape who I was and what I wanted to be about, and what I wanted to write about, and how I wanted the world to see me, and how I wanted to see myself. And also, the kind of writing I was interested in doing, which was using very classic rock & roll archetypes – cars, girls, Saturday night, the job, the end of the day . . . you're either going to turn them into . . . archetypes or clichés. And I did a lot of shaving away to [hopefully] turn them into something more than that . . . Those were the days I'd second-guess, third-guess, fourth-guess, fifth-guess and sixth-guess myself constantly, until I got exhausted, and then finally decide[d] on something and put it out. [2010]

By the end of April he had narrowed things down to twenty-two tracks, but he was still some way off done. As he said at the time of *Tracks*, 'It's never over until it's over. Everybody's telling you you're done and you take it home and it's just not right . . . [But] my life at the time [of *The River*] was extremely focused, probably to the detriment of the records.' He even tinkered with songs carried over from *The Ties That Bind*, starting with 'The River'. Not content with take five from the original August 26 session, he assembled seventeen imperceptibly different mixes of a near-identical retake and played them to CBS A&R man Peter Philbin, asking him which one was better, 'Which one is *better*??! Hey, flip a coin!' He was asking the wrong guy. He should have been talking to Plotkin. As one go-between put it, 'He was the one guy who could talk for an hour about the difference between mix twenty-seven and mix forty-two'. But others experienced the same OCD behaviour. In Springsteen's mind, he was focused on just one thing, the prize:

> **Bruce Springsteen**: In the studio, I'm conceptual. I have a self-consciousness . . . I often would try to stop that . . . [But] it's not a question of how you actually do it. The idea is to sound spontaneous, not *be* spontaneous . . . From the beginning I had an idea of what I felt the record should be . . . We started to work and I had a certain idea at the beginning. And at the end, that was the idea that came out on the record. It took a very long time, all the colouring and stuff, there was a lot of decisions [to make] . . . Right up until the very last two weeks, when I rewrote . . . 'Point Blank' – 'Drive All Night' was done just the week before that – those songs didn't exist in the form that they're on the record . . . I threw ['Ramrod'] ten million times off the record. Ten million times. I threw it off *Darkness*, and I threw it off this one, too . . . We [tend to] get into that little bit of a cycle. [1981]

Not surprisingly, elements of the music-media wanted to know what the hell was going on. His churlish response was, 'Spontaneity . . . is not made by fastness. Elvis, I believe, did like thirty takes of "Hound Dog".' (In fact, Presley recorded that song *plus* 'Don't Be Cruel' and 'Any Way You Want Me' in just two three-hour sessions.) But no matter how often he reiterated the mantra, 'You make your record like it's the last record you'll ever make,' every rock band since The Who knew if it took more than a month, they were doing something wrong. A Wayne King cover story in Anglophile music monthly *Trouser Press* that summer was among the first to seriously question whether the man still finishing up his fifth release in seven and a half years would be the same person who left the stage at Cleveland's Coliseum on New Year's Day 1979:

> 'In mid-April he took off to LA to mix the record; at press time he was still plugging away at it. Bruce Springsteen's history has shown that his greatest talent, a rock intuition second to none, is often at odds with a relentless sense of perfection. After *Darkness* he told a Boston newspaper that he was past the obsessively self-critical stage: "No more, hey, is this perfect? Just let me do it." Yet the time spent making his fifth record proves that idea wrong. All of rock's greats reach a point where they spend more time off the road than on, entrenched in the recording studio. Self-indulgent staleness sets in when live work is not interspersed meaningfully, enabling the artist to test out material live. Creating rock and then playing it to an audience has proven to be dangerous to creativity and communication.'

The dangers King outlined were all too real. Joel Bernstein ran into Bruce again at the Sunset Marquis that spring. Invited up to his poolside apartment, Bernstein found him there with a ghetto blaster and a bag full of tapes, one song per, flipping the cassettes in and out, supposedly sequencing *The River* ('I think he was doing it for weeks'). But if Springsteen was having a hard time making up his own mind, he also now had a number of other cooks who suggested he use *their* recipe.

The artist still took on board the opinions of Landau, as the person who 'listens on the most gut level, and simultaneously will look at the record and see what it's saying'; even if Landau had a protagonist with equal clout to contend with this time – Van Zandt. Landau later suggested, 'The album where Steve's influence was strongest was *The River*. [But] if Steve had had his way, there would have been only rockers on that album.' 'Restless Nights' for one, a song which Springsteen described on its live debut in November 2009 as 'Stevie's very favourite song of all time'. (At the end of a creditable stab at this forgotten classic, a mildly chastened singer pointed at his friend and said, 'Dammit, he might have been right all these years!') Springsteen would suggest in *Songs* it was he and Stevie who, in tandem, 'began to steer the recording of *The River* in a rawer direction.'

If so, any such rawness was lost in the transfer to vinyl. The record as released was his most thin sonic outing to date, sounding like something played on a Dansette even when put through a $1000 hi-fi. It sure as highwater didn't sound like another album made at Power Station that spring, the second long-playin' instalment by the duo who originally coined the term punk rock (in 1971!), before disassembling the boundary between performance art and rock: Alan Vega and Martin Rev, aka Suicide. If Springsteen seemed a most unlikely disciple, the Suicide effect would not become fully apparent until the next notch on his CBS contract:

> **Alan Vega:** Power Station was run by this engineer who [had] worked for us on the first Suicide album [at 914], Craig Leon. He didn't know what to make of Suicide, so he quit in the middle of it. The irony of it is, we [ended up] using Bruce's equipment. So we go to Power Station, and who's there, [Leon]. He hears Suicide are coming in and freaked out, 'I quit. I can't fucking stand [them]!' . . . [But] everybody wanted to

> be around Bruce. Bruce came by and he heard the first Suicide record, and thought, 'Holy shit!' And he started hanging out with me . . . We spent a lot of time in the men's room [smoking and drinking]. That culminated in the last day, [when] we played the entire thing [for the label]. Marty and I down the front. We didn't hear Bruce come in. Played the whole album and after the album was over, total silence. And out of nowhere, a voice, 'That was fucking great, man!' It was worth everything to hear that.

The voice's own offering was not so 'fucking great', but as he observed in 2010, 'Those were the days I'd second-guess . . . myself constantly, until I got [so] exhausted . . . [I] put it out.' What he left in the Station vault, as he duly admitted, was 'an entire album . . . "Restless Nights", "Roulette", "Dollhouse", "Where The Bands Are", "Loose Ends", "Living On The Edge of the World", "Take 'Em As They Come", "Be True", "Ricky Wants A Man", "I Wanna Be With You", "Mary Lou" – [that was] all three-minute, four-minute pop songs.' This didn't even take account of the irreparable harm done to certain songs during the process of 'second guessing'; or those that failed to make the transition from rehearsal room to recording studio. If it didn't take him too long to realize that the likes of 'Be True' and 'Roulette', 'would have been better than a couple other things that we threw on there', now was not the time to look back. The cupboard was bare. The process had not only worn away at his nerves, it had inexorably drained his not-so-plentiful bank account:

> **Bruce Springsteen**: In 1980 when we went to go on *The River* tour, I was just broke. After almost ten years in the music business I had about twenty grand to my name . . . I had gotten into a lot of trouble and made some bad deals and had to hire a lot of lawyers. And then nobody in the band had ever paid any taxes . . . So we got chased after for an enormous amount of back taxes . . . So between 1974 and 1980, I paid lawyers, the tax man, tried to keep the band afloat (which I barely could), and spent money in the recording studio. [2010]

For all his rhetoric about entering the adult world, he continued to disdain the very idea of keeping an eye on business. As he would inform *Uncut*, 'There was a lot of things I hated doing, business things . . . I wasn't even terrible at it, I just couldn't have cared less. I just wanted to be able to do what I wanted to do . . . I had a long period of time when I was pretty estranged from [the business side], and [Landau] kept the boat afloat.' He did so even in areas where they hardly needed a full-time crew. Like publicizing the fact that Bruce had taken two years to make a record, and in that time had done two gigs, and no interviews. Fortunately for all concerned, Debbie Gold had had enough: 'I was bored to death. I had an assistant. And this great office. And nothing to do.'

Her replacement was close at hand and a lot less ambitious; the wife of Dave Marsh, Barbara Carr. As Gold says, 'He found the right person. Who was never gonna move, who just wanted that power. I didn't have any interest in that. And it was time for me to go.' Meanwhile, Landau finally prevailed on Bruce to drop all this nonsense about theatres and agree to a full-blown US arena tour. Recalling their conversations on this topic in 2002, Springsteen described how Landau 'would say, "Well, you can . . . play a hall this size and it can still be great." He was constantly pushing the boundaries out for me a little bit.' In truth, it was time to replenish the coffers. A more realistic rocker opened up to Carr's husband on the ensuing tour:

> **Bruce Springsteen**: Until recently, there's been a lot of instability in everybody's life. The band's and mine. It dates back to the very beginning, from the bars on up to even after we were successful . . . And in the studio, I'm slow. I take a long time. That means you spend a lotta money in the studio. Not only do you spend a lotta money, you don't make any money . . . It's like you can never get ahead, because as soon as you get ahead, you stop for two years and you go back to where you were. [1981]

By then, the cash from a number one album, a Top Ten single and a highly lucrative arena tour was rolling in. *The River* – the weakest set of Springsteen songs issued in the E Street-era – was the smash hit *Darkness* was supposed to have been. And Bruce revelled in the moment. At Madison Square Garden on November 27, the week the album hit the top spot, 'Rosalita' got a new lyric: 'Well, this is last chance to let his daughter have some fun/ 'cause my brand new record, Rosie, made it all the way to number one, one, one, one'. No longer afraid of a little hype, 'Hungry Heart' was the lead-off single (with, for the first time, an unreleased

B-side, the blink-and-you'll-miss-it 'Held Up Without A Gun'). It was an old-style pop 45 with 'some eighties in there, too'; and the one song from *The Ties That Bind* left relatively unscathed. That he had perhaps unwittingly tapped into an audience unconcerned with content only became clear when these concert fans began to sing along to that despairing opening verse in a *celebratory* manner. 'Born In The USA', here we come!

Meanwhile, more astute reviewers – even those essentially positive about the album – were disturbed by the general drift in the lyrics towards repetition and cliché. That all-important *Rolling Stone* review – a Paul Nelson rave memorably headlined, 'Let Us Now Praise Famous Men' – duly praised the 'scope, context, sequencing and mood' of 'his summational record'. But Nelson also noted 'a few problems. Ever since he started conceptualizing and thinking in terms of trilogies, Springsteen has lost some of his naturalness and seemed more than a bit self-conscious.' Comparing it – as almost no-one else Stateside did – with *London Calling*, he suggested The Clash, in contrast, 'sometimes seem very innocent . . . [because they] still believe in total victory'.

Creem's Billy Altman, never a confidant, was not so inclined to candy-coat it: 'I really can't think of any other major star in the whole history of pop music whose range of thought and whose expression of those thoughts has been as limited as Bruce Springsteen's.' But it was *NME*'s pet iconoclast, Julie Burchill, who came closest to a grand slam. Finding the room to suggest 'Independence Day' was 'every bit as good as his fans will doubtless say it is', she also highlighted the fact that Springsteen had made an album with a rock soundtrack, but a country sensibility. Unlike him, she didn't think this was necessarily a good thing:

> Springsteen's morals, his melancholy, are rooted in American country rather than American rock. But time and trend taboos have made him irretrievably a rock singer with a rock audience. In country you can age gracefully without ever becoming cosy; in rock you have to tout your dead skin forever. This is great music for people who've wasted their youth, to sit around drinking beer and wasting the rest of their lives to.

Thanks to the recent change in Springsteen's set-up, Burchill's review would signal an end to easy relations between press and star. According to Nick Kent, 'Julie Burchill's negative response to *The River* created quite a

Child eat Humble Pie, circa 1969.
(The Brian Magid Collection)

The future's so bright, I forgot to shave. Greetings from promoland, 1973.
(Courtesy of CBS Records)

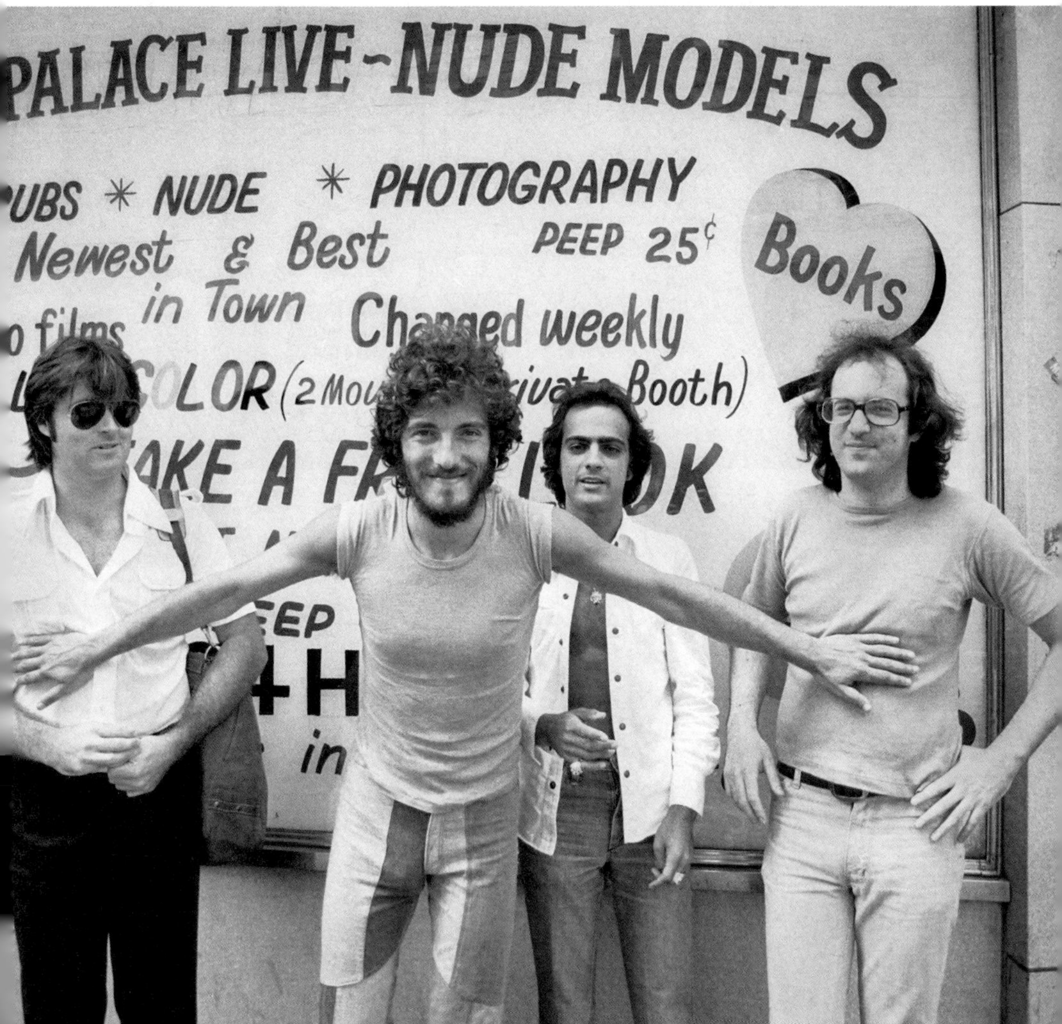

The *BTR* production team hold a staff meeting at their favourite spot, 1975.
(© Eric Meola)

Brothers under the Brooklyn bridge, 1978.
(© Rex Images)

A Recording Date: 1/82 Noise Reduction ☐ Yes ☒ No B

NEBRASKA	Ⓑ Deputy
Atlantic City	Reason to Believe
Mansion on the Hill	Child Bride
Born in the USA	
Johnny 99	
Downbound Train	
Losin' Kind	
State Trooper	
Used Car	
Open All Night	
Pink Caddilac	

RASTA RECORDS
4 Track Mixes

maxell UD XL II

The 'Batlan' version of the Nebraska tape, January 1982.
(The Brian Magid Collection)

Bruce about to nix the tie that binds, October 1979.
(© Joel Bernstein)

Mugging with Miami at Wembley, June 1981.
(© Harry Scott)

Turning the mike over to the Big Man, Wembley, June 1981.
(© Harry Scott)

Taking a breather at another marathon BITUSA performance, June 1985.
(© Rene Van Diemen)

Who do you love? Bruce and Patti on the Tunnel of Love Express, 1988.
(© Rene Van Diemen)

stir in the Springsteen camp. Delicate negotiations between CBS and *NME* to arrange an interview were abandoned, apparently after Bruce's management made their feelings towards the paper clear. *NME* most certainly would not have access to Springsteen during his Euro-tour.'

Barely had her cheeks settled into the still-warm chair of the departing Gold before Barbara Carr was applying her 'for me or against me' brand of PR, and in the process cold-shouldered the most important music weekly in the world. Not bright. And very unBruce-like. But Carr was cut from a different cloth – she genuinely believed Bruce was already too big to need the music press. From now on, one required a clean CV if wanting access to the big boss man. *Creem*'s Dave DiMartino got in under the wire – interviewing Bruce on the eve of the album's release, before s/he saw what Billy Altman thought – but from here on interviews were promotional, not confessional.

Not that Carr was entirely misguided in her analysis. There were sections of the *American* media for whom Springsteen was so totemic that any criticism needed to be spun with candy-cotton. Through the fall of 1980, Springsteen toured the arenas of America as if on a series of homecoming parades – while the reviews (again, *NME* and *Sounds* excepted) obligingly printed the legend. Even the normally level-headed Greil Marcus spoke of the approaching concerts in overtly mythic terms: 'The implicit promise of a Bruce Springsteen concert is that This Is What It's All About – This is The Rock. Whether the promise is more than a night's happy illusion is, at the time, less important than whether Springsteen can live up to it.'

The shows themselves were only very good in comparison with what other arena acts were offering in the name of entertainment that season, whether it be *The Wall* money-mart or the final descent of Led Zeppelin. By any Bruceian benchmark, they were a long way off *Darkness* standards, let alone the E Street Band's mid-seventies heyday. And a key problem was that Springsteen had decided to all but dispense with the pre-*Darkness* set-list. The 1980 shows were all about *The River*, with the odd, obligatory nod to its predecessor (four of the new album's concert highlights were from *Darkness*'s discard-pile).

And Bruce was quite unapologetic about his stance: 'The fans wanna hear everything. I know when I get to a concert, I wanna hear the hits . . . But you can't be afraid to play the new stuff, too. What's to fear – that they're not gonna clap as much?' What there was to fear was that the new songs would not measure up; that a stack-of-trax approach to a twenty-song double album – whatever its stronger moments contained – might just turn a three-hour performance into a promotional tool first, and a live experience second. But Springsteen was thinking about himself, and *he* couldn't wait to play the new songs:

> **Bruce Springsteen**: When I was in the studio and wanted to play, it wasn't the way I felt in a physical kind of way . . . I was excited about the record and I wanted to play those songs live . . . When I was in the studio, sometimes . . . I was wishing I was somewhere strange, playing. I guess that's the thing I love doing the most. And it's the thing that makes me feel most alert and alive . . . Nothing makes me feel as good as those hours between when you walk offstage, until I go to bed. That's the hours that I live for . . . I never feel as low, playing, as I do in the studio . . . / . . . I don't understand all those artists who . . . don't want to perform. Who wants to make records, for God's sake? What can be more boring than such a colourless, odourless, air-conditioned box and having to sing songs into a microphone when they are made for the people out there? [1981]

Failing to heed Wayne King's summer storm-warning – 'creating rock and then playing it to an audience has proven to be dangerous to [both] creativity and communication' – Springsteen now constructed a set-list which almost demanded proof of purchase of his new album before one got an E-ticket. Owners of *Greetings* and *The Wild, the Innocent* were sent to the back of the line, with 'Rosalita' as their sole companion. Large parts of the song-canon to date – as impressive as that of any seventies American rock artist – were airily dismissed, and when interviewers asked what gives, he replied 'I have very little to do anymore with my first two, even three LPs. I was much too young when I made those. I just talked a lot of nonsense.'

He even seemed to have it in for his 1978 LP, insisting he 'consider[ed] the *Darkness* LP a failure. *The River*, that's me. That's the best I can do.' He was dismissing The Album, not the songs – two-thirds of which continued to garner favour. As he told *Darkness* devotee Dave Marsh, 'I like the ideas. [But] I'm not crazy about the performances. We play all those songs ten times better live.' And he set out to prove it, recording shows in Tempe, Arizona in early November (from which the 'anti-Reagan' version of 'Badlands' on *Live 75-85* would later be pulled) and three nights at Nassau

Coliseum, at year's end, which all featured at least six from *Darkness*, along with the now-ubiquitous 'Fire', usually 'Because The Night', and between three and four *Darkness* outtakes masquerading as songs from the new album. Of these, an eight-minute 'Drive All Night' was usually a highlight; along with a recast 'Point Blank', which proved there was such a thing as life after studio-death, and that 'creativity and communication' was still possible in cattle-barns, ice-hockey arenas and airplane hangars. The shows proved gruelling for everyone. Playing anywhere between thirty-five and forty songs, sometimes spending three and a half hours onstage, Springsteen made the shows about stamina first, superlatives second.

And still he continued to talk in familiar tones about his enduring compact with the fans: 'There's a promise made between the musician and the audience. When they support each other, that's a special thing. It goes real deep, and most people take it too lightly. If you break the pact or take it too lightly, nothing else makes sense. It's at the heart of everything.' However, the occasional, nominal resurrection of a 'Spirit In The Night', a 'For You', or an 'Incident on 57th Street' – all songs which helped make his 'rep' – did not a rock messiah make. His idea of set-rotation had become *which* fifteen songs from *The River* to inflict on audiences.

After three months of sold-out arena shows, he concluded the year with three nights at Nassau's cavernous Coliseum. These sets were, on the face of it, everything longstanding fans yearned for. The final night, New Year's Eve, ran to 225 minutes and forty-three songs – a record-breaker in every sense. With unique 1980 performances of 'Rendezvous' and 'Held Up Without A Gun', cover versions of the Creedence classic 'Who'll Stop The Rain', Spector's 'Merry Christmas Baby' and Wilson Pickett's 'In The Midnight Hour' and a seven-song rock 'n' roll encore, it seemed he had once again pulled out all the stops. But, in truth, he was at times running on empty, putting heart and soul into songs from the new album, some of which barely deserved the time of day, but failing to raise his game on more worthy fare. Even a cursory comparison with the three September 1978 Capitol Theater shows – also recorded for a possible live album – finds precious few Nassau performances brooking comparison with their Passaic predecessors.

Nor did a three-week pit-stop in January fully recharge the batteries, and by the start of March he was on his last legs. With just twelve days separating his final US show in Indianapolis on the 5th from the start of his European tour in Brighton, he simply had to admit he was physically and mentally exhausted. The European tour would have to be delayed a fortnight, while the British shows which had been supposed to ease him into this potentially alienating experience, were moved to tour's end. It proved a smart move – the all-important London and Birmingham arena shows now became a fitting finale to proceedings, not a European appetiser. It also gave him time to rethink his approach, and even demo a couple of new songs he might spring on followers across the ocean.

In fact, the one song he worked into any kind of shape in those weeks had ideas enough for two. 'Fistful of Dollars' played with the idea that 'some gonna stand, man, some gonna fall/ And some ain't gonna get to play the game at all/ Well, they give you the worst and they take the best/ For a fist full of dollars and a little bit less'. The bulk of the song focused on a gamblin' man who is 'frightened of the dice they roll/ Where the highway ends and the sand turns to gold'; and though Atlantic City is not mentioned, its opening image was already pencilled in: 'Well, they blew up the chicken man in Philly last night/ Now that town sets in for a fight'.* Elsewhere he turned a self-conscious nod to Chuck Berry's 'Bye Bye Johnny' – 'Well, I drew my money from the Central Trust/ And I hopped with my guitar on a greyhound bus' – into a belated tribute of sorts to Elvis: 'Johnny Bye Bye'. But one verse is all he had, for now.

Presley was very much on Bruce's mind in the early weeks of the European tour, so much so that at his first ever show in Paris – between 'The Promised Land' and Woody Guthrie's rather more ironic 'This Land Is Your Land' – he talked about 'the last time . . . I'd seen Elvis in concert. My two favourite songs he sang was one called "How Great Thou Art", and "American Trilogy" . . . and I remember [this] 'cause I went hoping to see him do all old stuff, all the rocking stuff, but in the end it seemed like the songs that were closest to him, and that he sang with the most heart, was a song that was about the land that he grew up in and a song just about the God that he believed in . . . This is a song about freedom, it's . . . about not having to die when you're old in some factory, or about not having to die in some big million-dollar house with a lot of nothing pumping through your veins.'

---

* The line partially dates the recording by referencing the bombing of Philip Testa on March 15, 1981, a hit man for the mob known universally as 'The Chicken Man'.

The following night he opened the set – which had previously begun with the unremitting 'Factory' – with 'Follow That Dream', which was actually a hybrid of the 1962 Elvis original, a couple of phrases from Roy Orbison's 'In Dreams', and a Bruceian glossary on how to avoid the fate that befell Elvis: 'I need someone with a love I can trust/ And together we'll search for the things that come to us/ Baby in dreams, baby in dreams . . . You got to follow that dream wherever it may lead'. It was an audacious moment, setting things up nicely for a series of shows that reflected more the risk-taker of yore. He even talked like that man. As he said of this surprise opener the following week, 'I see it as catching a deep breath, before making the big jump . . . At the opening of a show, people don't expect intimacy, they want to get excited together, they want to jump up. So if you start calm, you take the people close to you from the beginning.'

It was a special night, which concluded with a first encore that included another favourite Elvis 'Hollywood' hit, 'Can't Help Falling In Love', a song he had recorded for *Darkness* and considered for the 1978 tour, telling Ed Sciaky, 'I really wanted to do [it] but we didn't get a chance to run it down . . . It was his theme song, which everyone relates to his Las Vegas period.' This was the Elvis the young Bruce had grown up with. It also reminded him of the Elvis he saw that night in Philadelphia, when it served as Presley's set-closer but delivered in the most desultory manner possible, connecting it to a parable Springsteen began to tell to press *and* punters alike:

> **Bruce Springsteen**: What my band and I are about is a sense of responsibility. If you accept it, that makes you responsible for everything that happens. People tend to blame circumstances, but in the end it's always your choice . . . / . . . You see, the sell-out doesn't occur when you take your first limousine ride. It happens here [in your heart]. And somewhere private. A lot of good people with something to say have fallen into that trap. It's when you get fat and lose your hunger, that is when you know the sell-out has happened . . . / . . . First the limousine, then the big mansions on the hill. I've always been suspicious of the whole [fame] package deal and I'm scared of it. I'm afraid because you just see too many people getting blown away, getting sucked down the drain. Elvis was the ultimate example of that. Here was a guy who had it all and he lost it, or maybe just let it slip through his fingers, 'cause somewhere,

> somehow, he just stopped caring. He let himself get fat and became a cartoon . . . a caricature. [1981]

Finally, on May 13, another special night, this one at Manchester's intimate Apollo Theatre, the parable became a pop song. On one level little more than a rewrite of the 'funeral' version of 1977's 'Come On (Let's Go Tonight)' with the opening couplet to 'Bye Bye Johnny' tacked on, 'Johnny Bye Bye' was also the first song since 'The Ties That Bind' he'd debuted in concert, not in the studio. The line he had used in the Paris 'This Land Is Your Land' rap had become the basis for a devastating closing verse: 'They found him slumped up against the drain/ With a whole lot of nothin' runnin' through his veins/ Well, bye bye Johnny, Johnny bye bye, you didn't have to die, you didn't have to die'. He was telling everyone that night, and throughout both legs of *The River* tour, that *he* wasn't gonna end up that way:

> **Bruce Springsteen**: Rock has never been a destructive thing for me. In fact, it was the first thing that gave me self-respect and strength. But I totally understand how it can be destructive to people . . . Look at all the examples of people in rock and what happened to them – people who once played great but don't play great anymore; people who once wrote great songs but don't write great songs anymore. It's like they got distracted by *things*. You can get hooked on things as much as you can on drugs. [1980]

One could easily get hooked on the star-trip. But not him. As he let *Rolling Stone* know after 'Johnny Bye Bye' finally received an official release, 'The type of fame that Elvis had . . . the pressure of it, and the isolation that it seems to require, has gotta be really painful . . . [But] I wasn't gonna get to a place where I said, "I can't go in here. I can't go to this bar. I can't go outside."' For Springsteen, it was still all about performing. And as he repeatedly insisted, 'I'm gonna perform as long . . . as I don't change into a parody of myself; and if I ever end up doing that, then I count on my good friends to tell me so.'

He had come dangerously close at various points the previous fall. Thankfully, he now remembered one element of those groundbreaking seventies shows he paid mere lip service to these days – doing great covers. They once provided both a point of reference and a way for Springsteen to embrace elements of popular song he loved, but could not emulate in his own songs no matter how hard he tried. They remained all-important reminders of what got him started and kept him going through the long years of obscurity, an explication of the whole E Street Band aesthetic. As he told Michael Watts before the London shows, 'Some people say rock & roll is fun, others say it's trite; to me, it's everything. I hear [The Drifters'] "When My Little Girl Is Smiling" and, wow, that's something to live by . . . Those moments are real.' He didn't attempt that one, but Arthur Conley's 'Sweet Soul Music' sometimes sufficed.

Starting on opening night in Hamburg – where every sixties Britbeat band once went to be blooded – Springsteen trimmed his own sails, giving half the songs from *The River* a rest; preferring to doff his cap to past travellers on this lost highway. In part, he felt unsure whether he was fully connecting with non-English speaking audiences. As he told a Belgian reporter later that month, 'At the beginning of this tour . . . they really were staring at us as if we were Pink Floyd, and then I decided to force a breakthrough by doing a number of rockers, six or seven of them right after one another, at maximum volume and without any comment in between the numbers. This had a result, but it was kinda creepy, because when I later started doing some slower numbers, they screamed for more rockers.'

When it got to encore time in Hamburg, he decided against ending with 'Devil In The Blue Dress', driving straight into a Creedence Clearwater moment instead. Elements of the German audience may have thought 'Rockin' All Over The World' was a Status Quo song, but it was a rousing finale to a show that had previously become overlong and needed pruning. A return to theatres in a number of cities (the arena-less north of Britain got five theatre shows: two each in Edinburgh and Manchester and one in Newcastle) signalled a general return to *Darkness*-length sets (25-30 songs) with a healthy smattering of covers, a handful of which became showstoppers.

If 'Follow That Dream' was a great way to kick off proceedings, so was another Creedence cover, the positively spooky 'Run Through The Jungle', which he introduced in Rotterdam on April 29 and retained for the duration. 'Can't Help Falling In Love' also continued to gain sporadic favour, as did 'Jole Blon', the closest Springsteen came to promoting the E Street Band's other 1980 vinyl offering, Gary US Bonds' *Dedication* (co-produced by Bruce and Stevie). But it was the stunning reinvention of Jimmy Cliff's 'Trapped', dropped into the set from nowhere at the opening Wembley show (his first London gig since Hammersmith '75), that really captured audiences' imaginations. A song he found on cassette at an airport duty-free shop, it had evidently struck a chord, because the last time he had sung a cover with this much emotional undertow, he was singing 'I Want You' to Suki Lahav.

One can't help wondering what girlfriend Joyce Heiser, who accompanied Bruce throughout the European jaunt, made of this paean to a suffocating relationship – 'Well, it seems like I've been playin' the game way too long/ And it seems the game I played has made you strong/ Well, when the game is over, I will walk out of here again/ I know someday I will find the key' – especially as that last line was Bruce's own lyrical addition. Fans didn't care. They felt like they had got the old Bruce back again.

Perhaps, though, it was this 'old Bruce', and his outmoded view of rock as a force for good, which had got him caught in a trap. After a show in Brighton, in conversation with Nick Kent, the one rock critic Carr had worked so hard to keep away from him, Springsteen talked for the first time about how 'rock has abused that ability to give that sense of *something better* to kids. A lotta kids in America and, I guess, here use a certain style of rock to just shut off. Completely! They just want to *forget*, to numb themselves from their existence. And that just horrifies me.' Could it be that Kent's co-worker, Julie Burchill, had been right all along; and his natural constituency really was country music's *cognoscenti*? Landau shared Springsteen's concerns, telling Kent, 'Great rock not only defines what is, but suggests what *might be*. And it's [that] sense . . . we're in danger of losing.' He just didn't expect Kent – who by May 1981 had substance abuse issues which made Elvis little more than a drugstore wannabe – to remember the conversation in the morning. Bruce, though, had only just begun having this little conversation with himself:

> **Bruce Springsteen**: I had to get out from under my misinterpretation of what the whole rock & roll dream was about. It took me a long time to do it. Partly because to do it means you have to accept death itself . . . In the end, you cannot live inside that dream. You cannot live within the dream of Elvis Presley or . . . The Beatles . . . You can live that dream in your heart, but you cannot live inside that dream . . . / . . . I guess I used

> to think that rock could save you. I don't believe it can anymore . . . You can dance, you can slow-dance with your girl, but you can't hide in it. And it is so seductive that you want to hide in it. [1987/1988]

He saw no future in the rock dream at precisely the point when, for many, he fulfilled the 'future of rock 'n' roll' epithet, having proven definitively that London – and indeed the whole of Europe – was finally ready for him. If he benefited from fans and (most) critics having no point of comparison with former glories, even critical comparisons with Dylan's own European arena tour barely three weeks later – to promote an album co-produced by Chuck Plotkin (at Debbie Gold's recommendation) – were invariably cast in Bruce's favour. In fact, the shows of born-again Bob were equally stamina-sapping, he had never been more committed to performing and his band was perhaps his most musical since The Band. Bruce's live reputation, though, had achieved (un)critical mass and he could do no wrong.

Landau knew he was onto a good thing, hurriedly booking his all-American boy to do thirty-two summer shows at some of the largest arenas in America, starting with a week of shows which opened the doors on the 20,000-seater Brendan Byrne Arena in East Rutherford, New Jersey. The six shows sold out in an instant, even before Springsteen decided to record the last four shows for that still-pending live album (he already had tapes of the last three London shows). By now, though, the sets were essentially set in stone. A 'Jackson Cage' for a 'Point Blank', an 'I Wanna Marry You' for an 'Independence Day' were almost the extent of any variants. This was very much a victory procession, or as Landau chose to spin it, 'The concept was to go back to cities that had been very special in Bruce's career. Basically, come in and stay for a while and play a little bit in depth.' In the process they made more money in two months than on the whole *Darkness* marathon. It was almost as if, this time, Springsteen knew he needed to hoard a few nuggets for the coming hibernation.

So it might seem on the face of it a rather strange time to develop a political conscience. But develop one Springsteen now did. He later suggested it was his trip to Europe that first opened his eyes: 'When you spend a good amount of time over [in Europe], you do have a moment to step out of the United States and look back with a critical eye . . . It's very difficult to conjure up a real worldview from within our borders.' In fact, the first flowering of a wider awareness had come earlier. His introduction to 'Badlands' at Tempe the previous November – 'I don't know what you guys think about what happened last night, but I think it's pretty frightening' – represented his first-ever political pronouncement onstage. I guess this was one vote Ronald Reagan didn't get the night he took the presidency.

By the following February, Bruce was informing *Rolling Stone*, 'The cynicism of the last ten years is what people adopted as a necessary defence against having tire tracks up and down their front and back every day.' No longer an innocent abroad, he was canvassing against arch-cynicism and advocating responsibility. As he subsequently said, 'If you're a citizen, and if you're living here, then it's your turn to take out the garbage.' On August 20, 1981 he signalled this new social awareness (and replacement belief-system) by donating all the proceeds from opening night at the unforgiving LA Sports Arena to the Vietnam Veterans Association, and prefacing his performance of 'Who'll Stop The Rain' that night with his first pre-scripted political speech:

> 'It's like when you feel like you're walking down a dark street at night and out of the corner of your eye you see somebody getting hurt or getting hit in the dark alley, but you keep walking on, because you think it don't have nothing to do with you and you just want to get home . . . Well, Vietnam turned, turned this whole country into that dark street and unless we're able to walk down those dark alleys and look into the eyes of the men and the women that are down there, and the things that happened, we're never gonna be able to get home.'

If a movie of a book had inspired the noirish *Darkness*, it was the book of someone's life which sparked this new concern. How ironic that the most famous New Dylan should alight on a biography of Woody Guthrie, seen through the prose of Joe Klein, as a way to reinvent himself. (There was a time, twenty years earlier, when Dylan was the New Guthrie.) In fact, Springsteen had been playing 'This Land Is Your Land' since the first night at Nassau (28/12/80), as if he already knew he wanted it on any resultant live album. Reading Klein, he had discovered this was a song which had been misrepresented since the day it was conceived, and he decided to reclaim it. Hence introductions like, 'This song was written a real long time ago . . . [It] was written to fight all the prejudice and all the hatred that gets passed on as patriotism or as nationalism.'

He finally sought to connect himself to that 'long tradition of artist involvement in the nation's social and political life. Woody Guthrie, Bob Dylan, James Brown, Curtis Mayfield . . . When they spoke, I heard myself speaking. I felt [that] connectedness.' And yet, he had admitted back in 1974 that he had never really listened to the protest songs of Dylan, only the electric Rimbaud. When the battle was outside a-ragin', he'd been back home reading *Rolling Stone*. Now a galvanized Springsteen was enthusing about how 'Guthrie and Dylan had the courage to comment on all that happened in America in the fifties and sixties . . . It's time that someone took on the reality of the eighties.' He may not have discovered a new religion, but he *had* found a soapbox.

With the tour over by mid-September, and the band taking a well-earned rest, he returned to his New Jersey home determined to write a 'This Land Is Your Land' he could call his own, one that would deal with 'the reality of the Eighties' by addressing a war from the sixties. Again, he initially looked for that story in picture form: 'I remember going to see *The Deer Hunter* with [the Viet-vet] Ron Kovic . . . he was looking for things that reflected his experience. The song came out of all that.' The song he was talking about was 'Born In The USA'. But that was not the song which came out first. Rather, he began something called 'Vietnam Blues' on his return east.

A 'stranger in his own home town' saga, 'Vietnam Blues' was neither 'Born In The USA' nor 'Shut Out The Light', though elements of both appeared therein, notably the prototype for the latter's first verse: 'The runway rushed up at me, I felt the wheels touch down/ Stood out on the blacktop, and took a taxi into town/ Got off down on Main Street, to see what I recognized/ All I seen was strange faces watching a stranger passin' by'. But 'Vietnam Blues' was some way from either offspring, and its refrain lacked universal resonance – 'You died in Vietnam, now don't you understand'. No, he needed something with a more Guthriesque quality. Something which suggested, whatever he'd been told previously, that this land was made for him and them.

Chapter 8: 1981–82 – Reasons To Believe

> I have the impression that I have only just begun to write since 'The River'; that I have [now] touched upon matters which will never leave me without inspiration: love, hate, sex, hypocrisy in marriage, adultery. Matters about which . . . very little . . . ha[s] been said in rock n roll. – Bruce Springsteen, 1981

> [The albums] after *Born To Run* . . . through *Nebraska* . . . were kind of my reaction, not necessarily to my success, but to what . . . I was feeling – what I felt the role of the musicians should be, what an artist should be . . . So I just dove into it. I decided . . . to move into the darkness and look around and write about what I knew, and what I saw and what I was feeling. I was trying to find something to hold onto that doesn't disappear out from under you. – Bruce Springsteen, 1984.

As Ralph and Carter Stanley harmonically pointed out, the darkest hour is just before the dawn. Well, throughout the fall of 1981 Springsteen spent all his time penning song after song with that four a.m. feeling, and when he wasn't doing this he was listening to Hank Williams, Robert Johnson and Suicide. (Thankfully, he excluded any British antidote to melancholy, as one spin of Richard Thompson's 'I'll Regret It All In The Morning' might just have tipped him over the edge.) He was shutting others out, repeating well-worn patterns of interpersonal behaviour again – in a partly-conscious attempt to drive another long-time girlfriend away:

> **Bruce Springsteen**: There's people who feel, 'I get what I need when I go onstage and I don't need the rest.' I felt like that for a long time. I always

> got to a point in relationships where if it got too complicated or there was too much pressure, whether it was right or not, I'd say, 'Hey! I don't need this!' . . . My fear of failure always held me back in dealing with people and relationships. I always stopped right before I committed to the place where, if it failed, it would really hurt. [1992]

The very person who had once proclaimed, 'I eat loneliness, man. I feed off it,' had again reached the place he would describe so convincingly in a 1984 introduction to 'Racing In The Street', 'It's hard to understand what brings people together and then what pulls 'em apart. You meet somebody, you think that they can take away all of your loneliness, when in the end nobody can take away the loneliness. You just hope that you can find somebody maybe that you can share it with.'

He still couldn't decide how much of his essential self he was willing to share with another person. It wasn't like he didn't know by now he was a difficult person to live with, or that he 'tend[ed] to be an isolationist by nature. And it's not about money or where you live or how you live. It's about psychology. My Dad was . . . the same way.' For Joyce, though, missing Karen Darvin's phone number from her address book, it was increasingly hard to bear. Barely had he returned from the road when he made it clear in gesture and deed that he wanted to be alone. She left her ex-boyfriend with no secrets to conceal, and a new notebook to write them in:

> **Bruce Springsteen**: That whole *Nebraska* album was just that isolation thing, and what it does to you . . . I wrote all those songs, and to do it right, you've got to get down in there somehow . . . [But] when that happens, there's just a whole breakdown. When you lose that sense of community, there's some spiritual breakdown that occurs. And when that occurs, you just get shot off somewhere where nothing seems to matter . . . / . . . At that point – well, that was the bottom. I would hope not to be in that particular place ever again. It was a thing where all my ideas might have been working musically, but they were failing me personally . . . I got to a point where all my answers – rock & roll answers – were running out. [1984/1986]

He needed to find another route out. Even before he began writing the songs that would form the cornerstones of *Nebraska* (and, ultimately, *Born In The USA*), he started searching for a new outlet from his inner turmoil. For the first time he decided to stop bottling up these neuroses, the self-same ones which had led him to quit a psychology course in college, and turn to a qualified therapist to help him address those 'moments when it was very confusing. Because [although] I realized that I was a rich man . . . I felt like a poor man inside.' Having pursued his singular goal – to be rich, successful, famous and *good* – with unswerving dedication for a decade or more, he found there were still more questions than answers. His new-found success merely raised ever more questions about who he was, and wanted to be. Experiencing an existential crisis of the soul, he sought outside help:

> **Bruce Springsteen**: I found I'd gotten very good at my job and because I was good at my job, for some reason I thought I was capable of a lot of other things, like relationships. If you're not good at those things and you're in your twenties, you don't notice it because you're too busy scuffling. But when you get a little older, you start to realize that there are all these other things that you're really bad at . . . basically your real life, your life away from your guitar, your music, your work, your life outside your work – you've been failing miserably at for a long time . . . I always enjoyed my work but when it came to functioning outside of that, I always had a hard time. [1992]

It took a great deal of personal courage to admit, as he did first in therapy and then in a number of 1984 interviews, that 'you're just somebody who plays guitar, and you do that good . . . but the rest of the time, you're scramblin' around in the dark like everyone else'. This process of personal development would ultimately take his songwriting in a more self-aware – though not necessarily such an abidingly creative – direction. For now, he was feeling the birth pangs of a born-again songwriter who, perhaps for the first time, was 'growin' into the particular shoes I was wearing'. And the songs flowed.

He was writing (and demoing on cassette) like there was no tomorrow. Like, indeed, it was 1976-7 all over again. As he later revealed to Chet Flippo, 'I just locked in, and it was real different for me. I stayed in my house, I just worked all the time . . . I realized that this was different from stuff I'd done before and I didn't know what it was.' Once again, his way of reclaiming the night was staying up late, writing. According to Springsteen, 'Mansion On The Hill', which he 'had the beginning of for some time', was the first song finished. Nodding to another major influence in its title – and perhaps finding at least one line in the Hank Williams original which struck home, 'I know you're alone with your pride . . . in that loveless mansion on the hill' – it was the first time he had written in such a nakedly autobiographical way since 'Randolph Street', a decade earlier. He yearned to experience those feelings in the here and now, still fearing the ghost of Johnny Bye-Bye:

> 'When I was a kid, my father used to drive me outside of town. There was this nice white house used to sit on this hill. As I got older, it took [on] more meaning. It became very mystical . . . like a touchstone. Now when I dream, sometimes I'm outside the gates looking in, and sometimes I'm the man inside.'*

To call 'Mansion' the earliest song written for *Nebraska*, though, would be untrue. There were at least two songs he worked on now which were lyrical recastings of 1979 *River* outtakes: 'Baby I'm So Cold', a reworking of 'Loose Ends' which he now set to the 'Follow That Dream' tune debuted the previous April, and 'Open All Night', originally 'Living On The Edge of The World'. A snatch of the latter appears at the end of the April 1981 home demos. Though lyrically it is still 'Living on the Edge of the World' (with a snippet of 'This Hard Land' thrown in for good measure: 'What happened to the seeds I've sown/ in this hard land?'), musically he has already made the switch to 'Open All Night'. Inspired by a William Price Fox short-story, it updated the sentiments of 'Drive All Night', with 'the hero brav[ing] snow sleet rain + the highway patrol for a kiss from his baby's lips.'

However, as he knew all too well, there *were* no 'baby's lips' waiting for him back home. His response was to turn the jagged 'Loose Ends' – written when Heiser was around – inward. A new verse now made the track sound right when reaching for those razor blades: 'We both made promises we couldn't keep/ Now last night, I found you crying in your sleep/ Baby, we used to walk on nights just like this/ And I would hold you in my arms, fill you with my kisses'. (By the time he was rehearsing the song for the *Electric Nebraska*, this pair of star-crossed lovers had also become 'like strangers who know too much about each other'.)

Another song which directly addressed a failed relationship that fall was the claustrophobic 'Fade To Black' – another component of spring '82 E Street sessions. Demoed when the emotions were red-raw, he pared its lyrics to the

* St Paul 29/6/84.

bone to provide his first film-treatment in song: 'Sunday matinee in a one-dog town/ You're two seats away, I move two seats down/ And the lights cut off, I walk out from my seat/ I walk you home, as the credits rise'. Skilfully using cinematic shorthand to advance the fateful narrative – 'Wipe the tears from your eyes, the first kiss I stole/ I walk you home, the credits roll/ Fade to black' – the song fits its author's description of the *Nebraska* material perfectly: 'The . . . record had that cinematic quality, where you get in there and you get the feel of life . . . some of the grit and some of the beauty.'

However, 'Fade To Black' was not destined to constitute part of *that* fabled demo tape. Nor was another of his Biblical mock-parables, 'Love Is A Dangerous Thing', which had a cast of characters including Eve, who 'tempted Adam with an apple/ You know the story in the end,' and Delilah, who 'took on Samson/ And left him slowly twisting in the wind'. Just no Jezebel.

Other songs demoed that fall – 'Johnny 99', 'The Losin' Kind' and the rock formation 'Born In The USA' – perhaps suggested a more enticing direction. In each case, he had created convincing characters caught in a moral bind. On the first two occasions they acted without thinking, while on the last occasion the protagonist went from one existential wasteland (home) to another (Vietnam) and back. Each song he was writing served to address, even embrace, the darkness, but the narration became almost exclusively third-person as Springsteen attempted to separate himself from invidious feelings of impotence and self-loathing, applying them to far more dysfunctional individuals than any previous singer-narrator. Rather than indulging in the kind of lachrymose self-pity found in most modern country music, he revisited its hillbilly roots and the traditional story-songs that were its bedrock, adopting a persona that was a cross between Luke the Drifter – the name Hank Williams gave himself when he wanted to spin parables-in-song – and the stoic Sun-era Johnny Cash, ever caught somewhere between heaven and hellraisin':

> **Bruce Springsteen**: All during the last tour . . . I listened to Hank Williams . . . That and the first real Johnny Cash record with 'Give My Love to Rose', 'I Walk the Line', 'Hey Porter', 'Six Foot High and Risin'', . . . 'Guess Things Happen That Way'. That, and the rockabilly . . . All that stuff just seemed to fit in with things that I was thinking about, or worrying about. Especially the Hank Williams stuff. He always has all that conflict, he always has that real religious side, and the honky tonkin' . . . side [as well]. [1981]

Like many who came before (and after), Springsteen's introduction to the works of Woody Guthrie had opened up an Anglo-American musical backdrop he had been blithely unaware of (even if Dylan had been mining it to the core for twenty years). It was a tradition which suggested that what happened at the Sun studios was as much an end as a beginning; that something unearthly went down south which changed the parameters of song forever, ultimately taking some of the traditional mystery out of the process. (Hence, presumably, why Springsteen recently described driving 'past Sun Studios. I just wanted to know it was there, that it was real. That all of that stuff *really happened*.') By fall 1981 Springsteen was in fast rewind when it came to the influences he allowed to impact on his songwriting craft:

> **Bruce Springsteen**: My music utilizes things from the past, because that's what the past is for. It's to learn from . . . I don't want to make a record like they made in the '50s or the '60s or the '70s. I want to make a record like today, that's right now. To do that, I go back, back further all the time. Back into Hank Williams, back into Jimmie Rodgers . . . The human thing that's in those records is just beautiful and awesome . . . It's got that beauty and the purity. The same thing with a lot of the great fifties records, and the early rockabilly. [1981]

What he says he found in many pre-rock 'n' roll reference points was a 'sense of consequences' that 'rock & roll didn't pick up from country and rhythm & blues'. And it was to country he now leaned. As he put it in 2012, 'Country's fatalism attracted me. It was reflective. It was funny. It was soulful. But it was quite fatalistic. Tomorrow looked pretty dark . . . If rock and roll was a seven-day weekend, country was Saturday night hell-raising, followed by heavy "Sunday Morning Coming Down". Guilt, guilt, guilt, I fucked up. Oh, my God.' And one of the things he now set out 'to do was provide that set of consequences' – though, in truth, most of the story-songs he was writing seemed more about *comeuppance* than consequence. The arbitrary nature of most punishments meted out on *Nebraska* reflected a worldview culled more from the works of Alan Vega rather than those devout sinners, Williams and Cash.

For Springsteen had not entirely surrendered his interest in modern music, or one of its more cutting edge cult-artists. He had only dug deeper since bonding with Vega at those Power Station sessions the previous year. And if few at the time would have considered Vega an obvious brother-in-song, Springsteen was keen to acknowledge his influence in a 1984 *Rolling Stone* interview: 'I like the band Suicide . . . They had that two-piece synthesizer-voice thing. They had one of the most amazing songs I ever heard. It was about a guy that murders [his family] . . . That's one of the most amazing records I think I ever heard.'

The song he was referring to was the psychotic centrepiece of Suicide's eponymous debut, 'Frankie Teardrop', which if it hadn't just reached the shops under its own steam, would have slotted right on *Darkness On The Edge of Town*: 'Twenty year old Frankie, he's married, he's got a kid/ And he's working in a factory/ He's working from seven to five . . . just trying to survive'. Frankie, though, 'can't make it, 'cause things are just too hard', and so he decides to kill himself, though not before he has 'picked up a gun/ Pointed [it] at the six month old in the crib', and then at his wife. But if Frankie is convinced he has escaped a world of existential terror, he awakes to find himself 'lying in hell'. The 'moralizing' coda is as unsparing as it gets: 'We're all Frankies/ lying in hell'.

A 'Hollis Brown' for the post-punk world, 'Frankie Teardrop' *literally* caused riots across Europe when Suicide were invited to support the likes of The Clash and Elvis Costello in 1977-78. It also provided Springsteen with a fictional role model for *Nebraska*'s most impenitent mass murderer, Charlie Starkweather; to go with the non-fictional role models of Starkweather himself, and the Gary Gilmore whom Norman Mailer had just epically depicted in his 'non-fiction novel', *Executioner's Song*. Because, as Springsteen openly admitted in 1987, 'In the end, I was probably using Charlie Starkweather to write about myself.' (Intriguingly, he once suggested in a 1975 interview that if he hadn't become a rock singer, he'd 'probably [have] done something crazy. Maybe robbed stores or something. That always appealed to me, robbing things.') Like the Dylan who saw something of himself in Lee Harvey Oswald, and nearly got metaphorically lynched at an Emergency Civil Liberties Committee dinner for saying so, Springsteen had come to feel just like Frankie and Charlie:

> **Bruce Springsteen**: There was something about ['Nebraska'] that was the centre of the record, but I couldn't really say specifically what it was, outside of the fact that I'd read something that moved me . . . I think in my own life I had reached where it felt like I was teetering on this void. I felt a deep sense of isolation, and that led me to those characters and

> to those stories . . . I was at a place where I could start to really feel that price . . . for not sorting through the issues that make up your emotional life . . . I just felt too disconnected, I just [felt I] wasn't any good, right at the moment that record occurred. [1999]

Having recently read a contemporary account of Charlie Starkweather's murdering spree, *Caril*, and garnered some further background from the co-author Ninette Beaver, a local reporter who covered the case, Springsteen's interest had been piqued by Terrence Malick's curiously amoral 1973 movie, *Badlands*. What led him there he couldn't say. It just 'seemed to be a mood . . . I was in at the time'. But if 'Nebraska' never excused the malevolent misfit his murderous mindset, he did seem to consider the Starkweathers of this world an outward manifestation of a deeper societal malady, something he made plain to audiences on the *Born In The USA* tour when introducing the song thus: 'I was reading in the papers about how television and all the media and stuff is bringing the whole world closer together. But it seems like in these times people [can] get isolated from their jobs; sometimes they [also] get isolated from friends and from their families, until you get that sense of powerlessness, and just explode.'

That he was mythologizing a particularly nasty specimen in Starkweather did not at this stage trouble him. Nor was he concerned by the clear historical liberties he was taking with what was, after all, a true story. (He had learnt that lesson from Guthrie, f'sure.) And the most egregious of those liberties came on the song's punch line. When 'they wanted to know why I did what I did', the mass murderer replied, 'I guess there's just a meanness in this world'. Needless to say, Starkweather never said anything of the sort. It is what another homicidal murderer said when about to murder a God-fearing old lady, this one the fictional creation of Flannery O'Connor in her seminal short story, 'A Good Man Is Hard To Find'.

O'Connor's character is only ever identified as The Misfit, and his explanation of where the world went wrong skewered Christ's message in a way only a lapsed Catholic could have accepted as an explanation for why a good man might be hard to find: 'Jesus was the only One that ever raised the dead, and He shouldn't have done it. He thrown everything off balance. If He did what He said, then it's nothing for you to do but throw away everything and follow Him, and if He didn't, then it's nothing for you to do but enjoy the few minutes you got left the best way you can – by killing somebody or burning down his house or doing some other meanness to him. No pleasure but meanness.' The murderer in 'Nebraska' applies a similarly warped worldview to the jurors who sentence him to death: 'They declared me unfit to live, said into that great void my soul'd be hurled'. However, it was only Charlie – and his fictional brother-murderer, Frankie – who envisaged life after death as 'that great void'. O'Connor fervently believed The Misfit would eventually be 'lying in hell'.

For Springsteen to have reached a place where he felt he 'wasn't any good – right at the moment that record occurred', openly identifying with those inner feelings of a callous murderer, suggests how little light now filtered through those blinds. Only later would he see the wider picture and acknowledge that a 'sense of consequences' was as important in one's life as in one's songs. As he said the night he rekindled that 'Nebraska' mindset onstage at the Christic Institute Benefit in November 1990, delivering his most powerful performance this side of a Portastudio, 'When I did the *Nebraska* album, I really didn't think anything about what its political implications were, until I read about it in the newspapers . . . But something I was feeling moved me to write all these songs, where people lose their connection to their friends and their families and their jobs and their countries, and their lives don't make sense to them no more.'

This was the overarching theme he took from Starkweather and Teardrop, Gilmore and The Misfit, constructing an album for 'every hung-up person in the whole wide universe'; peopled by folk who because they 'struggle to find the language . . . of the soul . . . explode into violence or [implode into] indifference or numbness', a view he only articulated after touring with the songs solo in 1995-96.*

Not that Alan Vega's influence was confined to his more Suicidal offerings. If Frankie Teardrop would inform *Nebraska*, so would Vega's eponymous 1980 solo debut, with its demo-rockabilly sensibility, specifically the eight-minute 'Bye Bye Bayou' which whoops and hollers like Jimmie Rodgers on a bed of nails. (In 2006, Bruce suggested, 'If Elvis came back from the dead I think he would sound like Alan Vega – he gets a lot of emotional purity.') Alan Vega certainly thought he'd heard

* All ten *Nebraska* songs were performed during the *Tom Joad* tour, and a triple bootleg-CD on the Godfather label, called *Broken Dreams & Reasons To Believe*, collects versions of all ten songs from said tour on disc two. (It does the same for the *BITUSA* and *Devils & Dust* tours, too.)

a ghost the day he visited his label and heard someone spinning Springsteen's latest:

> **Alan Vega:** I was on Zee Records, and I walk in, there's something on the turntable blasting out, and I'm hearing [all] these typical Alan Vega things – the whooping [&c.]. The music is very raw. And I'm just going, 'Man, did I do a record I forgot I did?' The yelps were me – and the music was *very* Suicide. Turned out to be 'State Trooper'.

Springsteen openly admitted, in handwritten notes to the songs which he gave to Jon Landau that winter, that 'State Trooper' was something he dreamed 'up comin' back from New York one night. I don't know if it's even really a song or not . . . It's kinda weird.' (I refer readers to Steve Wynn's cover version on the *Light of Day* Springsteen tribute 2-CD set for an even more Vega-like version.) In this unearthly concoction, he told the story of a man who professed to have 'a clear conscience 'bout the things that I done', without really explaining what these things might be. In the end, the driver asks someone to 'listen to my last prayer . . . [and] deliver me from nowhere', a rare expression of faith on a faithless record.

At least the other murder-ballad on the album returned its author to the land of fiction. 'Johnny 99' was the first of the 'desperado' songs written for *Nebraska*, predating even the title track. Johnny's 'explanation' for what drove him to his doom again pointed the finger at society – 'It was more 'n all this that put that gun in my hand' – replaced an original couplet that had more of the country in its blood, crossing 'Folsom Prison Blues' with *The Gunfighter*, 'Step in my way and I'll shoot you down/ Until the day that you understand'. (Anyone who doubts such a synthesis took place might want to refer to a 1996 observation on the subject, 'Since the early eighties, my musical influences . . . [have gone] back in a way [to] Hank Williams and some of the blues guys and folk guys, but films and writers and novels have probably been the primary influences on my work.')

Though Springsteen's 'Johnny 99' had no obvious real-life parallel, there was a probable literary source, the monumental *Executioner's Song*, the story of Gary Gilmore and the two senseless murders that led to his state-sponsored execution, published the previous year to enormous fanfare and justified critical acclaim. Like Gilmore, Johnny asks to be executed, rather than face life without parole. Unlike Johnny, though, Gilmore did not seek to excuse his crimes. (When asked what someone should say to his mother, Gary replied, 'I guess that it's all true'.) The penny-ante nature of the crime Johnny commits also replicated Gilmore's, even if Springsteen deleted the actual incident after that initial home demo: 'It's only $200, that was all I was asking for/ Judge, just $200 and I would have been on my way out the door/ He reached 'neath the counter and I saw something shiny in his hand/ He spewed blood like a fountain and I dropped my gun and I ran'.

Though the former was fictional, 'Johnny 99' and 'Nebraska' were very much two of a kind. Indeed, Springsteen paired them together when seeking to explain what he was reaching for on *Nebraska*: 'It's the inner thing that makes a song real to you. Whether it's . . . something like "Nebraska" or "Johnny 99", you kinda just gotta know what that feels like, somewhere.' He was still trying to figure out, 'How does it feel?' Hence a November '84 intro to 'Johnny 99', 'I went down to the bank that was about to foreclose on the mortgage of the house . . . and he tried to tell me that he knew how I felt . . . I said "Well, you walk around that desk and you sit in this chair and you walk in those shoes for a while."'

The rest of the songs now came with remarkable alacrity – even for such a prolific songwriter. As he admitted, 'I wrote almost all the *Nebraska* songs in about two months. Which is really fast for me.' And he was consciously applying a technique he'd already adopted in performance on 'Factory' and 'The River' – songs he claimed earlier that year he was 'singing through this other character. So I slowed down the tempos . . . not too much, but just enough so I could really dig into the songs and connect with the characters.' Well, he certainly 'slowed down the tempos' on most of these new songs, to wrist-slashingly slow.

The exception to this rule was 'Born In The USA', which gained tempo with each shift away from 'Vietnam Blues' and towards its anthemic destination. Five exploratory versions fill the pre-*Nebraska* demo tape (bootlegged as *Fistful of Dollars*). Initially in the same bluesy mode as 'Vietnam Blues', the song describes how this American-born protagonist ended up being shipped to Vietnam - 'I got in a roadhouse jam/ They gave me the choice: the barracks or the jailhouse/ With my country I did stand'.

But by the next take – thirty seconds over Saigon – everything has changed. As a despairingly driven riff replaces this deltaesque dirge, he finally has an opening: 'Got in a little hometown jam . . . so they put a rifle in my hand/ Born, baby, in the USA/ I believe in the American way'. That sardonic last line would have made Guthrie proud. But – like the one element he transferred to 'Shut Out The Light' ('in the dark forest . . .') – it wouldn't survive the honing process.

He already had more than enough songs for a much-needed return-to-form. But there was one other song that seemed to require sustained work before it was ready for the Portastudio, having begun life under the title 'The Answer'. Eventually recorded as 'The Losin' Kind', this 'one night of sin' was another mini-movie in song, living proof he wasn't bluffing when he said, 'When I write the song, I write it to be the movie – not to *make* a movie, to *be* a movie.'

It would become the only cut from the *Nebraska* tape to remain unreleased, its greatest crime being too many ideas for one song. The compressed narrative – 'It was around 3 A.M. we went out to this empty little roadside bar/ It was there the cash register was open, it was there I hit that guy too hard' – was exactly what he had been reaching for on 'Johnny 99'. In 'Losin' Kind', though, like any good film noir, all the action occurs in one night. He meets a girl, they get drunk, take off together, pull over at another bar, rob the till, club the barman, take off, crash the car, get rescued/arrested by a state trooper, who on the original pre-*Nebraska* demo delivers the immortal line, 'What did you think you were doin', son?' The song answered the patrolman by telling the loser's story. But in the end, Springsteen preferred the slighter 'Highway Patrolman', even though that song required a degree of exposition to make listeners empathize with its particular antihero.

If an adult narrator tauter than a tightrope was the main voice on the final collection, a painstaking Springsteen also occasionally adopted the all-seeing innocence of a child to provide an alternative angle but a similar moral. Again he was thinking along cinematic lines: 'I was thinking in a way of *To Kill A Mockingbird*, because in that movie there was a child's eye view. And *Night Of The Hunter* also had that . . . when the little girl was running through the woods.' And so on a couple of the lesser cuts – 'Mansion On The Hill' and 'Used Cars' – he constructed 'stories that came directly out of my experience with my family'. The two viewpoints – adult and child – were still inextricably entwined: '[*Nebraska*] sounds a lot like me . . . I don't mean in the particular details of the stories, but the emotional feeling feels a lot like my childhood felt to me.' It was a twist that again came directly from his reading of Flannery O'Connor, a connection he went out of his way to publicly acknowledge, partly to show how much broader his influences had become:

> **Bruce Springsteen**: There was something in those stories of [O'Connor's] that I felt captured a certain part of the American character that I was interested in writing about . . . She got to the heart of some part of meanness that she never spelled out, because if she spelled it out you wouldn't be getting it. It was always at the core of every one of her stories – the way that she'd left that hole there, that hole that's inside everybody. There was some dark thing – a component of spirituality – that I sensed in her stories, and that set me off exploring characters of my own. She knew original sin – she knew how to give it the flesh of a story . . . I'd come out of a period of my own writing where I'd been writing big, sometimes operatic, and occasionally rhetorical things. I was interested in finding another way to write about those subjects, about people, and another way to address what was going on around me and in the country – a more scaled-down, more personal, more restrained way of getting . . . ideas across. So [this was] right prior to the record *Nebraska*. [1997]

How ironic, then, that the one thing which should divide O'Connor from this acolyte was her devout Catholicism. However much she might be oppressed by a 'meanness' in this world – and she uses the term in both of her best-known short stories, 'The River' and 'A Good Man Is Hard To Find' – the promise of salvation remained a given. But Springsteen held his hands up and said, 'The *Nebraska* stuff was . . . kinda about a spiritual crisis, in which man is left lost. It's like he has nothing left to tie him into society anymore . . . When you get to the point where nothing makes sense . . . [and] you just feel that alone thing, that loneness – that's the beginning of the end.'

His rejection of the southern Catholic author's moral universe made *Nebraska* a far darker experience than even the bleakest O'Connor short story. And still he told the media, 'There was always hope . . . it's [just] seeing the cards the way they're dealt. If it's real, it's never depressing.' Perhaps he was remembering how *Darkness* had played in the wider world. Such 'realism' would inform everything from this point forward – the search for transcendence was permanently on hold (or at least in abeyance until he told *Mojo* in 2006, 'We live in a tragic world, but there's grace all around you'). Now it was just a case of holding on and enjoying the ride:

> **Bruce Springsteen**: If I was trying to capture anything on those [early eighties] records, it was a sense of a less morally certain universe . . . I was interested in trying to paint it as I saw it. With your own weaknesses and the places where

> you fail and get caught up in The Big Muddy. I was interested in taking a less heroic stance . . . Despite my protestations over the years in some of my [early] lyrics, there was a heroic posture to a lot of the music I created . . . and as you get older you realize how hard it is to do the right thing . . . [But] that moral certainty is attractive in a world that's so fundamentally confusing . . . Most of popular culture is based on childhood fairy tales . . . Even though some part inside of us yearns for a morally certain world, that world doesn't exist. That's not the real world. And at some point you've got to make that realization, make your choices, and do the best that you can. [1992]

The other iconic twentieth-century American artists he namechecked on *Nebraska*'s behalf – John Lee Hooker and Robert Johnson – had more in common with their fellow songwriter as regards their ambivalent relationship to their supposed saviour. In Johnson's case, it was a relationship he failed to resolve before the devil knocked on his door and told him it was time to go. Comparing oneself to these two iconic bluesmen set an awfully high bar, but set it Springsteen did. If, as he claimed in *Songs*, he was influenced by their records because they 'sounded so good with the lights out', how did he envisage making such an album with the E Street Band? Because when he started putting the *Nebraska* tape together – in late December 1981 – it was still 'merely' a demo for an E Street album, a way of ensuring they didn't disappear down the same tunnel of drudgery for a fourth time:

> **Bruce Springsteen**: I got tired of spending every single penny I had making records . . . When I came back from *The River* tour, it was the first time I had a little money in the bank, and I said, 'This time I'm not gonna go in and break myself again.' Because . . . if you were scrubbing away in the studio learning your craft, it was on your dime, my friend . . . And I was spending a lot of time learning what to do in the studio. An enormous amount: *The River* record went on for a year or two. So I told my roadie, go out and get me some little tape player . . . and I can tell if I have anything before I waste time and money in the studio with the band. So he came back with a little 4-track TEAC [Portastudio]. [2010]

What has never been satisfactorily resolved is just how long these fabled home 'sessions' lasted. Springsteen, in the above interview, recalled that 'there were maybe two or three takes of each . . . I mixed it through a

Gibson Echoplex, which is the sound of the echo on that record . . . onto another boom box. So the final mix came off the boom box you would take to the beach . . . I sat down, and in about three days I sang all the songs from *Nebraska*. I [already] had them written.' Dave Marsh, in his hagiographic *Glory Days*, implies it all came together in a single day – January 3, 1982 (the day it *was* put together); an assumption he may have taken from a usually-reliable source. In his November 1982 *Musician* review of the album, Paul Nelson describes 'one man, just sitting at home in front of a four-track cassette machine on the night of January 3, 1982, [who] felt he had to tell these stories . . . one take per tune'.

It was information Nelson could only have gotten from one of two sources. He or they wanted him to print this myth. Whereas the 'roadie' Springsteen sent out to buy that TEAC Portastudio, Mike Batlan – on hand throughout – specifically told journalist David McGee, 'Springsteen began organizing his work for *Nebraska* during the first week of December 1982 – that's when [I] was directed to buy the four-track . . . Actual recording began on the 17 or 18 December and ended around January 3.'

Batlan's seems the more credible scenario, given that TEAC's Portastudio was never the most user-friendly of tools, and 'bouncing' between tracks – to overdub an additional instrument or double-track a vocal – on a 4-track cassette running at 3¾ ips raised a whole set of issues. Even leaving aside such technical difficulties, to record and mix fourteen tracks in three days would be going some, especially when it involved some thirty-nine takes.* What he sent to Jon Landau sometime in January was a fifteen-song tape – the fourteen demos, as well as seven alternate takes and five alternate mixes, prefaced by a version of 'Johnny Bye Bye' which has long been assumed to be some lost outtake, but was probably a live take from Meadowlands. Accompanying the tape were three pages of notes.

---

* The take information on the fifteen songs is as follows:
Nebraska (Tk. 4); State Trooper (Tk. 5); Open All Night (Tk. 2); Johnny 99 (Tk.3); Highway Patrolman (Tk. 4); Pink Cadillac (Tk. 2); Downbound Train (Tk. 3); Mansion On The Hill (Tk. 1); Atlantic City (Tks. 2+4 were shortlisted, released take is one of these); Born In The USA (Tk. 1); Losin' Kind (3 takes – Tk. 2); Used Cars (Tk. 4); Reason To Believe (2 takes – Tk.1); Child Bride (no take info.). + My Father's House (2 takes, recorded May 25).
This would also appear to be the order in which the tracks were recorded, save for 'Child Bride', which was not backed-up on June 1 1982 and may have been recorded independently, i.e. earlier or probably later than the other thirteen January tracks. Peter Carlin repeats the recorded in-one-day legend in his biography.

In these notes Springsteen suggested 'Atlantic City' 'should probably be done with whole band + really rockin' out'; 'Born In The USA' should also 'be done very hard rockin''; and that 'Downbound Train' was an 'uptempo rocker [which] for full effect needs band'. But he was already expressing doubts about 'Losin' Kind' – 'I like the verses but I can't seem to find a better punch line' – and 'The Child Bride' – 'kind of a work in progress or more like without progress. I worked a real long time on this song and could never quite get it right.' Neither track would make the final cut. (In the latter's case, he simply lopped off the last two verses and recast it as 'Working On The Highway', in the process sacrificing one of the best verses from a highly productive writing season: 'There's nights I can't sleep, no matter how hard I try/ So from my window I watch the moonlight fall on the far hillside/ I imagine I put on my jacket, go down to this little roadside bar/ Pick a stranger and spin around the dance floor to a Mexican guitar'.)

The cassette sequence had evidently been thought out in advance. Just 'Child Bride' changed places from the original 14-track cassette, and only 'Highway Patrolman' (originally called 'Deputy') would be moved when the LP was sequenced in late May. On both Landau's full copy – discounting the 'live' 'Johnny Bye Bye' – and the released LP, 'Nebraska' opened proceedings, though Springsteen felt the song 'may need editing'. He thus set the overall tone before engaging the listener with a more commercial track, the accessible 'Atlantic City'.

'Atlantic City' had begun life nine months ago as part of 'Fist full of Dollars', but he had struggled to resolve this well-crafted song even as he began demoing (hence, his inclusion of three different takes with slightly different lyrics in the copy he made for Landau, and the two alternates on the 'album master' in June). But he certainly knew who he had in his sights – the underworld figures who had taken 'this old beach resort, one of those places that's fallen on hard times . . . [and] legalize[d] gambling . . . Now all they've got is big golden casinos next block away from the slums, and a mafia that fights for control.' The resignation in the singer's voice is there for all to hear when he sings to his gal, 'Put your make up on, fix your hair up pretty/ And meet me tonight in Atlantic City'.

'Reason To Believe', which seemed to end the 'album' on a note of hope, had no such vocal resignation, Springsteen bequeathing it a gutsy, devil-may-care delivery. Yet the singer questions the faith of each character, and in concert would sometimes preface the song with a statement suggesting he thought these believers were blundering in the dark, looking for a candle: 'This is about blind faith. Like, if your girlfriend comes home in the middle of the night and her clothes are all messed up; you see somebody pulling away from in front of your house, and you ask her where she's been, she says she's been with her girlfriends, you say, "Okay." That's blind faith . . . Or when the president says he's gonna do something about arms-control, that's blind faith too.'*

From the nihilism of 'Nebraska' to this no less desperate vignette was but a walk around the block of Reagan's America. The song asks of these folk – the man who can't accept he killed a dog, the woman pining for a long-gone lover, the parent of a dead baby, the jilted groom – what is it that gets you up in the morning? Springsteen gave no answers, not even a moralizing coda. And yet, he was still insisting, 'Maybe you've got to downsize some of your expectations . . . just in growing up, in accepting adulthood. My characters, I think that's what they do. They say, "Man, I had some shit thrown at me, but here I still am."'

That Springsteen himself had reached a point where he had lost any reason to believe was clear from other things he said, particularly when introducing it live: 'Sometimes people need something to believe in so bad that they'll believe in anything that comes along – just so that they got some reason to believe.' He later admitted this reflected his own mindset at this time: 'From "Badlands" through to "Reason To Believe", that's kind of an investigation of that place . . . that point – well, that was the bottom.'

When he finished compiling the tape, both the 'expanded' version he made for Landau and the one he carried around in his back pocket (and also copied for band-members), he was pleasantly surprised to find a consistency of tone and a near-seamless segue of styles that gave this demo tape a cohesiveness absent from the last E Street collection. Could it be that if you picked the right songs, the sequence would take care of itself?:

> **Bruce Springsteen**: [*Nebraska*] was something people weren't expecting, and it turned everything I'd done to that point on its head . . . I went for an emotional flatness that I felt was a part of the way those stories would get told . . . / . . . This junky equipment unintentionally [made] this very lo-fi, spooky [record]. I mean, I knew the mood I was going after, but a lot of it was just an accident. [2007/2010]

---

* Tacoma WA 17/10/84.

Landau was not so sure it *was* a demo tape. 'Right from the beginning,' he was 'somewhat skeptical . . . that some of this [*Nebraska*] material was gonna function better with a full rhythm-type thing . . . When you hear the *Nebraska* songs done even with a modest arrangement, in the [live] show . . . Bruce has to push harder . . . But on *Nebraska*, he's almost singing to himself.'[GD] Springsteen, though, had a thousand reasons to believe. Never had this band failed him. And when he resumed work with the guys, just three weeks later, they did not fail him now.

These sessions were not, however, starting the potentially torturous process of turning said demos into album tracks. They were recording songs Springsteen could donate to Donna Summer, and Gary US Bonds (who was about to embark on his second E Street Album, *On The Line*). The song they initially recorded for Summer Landau insisted was too damn good and instructed his employer to go write her something else. He would keep 'Cover Me' safe at home. Springsteen's response was to write 'Protection', which was still wasted on Summer (though she actually makes a very good fist of it). The original version, cut with the E Street Band at the Hit Factory on February 23, has a touch of 'Roulette' about it. It even shares that song's sense of paranoia: 'The phone rings in the middle of the night/ And when I pick it up, you won't answer/ A knock on the door, I rush down the stairs/ When I open up, there's no one there'. It proved that the E Streeters, even after a four-month break, could still cut up rough.

But rather than taking them straight into the studio to start work on an electrified *Nebraska*, Springsteen thought he needed another set of demos, now that he'd got the hang of TEAC's new toy. Somewhat predictably, the net result was another dozen songs he had no need of, and which merely served to muddy these already-black waters. Naturally, there were also more rough-cut gems left lying on the riverbank, come April.

Indeed, of the thirteen songs on the post-*Nebraska* winter '82 demos (later bootlegged from Batlan's copy as *Lost Masters X*), no less than eight would receive the E Street heat-treatment that spring: 'Downbound Train', 'Wages of Sin', 'Baby I'm So Cold', 'Jesse James and Robert Ford', 'Your Love Is All Around Me Now', 'True Love Is Hard To Come By', 'Fade To Black' and 'Glory Days'. Also probably recorded in these weeks was a solo slice of rockabilly called 'The Big Payback', which would appear as a European B-side to 'Open All Night'. Displaying a healthy regard for wordplay not always evident recently, it was another fine, but diversionary, howl: 'Well, it's a wham bam, thank you ma'am, god damn, look out Sam/ I took on that train rumblin' down the track/ They got your neck in the noose, your hands are tied up in back/ And you're a-workin' and workin' for the big payback.'

Many of the remaining songs he worked on represented a straight continuation of the *Nebraska* mindset, and so were in a sense already redundant. The most crafted of these – something he reworked the following year – was 'James Lincoln Deer'. The 1982 demo certainly had a *Nebraska* zip code, James being one of those now-familiar father-figures whose 'whole world went black' when he lost his job. He makes no apology when he shoots an innocent bystander in cold blood at a 7-Eleven hold-up: 'I held my pistol to his face/ His eyes caught fire with fear/ I said, 'Remember me before you die/ My name is James Lincoln Deer'. Something of an overreaction to unemployment methinks, but certainly a good argument for gun control. The subject was more overtly addressed on 'Ruled By The Gun', with its startling opening verse setting out the songwriter's societal stall: 'Everywhere I go I see people crying/ Every step I take I see young men dying . . . / They lay dead on the cathedral steps in the sun/ In a world ruled by the gun'. Neither song, though, would figure in Bruce's plans come April, when the band reassembled for rehearsals and recording.

Elsewhere, he re-examined failed relationship/s in the cold light of night, honing both 'Baby I'm So Cold' and 'Fade To Black' till they shone in the dark, and writing the equally arresting 'Your Love Is All Around Me'. It was an intentionally ironic title (à la 'Reason To Believe') for a song about a long-gone lover: 'I wake up in the morning and your picture's there/ The closet's filled baby with the clothes you used to wear/ I still got that ring baby on my finger/ Although you've gone away, your memory lingers'. The singer unashamedly proclaims, 'I'd rather live like this than let you go', suggesting a real edge of desperation. How desperate is only revealed at song's end: 'Oh, somebody turn out the light on me now/ Oh, let the darkness come in.' Rehearsed in April – with that clichéd 'ring on finger' rhyme superseded by the stark realism of 'Over in the corner sits your perfume/ As the first rays of sun hit this darkened room' – it was recorded at the May *BITUSA* sessions. But this was one song that went down, down, down and kept going.

At times, those April rehearsals – one of which has recently emerged – seem to have been more about introducing the band to the songs written in the interim than working up arrangements for those he'd demoed in January (only 'Reason To Believe' features on the known rehearsal). That was probably a mistake. Certainly, when sessions started for real at Power Station on April 26, they instantly hit a problem:

> **Bruce Springsteen**: We went into the studio a couple of times to record those [*Nebraska*] songs with the band, but it just didn't sound as good . . . / . . . The songs had a lot of detail so that, when the band started to wail away into it, the characters got lost. Like 'Johnny 99' – I thought, 'Oh, that'd be great if we could do a rock version.' But when you did that, the song disappeared . . . It needed that kinda austere, echoey sound, just one guitar – one guy telling his story. [1984]

They actually spent the whole first day recording 'Atlantic City', which, according to Landau, both Springsteen and himself had agreed 'sounded like it was gonna really lend itself to the band . . . [Yet] *that* was goin' nowhere. No way was it as good as what he had goin' on that demo tape. Then we tried "Nebraska" . . . Bruce had a whole little arrangement for it that had been rehearsed.'[GD] In fact, they tried a couple of other songs before attempting 'Nebraska': 'Johnny Bye Bye' and 'Born In The USA'. The latter track worked just fine. In fact, it seemed nobody wanted to stop playing when they finally hit that blasting gelatine groove:

> **Bruce Springsteen**: One night we did 'Born In The USA'. We just kinda did it off the cuff; I never taught it to the band. I went in and said, 'Roy, get this riff.' And he just pulled out that sound, played the riff on the synthesizer. We played it two times, and our second take is on the record. That's why the guys are really on the edge . . . There was no arrangement. I said [to Max], 'When I stop, keep the drums going.' [But] that thing in the end with all the drums, that just kinda happened. [1984]

> **Max Weinberg**: ['Born In The USA'] absolutely grabbed us. We played it [a second time] and got an even better groove on it. At the end, as we were stopping, Bruce gave me the high sign to do all these wild fills, and we went back into the song and jammed for about ten minutes, which was edited out. I remember that night as the greatest single experience I've ever had recording, and it set the tone for the whole record . . . It was really something to live up to.

Clearly, the problem was not the band's still razor-sharp chops but rather the fact that these songs – or some of them, anyway – did not suit the most rock-oriented musicians this side of the Rockies. Actually, Weinberg's account of the moment they nailed 'Born In The USA' is belied by the tape of the full *eight*-minute version. Not so much 'Hey Jude' as 'It's All Too Much', the additional four minutes proved this ain't the E Street Band Sancious quit. Pruned of its repetitious rump, though, the track was a lean, mean rockin' machine.

There were other magical moments at these sessions, which ran through April 30. Tellingly, the two other tracks which carried over to the 1984 E Street album – 'Working On The Highway' and 'Downbound Train' – were also songs Springsteen had rebuilt from the ground up since they were demoed. If on 'Working On The Highway' the whole underage element was quietly Tippexed out, leaving the listener to wonder exactly what crime left the narrator breaking rocks in the hot sun, the result was as much 'I Fought The Law' as 'Child Bride'. And it seemed to work. As for 'Downbound Train', I don't think I can improve on what Geoffrey Himes wrote in his excellent monograph on *BITUSA*:

> Downbound Train" was retrofitted with completely different music that liberated its lyric . . . Springsteen had overdubbed a heavily echoed, wordless moan onto the four-track demo. That moan, which echoed the lyric's reference to the train's "whistle whining", captured the lyric's mood of doom far better than the herky-jerky guitar figure. So he ditched the rockabilly guitar, slowed the tempo considerably, wrote an actual melody, and rebuilt the song around that moan, which now became a synthesizer riff.

When it came to the rest of the January demos, though, Landau and Springsteen were in full agreement: 'We're not [even] in the ballpark.' Chuck Plotkin concurred: 'Our treatment of the *Nebraska* stuff in the studio [was] . . . less meaningful . . . less emotionally compelling . . . less honest; we were reducing the stuff.'[GD] Springsteen proferred his own explanation in 1984, 'The minute [the E Street Band] start learnin' to play [a song], they start figurin' out parts and they get self-conscious. But the first two takes when they're learnin' it, they're worried about just hangin' on. So they're playing right at the edge, and they're playing very intuitively, which in general is how our best stuff happens.' He applied this lesson to the majority of E Street sessions from May 1982 to March 1984.

It may also explain why, after spending a whole day on 'Atlantic City', Springsteen and the band roared through twelve of the remaining fourteen songs on the January demo (the only exceptions being 'Pink Cadillac' and 'State Trooper') in just three days. There was even time for four Nebraskan afterthoughts: 'Jesse James & Robert Ford', 'William Davis', 'A Gun In Every Home' and 'On The Prowl'. The last two they cut on April 30, the last day the Streeters devoted to the so-called *Electric Nebraska*. When sessions resumed, the following week, they were working on an E Street Album, leaving Springsteen to decide what to do with these dirty dozen demos.

Maybe it was time to get back to writing about things which actually related to *him*. In which case, 'On The Prowl' was as good place to start as any. A song he later donated to Cats On A Smooth Surface – a favourite local rockabilly band – it delved deep in the dark forest that passed for Springsteen's psyche. The first anyone knew of such a song was when he dropped a portion of the lyrics into the middle of 'Lucille', during an August onstage jam session with the 'Cats' at Asbury Park's Stone Pony. Even divorced from its original context, that mid-song rap almost recalled his 'Sad Eyes' monologues, such was the intensity with which it was delivered:

> 'Now, every night I have a dream. I get up out of bed and I go looking for my baby. I go looking for my girl. When the clock strikes midnight I tear off the covers and I put on my jacket and I gotta go out on the prowl. Well, night after lonely night, my head don't touch the bed. I'm on a two-lane blacktop cruising in my rocket sled, I'm on the prowl . . . There's only one thing that I'm certain every mile, keep searching for a wild child, I'm on the prowl . . . They got a name for Dracula and Frankenstein's son, they ain't got no name now for this thing that I become. I keep looking, I keep searching, but every morning I ended up with the same thing.'

At another Stone Pony guest appearance with the 'Cats', six weeks later, he unveiled the song itself – the only stand-alone performance it ever received. How apposite that he should (only) perform it at the place, and in the very town, where he really was a predatory polygamist on the prowl for pussy. Because the song was a first-person narrative which walked a mile in his actual shoes, as casual liaisons became the name of the game, a substitute hobby until the real thing came along. 'On The Prowl' is a portrait of the 1982 Bruce Springsteen, single, successful and looking to get screwed. Lines like, 'In the morning I check my mirror/ And I hang my head and cry/ But at night I get a burning, burning, burning deep inside/ I'm on the prowl', were delivered at the only confessional he currently recognized, the stage of The Stone Pony, a stone's throw from the boardwalk.

Again, though, he looked to give the song away, perhaps because its subject matter was a little too close to the mark (no matter how humorously framed). But he also wasn't sure it suited the current E Street set-up. Rockabilly was another style of American popular music they had not fully mastered – which may explain why he also put 'Pink Cadillac' on the back burner.

As of April 30 the *Electric Nebraska* became another lost album, to go with 'Album #4' and *The Ties That Bind*. (Save that in this case no tape has ever leaked – partly because the New York-based collector Mike Batlan sold these tapes to in the late eighties was not as willing to share his booty as the party who bought the *Lost Masters* material.) Springsteen had arrived at the same point Dylan reached after four months of work with The Hawks on the successor to *Highway 61 Revisited* had yielded a single usable cut. As he told Robert Shelton on a flight from Lincoln, Nebraska (really!) in March 1966, 'It was the band. But you see, I didn't know that. I didn't want to *think* that.' Dylan acted decisively, hiring a set of hep Nashville cats to help him record *Blonde On Blonde* in just seven studio days. The Hawks would remain Dylan's live backup outfit for the next eight years, but it would be seven and a half more years before they joined him in the studio again, and only after they had proven their worth by making five frequently-superb studio albums of their own. As The Band.

It would take Springsteen a similar period to decide which direction home to take in the long run. Meanwhile, he would record the eight other songs needed for the last E Street studio album of the twentieth century, a handful of B-sides and at least forty songs not 'needed'. Between making and scrapping at least two 'alternate' E Street Band albums in 1982 and 1983, he would also record a solo successor to *Nebraska*. But, like both E Street 'albums', the *Nebraska* 'sequel' he spent the first three months of 1983 recording would go the way of all flesh and most post-1977 Springsteen/E Street Band projects. Thankfully, this was not the fate of the songs he had demoed back in January. These he had now decided to release – just not in the form he had spent the last six days trying to electrify.

Chapter 9: 1982–84 – Growin' Up

> When I was doing *Nebraska*, people would come up to me and say, 'Don't be so bummed out!' Sometimes I'd start thinking maybe [I was], but [then] I realized I was just growing up. – Bruce Springsteen, 1984

What happened next would prove to be a startling affirmation of both Springsteen's abiding creativity and the E Street Band's ability to raise its game when it mattered most. It had been nine years since they had cut *The Wild, the Innocent* in just a dozen sessions, and every album since had become exponentially more difficult. And yet in just ten sessions, over a thirteen-day period in May 1982 [3rd-14th], Springsteen and his band would record some twenty songs. From these they would cull an eleven-track album with real commercial clout, a rough-mix sequence being readied on July 5. Only for him to, you guessed it, change his mind.

The bulk of that album – seven from eleven – *would* eventually be released on an 18-million seller in June 1984, at which point Springsteen sought to explain what happened two years earlier: 'We initially went in the studio to try to record *Nebraska* with the band. [Instead,] we recorded the first side of *Born In The USA* . . . [In fact] if you look at the material, particularly on the first side, it's actually written very much like *Nebraska* – the characters and the stories, the style of writing – except it's just in the rock-band setting.'

The *Electric Nebraska* had not been entirely abandoned. Rather it was made to fit the proven E Street model. 'Born In The USA', 'Downbound Train' and 'Working On The Highway' – the three songs on that demo tape which suited both settings – were held over from the late April sessions and worked on some more, though they already knew the fourth take of 'Born In The USA' from April 27 was a keeper. Also retained was 'Gun In Every Home'. There was even time for another hit-and-hope electric 'Johnny 99' on day one. Nor was he inclined to let other songs rehearsed with the band go to waste. 'Baby I'm So Cold', 'Fade To Black' and 'Your Love Is All Around Me' were all brought to the studio for the first time. And yet he would later claim there was no specific plan when recording began:

> **Bruce Springsteen**: At the time we weren't consciously making a record. The *Nebraska* record had just come out [sic], and we had the bunch of cuts from the studio *Nebraska* sessions. It was just sitting there, waiting to be mixed . . . We did [the *BITUSA* material] in two weeks, the same two weeks we spent trying to record some new *Nebraska* stuff. [1986]

Songs like 'Wages of Sin', 'Your Love Is All Around Me', 'A Good Man Is Hard To Find (Pittsburgh)', 'Stop The War', 'Baby I'm So Cold' and 'Fade To Black', stockpiled during home sessions in February–March, represented the 'new *Nebraska* stuff'. Springsteen also had a ready supply of E Street-friendly rabble-rousers. The first (and best) of these they spent most of May 3rd recording. It was the point at which *BITUSA* became an album project in its own right. 'Murder Incorporated' in it's author's words, 'dealt with the paranoia and compounded violence of life in America: gated communities, the loss of freedom and the mistrust of your own neighbour'.

If 'Born In The USA' was an angry song, 'Murder Inc.' took that fury to another level and a whole other demographic. The setting is urban America, the mood – from the opening couplet – murderous: 'Bobby's got a gun that he keeps beneath his pillow/ Out on the street your chances are zero'; but it could just as easily be Saigon ('So you keep a little secret down deep inside your dresser drawer/ For dealing with the heat you're feelin' down on the killin' floor'). He never explicitly states Bobby is running from the mob – for whom the original Murder Inc. carried out 'hits' in the thirties and forties – but such is clearly the case. In the final verse, they get their man: 'Now the cops reported you as just another homicide'. As a counterpoint to 'Born In The USA', following that anthemic opener in the July 1982 sequence, it hit its target.

It was two days later that they next departed from songs considered for the *Electric Nebraska*, though the way Bruce talked about 'Glory Days' one could easily be misled into thinking it was something left over from the former project: 'What I wanted to do was to make it feel like you meet somebody and you walk a little while in their shoes and see what their life is like. And then what does that mean to you? That's kind of the direction my writing's going in, and in general it's just the thing I end up finding the most satisfying. Just saying what somebody had to say, and not making too big a deal out of it.'

Based on a real-life encounter with an old school friend in the summer of 1973 – as Bruce confirmed to a fellow classmate at their 1997 school reunion – 'Glory Days' first showed up on the winter 1982 home demos. Over eight years had passed since he, then a struggling recording artist with a single flop album, ran into ex-classmate Joe DePugh at The Headliner. DePugh had indeed been a star Little League pitcher and a teammate of Springsteen's in the Babe Ruth League 'back in high school'. After a try-out for the LA Dodgers, he ended up playing college basketball before becoming a self-employed contractor.

But 1973 was a long time ago. Something else must have triggered the song; and it was probably a movie Springsteen saw in November 1980 with a fan he met on the street, Woody Allen's *Stardust Memories*. In that underrated film, there is a memorable scene where the grouchy film director returns to his hotel after a long day only to be confronted by someone from his old high school, who has clearly been waiting all evening in the lobby. When he asks if the director remembers him, Allen replies, 'Sure, we used to play stickball together.' He asks what his school buddy is doing. The guy replies, 'I drive a cab.' 'There's nothing wrong with that.' 'Yeah, but look at me compared to you . . . the broads, you know.' It's a priceless scene and, although Springsteen told the fan who accompanied him to the Allen film he didn't feel this way, one can't help suspecting it reminded him of a similar incident from his own life.

In fact, when he first demoed the song, all he had was this scene with the baseball buddy, 'just talking about them glory days', and a verse about a father who at fifty-nine got put on the scrapheap after twenty years working 'in production on the Ford plant assembly line / Pluggin' in them, slappin' in them firewalls and windshields'. But by May 5 he had a song that walked the full mile with a skip and a beat. It was part of a highly productive session, resulting in 'Gun In Every Home', 'Stop The War', an even better 'Downbound Train', and two songs it would take him seventeen years to release, 'A Good Man Is Hard To Find' and 'My Love Will Not Let You Down'.

The former of these, logged simply as 'Pittsburg', took its full title and another reference to the meanness in this world from Flannery O'Connor's most famous short story. But the song itself is concerned with a broken-hearted woman who realizes that someday she's gonna have to tell her own daughter the facts of life: 'Now there's a little girl asleep in the back room/ She's gonna have to tell about the meanness in this world/ And how a good man is so hard to find'. Lyrically at least, 'My Love . . .' was something of a natural successor to 'On The Prowl', with lines like, 'At night I walk the streets lookin' for romance/ But I always end up stumblin' in a half trance'. Like in that song, he is primarily concerned with physical potency – love as a four-letter word spelt l-u-s-t. He even adopts a suitably sacrilegious image to depict the virgin he is planning to deflower tonight: 'I see you standin' across the room watchin' me without a sound/ But I'm gonna push my way through that crowd, I'm gonna tear your holy walls down'.

By the end of that first week of sessions he had the makings of a weighty eighties E Street album. They weren't hanging around. As Weinberg would inform *Musician*, 'There was very little rehearsal. We just went in without ever really running the songs down and recorded everything live . . . Sometimes the band didn't even know the chords.' Springsteen was determined to get the band's first instincts – and to hell with second-guessing. His own memory of these sessions certainly chimes with Weinberg's: 'We didn't do any more than five takes on any one song. If it got any more than that we'd choose an earlier take . . . We put some more guitar on some of the tracks and some backing vocals, but they were all done real live and quick.' Could it be this was how they made all those great records he had heard growing up?

But when the band returned to Power Station on the following Monday (the 10th), he was preparing to take them down the dark end of the street. Over the next two days, he would summon forth 'Johnny Bye Bye', 'Your Love Is All Around Me', 'Fade To Black', 'Baby I'm So Cold', 'Wages of Sin' and something logged as 'Stay Hungry (Common Ground)' – all songs with the kind of wind-chill factor that came whistling straight from *Nebraska*.

He also brought with him the freshly-minted 'I'm On Fire'. Actually, according to the man himself, the latter came to him 'one night in the studio when [he] was just goofing around with a Johnny Cash and the Tennessee Three rhythm'. 'I'm On Fire' may have pared its imagery to the point of parsimony, but it communicates its dirty little secret just fine. A straightforward song of adulterous desire, the narrator's ardent professions of lust again mask a secret sorrow: 'Sometimes it's like someone took a knife baby, edgy and dull/ And cut a six-inch valley through the middle of my soul'.

Finally, on the 12th, after reviving 'Cover Me' and overlaying it with bongos, he produced the ultimate anti-relationship song, 'Down, Down, Down' (issued as 'I'm Going Down'), a cut he would preface in concert with a humorous but oh-so-telling summation of relationships – the gospel according to Bruce:

> 'Here´s a song about relationships, how when you first meet somebody, you´re kissing all the time and holding hands every place you go. It´s like, if you´re gonna go out to the movie, she says, "Oh, honey, I don´t care, we can see whatever you wanna see," and you say, "No, we can see whatever you wanna see." Whatever they wear, it's like, "Oh honey, you look so beautiful tonight", and, "Gee, do you wanna go out tonight?" "Oh, I don´t care what we do, as long as I´m with you" . . . / . . . You come back about four or five months later and you hear, "Are you gonna take me out tonight or do I have to sit here and look at your face?", "Are you gonna make love to me tonight, or are we waiting for the full moon again?" . . .. In the end you´re sitting there and she´s sitting there, it's just a cold hard stare.'*

Already, in just eight sessions, they had recorded enough world-weary world-beaters for a three-sided album. Judiciously pruned, it could have been potentially the equal of *Darkness*, returning him to the road he spun off when heading down to *The River*. But after a series of bold steps forward in the first eight sessions, he took two steps back at the last two. First, he returned to an idea originating in a song called 'Stay Hungry', which now became 'This Hard Land' (the final line of which reads, 'If you can't make it stay hard, stay hungry, stay alive if you can'). A song conceived

* Meadowlands 17/8/84 + Hartford 7/9/84.

from a stray couplet in an early version of 'Open All Night', it was a ponderously self-important résumé of every *Bound For Glory* cliché that had ever captured the Jersey boy's heart. Evidence he thought he'd stumbled onto the set of some John Ford movie comes thick and fast: 'We're ridin' in the whirlwind searchin' for lost treasure / Way down south of the Rio Grande / We're ridin' 'cross that river in the moonlight / Up onto the banks of this hard land'.

The session on the 13th then ended with an unexpected revival of a song he originally wrote for *Darkness*, 'Darlington County'. Perhaps he really was looking to connect the dots. Conclusive evidence was provided the following day, when he wrapped up 'Another Side of the E Street Band' with a reinterpretation of the song that in 1976 changed everything, always, 'Frankie'. However, a few lyrical changes were intended to demonstrate a shift in perspective. In the 1982 version, possibilities have been shut down. Escape is no longer an option as Springsteen penned the chilly couplet, 'Well, everybody's dyin', this town's closin' down / They're all sittin' down at the courthouse, waiting for 'em to take the flag down', to replace the fieriest image in the original, a summation of a greater *Darkness*, 'There's machines and there's fire on the outside of town'.

Other lyrical tweaks suggested a similar failure of nerve. That glorious original-sin image, 'Living and dying like I was born to do', has been replaced with the anodyne, 'Now and forever, my love is for you', while the transcendent, 'In the darkness there'll be hidden worlds that shine' has become enclosed in four walls: 'I don't know what I'm gonna find . . . maybe a world I can call mine.' In keeping with the austere vibe of recent songs, there was not even a sax coda to convince us it's still gonna work out fine. Whatever its lapses, though, this former classic gave him a second album in less than six months. If only Springsteen were willing to allow himself to be convinced:

> **Bruce Springsteen**: What takes so long is finding out what the idea is. You have a feeling that you go by. After *Nebraska*, you have to come from there and get back to somewhere very different. We recorded a lot of [other] stuff when I did *Nebraska*. But I just didn't seem to have the whole thing as to what I wanted to do . . . I [felt I] had recorded a bunch of songs. I never had an album. Because if I had an album, I would have put it out. [1984]

That was not quite the whole truth. Throughout June, Plotkin, Springsteen and co., worked on mixing *both* albums. The one with the E Street Band received the following sequence:

> **Side 1**: Born In The USA. Murder Inc. Downbound Train. Down Down Down. Glory Days. My Love.
> **Side 2**: Working On The Highway. Darlington County. Frankie. I'm On Fire. This Hard Land.

The other LP took nine demos from the January 3 tape (having decided, once and for all, that three of them belonged to an E Street album), and added something equally home-grown but more recent to the mix. He initially intended to prepare both artefacts for release – after which, he would toss a coin. (As he told *Mojo* at the time of *Tracks*, 'I was going to put out [*Nebraska* and *Born In The USA*] at the same time as a double record. I didn't know what to do.') Slowly, though, *Nebraska* began to take precedence over the E Street Band's answer-album.

Perhaps, rather than putting out another double record, he could issue the two in close succession. The E Street LP could wait. And wait. The end result would be, as Geoffrey Himes suggests, all 'those extra songs, products of the most fertile songwriting period of his career, [which] could have reached the public as fresh fruit, contemporary commentaries on the world of the mid-80s, instead petrifying into historical artefacts, released in the late 90s on various anthologies.'

By mid-July, *BITUSA* was on semi-permanent hold. The sequencing of *Nebraska* was, thankfully, a lot more straightforward. After all, he only had twelve tracks – the eleven original January demos (minus 'Born In The USA', 'Downbound Train' and 'Working On The Highway') and a song he had recorded with the same Portastudio setup in two takes on May 25, eleven days after time was called on E Street duties. 'My Father's House' was partly a reworking of a song he had spent the whole of May 10 working up with the band, 'Wages of Sin', and wholly the creative by-product of recent therapy sessions:

> **Bruce Springsteen**: I had this habit for a long time. I used to get in my car and drive back through my old neighbourhood, the little town I grew up in. I'd always drive past the old houses I used to live in, sometimes late at

night. I got so I would do it really regularly – two, three, four times a week for years. I eventually got to wondering, 'What the hell am I doing?' So I went to see this psychiatrist . . . He said, 'What you're doing is, something bad happened, something went wrong, and you're going back thinking you can make it right again . . . to see if you can fix it, if you can somehow make it right . . . Well, you can't.' [1990]

A new-found maturity here invaded his songwriting, albeit mining images familiar to any long-time fan: 'My father's house shines hard and bright, it stands like a beacon calling me in the night / Calling and calling, so cold and alone / Shining 'cross this dark highway where our sins lie unatoned'. Co-opting the last verse of 'Wages of Sin' – with its image of a young boy running home 'with the devil snappin' at my heels' – Springsteen crafted a song which was deliberately and self-consciously 'meant to evoke emotion - to individualise personal emotion in the listener'. He did this by relating a story 'that came directly out of my experience with my family' in the form of a dream. He instinctively knew he required this one song to remind himself you can't go home again, and to intersect 'Open All Night' and 'Reason To Believe'. Now he just needed to lose a coupla others:

Bruce Springsteen: When I wrote the *Nebraska* stuff, there were songs I really didn't get – because I didn't get the people. I had all the detail, but if you don't have that underlying emotional connection that connects the details together, then you don't have anything. There were songs that didn't get onto *Nebraska* because they didn't say anything in the end. They had no meaning. [1984]

The losers in this lottery were 'Pink Cadillac' and 'The Losin' Kind', though both had been transferred to four-track half-inch tape on June 10, when work began in earnest on turning this 'crappy cassette' into a proper album. This took over two months – longer than it took to write and record the record – because, as Springsteen noted, 'It was hard to get on an album; that took us some time, because the recording was so strange that it wouldn't get onto wax . . . / . . . It's amazing that it got there, 'cause I was carrying that cassette around with me in my pocket without a case for a couple of weeks, just draggin' it around.'

By 1982, bootleggers had been transferring acoustic demos from cassette to vinyl for thirteen-plus years. But Springsteen wasn't prepared to just put the tape out 'as is' (as an Italian bootlegger did in 1996, when he got his hands on that original 14-track 'master' cassette – see photo insert). Even with just a four-track cassette to work with, he did nine separate mixes of 'Used Cars', with 'more slap', 'more echo', 'brighter'; and added a synthesizer to 'My Father's House'. A synthesizer was also added to 'State Trooper', making its Suicide nomenclature explicit – a decision he wisely reversed. As such, it was August 16 before there was a production master for a ten-song edit of a cassette demo.

Now they just needed to market a non-E Street Bruce Springsteen album of solo demos in bootleg sound quality to a mass audience. Again, they relied on the no-hype template of *John Wesley Harding*, issued eighteen months after the kaleidoscopic *Blonde on Blonde*. They even took a leaf from Columbia's old Dylan press ads, turning the famous 'Nobody Sings Dylan Like Dylan' into 'Nobody But Springsteen Can Tell Stories Like These'. Nonetheless, the label was heavily reliant – in a way they hadn't been since 1973 – on good reviews to help sell fans on this daring departure. Springsteen professed not to give a damn:

> **Bruce Springsteen**: [*Nebraska*] was the only record where after it was done, I really didn't care what people thought about or said about it. I just thought it was right. It rang true . . . [And] what made the record work [was] the sound of real conversation. [1984]

In fact, Greil Marcus had predicted a co-relationship between Dylan's 1967 album and Springsteen's 1982 offering some eighteen months earlier: 'As Jon Landau . . . wrote in 1968, an awareness of the Vietnam War could be felt all through Bob Dylan's *John Wesley Harding*; it is an almost certain bet that the songs Springsteen will now be writing will have something to do with the [election] of November 4. Those songs likely will not comment on those events, [but rather] reflect those events back to us, fixing moods and telling stories that are, at present, out of reach.' He was bang on. But even as *Nebraska* directly addressed Reagan's America, Springsteen was insisting he still saw himself as an apolitical man in a political world:

> **Bruce Springsteen**: I didn't think about the politics of *Nebraska* until I read in a review that it had a variety of political implications. At the time that was my most personal record – it reminded me of the way my childhood felt, the house that I grew up in. I was digging into that . . . The political aspect wasn't something that was really on my mind at the time, it was more just people struggling with those particular kinds of emotional or psychological issues. [1999]

Just about every review commented on the social and political climate in which *Nebraska* had been made. The reviews themselves, though, were decidedly mixed, even if Robert Hilburn later claimed the album 'was instantly hailed by the critics as a masterpiece of boldness and individuality'. Hilburn himself certainly hailed it as such, suggesting that in its 'best moments, Springsteen combines a captivating sense of cinematic detail with an endearing sense of America that we have not approached in pop music (sic) since the early works of John Prine and The Band'.

Another old-time advocate, Paul Nelson, had larger doubts: 'Initially, *Nebraska* sounded so demoralized and demoralizing, so murderously monotonous, so deprived of spark and hope that, in comparison, the gloomy songs from *Darkness on the Edge of Town* and *The River* seemed not altogether unhappy.' Gradually, though, over the course of his *Musician* review, he allowed those doubts to dissipate (though not wholly fade away) as he 'found a road map that took me to the right places'.

Richard C. Walls, in *Creem*, was another one who damned with faint praise: 'I like this album. Its singular gloom seems appropriate to the times and its underlying compassion is restrained and moving, though I suspect that most people will find it more admirable than likeable.' With *Rolling Stone*'s review predictably uncritical, it was left to English music weekly *Sounds* to crack the kernel and rub the nub: 'The whole deal sounds like a return to basics, capturing the rough, natural feel of the songs with no embellishment. Or depending on your view, it sounds like a bunch of demos.'

What wasn't on the cards was any kind of promotional tour or bout of interviews. As Springsteen himself noted in 1996, *Nebraska* was 'enough of an accident that I didn't really think that [it] was something I was going to tour with'. In fact, he pretty much disappeared from view in the months after *Nebraska*'s September 1982 release. Even the stylized promo video for 'Atlantic City' failed to feature the song's *auteur*. He was busy relocating operations to Los Angeles, where he could further cut himself off from the humanity he professed to embrace in song:

> **Bruce Springsteen**: I had a small place in California from the early eighties on, and it was a place where I could go and I had my cars and my motorcycles . . . You can be out of Los Angeles in thirty minutes and hit the edge of the desert and travel for a hundred miles. There is still a lot of nothing out here and I loved it. [1999]

It was there, in January 1983, that Springsteen resumed work on *Nebraska* Mk.2. Or, as he later put it, 'When I stopped the *Nebraska* record, I just continued [recording] in my garage, in Los Angeles. I improved the recording facilities somewhat; I just got an eight-track board. I drove across the country and I got to Los Angeles and I just set up . . . [and] continued [recording], because I was excited about the fact that I felt the *Nebraska* stuff was my most personal stuff.' With only Mike Batlan and personal assistant Obie Oziedzic on hand, Springsteen began experimenting with the drum computers and digital synthesizers that had been Suicide's private domain until The Human League nabbed the idea and sold it to the masses:

> **Mike Batlan**: We were working four to ten hours every day. Bruce was learning about all this new technology that showed up on *Born In The USA*. He was experimenting with 24-track, cutting complete songs – and he was starting to sound like the E Street Band. He was really good . . . Those six months were a period of real growth for Bruce . . . [He] was alone – Chuck Plotkin wasn't around, Jon Landau wasn't around – he had no serious girlfriend, he was hanging out.

At least one E Street Band member was seriously worried – the one most directly affected by Springsteen's flirtation with drum machines, Max Weinberg. He called Batlan up for reassurance 'that Bruce wasn't preparing to release a sophisticated 24-track recording with machines standing in for the E Streeters'. With a fine E Street album already in the can the boss had no need to make another, and anyway, as Landau later observed, 'He was[n't] ready to suddenly switch back into the *Born In The USA* mode.'

Yet almost the first thing Springsteen did that winter was complete the sister-song and flipside of 'Born In The USA', 'Shut Out The Light'. Finally, the songwriter had figured out what to do with that evocative opening to 'Vietnam Blues'. He has come home but not to a homecoming parade, and the first thing he needs is a drink. Meanwhile, the girl he left behind fixes herself up for her returning hero. But he ain't the man she knew before. The segue from first verse to chorus uses cinematic shorthand to make its point: a close-up of a man in bed, it is four a.m., he is staring at the ceiling wondering why he can't move his hands – cue chorus, 'Oh mama, mama, mama come quick/ I've got the shakes and I'm gonna be sick/ Throw your arms around me in the cold dark night/ Hey now mama, don't shut out the light'. For in that darkness he knows he will see the same recurring vision: 'Deep in a dark forest, a forest filled with rain/ Beyond a stretch of Maryland pines, there's a river without a name.'

Like 'Born In The USA', the song was then trimmed of some fat pre-release. In this case it lost lines which made the debt to John Prine's 'Sam Stone' explicit – depicting him locking the back bedroom door each evening before lying back to indulge in 'a few habits he'd brought back from over there'. All in all, 'Shut Out The Light' showed the new-found lyrical sophistication of 'My Father's House' was no fluke. Nor was it the only idea dating back to 1981 worked on that winter. 'Johnny Bye Bye' – the only other song from these sessions officially released in the eighties – and 'Follow That Dream' were both demoed a number of times, in the former's case beefed up with a cryptic last verse that later got the chop: 'In the Nevada desert a young boy travels alone/ Walking five thousand miles trying to get home/ Stars rising in the black and endless sky/ He stares up into the darkness, he looks down and walks on'.

And still the question remained: what was he intending to do with these tracks? All twenty-two of them? A curious document from the time suggests he still planned to release his 1982 E Street Album – now provisionally entitled *Murder Incorporated* – with a single change, 'Johnny Bye Bye' for 'Darlington County'. Five songs, all recorded at these January home-sessions, were down as potential B-sides: 'Sugarland', 'Follow That Dream', 'Don't Back Down', 'One Love' and 'Little Girl Like You'. But 'Shut Out The Light', recorded at the January 19 session, was tellingly absent from this list, probably because he had already earmarked it (and other weightier songs recorded between January 18 and February 17) for a more serious-minded project.

After all, neither 'One Love' nor 'Little Girl (Like You)' were about to change the parameters of popular song. The former was little more than a cut-up of every rock-chick cliché he could recall that day, 'Come on baby, rock me all night long/ I been searchin' for you for so long/ You're the one, yeah, you're the one for me'; and no amount of vocal commitment was ever gonna raise it higher. 'Little Girl' was the proclamation of an infamous prowler, claiming those days are done: 'Seen a lot of girls, had a lot of fun/ Ran around a lot, now my runnin's done', which he wisely left unreleased (given its condescending lines about how he's 'got a plan, but it's one made for two/ So I need a little girl like you'). Likewise, 'Don't Back Down' may have raised Cain, but he was still working with less than earth-shattering material ('A time comes and you just gotta . . . make a stand somewhere').

Of the five potential B-sides just 'Sugarland' had real potential, with its well-honed sense of despair that many a contemporary American farmer would have recognized: 'They're grazin' the field covered with tar/ Can't get a price to see my way clear/ I'm sitting down at the Sugarland Bar/ Might as well bury my body right here'. Of the other songs demoed that month, just one would make *BITUSA*. 'Your Hometown' aka 'My Hometown' was a song 'about the place where you live, and sharing the responsibility in it; and how you can run, but you can't hide'. On the initial demo the lonely rock star even embraced a more ordinary life: 'Now there's a hill outside of town where me and my wife/ Watch the stars rising brightly in the black endless sky/ I'm thirty-five, we got a boy of our own'.

But he had not quite relinquished those Nebraskan narratives, penning a new song about the Ku Klux Klan as seen through a child's blinkered eyes: 'I was ten years old when my Pa said, Son, some day you will see/ When you grow to wear the robes like your brother and me'. But compelling as 'The Klansman' may be, it was a curio, something written as if this were the late fifties and Springsteen was channelling Guthrie, rather than addressing his own generation.

Two other songs created characters straight out of an O'Connor short-story, 'Delivery Man' and 'Betty Jean' (who is described in *both* songs as having 'eyes like a jack rabbit starin' dead in your high beams'). The former song ends in riotous fashion, with the narrator and his sidekick Wilson chasing the chickens they lost on a low bridge across the road as the highway patrolman pulls up; at which point the song abruptly ends. 'Betty Jean', sung in his best Robert-Gordon-meets-Buddy-Holly voice, was probably one he intended to rev up, too, with its share of good one-liners – 'We were married in the Spring out on 531, had fifteen kids and I hate every single one'; 'Stretched out on the hood of my GTO/ she's filin' her nails shoutin', Go, Bobby, go!' – placing us firmly in trailer-trashland. But after sessions on February 15th and 17th gave Springsteen three more songs to lose – 'Seven Tears', 'I Don't Care' and 'The Money We Didn't Make' – he called a three-week hiatus on the sessions; probably in part to decide whether to release *Murder Inc.* as is. He chose to just say no.

On March 9 he was back again at Thrill Hill West, his jokey name for this LA home setup, working through April 23. This go-round the songs were mostly reworked older ones. 'Johnny Bye Bye' was done again, as were 'Don't Back Down', 'Jim Deer' and, surprisingly, 'The Losin' Kind'. Two of the songs he re-examined, 'Jim Deer' and 'Fugitive's Dream' (both recorded at the January 20 session) were transformed into 'Richfield Whistle' and 'Unsatisfied Heart' respectively, as Springsteen continued to point his songs in a Nebraskan direction.

'Richfield Whistle' intricately wove a number of *Nebraska*'s strands – the man who never had a chance, the dreams he shared with a loving wife, the single misjudgement, the senseless murder, the comeuppance – in a six-and-a-half minute narrative that was another nod to *Executioner's Song*: 'Well, that night me and Pat, we had a fight/ I was out drivin' 'round in the rain/ With a fifth of gin and a half-tank of gas and ten dollars to my name/ I passed a deserted liquor store way out on Highway One'. But by April 1983 everyone knew how the story ends.

'Unsatisfied Heart' also ploughed over-cultivated territory, beginning with a man who 'was respected and satisfied/ . . . had two beautiful children and a kind and loving wife'. Then, 'one day a man came to town, a man with nothing and nowhere to go/ [Who] came to my door and mentioned something I'd done a long time ago'. It ends with that all-too-familiar dream of how it used to be: 'Night after night the same dream keeps comin' round/ I'm standing high on the green hills on the outskirts of town.'

Good as both songs were, it was time to return to *The River*'s edge.

Even if he had to do it circuitously, he needed to write some band-friendly material they could record. By now, Springsteen had decided if there was to be an E Street Band album after *Nebraska*, it wouldn't be *Murder Inc.* Talking to *Rolling Stone* in April about the (non-)prospect of a tour, he struck an ominously familiar note, 'We'd like to . . . but it depends on the record. I don't have much control over that myself. I just gotta wait till the record feels right.' For this to happen, his songwriting would need to maybe lighten up.

So he wrote the shamelessly nostalgic 'County Fair', about a Carol who was presumably as fictional as the fabled Chuck Berry heroine, recalling the time he pulled her 'close to my heart/ . . . I wish I never had to let this moment go'. After which, his next heroine-in-song would be the anti-Carol. Cynthia was the name he gave to this modern-day Pretty Flamingo. And like that mythical figure, 'Cynthia' will never be his: 'Cynthia, when you come walkin' by, you're an inspiring sight/ Cynthia, you don't smile or say hi, but baby that's alright . . . I just like knowin', Cynthia, you exist in a world like this.'

Before the spring was through, both songs would receive the E Street stamp of approval. First, though, Landau sat him down for a long chat. What he told him was the result of hearing the songs Springsteen had spent the past three months recording. And it distilled down to a single point: 'The problem with the *Nebraska* thing as a permanent approach . . . is that . . . you have so many capabilities that are not utilized, that it seems like it's less than you can be.'[GD] It was time to submerge the whole wrecking crew in studioland again:

> **Chuck Plotkin**: One of the things that happens when you work for Bruce, you go down – as if in a submarine – for a period of time, and when you resurface, you realize that you've let the rest of your life go to seed. Whenever I've finished working on a project, it takes six to eight weeks to regain my bearing. My tax returns are always late. I'm scrambling around trying to pay my bills. I get home . . . and the phone's been shut off, the gas doesn't work.

In an almost exact replication of the previous spring's trials and tribulations, Springsteen recalled the E Street Band to Power Station May 23 and began recording a bunch of songs he'd already demoed solo, a fair few of which – like 'Richfield Whistle' and 'Sugarland' – did not obviously lend themselves to the E Street ethos. Finally, he turned to the kind of songs which actually suited them. And after they stockpiled enough songs for a whole new album and mixed and sequenced it, he scrapped the whole thing and started again. However, this time there was a significant change in the dynamic. Two of the key contributors – Chuck Plotkin and Steve Van Zandt – were becoming exasperated by Springsteen's working methods. And in Plotkin's case this meant that by the end of proceedings they were barely speaking:

> **Chuck Plotkin**: It looked for a long time like we could end up with *Nebraska II* . . . Bruce would ask me what I thought about a guitar solo, and I'd say, 'I don't know. I don't know what the song's about. I don't know whether the guitar solo's the right guitar solo, because I'm not getting any hit off the song.' . . . After two or three of those responses, he just stopped asking me what I thought . . . I was there every day [for two months] and hardly ever expressed an opinion because he stopped asking me. [GD]

Van Zandt, too, had his mind on other things. The previous year, he had taken advantage of another lull in E Street activities to record a decent solo album, *Men Without Women*. Not surprisingly, when he ventured out to promote the record live, he was asked about his status in Springsteenland. He answered unambiguously, 'I haven't left the E Street Band, and I don't see any serious reasons why I should unless it conflicts with what I'm currently doing.' Nonetheless, those intimate gigs reminded him why he did this in the first place.

He may well have been having a go at his old friend when he told a journalist on his second solo tour, 'Rock 'n' roll has never stopped being the most important art-form of our time. It's never changed, it's never lost the power to *communicate*, the power to affect people, it's just that nobody's using it.' By the time of the 1983 E Street sessions, Van Zandt had started a second solo album, *Voice of America*, where he finally found his own voice, having been as inspired by Guthrie's scoundrel-free version of patriotism as his friend. Songs like 'I Am A Patriot' and 'Vote (That Mutha Out)' were stripped of ambiguity, raising a clarion call for change. And though he lent a hand to the May–June E Street sessions, they would be his last this side of the millenium:

Steve Van Zandt: At the time I joined Bruce I didn't know what would happen. I might have just been there for one tour, but I ended up staying for seven years because I was able to contribute along the way to his thing. But with [*Voice of America*] it became obvious that, artistically, I had something that was just too important [to stay].

Springsteen seems to have been fully aware of the shift in dynamic, though he made light of Plotkin's despair in typically humorous fashion during his 1998 Rock n Roll Hall of Fame induction speech, thanking Plotkin and engineer Toby Scott for remaining 'in the saddle as often the years went by, wondering if we'd ever get the music or if they'd ever get a royalty check. They kept their cool and their creativity . . . Of course, they're basket cases now.'

His response to Van Zandt's imminent defection was more immediate. He wrote one of his great songs of camaraderie, 'None But The Brave', ostensibly to a girl: 'These nights I see you, my friend, the way you looked back then/ Ah, on a night like this, I know that girl no longer exists/ Except for a moment in some stranger's eyes . . . In my heart you still survive/ None, baby, but the brave'. If the girl herself was a fiction, all the people he was celebrating were wholly real. As he admits in the *Essential* liner-notes, the song was 'set in the bars and 70s circuit in Asbury Park'.

Even as he wrote this farewell to former brothers- and sisters-in-arms, he was still convinced the E Street Band gave him some X factor otherwise missing from his studio work. Recalling these sessions, he talked about the process in comradely terms, 'We get together and the band plays and sometimes we get something and sometimes we don't, but we do have a feeling that everybody's chipping in and working on a project . . . [that] something['s] going on.' He clung to this garage-band mentality even when his was the last gang in town, tellingly stating the following year, 'The people that I'm fortunate enough to have around me have been there since I was young, they're the same guys . . . It's hard . . . just holding onto relationships.' As he knew only too well, a good band is hard to find. And these guys still could make things happen in the most unpropitious circumstances:

Max Weinberg: I remember one night when we were completely packed up to go home and Bruce was off in the corner playing his acoustic guitar. Suddenly, I guess the bug bit him, and he started writing these rockabilly

> songs. We'd been recording all night and were dead tired, but they had to open up the cases and set up the equipment so that we could start recording again at five in the morning. That's when we got 'Pink Cadillac', 'Stand On It' and . . . 'TV Movie' . . . Bruce got on a roll, and when that happens, you just hold on for dear life.

Yet none of the songs from that highly productive night would make the 1983 sequence, let alone the 1984 album. In fact, the series of E Street sessions which ran from May 23 through June 16 would not produce a single song on the latter, multi-platinum smash. The one song from this long hot summer of sessions which *did* make the final cut would be an afterthought. ('My Hometown' was cut on June 29, when Plotkin had already started mixing tracks for the July 26-27 sequence.)

Predictably, there were a number of ripsnorters cut in these weeks that never made the light of day. These included a song logged as 'Just Around The Corner To The Light of Day', which would last longer in the live set than most of *Born In The USA*. It represented an overdue return to writing about cars and girls ('Been driving five hundred miles, got five hundred to go/ I got rock and roll music on the radio'). Equally enduring was a song logged as 'Gone Gone Gone', about those 'people who came down from up north looking for work in the oil fields and the refineries; then when the price of oil went bad, they were shutting down the refineries . . . [and] they [were] just telling 'em to move on.' The final lines said it all: 'You ain't gonna find nothin' down here friend/ Except seeds blowin' up the highway in the south wind/ Movin' on, movin' on, it's gone, gone, it's all gone'. Neither track even made the July 1983 sequence, though the latter was belatedly introduced into the live set the following July under the title 'Seeds'.

Those that *did* make the twelve-song shortlist included 'None But The Brave', 'Drop On Down and Cover Me', a recast 'Cynthia' and a reunion with an old friend in need of a shooter, 'Janey, Don't You Lose Heart'. Both 'None But The Brave' and 'Cynthia' would be bootlegged to Betsy and back, before being released on *The Essential* and *Tracks* respectively. Yet the also bootlegged 'Drop On Down and Cover Me' – which reworked 'Cover Me', a song Springsteen had never been convinced about – was probably the best of the lot. It remains unreleased, even though it took the architectural outline of the original song – and its first two verses – and immeasurably improved it with a less-clichéd catchphrase and a sturdier musical structure which lent it some of that E Street electricity. With the band rebounding off every phrase, this time Springsteen's plea for understanding sounds heartfelt, not histrionic: 'Inside I feel the pain/ The hatred and the sorrow/ I wanna shut the light, baby . . . Drop on down and cover me/ I just wanna close my eyes and let your love surround me'.

Initially, Springsteen seemed to wholly realize which songs from the 1983 sessions played to everyone's strengths, compiling an album on July 26-27 that was part-*Murder Inc.*, part *Nebraska Mk.2*, part-return to form:

> **Side 1**: Born In The USA. Cynthia. None But The Brave. Drop On Down & Cover Me. Shut Out The Light*. Johnny Bye Bye*.
> **Side 2**: Sugarland*. My Love Will Not Let You Down. Follow That Dream*. My Hometown. Glory Days. Janey Don't You Lose Heart.

Just three songs from the 1982 sequence had survived thus far, outnumbered by the four from the winter 1983 solo sessions (asterisked) and five from the recent E Street sessions. But it was another multi-layered album, which fully acknowledged his development as a songwriter post-*Nebraska*. It was also apparently just another work in progress. Just as with *The Ties That Bind*, four years earlier, poor Plotkin had barely sequenced a releasable artefact when Springsteen was back in the studio working on a new song – in this case the day *after* they agreed the 'final' sequence for a sixth E Street album, July 28.

On the face of it, 'Bobby Jean' was just an inferior 'None But The Brave', addressing another gal who 'liked the same music . . . liked the same bands . . . liked the same clothes . . . [and] told each other that we were the wildest'. But with Little Steven's imminent departure from the band still secret, the song was another coded message, with Bruce waving farewell to Bobby *and* Jean: 'Now there ain't nobody, nowhere, no-how, gonna ever understand me the way you did'. Unfortunately, 'Bobby Jean' was one of the worst things recorded that summer – a misguided snapshot on a rose-tinted past. Even more unfortunately, it convinced its author he should keep going:

> **Bruce Springsteen**: What I take a long time doing is not the recording, it's the conceptualizing; where I'll write three or four songs, and the fifth one I'll keep . . . The main thing with my songs now is that I write them to be

> complete things, filled with a lot of detail about what people are wearing, where they live . . . I'm pretty harsh with the stuff myself. I have a good sense of when I'm doing my best. Which is why it takes a long time, 'cause a lot of times I don't think I'm doing my best. [1984]

In truth, he had long stopped making sense when working at optimum level with the E Street Band in the studio. Working solo on *Nebraska* and in the winter of 1983 he had worked quickly and efficiently towards a clear goal. (Even if the latter sessions yielded just four tracks on the album he scrapped in 1983, and none for the album he released in 1984, they were a necessary bridge from *Nebraska* to *Tunnel of Love*.) He had reached a point where surrendering the slightest element of control short-circuited *any* decision. As he told Dave Marsh after *BITUSA* appeared, 'I enjoy having control over what I'm gonna say . . . I work somewhat collaboratively but not nearly as much as, say, a video, with a director . . . On the records I'm the director.'

To maintain that unswerving self-belief it took not only extraordinary willpower– which he had in spades – but also unerring judgement as to what works, and what doesn't. That was not something he had regularly displayed at eighties E Street sessions. Even when lightning now struck, he didn't know what to do to conduct it. Hence, by the eleventh summer of the band, they were often just riding the wave of electricity till exhaustion set in.

With Van Zandt's mind elsewhere, and Plotkin not even sure what he was doing there, the boss turned to that audience-cipher, Landau, for an opinion as to what album they should release. Landau's response shocked him. Two of his suggestions – 'Protection' and 'Cover Me' – had been recorded in the winter of 1982, pre-*Electric Nebraska*. And just three tracks came from the recent E Street sessions, 'My Hometown', 'Bobby Jean' and 'Janey, Don't You Lose Heart'. The rest – 'Follow That Dream' excepted – all came from May 1982. Landau's vision shaped Springsteen's, but as the singer said in 1984, he still 'just wanted it to feel like an everyday "Darlington County" kind of thing'. And he started by restoring that lost 1977 song to the equation. He just needed one or two more songs to round things off, set to the sound of a band and two co-producers smashing their heads against the studio wall. He had worn his perennial themes clean through, but he refused to accept this – for now:

> **Bruce Springsteen**: I came out of a working class environment, played in working class bars, and my history just drew me towards these topics naturally . . . Those were the things that felt urgent [to me] . . . and I'm proud of that music. But I felt at the end of *Born In The USA* that I'd said all I wanted to say about those things . . . I lived in New Jersey for a very long time and I'd written about a lot of things which were very tied into my past, a lot of ghosts you're chasing . . . I'd taken that as far as I could. [1992]

He – and he alone – thought they had more work to do. In mid-September the Van Zandt-less band spent three more days in the studio, cutting 'Glory of Love' and 'Brothers Under The Bridges'. With the latter, he went back to 'the edge of town' (he even throws in a second use of 'trestles') as two brothers 'watched from the tall grass as the challenges were made and the duels went down'. Hiding on the backstreets, they long to belong: 'Yeah, someday [we'll] run with the brothers under the bridges.' But then the dream ends and we are in the bleak present, as the haunted narrator hears 'a cry in the distance and the sound of marching feet come and gone'. Evidently, his brother died in Vietnam, leaving the narrator sitting down 'by this highway figuring just where I belong'. Perhaps he was looking for a song to bookend an album that contained only one song for certain, the opener 'Born In the USA'.

With fifty-plus songs already in the can, he worked on through the fall. Another three days of sessions the last week in October produced two more lost songs – 'Shut Down' and '100 Miles from Jackson' – and another affirmative anthem which fell short of 'None But The Brave'. 'No Surrender' subtextually suggested Van Zandt thought his old friend was losing his way, a view Springsteen challenges lyrically, addressing his friend's concerns in martial terms: 'There's a war outside still raging/ You say it ain't ours anymore to win', before laying claim to a grander vista, 'A wide open country in my eyes/ And these romantic dreams in my head'. It was a defiant statement, but not one he was sure he wanted fixed to disc. Ironically, it was Van Zandt who ultimately persuaded him to include the track, arguing 'that the portrait of friendship and the song's expression of the inspirational power of rock music was an important part of the picture'.

November was almost over when Springsteen called the band back for *another* three days of sessions. These proved equally productive, resulting in five new songs* and yet more work on 'Sugarland', 'No Surrender' and 'Bobby Jean'. But still, he refused to put the album to bed. Even Landau felt alienated by the process now: 'I felt like, "Let's get on with it now." So I started to behave somewhat differently than I have in the past.' But he was still up against 'the strongest will [he'd] ever encountered'; a comment made in 1975, when Paul Nelson first suggested that in the studio, 'it was Springsteen himself who was responsible for the technical agony and ecstasy . . . [because he] was astigmatic and short-sighted, a perfectionist who frequently took the long way around simply because he didn't know the short one'.

Unable to get any handle on what he was now trying to say, Springsteen did what he had learned to do in such a situation – he just kept recording. New year brought a new start on an album he near-as-dammit finished eighteen months earlier. On January 12 1984 he brought two terrific songs to the studio, neither of them needed, 'Rock Away The Days' and 'Man At The Top'. The former took a number of elements from other 'wrong side of the tracks' songs demoed previously, including the prison record, the ubiquitous bar-fight that turned nasty (Billy pulls out a razor), the car crash that may or may not have killed Billy, the little lady who stands by her man, before sticking on a happy ending of sorts: 'Well, rich man want the power and the seat on the top/ Poor man want the money that the rich man got/ Honey, tonight I'm feeling so tired and unsure/ Come on in Mary, shut the light, close the door'.

It seemed intended to segue into a song written about the greasy pole that leads to stardom. For the big boss man had arrived at this session with a perfect album-closer, a summation of all the doubts he fought so hard to overcome: 'Here comes a kid with a guitar in his hand/ Dreamin' of his record in number one spot/ Everybody wants to be the man at the top'. At the same time, he seemingly welcomed the opportunity to drain the poisoned chalice: 'Man at the top says it's lonely up there/ If it is man, I don't care'. But 'Man At The Top' was not to be taken at face value. As he said the first time he played the song live, 'This is a song for election year'. His target was everyone who bought into a perverted version of the American Dream 'from the big white house to

* The five new songs were as follows: 'Shut Down', '100 Miles From Jackson', 'Swoop Man', 'Roll Away The Stone' and 'Under The Big Sky'.

the parking lot', written by someone whose lifeblood remained 'my relationships with my friends, and my attachment to the people and the places I've known . . . To give that up for, like, the TV, the cars, the houses – that's not the American dream. That's the booby prize.' This was one chastened man, returning from the wilderness:

> **Bruce Springsteen**: I do not believe that the essence of the rock & roll idea was to exalt the cult of personality. That is a sidetrack, a dead-end street . . . I think I made the mistake earlier on of trying to live within that . . . rock & roll dream. It's a seductive choice, it's a seductive opportunity. The real world, after all, is frightening. In the end, I realized that rock & roll wasn't just about finding fame and wealth. Instead, for me, it was about finding your place in the world, figuring out where you belong. [1987]

As Clemons let slip in his resolutely unopinionated autobiography, 'Bruce . . . was a very reluctant star. He never wanted to be Elvis. He saw himself more like Dylan. But the power of the songs made the pull of giant stardom irresistible.' But rather than addressing these fears on record, Springsteen spent the next month worrying about writing a hit single. Landau had told him he couldn't hear one on the album they had almost finished sequencing. He says he wanted 'the type of single . . . that would truly represent what was going on'. What he got was 'Dancing In The Dark', a song that addressed Springsteen's mental bind by wrapping it in a seductive synthesizer-wash and setting it to repeat spin:

> **Bruce Springsteen**: Jon had been bothering me to write a single, which is something he rarely does . . . I had written a lot of songs and was kind of fed up with the whole thing. We'd been making the record for a long time and I was bored with the whole situation . . . That particular night I came home and sat on the edge of my bed and the thing I remember thinking first was that we had a record, but it wasn't necessarily finished; I could change the whole thing right now if I wanted to. [1987]

The following day he brought the song to the studio, even as 'final' mixes were being prepared for the likes of 'Johnny Bye Bye', 'Pink Cadillac', 'Man At The Top', 'Invitation To The Party' and 'My Love Will Not Let You Down', none of which made the album. (Even the mixing of 'Dancing

In The Dark' was interrupted by attempts to record two new songs, 'Refrigerator Blues' and 'Ida Rose (No One Knows)'.) It was the twelfth anniversary of the day a young Bruce turned up at Mike Appel's office for a second time and played him seven songs. They included 'If I Was The Priest', 'For You' and 'Saint In The City'. Now he was laying down the final song on an album he had started recording more than two years earlier, with 'Cover Me'.

And still Sony were breathing down his neck, sending out at least one copy of the album without 'I'm Going Down', one of a number of throwaway songs Springsteen had penned back in May 1982 for a pop album, and now decided to throw back into the mix. The 46-minute LP he finally okayed showed all the marks of an exhausted director who was over budget and had to face an impatient studio head. As he wrote in his *Songs* essay, 'I put a lot of pressure on myself over a long period of time to reproduce the intensity of *Nebraska* on *Born In The USA*. I never got it. [Yet] there was something about the grab-bag nature of . . . the album that probably made it one of my purest pop records.' First and last track excepted, it was as random a selection of songs from these sessions as any simian, taking a tea-break from work on Beethoven's Fifth, woulda made. It was destined to sell eighteen million copies worldwide.

Chapter 10: 1984–88 – None But The Brave

> You can make a very good living – a *very* good living – selling a couple of million records and selling out arenas. I don't think we needed to be any more successful. – Steve Van Zandt, *Mansion On The Hill*, p339

> I drew a lot of my earlier material from my experience growing up, my father's experience, the experience of my immediate family . . . But there was a point in the mid-eighties when I felt like I'd said pretty much all I knew how to say about it all. – Bruce Springsteen, 1997

Five years after a completed *Born In The USA* sent Springsteen and the E Street Band into the commercial stratosphere, the leader finally disbanded the group which had been such an integral part of his glory days. By the end of the *Born In The USA* tour, on October 2 1985, they had already achieved everything they ever set out to do. Not perhaps quite realizing that they were only marking time, they would fill the ensuing four years with issuing the most extravagant testimony to their live prowess imaginable, the misnomic five-LP set, *Live 1975-85*, and the completion of another lengthy world tour and an abbreviated Amnesty tour that served to confirm they were done as a force in rock.

In truth, the band had been living on borrowed time ever since *Nebraska* gave Springsteen full control of the album-making process. Once Springsteen began 'writing about men and women – their intimate personal lives', he no longer needed that communal spirit and integrated purpose the E Streeters had brought to every session since August 1972. In fact, the E Street Band would never again put themselves through the punishing regime demanded by their boss on their last four albums. Instead, Springsteen confirmed all Weinberg's worst fears by making an album in 1987 that was solo in every sense of the word, *Tunnel of Love*, before asking the E Street Band to make the songs come alive in their increasingly part-time hands, in venues that removed all the intimacy from said material. It was a doomed attempt to replicate the strategy from the *Born In The USA* tour, but with a non-E Street, un-bombastic album.

The military precision with which that earlier album and attendant fifteen-month world tour had been marketed was something to behold: every single, every broadcast of a UK TV special, every incremental stage from arenas to stadia strategized in advance. And, like all good armchair generals, Landau had learnt well from recent history. If he had a campaign plan, it was closely modelled on the one another repeatedly inventive solo artist of the seventies, David Bowie, adhered to for his 1983 album/tour, *Let's Dance*, which spawned three major hit singles and gained a whole new audience for an artist whose critical reputation Stateside had always exceeded his second-league album sales. That audience was even prepared to trek out to hockey arenas to hear their favourite songs ricochet off asymmetrical walls. Like Bowie, Bruce had shaken off the influence of an ex-cheerleader-manager and was entering these accursed arenas with both eyes open:

> **Bruce Springsteen**: In the end, it was a variety of things that kinda threw the argument in [the] direction [of going for it], but my feeling was that I'd created an opportunity for myself and why cross the desert and not climb the mountain? . . . / . . . You could [certainly] make an argument that one of the most socially conscious artists of the second half of this century was Elvis Presley, even if he didn't start out with any set of political ideas that he wanted to accomplish. He said, 'I'm all shook up and I want to shake you up,' and that's what happened. He had an enormous impact on the way people lived. [1986/1997]

Even as he was okaying the release of 'Johnny Bye Bye' (one of five *BITUSA* outtakes issued as B-sides on a steady stream of *BITUSA* 45s), he was aiming to have a similar 'impact on the way people lived'. Yet he remained wary of becoming the man at the top. Crossing paths with his old mentor, John Hammond shortly after he delivered *BITUSA*, he informed the now-retired producer, 'When you start to get real popular, you have to be careful that there isn't a dilution into some very simplistic terms of what you're doing.' Very careful.

But proof that he could be the exception to the rule, could buck the trend and stay hungry, stay true, would as ever have to be provided down on the acoustic killing floors of those American astrodomes which threatened to become rock music's final resting place. It was here Landau had booked shows all through the summer of '84 and into the fall, with record-breaking extended residencies at New Jersey's Meadowlands, Philadelphia's Spectrum and LA's Sports Arena all selling out in record time. But before Bruce could reaffirm his vows, the E Street Band needed to assimilate two new members into a set-up which had gone unchanged in nine years. The most significant change – musically – was the addition of Nils Lofgren, ex-Crazy Horse and Grin, replacing Miami Steve. It was a change that had long been in the offing, but was only confirmed the June night Nils took to the Stone Pony stage with the E Street Band to run down a dozen songs from the nascent set:

> **Nils Lofgren**: It was six or seven months prior to the release of *BITUSA* that I'd gone up to Jersey to spend a weekend with Bruce, just hanging out . . . It was the end of '83 and that was the first time that I was actually out on the street without a record deal . . . I was talking to Bruce on the phone, and he could hear that I was down in the dumps, so he said, 'Why don't you come up and hang out?' I did, and he just happened to have pretty much the finished . . . *BITUSA*. We listened to it a lot, and I was amazed at what a great record it was. We jammed a lot in Jersey clubs and spent some time together . . . At that point MTV was announcing that there would be a replacement for [Little] Steven [which] was very premature. I could tell as I was watching MTV with Bruce that he was . . . upset with that . . . I just took the opportunity – even though Bruce said there wasn't any truth to that at the time, and I don't believe either he or Steve had made any decisions yet – I just said, 'Well, if you ever needed a guitarist, I would certainly want an audition.' I think that was a little bit of a surprise, because Bruce had always known me as a solo artist . . . It was about six months later that he and Steve finally . . . came to the uncomfortable decision that Steve needed to go do his own music . . . Bruce called me and said, 'Why don't you come up, hang

> out, and we'll do some jamming with the band.' Bruce is very low-key about things, and when he said 'jam with the band', I knew that he wasn't going to put the E Street Band together just for fun to jam with me. I took that as meaning, 'Let's see how it feels with you playing with the band and me.' . . . When I got up to Jersey, we went to Big Man's West in Red Bank, which had closed prior to that, and we jammed for a few days . . . I got the job about four weeks from opening night.

Springsteen had found a pedigree replacement for his old friend, someone he 'knew . . . felt about music and rock & roll the way I did'. The other addition was more of a gamble, and the one that ultimately turned his life around. Patti Scialfa, a local girl who had attended Asbury Park High School, had been a singer in Cats On A Smooth Surface and had worked with Southside Johnny, so knew the lie of Bruceland. And unlike Bruce she had a music degree. Letting a girl into the all-male E Street Band was a risk he had to take because Lofgren had contracted mononucleosis, which meant backing-vocal duties were out of the question. If Lofgren had just three or four weeks to learn the ropes, Scialfa had three or four days. Much was expected of them both.

It had been three long years since the last tour; a hiatus so extensive it prompted Springsteen to joke, after song #4 on opening night, 'I should've wrote, right?' That first show, St Paul's Civic Centre on June 29, suggested Springsteen was determined to strike some kinda balance between old and new – just not one that included anything save 'Rosalita' from his first two albums. In a 32-song set, eight songs from *BITUSA* vied with five from *Nebraska* and seven from *The River*, every one of which – save the title track – was a crowd-pleasing pastiche-rocker. Already he was fighting to maintain light and shade when playing to vast audiences of party animals and, by the second week, picnic-goers.

The acid test was how well *Nebraska*'s songs played to the madding crowd. On that first night, where four of its five tracks were judiciously placed in the first half of the show, it was 'Johnny 99' and 'Atlantic City' which were received best. But he still felt the need to punctuate them with explanatory raps. Some of these were genuinely illuminating; some were just there to get the audience to settle down and pay attention; the pithier, the better. ('This is a song about family and trying to do the right thing'; 'The factories close down but the mansion on the hill remains'.)

The second night in St Paul saw a show coalesce around half a dozen *Nebraska* songs, including the title track, chillingly introduced as 'about being so lonesome you could cry'. But it would be the last time he played more songs from his 1982 LP than *BITUSA*. After the show he acknowledged that integrating this more difficult material into an arena show was proving his greatest challenge: 'There's a good amount of the audience that has [*Nebraska*], but I don't think it compares to the percentage that has the other records. But I felt that the audience [tonight] was real responsive . . . It's just a trick of getting in and getting out of it.'

That second show was also the first to open with 'Born In The USA', which very soon became the defining moment to each night's performance. Self-consciously imposing himself against a backdrop of an American flag – on album and $10 programme – had none of the frisson of Dylan in Paris in 1966, when a similar gesture riled the anti-American French crowd. It merely served to obscure the message of the song and its contextual counterparts. But to the crowds, and particularly new fans, it promised a very special night, even if Springsteen was now setting his sights somewhat lower than in the E Street Band's seventies heyday:

> **Bruce Springsteen**: Somebody comes out, they shout and yell, they have a great night, it's a rock & roll show. It [also] makes . . . them think about something different . . . I think it can do that . . . At the same time it could be just a good date . . . Whatever they want to take from it. [1984]

With Landau's help, he was becoming reconciled to the gulf separating the polarities of crowd-pleasing and performance art. Looking back in 1987, he addressed this duality: 'When I walk out on stage I've got to feel like it's the most important thing in the world. Also I got to feel like, well, it's only rock 'n' roll. Somehow you got to believe both of those things.' Once the fiercest believer on the planet in the power of rock to *redeem* its recipients, he had become besieged by doubt at the exact point when he had the music-world in the palms of his hands. He even suggested that moments like when the audience sang over the singer on 'Thunder Road' made it 'more powerful. It's like songs [like] that are little touchstones. That's when the rock 'n' roll thing is really happening, it's realized.'

The Springsteen of old – the man who insisted in February 1975, 'I'm not into people screamin' at me, like Bowie. Once they do that, it's over . . . I'm there for me, y'know, that's all. If they can dig it, cool; if not, they don't have to come' – would never have dreamed of allowing such moments to interfere with such a singular vision. Now there were several such stage-managed displays of showmanship, down to the lucky girl pulled up from the audience to schmooze with the boss on 'Dancing In The Dark'. It replicated a 'live' video shot at the first St Paul show to promote the single, but too late to stop it stalling just short of the number one spot, held off by the incomparable 'When Doves Cry'. Even turning the song over to mixmaster Arthur Baker to make a disco-mix of it – the more apposite setting – failed to claim the Prince audience; though it certainly riled his more purist fans. His response to the inevitable criticism suggested such fans shouldn't be so precious about songs *he* spent two solid years working and reworking till they were exactly how he wanted them: 'I figured . . . that the people that didn't like it would get over it.'

The album suffered no such setback. It entered the Top Forty the week before St Paul and hit the number one spot on July 7, where it stayed for the four weeks it took *Purple Rain* to repeat the success of 'When Doves Cry'. *BITUSA* remained in the Top Forty for 96 weeks, even returning to number one after Prince's twenty-four week stint; aided and abetted by the relentless slog of shows and a steady stream of spin-off hit singles, à la *Thriller*. In fact, the carefully-orchestrated Springsteen hype managed to produce seven Top Ten singles from an album on which Landau had initially heard only two.

But it was the response to the shows that would decide the album's long-term fate worldwide, and this time he was determined to give it a genuinely global sweep, taking in Japan and Australia as well as Europe. Perhaps surprisingly, given past E Street performance history, the shows very quickly settled into a pattern. The one regular cover was an encore version of 'Street Fighting Man' that seemed to have been included for a single reason; the line, 'What can a poor boy do 'cept to sing in a rock & roll band'. The outstanding cover in the 1984 sets, Dobie Gray's 'Drift Away', was performed just twice. The first of these was the final night of a ten-date residency at the Meadowlands Arena, where Miami Steve brought his horn section to the party, but Springsteen had only arranged to tape the first two shows for a possible live album, so missed the tour highlight to date.

Also not recorded to multitrack was the version of 'Man At The Top' he debuted at Alpine Valley the second week in July. Here he found himself at one of those out-of-town, open-air venues America favours, with a lawn stretching to the horizon, wondering what he had let himself in for. With more punters lugging picnic chairs, tables, hampers and coolers than hard core Boss fans, this was a party with full catering. Meanwhile, Springsteen had been in full damage-limitation mode for the past two weeks, telling Chet Flippo he ain't changed: 'I could easily go out and do just what I did before. But now we're playing outdoors on this tour, which I hadn't done before . . . I want to just step out and see what works.'

Well, two-thirds of the way through his first show on the picnic circuit, he was fighting to be heard. Abandoning the second *Nebraska* slot, he instead declaimed a strident acoustic arrangement of 'No Surrender' (a song he'd attempted this way in the studio), and when that didn't do the trick, decided to show how the American Dream looked from the other side of the mirror, 'Been going on forever, it ain't ever gonna stop/ Everybody wants to be the man at the top'. Rather than appreciate the moment, Alpine Valley rang to the sound of twenty thousand hands clappin'. In such a setting, it wasn't just the *Nebraska* songs' days which were numbered:

> **Bruce Springsteen**: I've had some beautiful nights outside with the moon coming up and people having a great time, but it's a different kind of experience . . . The bigger the place gets, the more you concentrate on focusing people, getting their attention in the first place . . . In a club you have everybody's attention and so you can change a string, tell a story and they'll watch. [1992]

In fact, Springsteen had been sold on stadia even before he considered descending the mountain to the valley below. If seeing The Who at his hometown Convention Hall in 1967 had shown him the virtues of a good education in maximum r&b, catching them at a stadium show in 1982 – when very much on their last legs – somehow convinced him such a transition need not have a downside. Having, by his own admission, 'agonized tremendously over it when we were moving from theatres . . . this time out, we planned from the beginning, before the tour started, that we'd end up in the stadiums.'

But if Springsteen did not realize the toll it was taking, those who had just joined the organization saw the change. As video operator Arthur Rosato – fresh from working five years for Dylan – recalls, 'Bruce got more remote as the gigs and entourage got bigger.' It wasn't only new members of the entourage who found it increasingly hard to recognize the firebrand of yore. By tour's end, the disaffected would be as rodents on a sinking ship. Marc Brickman, who had been doing the lighting since 1974, left first, supposedly 'over personality clashes with Landau and George Travis, Springsteen's authoritarian road manager'. Doug Sutphin quit after being docked a week's pay for touching Nils Lofgren's guitar. Mike Batlan joined the exodus when he was similarly fined for not mooring Bruce's canoe properly. (The latter two would subsequently attempt to sue Springsteen for overtime payments and constructive dismissal.) Bruce's blue-collar credentials were beginning to look ever-so-slightly frayed.

If he'd lost his ability to communicate with his co-workers, though, Springsteen continued to claim that 'if there happen to be sixty thousand out there . . . I'm basically trying to reach as many of them as I can, in as personal a fashion as I can.' *Ce n'est pas possible.* Such was his dislocation from his former redeemed-by-rock Self that he even refused to rock the boat when he found himself at the centre of a political storm entirely of his own making. It was one that had been brewing ever since he turned 'Born In The USA' into an Anthem first, and an anti-war song a poor third. Initially, he continued his well-worn strategy of directing critics towards his songs, and away from any personal declaration of political allegiance, telling *Musician* that summer: 'I don't know that much about politics . . . My politics are in my songs, whatever they may be . . . I feel that I can do my best by making songs. Make some difference that way.' The concert raps continued speaking in terms familiar to any audience member who attended the *River* tour. But at a September show in Pittsburgh he prefaced 'The River' by alluding to a severed bond between electorate and politician:

> 'There's a promise getting broken and I think that in the beginning the idea was we all live here like a family, where the strong can help the weak ones, the rich can help the poor ones . . .. I don't think it was that everybody was gonna make a billion dollars, but it was that everybody was gonna have the opportunity and a chance to live a life with some decency and some dignity and a chance for some self-respect, and I know you gotta be feeling the pinch here where the rivers meet.'

Few of those hollering throughout this rap realized he was having a go at the President, but he was. It was in response to a remark Reagan had made at a Jersey re-election rally three days earlier, suggesting it was *his* job to 'help make those dreams' Springsteen sang about 'come true'. Already, the previous night in Pittsburgh, in an intro to 'Johnny 99', Springsteen had suggested the old ham check out his last but one album: 'The President was mentioning my name in his speech the other day, and I got to wondering what his favorite album of mine must've been, you know . . . I don't think it was the *Nebraska* album.' But if he thought that was the end of the matter he was sorely mistaken. A number of non-believers in the media had been looking for a reason to wield the rod of rhetoric, and it came when his sole response to Reagan's opportunistic namecheck was a coupla prefatory raps. It brought a vat of well-seasoned scorn from part-time rock critic and full-time curmudgeon Richard Meltzer down on him – part of a ten-page moratorium on 'The Meaning of Bruce' in *Spin*:

> 'A couple weeks left till the election – remember? – and Reagan starts quoting Bruce. But instead of saddling his *sturm und drang*, riding out and yelling, . . . "Our President wants us dead!" . . . the little cocksucker passes it on to his publicist Barbara Carr, who passes it to her wonderful husband David . . . [who] did an outstanding hem-haw on page one of the respected news-sheet I happened to catch. Something to the effect that if the President would only look at such and such a Springsteen album cut, he clearly would see that *au contraire* blah blah blah. Don't say anything, don't stir anything, don't lose a single customer! Fuck these people!!'

In fact, Springsteen did respond; informing *Rolling Stone* he thought Reagan's comments felt like 'another manipulation . . . I had to disassociate myself from the President's kind words'; before going on to discuss how 'the social consciousness that was a part of the Sixties has become old fashioned . . . you go out, you get your job, and you try to make as much money as you can and have a good time on the weekend. And that's considered okay.' The fact that his own concerts had become merely another way to 'have a good time on the weekend' went unremarked. All in all, it was a mealy-mouthed retort from someone who when he got steaming mad had been known to cuss out the world.

But Meltzer's was only the first lash to be applied to Saint Bruce's increasingly broad back. An equally steamed James Wolcott in *Vanity Fair* targeted all the apologists who refused to accept their boy was sending mixed messages, scrambling communication between artist and audience: 'Critics have . . . fretted over the fact that audiences react to 'Born In The USA' as a rouser rather than take heed of its whipped-dog lyrics. It seems to me that the fans have the saner response. The thunderboom beat of "Born In The USA" is more compelling than its case history about a small-town loser being sent to 'Nam to "kill the yellow man", just as the saloon esprit of "Glory Days" carries more conviction than its ironic message.'

Springsteen insisted he didn't see it that way. His response to Wolcott and his kind was, 'If somebody doesn't understand your song, you keep singin' the song.' He was drilling the *wrong* message home; a view to which he only acceded after opening the paper one day in 1987 and seeing 'where they had quizzed kids on what different songs meant, and they asked them what "Born In The USA" meant. "Well, it's about my country," they answered.' He finally came to realize that 'in order to understand ["Born In The USA"]'s intent, you needed to invest a certain amount of time and effort to absorb both the music and the words. In fact, he had constructed a song whose martial music set itself in counterpoint to the message – his fault, his mistake – and rather than driving its essential point home by reverting to its original, Guthriesque guise and stop opening with it, became the anthemic introduction to every *BITUSA* show from August 1984 on, save Independence Day at Wembley Stadium. Appeasing understandable feelings of guilt by donating a small part of every night's takings to 'good causes', he seemed to think this laudable gesture retained a grassroots connection to 'his' kind:

> **Bruce Springsteen**: When rock music was working at its best, it was doing all those things looking inward and [also] reaching out to others . . . At your best, your most honest, your least glitzy, you shared a common history and you attempted both to ask questions and answer them in concert . . . [But] there was a point in the mid-eighties where I wanted to turn my music into some kind of activity and action, so that there was a practical impact on the communities that I passed through while I travelled around the country . . . Those meetings and conversations kept me connected so that I remember the actual people that I write about. [1997]

At this juncture, he still 'believed that it was good for the artist to remain distant from the seat of power, to retain your independent voice'. And that 'independent voice' continued to express itself between songs at the shows, even if less and less of the downbeat songs written between 1977 and 1982 were permitted entry to the three-hour sets. The most powerful of the nightly raps probably came before 'Racing In The Street', when he talked of a time 'I took the car out, and when I won that it was the only time I really felt good about myself . . . to have just one thing that you do that makes you feel proud of yourself, I don't think that's too much for anybody to ask'. Such stories operated as parables, not personal insights.

Not that this was the only modern parable at shows which were at times akin to a revivalist meeting. For an ex-Catholic like Springsteen, the parable form itself remained ripe for parody, as he did rather memorably in the long intro to 'Pink Cadillac' that began to assume epic proportions just as he realized he had left another rockabilly rocket off an album of his. What had begun as a spoof on the 'commie' scare-stories of the fifties – in which 'Russian infiltrators [hope to] have so weakened the morals of American society that by 1985 they're planning to have sex on the streets of every street corner coast to coast and the music that they're playing to ruin the morals of an entire generation is that dirty filth, rock and roll' – by the first stadia shows in January 1985 had become his own blasphemous account of the Garden of Eden. Whatever would the nuns of Freehold think?:

> Now, the Garden of Eden was originally believed to have been located in Mesopotamia, but the latest theological studies have provided conclusive evidence that its actual location was ten miles south of Jersey City, off the New Jersey Turnpike. That's why they call it the Garden State. In the Garden of Eden, there were none of the accoutrements of modern living . . . you didn't go get your Pop-Tarts and put 'em in the toaster and jump in the sack and watch Johnny Carson – no Sir! In the Garden of Eden there was no sin, there was no sex. Man lived in a state of innocence. Now, when it comes to no sex, I prefer the state of guilt that I constantly live in. But before the tour I decided to make a spiritual journey to the location of the Garden of Eden to find out the answer to some of these mysteries and so I hitchhiked on out there and I found out that that spot was now taken up by Happy Dan's

> Celebrity Used Car Lot. I walked in, I said, 'Dan, I wanna know the answer to some of this conflict, I wanna know what temptation is all about, why does my soul pull me one way and why does my body pull me the other all the time?' He said, 'Well, Son, in the Garden of Eden there were many wondrous things: there was a Tree of Life, there was a Tree of Knowledge of Good and Evil, there was a man, Adam, there was a woman, Eve, and let me tell you she looked so fine and when Adam kissed her, it was the first time that a man had ever kissed a woman. And she had legs that were long and soft to the touch, and when Adam touched her, it was the first time that a man had ever touched a woman. And then they went out into the green fields and they lay down and . . . well, let's just say it was the first time. But there was something else in the Garden of Eden on that day, old Satan came slithering up on his belly and somehow he turned their love into a betrayal and sent them driving down into the darkness below. But that's alright because if you've got the nerve to ride, I've got the keys to their getaway car . . . the first . . . pink . . . Cadillac.'

The 'Pink Cadillac' rap slowly but surely took over from the more jaundiced portrayal of relationships with which Springsteen had been prefacing 'I'm Going Down' the previous fall. In these raps, the sexual dynamic had begun with, 'Every place you go, you can't keep your hands off 'em, you're touching 'em all the time and you wanna make love to 'em all the time,' only to end thus, 'If you come back about six months later . . . it's like, 'Ain't I gonna get a goodnight kiss?'

At the same time, he insisted, 'I'm just not really looking to get married at this point. I've made a commitment to doing my job right now.' But by the time of the 27th Annual Grammy Awards ceremony, on February 26 1985, his point of view had switched 180 degrees. The reason was Julianne Phillips, a young actress who could have stepped right out of a Chuck Berry song. American Pie-pretty, she came from good solid Catholic stock. She was also someone to hang onto when the world started spinning. But what she had on Karen or Joyce was anybody's guess. Whatever it was, in the matter of a couple of months bad-boy Bruce had gone from on the prowl to looking to settle down. Inside, though, the process had taken somewhat longer:

> **Bruce Springsteen**: For a long time there were a whole lot of things I was trying to avoid. Part of it [was] because I thought, 'If I don't do this and I

> don't do that, well, maybe I won't get any older.' . . . [But] for quite a few years previous to when I got married, I was going in that direction. Not necessarily that marriage is the only thing that puts you in that place, but it is one of the things. And I realized that you can't live within that rock 'n' roll dream that I had in my head . . . / . . . When I was young, I had this idea of playing out my life like it was some movie, writing the script and making all the pieces fit. And I really did that for a long time . . . And it's bad enough having other people seeing you that way, but seeing yourself that way is really bad. It's pathetic . . . I had locked into what was pretty much a hectic obsession, which gave me enormous focus and energy and fire to burn, because it was coming out of pure fear and self-loathing . . . [Finally,] I realized my real life is waiting to be lived. All the love and the hope and the sorrow and the sadness – that's all over there, waiting to be lived. And I could ignore it and push it aside, or I could say yes to it. [1987/1992]

In fact, the (re-)introduction of his favourite Elvis tune, 'Can't Help Falling In Love' at the January 10 Louisville show – with an extra notch of vocal commitment – probably signalled a newly besotted Springsteen; so in love that the words to that Percy Sledge classic, 'Take Time To Know Her' temporarily slipped from his mind. Springsteen and Phillips tied the connubial knot on May 13 at Our Lady of the Lake, the parish church of Julianne's family, set in Lake Oswego, an affluent suburb of Portland OR. Springsteen now looked forward to a life as far removed from his songs' heroes and villains as possible: 'The night that I got married, I was standing at the altar by myself, and I was waiting for my wife, and I can remember standing there thinking, "Man, I have everything. I got it all." And you have those moments.' The feeling didn't even last through 1987. Because, as he later ruefully observed, 'You end up with a lot more than you expected.'

If the groom entered matrimony with his eyes wide shut, his bride evidently kept her 20/20 vision throughout. Just a few months later, she informed an entertainment journalist, 'I don't feel I married a superstar. He's my husband and I love him very much, but he's a normal human being with faults.' By then, she was advancing her short-lived film career, and Bruce was back in the stadia of America.

The second instalment of her honeymoon had been an all-access pass to a series of stadia shows across Europe, beginning in the bucolic setting of Slane Castle in Ireland on June 1, somewhat spoiled by 150,000 Irish drinkers holding their second annual convention, this year to an E Street Band soundtrack. Springsteen did his best to inject some much-needed romance into the proceedings, singing a solo version of Brian Wilson's 'When I Grow Up (To Be A Man)', prefaced by an admission that 'I'm thinking a lot of different things standing here today. I guess this song kind of sums it up.' Intended as an affirmation of a grown-up Bruce, lines like: 'Will I look for the same things in a woman that I dig in a girl?' would soon enough look like a double-edged query.

If there were moments when the Slane show became more about crowd control than crowd-pleasing, there was no turning back. The course was set. Over the next four months he would play forty-five stadia shows, reaching more folk than in all his seventies odysseys. Sadly, by the time he played three nights at London's Wembley Stadium in early July the set was hopelessly out of kilter. Pick the right night and you might get two *Nebraska* songs. In fact, he was doing as many *BITSUSA* outtakes. ('Seeds' and 'Pink Cadillac' were now nightly highlights.) As for the ten *BITUSA* tracks he performed nightly, they had become an excuse to Singalonga-Springsteen.

On September 27, the travelling band rolled into LA's 90,000-seater Coliseum for the final four *BITUSA* shows, and again the tapes would be rolling. He even produced a couple of surprises that first night: a live debut for 'Janey Don't You Lose Heart', the song originally supposed to close the 1983 *BITUSA*, and a cover of Edwin Collins' 1969 anti-war anthem, 'War' – because 'the values from that time are things that I still believe in. I think that all my music, certainly the music I've done in the past five or six years, is a result of that time and those values.' He was apparently 'looking for some way to reshape that part of the show to make it as explicit as [possible], without sloganeering'. But his lung-busting performance merely stripped the paint from the walls of the Coliseum, and the scales from the eyes of anyone with ears. He was done. And he sorta knew it:

> **Bruce Springsteen**: At the end of the *Born In The USA* tour and after we made the live album, I felt like it was the end of the first part of my journey . . . By the end of the whole thing, I just felt 'Bruced' out. I was

> like, 'Whoa, enough of that.' . . . Eventually it oppresses you . . . / . . . Success at that level is a tricky business because a lot of distortion creeps in and . . . it was fascinating realising that you really do comment on a lot of different levels . . . I found very often that your success story is a bigger story than whatever you're trying to say on stage . . . When you lock into it on a very big level, it's a big wave that you ride and you try and stay on and think, . . . 'What did I accomplish? Where do I feel I've failed?' I thought about all that stuff after we came home. [1992]

Proving that some things never change, he still 'thought about things' way too much. What he most needed was some downtime, and some tlc. from Mrs Springsteen. But if Ms Phillips thought her husband was about to take a break from all that jazz, she didn't know her man. He wasn't listening to her importunings. Maybe all those stadium shows had done some permanent damage to his hearing. Certainly, on the evidence of his 1986 listening sessions, he could no longer tell the difference between strong singing and shouting. Starting in the new year, he began drawing up plans for the greatest live album ever made. They were first formulated after Landau sent him a four-song sample from the final Coliseum show:

> **Jon Landau**: Bruce is a perfectionist. And he wants to give the best; the live album had to be special. If he had released it earlier, it would have been just the normal stuff. The public would have liked it, but it wouldn't have been an event; and that's what he wanted . . . One really important part of the [*Live 1975-85*] set is 'Born In The USA', 'Seeds', 'The River', with that long talk about the draft, 'War'. Actually, everything started with that part. We played them, and then we understood it was not only fantastic live material, but that these four songs together were telling different things, things never heard before on any of our albums. [GD]

Things like how to *really* over-PROJECT. What Springsteen didn't do was ask his label to pull tapes from Max's January 31 1973 as a point of comparison. Or Joe's Place, a year later. Or give a serious listen to the Main Point the following February. In fact, it would appear he chose not to listen to any show before 1978 (except the first five minutes of the Roxy '75, before the band played). It was a point maybe lost on a post-stadia Springsteen but it was not lost on reviewers of the resultant artefact, *Live 1975-85*, certainly not on *Sounds'* Billy Mann:

> '[Perhaps] there were no recordings from that earlier period of a quality that would satisfy Springsteen the Perfectionist. But as Mike Appel had already pencilled in a double or triple live set to follow *Born To Run* (a move Springsteen resisted as too "easy") and despatched crack producer Jimmy Iovine to preside over live recordings in New York, Philadelphia and Toronto, this is an unlikely explanation . . . It is significant [precisely] because by 1978, which is effectively when this live thing starts . . ., many would argue that a lot of the experimentation of the earlier live work – the reworking of old songs into fresh musical statements – had been replaced by the obligation to perform to large rock audiences in a characteristic Rock way.'

In fact, what Landau and Springsteen – with due diligence – set out to produce was the exact opposite of the May 1974 show that once convinced the former he had seen 'the future of rock 'n' roll'. For Springsteen, the pressure to do such a set had become overwhelming. As far back as 1981, he gamely admitted, 'I have this live reputation and I cannot allow myself anything less than to produce the best live LP ever. Perhaps I have to make another five LPs like *The River*, and then compile the best songs from those.' He had made five LPs, but only released two of them. Then in 1984 he spoke about how he particularly wanted to find definitive live readings of the songs on *Darkness*: 'I always felt it was a little dry recording-wise. I felt like I oversang . . . I'd be interested in getting different versions of a lot of those songs . . . just the best of that stuff.' Yet of the six *Darkness* songs on *Live 75-85*, only 'Adam Raised A Cain' came from the requisite era. As for oversinging, nothing from *Darkness* came close to those Coliseum concerts. One-two-three HUH!!!

But there was now a commercial imperative underlying the gesture. A multi-volume set on the back of Dylan's surprisingly successful five-LP *Biograph* was no longer such a scary prospect for Sony (who had their eye on CD sales as much as vinyl). As Mike Appel noted at the time, his former client had finally 'realized he couldn't follow *Born In The USA* with anything but a live album for the . . . same [reason] I'd offered ten years ago: that it would be impossible to immediately follow up a studio album as strong as either of the *Borns* with another studio album.' Landau meanwhile assured fifteen million fans said collection did 'not detract in any way from your memories of Bruce live'. Assuming said memories were as short as his, or as shot as his ears.

Plotkin was back on board, too, and had more of an excuse for omitting all evidence of the pre-*Darkness* band. He wasn't there then. But he was now, as he and Bruce 'spent about six hours a day, five days a week, essentially trying to come up with the right songs to use, come up with little segments of sequences, and to come up with the right takes of the songs'. Yet there was precious little evidence of such deliberation in the set released, which blithely disregarded every show pre-1978, with even multitrack tapes from a dozen shows in that peak year – from Berkeley in July to two San Francisco shows in December – discounted, save for half a dozen full songs and a mutilated 'Backstreets' from the Roxy, and a solitary 'Fire' from the second Winterland.

The remaining 43 songs were all culled from eighties shows, with those from *Born In The USA* and the sparsely-represented *Nebraska* largely taken from summer '85 stadia shows. If, as Springsteen claimed on its release, 'We started with the idea that there was a certain amount of [good] material from each phase of the band,' most of it was caught between the grooves. He had managed a rare coup – using only the finest ingredients, he'd produced a turkey few could finish just in time for Christmas 1986. The initial rush of sales, fed on the hype-to-end-all-hypes and fans starved of living proof of the live E Street experience, sent the album to the top of the charts, with three million shipped. But by new year boxes were piling up in the warehouses of Tower Records &c., prompting *Rolling Stone* to suggest as many as 750,000 copies were gathering dust.

As paydays go, it was a bonanza for the band, who had been twiddling their thumbs for the past fifteen months. But then news reached the musicians that Springsteen was back in the studio, as of January 20, 1987, without making the requisite call to former brothers-in-arms. Landau may have just told a French reporter 'the E Street Band can play everything Bruce writes', but his client was no longer reading from the same book. He was out in LA, looking to repeat the winter 1983 experiment.

Sure enough, on day one an inspired Springsteen cut three songs, 'Walk Like A Man', 'Spare Parts' and 'If You Need Me', the latter pair first and second takes respectively. A second session four days later was even more productive, with five songs recorded (two of which – 'Pretty Baby, Will You Be Mine' and 'Things Ain't That Way' – would go unused). A rough idea for a song listed as 'Is That You?' at a February 5 session became 'Brilliant Disguise' by month's end. In just eighteen sessions he had enough songs to leave off the resultant album the most personal, 'The Wish', addressed to the woman he loved most – his Mum. What was on there suggested he had yet to find a bridge across troubled marital waters, even if he tried putting his best spin on things in interviews:

> **Bruce Springsteen**: When this particular record came around, I wanted to make a record about what I felt, about really letting another person in your life and trying to be a part of someone else's life. That's a frightening thing, something that's always filled with shadows and doubts . . . My main concern is writing that new song that has that new idea, that new perspective. [1988]

Only when the album was all but done, on May 25, did he invite the entire E Street Band (Federici excepted) to add some musical colour to the recently-written 'Tunnel of Love' and, while they were at it, 'Valentine's Day'. Initially, though, 'Tunnel of Love' was the title track to an album it nearly didn't appear on. ('Lucky Man' occupied its slot.) Finally, though, he went with the catchier option, incorporating two songs the band knew should he decide to play with them again after the record appeared. That the album would need some promotion became immediately apparent on its October 6 release, when it spent just a single week in the top spot and the lead single, 'Brilliant Disguise', even with another non-album B-side, failed to emulate 'Dancing in the Dark's' cross-generational appeal. Although initial reports suggested he might tour solo, he changed his mind and made that SOS call to his trusty sidekicks:

> **Nils Lofgren**: In the fall of '87, we went up to Jersey for a series of weekends where we'd get together and just jam with Bruce. It was just kinda an exploratory gathering for Bruce to bounce around ideas and just see how he felt about it. And I think after three weekends of that, we all went home . . . Somewhere after that exploratory series of rehearsals or jams, Bruce decided to do the *Tunnel of Love* tour. So we knew about it before the end of the year.

Actually, he needed to get away; and what better excuse was ever invented than, 'I gotta go on tour with the band (y'know, the one with that hot, single, redhead backing singer).' But he already knew this route contained one road he had to walk alone. Indeed, it was a surprisingly sanguine Springsteen who inducted his musical mentor, Bob Dylan, into the Rock and Roll Hall of Fame that January with a speech describing how the elder statesman's music had helped this boy grow up to be a man: 'When I was fifteen and I heard "Like A Rolling Stone", I heard a guy like I'd never heard before, a guy that had the guts to take on the whole world and make me feel like I had to, too. Maybe some people mistook that voice to be saying somehow that you were going to do the job for them, and as we know as we grow older, there isn't anybody out there that can do that job for anybody else.'

The weight of expectation, which had proven such a burden to Dylan through the sixties and seventies, now weighed as heavily on the last of the New Dylans. But with the *Tunnel of Love Express*, he was determined to throw it off. As he informed *Rolling Stone* on the opening week of the tour: 'The idea on this tour is that you wouldn't know what song was gonna come next. And the way you do that is you just throw out all your cornerstones, the stuff that had not become overly ritualized on the *Born In The USA* tour, but would have been if we did it now.'

Certainly opening night at Worcester's Centrum contained its share of left-field inclusions. Of the two songs entirely new to Bruce fans, 'I'm A Coward (When It Comes To Love)' and 'Part Man Part Monkey', and those resurrected *River* outtakes, 'Be True' and 'Roulette', it was the professions of abiding faithfulness in songs one and three which cut the least mustard. *BITUSA* also contributed its share of outtakes – 'The Light of Day' and 'Seeds' – to the mix, while a belatedly acoustic 'Born In The USA' was another part of a process he later called 'taking the whole thing down, making it feel more human-scaled, less iconic and more about everyday issues; which I [also] thought the *Tunnel of Love* record . . . dealt with.'

Perhaps the most telling set changes, though, were the substitution of 'Can't Help Falling In Love' with 'Have Love, Will Travel' midway through the five-month tour, and a belated switch from 'Ain't Got You' to 'Who Do You Love?' as precursor to 'She's The One'. It was a message his baby back home did not receive right away, but the redhead sharing his mike nightly did. When the paparazzi snapped Bruce and Patti canoodling on a hotel terrace, it was evident some E Street members were more equal than others. It wasn't just the end of the marriage, it was time's up for this band of blood brothers.

As a final gesture, and one more way of avoiding going home, Springsteen agreed to share nineteen stadium dates in September and October with Sting and Peter Gabriel, raising money for Amnesty International. It was a strangely muted end to the E Street era. The sets themselves lasted barely long enough to raise steam, let alone hands. And the set-lists – save for an E Street arrangement of 'Chimes of Freedom' almost as powerful as 1975's 'I Want You' – were entirely predictable. And the backlash kept raining down, John Lombardi in *Esquire* delighting in depicting the crowd as 'louder than the band because it apparently needs to be . . . For Bruce and his fans, noise ha[s] replaced action in the modern scheme of things.'

Springsteen, to his credit, remained stoic in the face of deserting crew members, a disaffected wife and an alienated critical consensus. As he philosophically observed on his return in 1992, 'As far as the whole myth thing goes . . . it ends up being dismantled for you anyway. It doesn't matter whether you do it or not, somebody's going to do it.' He did at least now have a woman, in Patti Scialfa, who understood him *and* his music. (And wanted kids, pronto.)

For his band, though, the future was decidedly uncertain. Lombardi's December 1988 *Esquire* 'Saint Boss' piece quoted an anonymous inside source who had heard 'Bruce [was] breaking up the band because it "was no longer efficient".' Some of the band felt it was about time. Federici, for one, opined that what had 'started out as a band . . . turned into a super, giant corporate money-making machine.' But even Federici thought that a year of silence and then a single phone call was not the way to go about it: 'I thought the way the band broke up was really crappy. It left a sour taste in everybody's mouth; we really didn't know what happened, if we were "fired" or "let go" – any of those words are not good. They don't sound nice.' 'Busy hands' Bittan also thought it was handled badly, although he was the one band member Springsteen recalled when starting work on another solo album in January 1990:

Roy Bittan: I got the same phone call that everybody else in the band got . . . I think he felt like he had come to a certain stage with the band

> where he thought he had finished something, and he wanted to move on somewhere or at least explore . . . On the other hand, emotionally, I think that I speak for everybody, we all felt that we had invested a lot in this situation. We had all really given the best years of our lives to the band, to Bruce, and that we were a big part certainly of what Bruce is about. It was difficult to be told . . . that we were not supposed to be part of it anymore.

The most enraged of the E Streeters was the one who perhaps feared he had the least future as a jobbing musician on other artists' albums and tours – Max Weinberg. That he had enjoyed ten times the career and a hundred times the rewards of the men he replaced in the E Street Band counted not a jot. He even phoned Dick Wingate, who had not worked for Bruce since 1979: 'He was fucking furious. He was really pissed! I guess there was some financial offer he wasn't very happy with. He felt the way it went down was really bad.' And three years later, he had still not quite calmed down. Talking to *Backstreets* in the winter of 1992, Weinberg spoke of a deep and debilitating disappointment:

> **Max Weinberg**: Initially, it was very difficult to accept. In fact, I didn't accept it at first; I denied it . . . because it was never truly articulated to me that the relationship the E Street Band had with Bruce was definitely over. I had to figure that out for myself . . . I spent a large part of my life as a member of the E Street Band . . . I never saw it as just a 'job'. You know, one of the things that made what happened a bit more difficult was that six weeks before I got the phone call from Bruce, I had read . . . how he was in LA recording with studio musicians . . . Now that hurt.

But Springsteen had simply faced up to the inevitable truth. The E Street Band – America's finest live rock band in their day – had become an anachronism; a way of ensuring he could fill arenas, but only if he wanted to be a nostalgia act. He had arrived at a different shore. As he said, shortly after Weinberg let rip, the music he was making now was 'about somebody walking through that world of fear so that he can live in the world of love'. It just happened to come from a man who once spit in the face of these badlands with a band of brothers who for fifteen years never stopped feeling the self-same way.

November 22, 2009 – Everything That Dies, Some Day Comes Back

> I think we got to a place where everybody realizes that this is a very singular thing . . . this group of people playing together in this fashion . . . We wanted to live up to that thing, and we wanted to continue to serve in the fashion that we served before with our audience . . . Every person on the stage is very singular and we do something that is very unique together. And I think that unspoken recognition was a part of the resolution of whatever [bad] feelings someone might have had from [when we broke up]. – Bruce Springsteen, 2001

Ten years of intermittently burning down the reunion road had brought the E Street shuffle to Buffalo in upstate New York at the end of another marathon year of touring. After nigh on ninety dates promoting the third E Street Band album of the 21st century, *Working on a Dream* – and a decade after a 1999 reunion tour turned inexorably into the second E Street era – Bruce had decided to return to the starting point, 'the miracle . . . the record that took everything from way below zero to One'. He and a reconstructed E Street Band, including both Miami Steve *and* Nils Lofgren, were going to play *Greetings from Asbury Park*, for 'one time only'. And, completing the circle, he had asked Mike Appel to join them for this symbolic moment of closure:

> **Mike Appel:** Bruce just called up out of the blue. I was in a diner with my son. 'Who's this [on the phone]?' 'It's Bruce.' 'What on earth are you calling about?' 'Well, it's the last date of the tour and we're gonna do the *Greetings From Asbury Park* album. We never did it [live]. I'd like you to be there.' 'Bruce, it's twelve noon now. How am I gonna be there?' 'Don't worry

'bout a thing. Go to your house. I'll arrange everything.' So we return to the house. An hour later, a limousine picks us up, takes us to the airport. Of course, they have their own jet. We all went up there with the E Street Band.

For the past month, Springsteen had been selectively performing each of the six first-era E Street albums in their entirety – even *The River* – as a way of making these final shows, after three years of almost continuous recording and performing, something special. (Of the six, the attempt to replicate *The Wild, the Innocent* proved the most hit and miss.) It was a tacit acknowledgment from an older, wiser Springsteen of the E Street Band's central importance to those genre-defining records: 'As I said when I inducted U2 into the Rock and Roll Hall of Fame, one of the rules of rock & roll is, "Hey asshole, the other guy's more important than you think he is!" It can take time away from people to get a [real] view on that.'

It was also a logical extension of the 'let's present the past in modern dress' *modus operandi* Springsteen adopted the minute he brought the band back to life in the winter of 1999 – when the album they were primarily promoting was a four-CD retrospective of (mainly) songs left off the E Street Band albums: legendary lost songs like 'Hey Santa Ana', 'Seaside Bar Song', 'Zero and Blind Terry', 'Thundercrack', 'Rendezvous', 'Don't Look Back', 'Restless Nights', 'Roulette', 'Loose Ends', 'I Wanna Be With You', 'Cynthia', 'My Love Will Not Let You Down', 'Frankie' and 'The Promise', every one of which he would perform at some point in the ensuing decade – 'Restless Nights' excepted. That one he saved for his 2009 shuffle off to Buffalo.

By this time, the brand-name backing band contained just two members who had played on that original 1973 artefact – Garry Tallent and Clarence Clemons. Danny Federici's death in 2008 had robbed this newly revamped E Street combo of an irreplaceable original member. And by November 2009 Clarence Clemons was not a well man, either. Another E Street tour for him looked increasingly unlikely. But the Big Man had a big heart, even if it looked at times like he was gonna leave part of it in Buffalo. As Appel wrote after that final public performance, 'It ain't easy blowing a saxophone all night . . . when you're sick.'

Thankfully, the *Greetings* album had only ever required Clarence's clarion blasts on two songs, 'Blinded By The Light' and 'Spirit In The Night' – though 'Growin' Up' and 'Does This Bus Stop' followed suit in concert. It was an album much of which had been written at, and for, piano; containing some of Springsteen's most personal songs. And so it was that, on this November night, Roy Bittan got to put years of musical virtuosity into the parts of 'Lost In The Flood', 'The Angel' and 'For You' Springsteen wrote for and by himself.

The greatest challenge for Springsteen and Bittan in Buffalo was to make 'The Angel', the one *Greetings* song the E Street Band had *never* manhandled, rise from its 'marble dome'. Somehow, with Soozie Tyrell's violin effortlessly slipping into the cracks 'twixt vocal and piano, they made this wordy work a little more heavenly. 'Lost In The Flood' was also given a wailing guitar coda by the ex-Steel Mill lead guitarist, while 'For You' was transported back in time to the Roxy, and a younger Greg Kihn copycat. Somehow the elements of a rekindled E Street Band were setting off sparks and bridging the years – their failing flesh willing to fuel fans' fantasies one last time.

But *Greetings* was just the starting point for a night of rock 'n' roll reconciliation. By 2009 Springsteen had eight more albums to add to the eight he had made in the first E Street era. And so, although he acknowledged the audience's desire to hear the 'old stuff' – even when drawn from 1999's *Tracks*, as 'Restless Nights' and 'My Love Will Not Let You Down' were – he was 'still try[ing] to keep a schematic that remains centered around our newest material'. Even if he knew this was a losing battle. And had been ever since the band reformed in 1999 without a new record to promote, and only three fair-to-middling albums of Springsteen originals (*Lucky Town, Human Touch* and *The Ghost of Tom Joad*) separating them from their decade-old dissolution. But still, he liked to think, 'On any given night I'm playing to many of my audiences out there. There's the *Tom Joad* audience, there's the 'Dancing In The Dark' audience, but hey, they're all there at that particular moment.'

In upstate New York – which had last seen Springsteen before *Magic* and *Working On A Dream* tripled the count of 21st century E Street albums – he chose to play as many covers as second-era originals. All were certainly familiar to any serious Bruce taper: 'Merry Christmas Baby', 'Santa Claus Is Coming To Town', 'I Don't Wanna Hang Up My Rock & Roll Shoes' and – as final encore – 'Higher And Higher' and 'Rockin' All Over The World'; each a song Springsteen had claimed for his own three decades earlier. All affirmed the promise he had often spoken about, at a time in his life when everything was at stake and there was all to play for. The nights when miracles were commonplace. Back in the glory days.

Further Notes on Springsteen Songs

Part One: 1972–1978

The notes below provide additional commentary on the 300 songs written by Springsteen in the twelve years (to the day) that separate his audition for Appel in February 1972 from the recording of 'Dancing In The Dark' in 1984. Included is full studio data for each track, culled primarily from Sony's own database of the sessions, and where applicable the first documented live version. Session dates in square brackets indicates a possible mix session, as opposed to a full recording session with the band. In the case of certain early compositions, a second documented live version is included in brackets, to indicate where the first recording may be sonically challenged (i.e. crap). The short codes for the album on which a given track appears are as follows:

18TR – 18 TRACKS
BITUSA – BORN IN THE USA
BTF – BEFORE THE FAME
BTR – BORN TO RUN
DA – DARKNESS ON THE EDGE OF TOWN
GH – GREATEST HITS
GR – GREETINGS FROM ASBURY PARK
NE– NEBRASKA
PS – PRODIGAL SON
RI – THE RIVER
TE – THE ESSENTIAL . . .
TP – THE PROMISE
TR – TRACKS
WI – THE WILD, THE INNOCENT & THE E STREET SHUFFLE

[TR]* and [TP]* indicate that the original studio recordings were overdubbed decades later, prior to release on *Tracks* or *The Promise*.

1972–1978

I) 1–17. Songs demoed in 1972, but not recorded for *Greetings*:

1. IF I WAS THE PRIEST

Known studio/demo recordings: Mike Appel's Office, New York April 1972; 'John Hammond session', CBS Studios, New York 3/5/72; Pocketful of Tunes Studio, New York May–June 1972. [BTF]

Remarkably, given the plethora of archival releases in recent years, 'If I Was The Priest' still remains unreleased by Sony. Reportedly performed at The Student Prince in the fall of 1971, it is the song that opened the door to a new world of singer-songwriting for the young Jersey devil. As one of the songs that convinced John Hammond Senior the boy deserved a record contract, and as the one track demoed in 1972 which directly led to a pre-fame cover version – by The Hollies' Allan Clarke – one might have expected its official appearance before now. As it is, its only quasi-legal release was on the *Before The Fame* 2-CD set which Springsteen went to such trouble to put out of circulation.

2. SOUTHERN SON

Known studio/demo recordings: 'John Hammond session', CBS Studios, New York 3/5/72; Pocketful of Tunes Studio, New York May–June 1972. [BTF]

This weird little ballad about a displaced child of the Union remains one of just two tracks Springsteen played to Hammond at his May 3 CBS audition that were not worthy of consideration for his debut album. One of that small body of 'cowboy' songs he wrote during or shortly after his trip to California, there isn't a great deal separating the Laurel Canyon demo from the Hammond demo. It was the former which first passed into collector circles, via the so-called London publishing demo.

3. RANDOLPH STREET

Known studio/demo recordings: Jim Cretecos apartment, New York April 1972. [BTF/PS]

One of half a dozen songs Springsteen recorded at the apartment of Jim Cretecos, Appel's partner, in the weeks before he made a proper demo tape with John Hammond, 'Randolph Street' was not a song anyone else was likely to cover. [see discussion in main text p. 4]

4. BABY DOLL
5. BORDER GUARD
6. WAR NURSE*
7. JESSE*
8. HOLLYWOOD KIDS

Known studio/demo recordings: Jim Cretecos apartment, New York April 1972. [BTF], * also [PS]

These five songs – not one of which reappeared post-Hammond, even as a publishing demo – fully testify to the then-output of this prodigious son, though such fecundity came at a price: quality control. 'Baby Doll', the oldest of these songs, was the one which failed to impress Appel at their November 1971 meeting. It may not be as bad as Appel has suggested, but nor is it 'Pinball Wizard' (baby doll is playing at being deaf and dumb). The messianic 'Jesse' is half a good idea ('Oh Jesse, he says you wear a cross 'round your neck and come on with nails in your hands'), but at no point does Springsteen figure out what sets the lad apart from other false prophets. Similar flaws impair Springsteen's paeans to the Border Guard, the War Nurse and the Hollywood Kids. One somehow doubts Cretecos thought this home-tape would yield its own payday twenty years down the line, when any scraps could be served up as 'lost songs' of The Boss.

9. PRODIGAL SON

Known studio/demo recordings: Jim Cretecos apartment, New York April 1972. [BTF/PS]

Long-rumoured to be an important early song, 'Prodigal Son' was one of the major finds among the pre-Hammond tapes served up on the 2-CD set of the same name in 1994, before the injunctions started a-flyin'. It would be superseded by 'Lost In The Flood' when it came time to get serious.

10. FAMILY SONG
11. CAMILLA HORN
12. ELOISE
13. MARIE

Known studio/demo recordings: Pocketful of Tunes Studio, New York April–May 1972. [BTF/PS]

The least consequential song from another batch of demos turns out to be the most intriguing. 'Eloise', or the extant one-minute snatch which provides the gist of another girl-name song, is not only sufficient to reveal another lyric about an all-seeing woman whose power 'late in the night . . . comes over me', but also the melodic template for what will become 'Growin' Up'. Of the other three songs cut here, Springsteen and/or Appel evidently rated 'Marie' the highest, as only this cut made the London publishing demo [see discussion of 'Family Song' in main text p. 42].

14. SHE'S LEAVING
15. THE SONG (I HEARD THE WORD)

Known studio/demo recordings: Pocketful of Tunes Studio, New York May–June 1972.

Two more songs which feature on the London publishing demo, making them well known to the bossman's collecting fraternity. More surprisingly, neither appeared at the *Greetings* sessions, even though 'The Song' was included in a list of possible album tracks that summer, under its alternative title, 'I Heard The Word'. 'She's Leaving', one suspects, was already too old, having in a previous life been part of the Bruce Springsteen Band repertoire. As such, it represents an important bridge between the big fish in a little pond that was Asbury Park Bruce and the CBS Recording Artiste he was by the time he demoed it in New York.

16. HENRY BOY
17. NO NEED

Known studio/demo recordings: Pocketful of Tunes Studio, New York June–July 1972.

This pair probably constitute the last tracks recorded at the little demo-studio in New York Appel and Cretecos had been using in the lead-up to inking the CBS deal, and the release of funds that brought. Both made it onto the London tape, but not to the *Greetings* sessions, though 'Henry Boy' – another refugee from the rhyming dictionary with its 'trip for dippers . . . get[ting] clipped by rippers' &c. – did appear on the same provisional first album check-list as 'The Song'; and was certainly performed at Max's that August (a crude video recording exists).

II) 18–28. Songs both demoed & recorded for *Greetings* June 1972:

18. COWBOYS OF THE SEA

Known studio/demo recordings: 'John Hammond session', CBS Studios, New York 3/5/72; Pocketful of Tunes Studio, New York May–June 1972; 914 Sound Studios, Blauvelt NY June 1972. [BTF]

The one Bruce Springsteen Band-era track Springsteen cut at the first set of *Greetings* sessions in June, 'Cowboys of the Sea' circulates only as a solo performance from 914. However, as the one song that already had a full band arrangement (with the same rhythm section that whip up a storm on a February 1972 Richmond show), it seems probable a full band version was attempted at these sessions, though neither it nor the extant solo outtake feature in the Sony logs.

19. ARABIAN NIGHTS

Known studio/demo recordings: Mike Appel's Office, New York April 1972; 'John Hammond session', CBS Studios, New York 3/5/72; 914 Sound Studios, Blauvelt NY 7/6/72 + 27/6/72. [BTF]

One of seven 'new' songs Springsteen presented to Cretecos and Appel at their Valentine's Day 1972 meeting, 'Arabian Nights' was also one of three tracks he recorded for Appel in April, presumably to give him something to hawk around the labels. By now, the shoreline kid is running riot with that rhyming dictionary. One of ten tracks included on the version of *Greetings* delivered to CBS in August 1972, only to be told to try again.

20. MARY QUEEN OF ARKANSAS

Known studio/demo recordings: 'John Hammond session', CBS Studios, New York 3/5/72 [TR]; 914 Sound Studios, Blauvelt NY 26–27/6/72. [GR]
First documented performance: Max's Kansas City, New York 31/1/73.

If the main mystery remains what did the songwriter ever see in 'Mary . . .', a more minor mystery is what prompted a song on that perennial theme, the love of an aristocrat for an acrobat. A song he has consistently championed, 'Mary . . .' would feature live and in regular acoustic radio sets through March 1974.

21. GROWIN' UP

Known studio/demo recordings: 'John Hammond session', CBS Studios, New York 3/5/72 [TR]; 914 Sound Studios, Blauvelt NY 7/6/72 + 27/6/72. [GR]
First documented performance: The Main Point, Bryn Mawr PA 31/10/73.

Springsteen evidently turned up at his make-or-break May 3 session with the legendary John Hammond Snr. quite prepared to play songs he'd barely finished. 'Growin' Up' was one such. Never demoed for Laurel Canyon, he pulled it out mid-session, to Hammond's discernible delight. Applying metaphorical Band-Aids to the psychological scars from twenty-plus years on the boredwalk, Springsteen had finally learnt to laugh at the past. As a welcome by-product he unveiled a genuine lyrical gift right from that dazzlingly Dylanesque opening, 'I stood stone-like at midnight/ Suspended in my masquerade'. Recorded at the first *Greetings* session in early June – almost certainly in the same acoustic guise as the other three tracks cut that day – it received an electric rearrangement later in June, when prototypical E Street elements were finally to hand.

22. DOES THIS BUS STOP AT 82ND STREET?

Known studio/demo recordings: 'John Hammond session', CBS Studios, New York 3/5/72 [TR]; 914 Sound Studios, Blauvelt NY 26-27/6/72 + 12/7/72. [GR]
First documented performance: Max's Kansas City, New York 31/1/73.

Though demoed for Hammond in acoustic guise, having been largely composed on a bus-ride back to Jersey one afternoon, 'Does This Bus Stop' should have stood as fair warning that this was someone itching to rock out. Even the faux-rock arrangement made to suffice on *Greetings* is the barest of prototypes for the gung-ho live versions which would prove such a highlight at the 1973–74 shows, the Big Man stamping his presence on a song he shoulda got his mitts on when they were rolling studio tape.

23. IT'S HARD TO BE A SAINT IN THE CITY

Known studio/demo recordings: 'John Hammond session', CBS Studios, New York 3/5/72 [TR]; ?Pocketful of Tunes Studio, New York June 1972; 914 Sound Studios, Blauvelt NY 26–27/6/72 + 26/10/72. [GR]
First documented performance: My Father's Place, Roslyn NY 31/7/73.

The song that seems to have sold both Appel and Hammond on Springsteen's talent, 'Saint In The City' was played at both the February 14 and May 2 'auditions', for which no tapes exist. A blast of bravado from a scuffling songwriter with little to lose, the song flew off the page, one of those 'fifteen-minute blasts' he talked about. Though soon revamped in an electric guise, solo versions produced by Hammond in May and Appel in June are extant (in the former's case, on the official *Tracks* boxed set). The superior solo take on the Appel tape is generally considered a publishing demo. However, it is probably a *Greetings* outtake (as suggested on *Unsurpassed Masters* 4) from the June 26 session, one of three acoustic tracks cut that day.

24. THE ANGEL
Known studio/demo recordings: 'John Hammond session', CBS Studios, New York 3/5/72; 914 Sound Studios, Blauvelt NY 26–27/6/72; 29/6/72 + 26/10/72. [GR]
First documented E Street performance: HSBC Arena, Buffalo NY 22/11/09.

'The Angel' demands our attention based largely on the power of some patchy poetry ('The interstate's choked with nomadic hordes' – natch) and a grand solo piano performance. Yet it seemed to hold Hammond; and after it was cut at 914 in June (with an overdubbed bass from Richard Davis), it featured on all the various provisional track-listings for *Greetings*.

25. JAZZ MUSICIAN
Known studio/demo recordings: 'John Hammond session', CBS Studios, New York 3/5/72; Pocketful of Tunes Studio, New York May–June 1972; 914 Sound Studios, Blauvelt NY 27/6/72. [BTF/PS]

One of three songs bumped from *Greetings* when Springsteen went back in and cut 'Blinded By The Light' and 'Spirit In The Night', 'Jazz Musician' was probably one thesaurus-swallowing song too many. Which isn't to say it doesn't have its moments. One couplet was so memorable it made it all the way to 'Tenth Avenue Freeze Out': 'Oh, now the Park is dark, but the sidewalk's bright/ And alive with the light of the living.'

26. TWO HEARTS IN TRUE WALTZ TIME
Known studio/demo recordings: 'John Hammond session', CBS Studios, New York 3/5/72; 914 Sound Studios, Blauvelt NY 27/6/72 + 29/6/72. [BTF]

With such a great title, it is something of a disappointment to hear the resultant song, which reads more like the first draft of a potentially good idea (Springsteen evidently felt the same way – a song of the same name reappears on a winter 1974 list of possible songs for 'Album #3'). Yet 'Two Hearts' was seriously considered for *Greetings*, appearing on an August short-list.

27. STREET QUEEN
Known studio/demo recordings: 'John Hammond session', CBS Studios, New York 3/5/72; 914 Sound Studios, Blauvelt NY 7/6/72.

Before he had heard a note of Robert Johnson, Springsteen has taken the motif of 'Terraplane Blues' and written a song about a girl made of car parts (or vice versa). A deliciously raunchy early song that was cut the first day of sessions for *Greetings* , using an electric piano, and was never heard of again, only seeing out her days as opening track on the London publishing demo.

28. LADY AND THE DOCTOR
Known studio/demo recordings: Mike Appel's Office, New York April 1972; 914 Sound Studios, Blauvelt NY 7/6/72 + 27/6/72. [BTF/PS]

Another song about two ill-suited lovers from different social strata, a theme to which Springsteen showed an abiding attachment, 'The Lady and the Doctor' in all likelihood was cut for *Greetings* in both solo and band guises. If so, the latter remains uncirculated. [See discussion in main text p. 43].

III) 29–35. Other songs recorded for *Greetings from Asbury Park*:

29. VISITATION AT FORT HORN
Known studio/demo recordings: 914 Sound Studios, Blauvelt NY 27/6/72. [BTF/PS]

Known for many years in collecting circles under the anomalous title 'American Song', 'Visitation at Fort Horn' was supposedly cut from the album at the last minute. It certainly appears on all three 'provisional' track listings for *Greetings*, including the one delivered to CBS in August 1972. What undoubtedly did for it, at least in part, was its near eight-minute length (though the album would still only have clocked in at forty-five minutes). [See discussion in main text pp. 46–7].

30. LOST IN THE FLOOD

Known studio/demo recordings: 914 Sound Studios, Blauvelt NY 27/6/72. [GR]
First documented performance: New Gymnasium, Richmond VA 14/2/73 [Berkeley CA 2/3/73].

If Springsteen happily revealed his blasphemies to Hammond in the form of 'If I Was The Priest', he was just warming up. By the time of the first 'band' sessions for *Greetings* he had written this amalgam of irreligious and Dylanesque imagery. 'Lost in the Flood' may well be the great 'lost' song on a debut record teeming-with-ideas. 'Lost' in the sense that it never really retained any solid hold on the live set, and great, because it is.
Note: The 'sound effects' on the album version were apparently overdubbed by Van Zandt.

31. FOR YOU

Known studio/demo recordings: 914 Sound Studios, Blauvelt NY 27/6/72 + 26/10/72. [GR]
First documented performance: New Gymnasium, Richmond VA 14/2/73 [Washington 6/12/73].

Though 'For You' seems to have only ever been recorded as a band performance at the album sessions, it was consistently performed through 1975 solo at the piano. Only in 1978 was it given the full E Street Band treatment, with a frenetic, hell-for-leather rendition from the Roxy later being issued on the first tie-in single from 1986's *Live 1975-85*, 'War', where its still-raw emotions cast in high relief its more bellicose A-side.

32. THE CHOSEN

Known studio/demo recordings: 914 Sound Studios, Blauvelt NY 11/9/72

The biggest mystery thrown up by the Sony *Greetings* session-logs is a song recorded at the penultimate session, listed as 'The Chosen', probably the same song he discusses with Paul Nelson in December for a piece that never ran: 'I tried to get [the song] on, I fought like a mother, but it came out like nine minutes something. But we had a steel player on it and we had Clarence, who played a great solo.' The mention of Clarence dates this track to the last two sessions, i.e. September 11 or October 26, but Springsteen claims he can't remember its title. The one line he does mention, 'Blow the whistle from the mountaintop', doesn't fit any known song of the period. Another possible title for this song could be 'Let The Words', a title on a provisional sequence compiled *after* the September 11 session.

33. SONG TO THE ORPHANS
Known studio/demo recordings: 914 Sound Studios, Blauvelt NY 19–20/2/73 [PS]
First documented performance: Max's Kansas City, New York 31/1/73.

Perhaps 'The Chosen' is not so much a lost song as an alternate title for something definitely written at this point. 'The Chosen' would actually be an apposite title for this important song, which Springsteen was still performing in the winter of 1973 (when he also cut the solo demo that features on the London publishing demo). Surprisingly, given its omission from the voluminous *Tracks*, the song was revived at a solo show in November 2005, Bruce doing a creditable job of the words but rather steamrollering a once-distinctive tune.

34. BLINDED BY THE LIGHT
Known studio/demo recordings: 914 Sound Studios, Blauvelt NY 11/9/72. [GR]
First documented performance: New Gymnasium, Richmond VA 14/2/73 [Berkeley CA 2/3/73].

According to Springsteen in *Songs*, both 'Blinded By The Light' and 'Spirit In The Night' were written to order – after Clive Davis told him there was nothing on the provisional album which could garner radio play. But that isn't quite what he said at the time. To Paul Nelson, he implied 'Blinded' was first attempted in the same style as the other tracks, but 'wasn't really an acoustic song'.

35. SPIRIT IN THE NIGHT
Known studio/demo recordings: 914 Sound Studios, Blauvelt NY 11/9/72 + 26/10/72. [GR]
First documented performance: Max's Kansas City, New York 31/1/73.

The 'other' song written in response to Clive Davis's request for some 'single' material, 'Spirit In The Night' was issued on single hard on the heels of 'Blinded By The Light' in 1973, without result. By then, 'Spirit In The Night' was already a live staple, and remains the best-known song on *Greetings*.

IV) 36–51. Songs demoed and/or performed January–June 1973:

36. BISHOP DANCED

First documented performance: Max's Kansas City, New York 31/1/73. [TR]

Thanks to the magic of bootlegging, specifically classic late-seventies vinyl boot *Fire On The Fingertips*, 'Bishop Danced' enjoyed favour among Bruce collectors long before its appearance on *Tracks* (1998). Many listeners to that set would have been familiar with the version chosen, which – despite its erroneous date attribution – was the self-same January 1973 Max's version broadcast by the King Biscuit Radio Hour, and released by an English bootlegger five years later (where it was given the title, 'Mama Knows 'Rithmetic').

37. THUNDERCRACK

Known studio/demo recordings: 914 Sound Studios, Blauvelt NY 22/6/73; 7 + 9/8/73. [TR]*

First documented performance: Max's Kansas City, New York 31/1/73.

'The song 'Thundercrack' was something that we wrote as the showstopper . . . That was 'Rosalita''s predecessor . . . It was one of the few songs that actually was finished when I went and found it [for *Tracks*] . . . It was probably 80% done – we had to shape it a little bit, but I wanted to get that on . . . I found a version which was actually pretty good, called up Vini Lopez and I said, 'Vini, I have some singing for you to do.' - Bruce Springsteen, 1999.

'Thundercrack' was another early cut which first found a wide(r) audience in bootleg form, initially on *The Jersey Devil* (from a Main Point, April 1973 radio broadcast), and then on *Fire On The Fingertips*, from Max's. The latter supposedly came from an English publishing acetate compiled by someone at Laurel Canyon, who one must suppose had access to the June studio outtake, but presumably thought it wasn't up to snuff, so included the live version instead. Its release on *Tracks* only served to prove the compiler of the publishing acetate had been right all along.

38. SAGA OF THE ARCHITECT ANGEL

Known studio/demo recordings: 914 Sound Studios, Blauvelt NY 29–30/1/73.

First documented performance: Max's Kansas City, New York 31/1/73.

39. JANEY NEEDS A SHOOTER

Known studio/demo recordings: 914 Sound Studios, Blauvelt NY 29–30/1/73.

Not only were these two titles recorded at the same demo session/s, but they both seem to have survived as song-ideas long after other discards from this prolific period fell by the wayside. In the case of 'Architect Angel' – which he claimed he 'wrote for John Wayne', the night he debuted it – the title appears on provisional lists for *The Wild, the Innocent, Born to Run* and *Darkness on the Edge of Town*. Not that there is any evidence to suggest it was *recorded* for any of these, unless the demo version cut in January 1973 was meant to suffice for the second album. (It already had a past, deriving melodically from a 1971 Bruce Springsteen Band song, 'Talkin' About My Baby'.) When it comes to 'Janey Needs A Shooter', two terrific performances from 1979 demonstrate that the basic idea – girls like sex, too – survived the dramatic transition in Springsteen's songwriting from *The Wild, the Innocent* to *Darkness* essentially intact. [See discussion in main text pp. 67–8].

40. BALLAD OF A SELF-LOADING PISTOL
41. WINTER SONG
42. I MET HER IN A TOURIST TRAP IN TIGUARA [UNCIRCULATED]

Known studio/demo recordings: 914 Sound Studios, Blauvelt NY 29–30/1/73.

The three other songs demoed across the same two days at the end of January 1973, presumably with a view to inclusion on the second album. (Otherwise, why lodge copies with CBS?) Of the trio, 'I Met Her In A Tourist Trap in Tiguara' remains uncirculated. The other two tracks surfaced in the early nineties as part of Yellow Dog's *Unsurpassed Masters* series, though 'Ballad of a Self-Loading Pistol' had been rumoured to exist since the late seventies, having apparently been pressed to acetate by Laurel Canyon. Whether the story in 'Winter Song' of a visit to a 'Pennsylvania mountain' brothel has some basis in reality I leave to more intrepid investigators, but Winter is not the last lady of the night to trade swords for candy in a Springsteen song.

43. TOKYO (AND THEN THE BAND PLAYED)

Known studio/demo recordings: ?914 Sound Studios, Blauvelt NY 19–20/2/73. [BTF]

First documented performance: The Main Point, Bryn Mawr PA 24/4/73.

44. VIBES MAN

Known studio/demo recordings: ?914 Sound Studios, Blauvelt NY 19–20/2/73.

Extant Laurel Canyon demos of 'Tokyo' and 'Vibes Man' have been consistently dated to 1972 in Springsteen tapeographies. But this presents problems. One, there is documentary evidence Springsteen cut further demos on 19–20 February 1973 (presumably at 914). The only demos that could fit such a timeline are 'Song To The Orphans' (which otherwise dates from summer 1972, alongside 'Henry Boy' and 'The Song'), 'Vibes Man' and/or 'Tokyo'. ('Tokyo' made its live debut in April, but is not on live tapes from February, while 'Vibes Man' became the coda to a song also debuted in April 1973, 'New York City Song'.)

The main argument against 1972, though, is stylistic. 'Tokyo' and 'Vibes Man' lend themselves to the E Street Band – unlike 'Henry Boy', 'The Song', 'Southern Son' &c. As Springsteen himself said, 'When I went on the road . . . I began to just write with the band in mind, with the idea of mixing those two things.' That 'Tokyo' was written 'with the band in mind' was demonstrated by its evolution into 'And Then The Band Played', a jazzier hybrid which survived in the live set till June 1974. And yet, the solo demo of 'Tokyo' remains the only known studio recording of the song.

45. NEW YORK CITY SONG
Known studio/demo recordings: 914 Sound Studios, Blauvelt NY 20 or 22/6/73.
First documented performance: The Main Point, Bryn Mawr PA 24/4/73.
as NEW YORK CITY SERENADE
Known studio/demo recordings: 914 Sound Studios, Blauvelt NY 28/6/73; 7/8/73. [WI]
First documented performance: Max's Kansas City, New York 18/7/73.

To portray 'New York City Song' as an early version of 'New York City Serenade' is to do a gross disservice to the former song. In fact, Springsteen not only consistently performed 'New York City Song' at the spring shows (and an atmospheric acoustic version for WGOE in May), but also recorded this original song at the first sessions for his second album. Though not in general circulation, Brucebase describes it as 'piano based with sparse band backing'.

But when they resumed work on *The Wild, the Innocent* on June 28, David Sancious was on board and ready and willing to offer arrangement suggestions, presumably the by-product of rehearsals for a jazzed-up 'Vibes Man' – though he would coyly insist, 'I don't think they constituted the arrangement.' 'New York City Serenade' would receive another test run three weeks later at a residency at Max's, acquiring a *West Side Story*-esque piano introduction as Sancious began to encourage a more grandiose Bruce to emerge from his chrysalis.

Note: The original, slightly longer mix of the album version would anticipate the calamitous 914 *Born To Run* sessions, featuring strings, group vocals and congas.

46. WILD BILLY'S CIRCUS STORY

Known studio/demo recordings: 914 Sound Studios, Blauvelt NY 14/5/73; 25–26 + 28/6/73. [WI]

First documented performance: Max's Kansas City, New York 31/1/73.

According to Brucebase, this song was recorded for *Greetings* in its 'Circus Song' guise. In fact, that version was recorded for the second album, on May 14, when they cut eight takes of what is essentially the same beast, save for a later-deleted section at song's end where Springsteen riffs on the liars' response to Billy's circus: 'Hear the liars, they're outside crying . . . they're inside sighing . . . listening to the barkers . . . watching the centre ring . . . up on the trapeze . . . feel their fire . . . they're all scared of dying'. He returned to Wild Billy at the sessions proper in late June; and this time 'the circus boss leans over and whispers into the little boy's ear . . . All aboard, Nebraska's our next stop'.

47. FEVER

Known studio/demo recordings: 914 Sound Studios, Blauvelt NY 16/5/73. [18TR]

First documented performance: Liberty Hall, Houston TX 10/3/74.

Though it took Springsteen a quarter-century to finally release the legendary 'Fever', it is hard to imagine he had many serious fans who had not already found a way to get hold of this outta-nowhere classic, cut one afternoon in May 1973 – supposedly in a single take (marked on the box 'demo'). Talking about the song the following March, Springsteen claimed, 'We did it when we were recording the second album . . . as a demo tape for . . . I don't know what for.' Originally called '(I Got The) Fever For The Girl', the song nudges eight minutes in its original 'sneaky mother' guise, and would have been almost impossible to edit down to single-length, relying as it does on the whole slow-burn arrangement for its smoky power.

48. SECRET TO THE BLUES

First documented performance: Coliseum, Richmond VA 31/5/73.

49. YOU MEAN SO MUCH TO ME BABY
Known studio/demo recordings: WGOE-FM, Richmond VA 31/5/73.
First documented performance: My Father's Place, Roslyn NY 31/7/73.

By the end of May 1973, Springsteen had stockpiled an impressive array of songs for his next album. And yet still he revived two r&b-infused throwbacks he was happy to play live, but was never gonna allow to impact on the serious statements of Album #2. Like 'Fever', 'Secret To The Blues' and 'You Mean So Much To Me Baby' had their antecedents in the Bruce Springsteen Band. In fact, 'Secret To The Blues', a song that lasted only a matter of weeks in the live set, was a version of a 1971 favourite, 'The Band's Just Boppin' The Blues'. Offering the sage advice to 'sit back and hang loose/ 'Cause that's the secret of the blues', it was more throw-away than throwback.

'You Mean So Much To Me Baby', which had a lot more going for it, survived in the live set as long as Mad Dog. Only marginally rearranged from its summer 1971 guise – when it had a full girl-chorus and gratuitous guitar workout – the song first pops up in an acoustic session for WGOE, a Richmond, Va. radio station that had been championing his work since the Steel Mill days, perhaps as a nod to some old fans. Subsequent live versions hint at a direction he may well have gone in had Sancious stayed on board.

50. ROSALITA
Known studio/demo recordings: 914 Sound Studios, Blauvelt NY 23/9/73. [WI]
First documented performance: New Gymnasium, Richmond VA 14/2/73 [Philadelphia PA 6/6/73].

Beginning life as more shaggy dog story-in-song than show-stopper, 'Rosalita' would prove the hardiest of the 'Mad Dog'-era E Street songs, surviving through the *Born In The USA* tour as the one sop to former glories. By then it was the dying embers of a song which, back in the day, made sparks fly every night. First performed in February 1973, it featured a story about how he was coached by various fellow vagrants he met in jail, when arrested for loitering during the five years he spent hitchhiking around the country from the age of eight! [see p. 64] But by the time the song reappeared in the live set in early June, at arena shows with Chicago, it had been stripped for action. Lyrically all but finished, this live version confirms the link with the Rosalie in 'Tokyo', referring to her 'sweet samurai tongue'.

51. HEY SANTA ANA

Known studio/demo recordings: 914 Sound Studios, Blauvelt NY 22, 26 + 28/6/73; 1/7/73. [TR]

First documented performance: The Main Point, Bryn Mawr PA 24/4/73.

Once again Springsteen's fascination with Wild West mythology gets the better of him, as he finally constructs a New Mexico mini-movie worthy of the theme. However, 'Hey Santa Ana' would suffer the same fate as that other 'how the West was lost' travelogue recorded for *The Wild, the Innocent*, 'Evacuation of the West'. Back in June, Springsteen presumably planned a more pan-American statement than the album he eventually released. [See discussion in main text p. 69].

V) 52–60. Other songs recorded for *The Wild, the Innocent,* July–September 1973:

52. PHANTOMS (OVER THE HILLS OF ST GEORGE)

Known studio/demo recordings: 914 Sound Studios, Blauvelt NY 22, 26 + 28/6/73; 1/7/73.

First documented performance: Broome County Veterans Memorial Arena, Binghampton NY 13/6/73.

Another legendary song that finally made its way into general circulation with bootleg label E Street Records' riposte to *Tracks*, the 3-CD *Deep Down In The Vaults*, 'Phantoms', as long rumoured, turned out to be a prototype for 'Zero and Blind Terry' (musically they are all but identical – even down to the 'oh-ho-ho' backing vocals). According to the Sony logs, though, he continued working on 'Phantoms' on July 1, despite cutting 'Zero and Blind Terry' at the June 28 session. The song was performed live in June, suggesting he genuinely rated this song about an outlaw who learnt the hard way, 'To be free is to be lonely'.

53. ZERO AND BLIND TERRY

Known studio/demo recordings: 914 Sound Studios, Blauvelt NY 28/6/73; 7/8/73. [TR]

First documented performance: Max's Kansas City, New York 18/7/73.

This song was worked on at two separate sessions for *The Wild, the Innocent*, five weeks apart, throwing up the intriguing possibility that the earlier version was quite different from the released take. Or not. According to the *Tracks* session data, the version on the 1998 set comes from the June 28 session. This is confirmed by the logs, which show that the June 28 version was referenced on November 5, 1997. But this does not explain the overdubs on the version used on *Tracks*. Sancious's piano was certainly not recorded on June 28, nor presumably were the acoustic guitar and backing vocals found on that *Tracks* mix (the basic track was sent out as a publishing demo in its raw original mix – before a flute was removed from the backing). The vocals were also probably overdubbed in August. There are slight lyrical changes to the final verse as performed at Max's in mid-July, which fails to specify whether Zero and Blind Terry got away. In all likelihood it was the June 28 basic track that was overdubbed on August 7.

54. E STREET SHUFFLE

Known studio/demo recordings: 914 Sound Studios, Blauvelt NY 28/6/73. [WI]
First documented performance: The Spectrum, Philadelphia PA 6/6/73 [The Main Point, Bryn Mawr PA 31/10/73].

According to Brucebase, this was a song 'Bruce hadn't even rehearsed . . . until David [Sancious] joined'. In fact, it was one of two songs preserved from the June 6 Spectrum show. Likewise, an early set of lyrics, reproduced in *Songs*, rather suggests it was a song Springsteen had been playing with for a while before Sancious joined the band and solidified his intention, which was 'to describe a neighbourhood, a way of life . . . the dance you did every day and every night to get by'. However, there was as yet no E Street Band to attach said shuffle to.

55. SEASIDE BAR SONG

Known studio/demo recordings: 914 Sound Studios, Blauvelt, NY 22, 26 + 28/6/73; 1/7/73; 24/7/73. [TR]
First documented performance: Veterans Memorial Arena, Binghamton NY 13/6/73.

This flippant little funster was repeatedly logged on the studio reels as 'Johnny & The Hurricanes Song'. The message of the song proved ultimately an enduring one (as did the image, 'The highway is alive tonight!'), even if the song itself did not even make the ten-song shortlist for Album #2. Only when the reformed E Street Band began taking *Tracks* on the road would Springsteen decide he did like to be beside the seaside bar.

56. EVACUATION OF THE WEST

Known studio/demo recordings: 914 Sound Studios, Blauvelt NY 22 + 28/6/73. [BTF/PS]

One wonders whether Springsteen was a little miffed when this terrific track popped up on *Prodigal Son* in the mid-nineties, after being rumoured for over a decade. Another of those songs transferred in early November 1997 during the track-selection stage for *Tracks*, 'Evacuation of the West' – or, as it was sometimes called, 'No More Kings In Texas' – was a type of song that, like the cowboy subject matter, had its day before Springsteen started his second album selection process.

57. KITTY'S BACK

Known studio/demo recordings: 914 Sound Studios, Blauvelt NY 28/6/73; 24/7/73; 23/9/73. [WI]

First documented performance: University of Massachusetts, Amherst MA 25/11/73 [Washington 6/12/73].

Still a feature of the live set in summer 1978, long after David Sancious had carved a career of his own, 'Kitty's Back' really should have been put to bed the day David gave Bruce notice. One of the songs on *The Wild, the Innocent* stamped and franked by Sancious, 'Kitty's Back' was, by Sancious's own admission, a track where they already 'had the basic thing. [But] I did the organ solo, electric piano.' And gave it life.

58. FOURTH OF JULY, ASBURY PARK (SANDY)

Known studio/demo recordings: 914 Sound Studios Blauvelt, NY 9/8/73; 23/9/73. [WI]

First documented performance: Max's Kansas City, New York 18/7/73.

'Sandy', as this Springsteen classic is known to all but the most pedantic, was evidently written during the making of the second album. In *Songs*, he claims he 'used the boardwalk and the closing down of the town as a metaphor for the end of a summer romance and the changes I was experiencing in my own life'. It certainly has that end-of-season, end–of-pier feel. Bruce was presumably excited by the song, because he seemed anxious to play it, performing it throughout the mid-July Max's residency (his third) and giving it a radio debut on his end-of-month My Father's Place broadcast, in what may still be its definitive live incarnation.

59. INCIDENT ON 57TH STREET
Known studio/demo recordings: 914 Sound Studios, Blauvelt NY 23/9/73. [WI]
First documented performance: Muther's Music Emporium, Nashville TN 29/1/74.

If 'Sandy' opened the door, 'Incident on 57th Street' was where Springsteen stepped on through. His early masterpiece, it is the kinda epic song he had spent his youth imagining and the past 18 months working toward. It was also the last song he wrote and recorded for that second album. Presumably it did for 'Zero and Blind Terry', being a richer reworking of the ganglands of New York motif. It may also have done for 'Mad Dog' Lopez, being a song Springsteen was reluctant to rework live as long as he had a drummer who liked cutting loose.

60. FIRE ON THE WING
Known studio/demo recordings: 914 Sound Studios, Blauvelt NY 7/8/73.

If 'The Chosen' stands as the great lost track from *Greetings*, 'Fire On The Wing', a song recorded at the same session as the likes of 'Zero and Blind Terry', 'Thundercrack' and 'New York City Serenade' is an equally mysterious omission from *The Wild, the Innocent*. But, unlike 'The Chosen', it was not entirely forgotten. When compilation reels were put together for the *Tracks* project on November 4–5 1997, 'Fire On The Wing' was transferred from its 16-track master.

VI) 61–68, Songs performed and/or recorded at 914 between March 1974 and February 1975:

61. ANGEL'S BLUES (RIDE ON SWEET WILLIAM)
First documented performance: Liberty Hall, Houston TX 10/3/74.

When Springsteen debuted 'Angel's Blues' in Houston during a three-night March 1974 residency, it had been six months since he had debuted any new songs. This was a new experience. As he later said, 'I've always [previously] had songs going into the studio.' Rarely, though, can he have chosen to debut such a half-formed song in concert, even one which in the final spoken section directly anticipates 'Thunder Road': 'She gets in my car and I take her home. She lives on 16th and E Street. [She] steps out of the car and goes up the driveway , into the house and she's gone . . . But that can't be the end of this story, 'cause I'm sittin' in the driveway and the door opens a little bit and she comes out with a suitcase. She's all packed and she's gonna come with me.' Thankfully, the song-exchange process was one at which he had become quite adept. As he informed *Musician*'s Bill Flanagan, 'In those [early] days I used to switch and trade [lines] all the time. You could do it with a lot of that stuff.'

62. A NIGHT LIKE THIS (ANGEL BABY)
Known studio/demo recordings: 914 Sound Studios, Blauvelt NY 16/10/74.
First documented performance: The Toledo Agora, Toledo OH 2/6/74.

When Springsteen sketched out a provisional track-listing for album #3 in the spring of 1974, it seemed destined to include a fair few discards from that difficult *second* album, including 'Architect Angel', 'Thundercrack' and 'Janey Needs A Shooter'. Only two songs on said list would end up performed – 'Jungleland' and 'Angel Baby', aka 'A Night Like This' – and then recorded. In the latter's case, a single performance, opening song in Toledo in June, gave it a test run some four months before it was attempted in the studio. What begins as another solo barroom-stool reverie is punctuated at various junctures by Big Man sax breaks and, at song's end, by Federici's trademark accordion, evocations of the early E Street sound. It is a song with a story to tell, anticipating 'Lonely Night In The Park'.

63. BORN TO RUN
Known studio/demo recordings: 914 Sound Studios, Blauvelt NY 21/5/74; [6/8/74]; 17/3/75. [BTR]
First documented performance: The Bottom Line, New York 13/7/74.

Much has been written about the genesis of Springsteen's first rock anthem of note, 'Born To Run', much of it misleading or plain wrong. The first myth to counteract is that the song was always the intended centrepiece of his third album. It was initially intended to be a single, a stand-alone (i.e. non-album) single. Quite why it was not released at the time it was 'leaked' to various pro-Springsteen radio stations in early November 1974 has never been satisfactorily explained. Somebody presumably high up at CBS changed their mind. As a result, Springsteen was deprived of what surely would have been a major hit just when he needed it most. He also had an excuse to give it another mixdown, returning it partly to the mire.

64. SO YOUNG AND IN LOVE
Known studio/demo recordings: 914 Sound Studios, Blauvelt NY 1/6/74 & ?26/6/74. [TR]
First documented performance: AA Arena, Miami FL 23/11/02.
as A LOVE SO FINE
First documented performance: Kean College, NJ 22/9/74.

When Bruce heard 'So Young And In Love' on tape for the first time in twenty-plus years, compiling *Tracks*, he was bowled over – 'Beautiful ensemble club playing, very exciting. Meant to blow your head off.' He also seems to have fondly imagined it was an outtake from the *Darkness* sessions, crediting the song to the Record Plant and engineer Jimmy Iovine, not to 914 and Louis Lahav. The recording date given on *Tracks* was a clue – 6/1/74 – even if it was patently incorrect (on January 6 the boys were in Boston, recording a live show at Joe's Place). Lahav was an Israeli, and would have almost certainly used European dating when logging tapes, making 6/1/74 June 1, not January 6 (ditto 'Jungleland'). Sure enough, the boys were in the studio that week working on 'Born To Run', and probably intended 'So Young And In Love' to be its B-side. Like 'Born To Run', the song was initially cut as a basic instrumental track, with vocals then added to the E Street equation, possibly on June 26, as something marked 'Bruce Springsteen Voice Track' was recorded on that date.

By October 1974 he had rewritten the hook, trading one cliché ('so young and in love') for another ('we got a love so fine'), though only after an intermediary live debut took its chorus from 'A Night like This. According to Brucebase, Springsteen recorded 'A Love So Fine' on October 16. There was a session on that day, though the Sony logs say nothing about 'A Love So Fine'. However, a two-inch master reel has 'A Love So Fine' and 'Born To Run' paired, suggesting this might be the master for an aborted 'Born To Run' single. To add fuel to this speculative fire, an instrumental backing track of 'A Love So Fine' had been in circulation since the late seventies and – surprise, surprise – it is the same backing track as 'So Young And In Love' on *Tracks*. No studio vocal of the 'A Love So Fine' version circulates, though there are live versions aplenty through February 1975.

65. JUNGLELAND
Known studio/demo recordings: 914 Sound Studios, Blauvelt NY 1/8/74; Record Plant, New York 18, 23 + 25/4/75; 14, 19–20/7/75. [BTR]
First documented performance: The Bottom Line, New York 13/7/74.

It was during a July 1974 Bottom Line residency that Springsteen finally decided to debut 'Jungleland' in the city that birthed it. Thankfully, there is a good-quality raw soundboard of one of these versions, quite probably taped at Springsteen's behest. The song at this juncture is still very much of a piece with other jazzed-up mini-operas from *The Wild, the Innocent*, and Sancious is still Bruce's bag-man. The song resolves itself quite differently, with a coda which holds out the hope that everything may end okay, à la 'Zero'. It is this version that the E Street Band set out to record two weeks later at 914, even as Sancious and drummer Carter were giving their notice and moving on. This early studio version retained the superior 'masters of flesh and fantasy' image. However, he has already starting playing with that final verse, evidently unhappy with it. So the coloured girls are now jungle girls who 'stand by fire angels fallen in the city', the Magic Rat reappearing just in time to save 'her from the edge of an on-coming train'. But the take never quite gels. By the time of the fabled February 1975 Main Point show, the original final verse has been shunted before 'streets on fire in a real death waltz'. Sadly, he would not keep either the epiphanic chimes or that lovely coda where 'the animals on the corner sing', another allusion to 'Jungleland's origins in 'Zero and Blind Terry'. [See discussion in main text pp. 87–8]

66. SHE'S THE ONE

Known studio/demo recordings: ?914 Sound Studios, Blauvelt NY 16/10/74; Record Plant, New York ?4–5/75; 24–25/7/75. [BTR]

First documented performance: Avery Fisher Hall, New York 4/10/74.

'She's The One' seems to have been a song Springsteen did not resolve to his satisfaction till the very last session for *Born To Run,* in late July 1975. And yet, it was a song he had been playing nightly since early October 1974 – when he also recorded the original studio version that appeared on the legendary *E Ticket* vinyl boot. Nor did the arrangement of the song change in any meaningful way in the interim. It stayed a 'Mona'-esque take on that Bo Diddley beat which was in some quarters single-handedly held responsible for a perceived slide in American morals in the late fifties. It was the lyrics that tortured him, as she had.

67. WALKING IN THE STREET (LOVERS IN THE COLD)

Known studio/demo recordings: ?914 Sound Studios, Blauvelt NY August or October 1974.

Another 'lost' *Born To Run* song from the 914 sessions that ended up on the first Springsteen studio bootleg, *E Ticket*, 'Walking In The Streets' may have served as a prototype for 'Thunder Road', but Springsteen clearly saw it as a song in its own right. Not only did he hunt high and low for a master-tape to include on *Tracks*, but he rehearsed the song at the Fort Monmouth Post Theater in January 1999, a version he taped for purposes unknown (quite possibly for inclusion on *18 Tracks*, alongside the 1999 version of 'The Promise' he recorded ten days later at Boxwood Studios). One image transposed from 'Walking In The Streets' – 'Babe, I can't lay the stars at your feet/ Oh but I think we could take it all, just you and me' – would survive intact to the live debut of 'Thunder Road (Wings For Wheels)' in February 1975. The song itself was bootlegged as 'Walking In The Street', its repeated refrain being 'Walking in the street with love from above', so God knows what the origin was of 'Lovers In The Cold', the title used by a number of bootlegs and discographies.

68. THUNDER ROAD (WINGS FOR WHEELS)
Known studio/demo recordings: ?914 Sound Studios, Blauvelt NY October 1974/ February 1975; Record Plant, New York 18–19+23/4/75; 15–16/7/75. [BTR]
First documented performance: The Main Point, Bryn Mawr PA 5/2/75.

'Thunder Road', like the three other *Born To Run* songs first recorded in 1974, has a protracted history. The opening couplet apparently dates back to a lost 1972 song called 'Angelina', one of a number of ladies' names Springsteen went through before settling on Mary. A solo prototype from fall 1974, 'Chrissie's Song', explicitly names Thunder Road; 'Leave what you've lost, leave what's grown cold – Thunder Road', but makes no reference to Glory Road, its original title. By the time something recognisably 'Thunder Road'-ish made its live debut, on a momentous February night in Bryn Mawr, 'Chrissie' had been replaced by 'Angelina'. The song that night is quite a different beast from the earlier solo take; but we are still some way from the finished song, 'debuted' in July at Providence. In particular, he sings, 'I don't know but I been told/ There's something waiting for us down that dirty road/ If we take our chance', lines absent from all the known studio versions.

VII) 69–75. Other songs recorded for *Born To Run* April–July 1975:

69. BACKSTREETS
Known studio/demo recordings: Record Plant, New York 25/4/75; 19, 23/5/75; 6+18/7/75. [BTR]

First documented performance: Civic Theatre, Akron OH 8/8/75.

'There's been guys that have worked with me in the band that for one reason or another went their own ways, who I don't see as much as I used to. But when I see 'em, it's like they never went away.' – intro. to live 'Backstreets' at the LA Sports Arena, 28/8/81.

If, as Springsteen wrote on the original draft of this key song, The Shirelles' 'Sha La La (Baby It's You)' was a direct inspiration, then the song travelled a long way in a short time. This was a song that came together in the studio by taking 'a different approach toward some of the lyrics, [so] if you read them on paper sometimes they don't look that good, but when you hear them, they've got the right *feel* – like some of the sixties songs'. Say, something by The Shirelles cross-bred with elements of a prototype 'She's The One'.

70. LONELY NIGHT IN THE PARK

Known studio/demo recordings: Record Plant, New York 4-5/5/75.

'Lonely Night In The Park' was one of two *Born To Run* songs placed on the July 2, 1975 album-sequence, but deleted after Appel made his feelings known. As such, it is slightly surprising it was not one of the songs chosen for *Tracks* – or indeed, *The Essential Bruce Springsteen* bonus disc – and had to await Sirius's 2005 inaugural broadcast of a dedicated Bruce Springsteen digital radio station for fans to evaluate its worth. If it had long been known that the song contained elements of 'A Night Like This', its 2005 broadcast revealed this candidate for a break-through album still had very much the feel of a demo.

71. TENTH AVENUE FREEZE OUT

Known studio/demo recordings: Record Plant, New York 5, 16/5/75; 13/7/75. [BTR]

First documented performance: Palace Theatre, Providence RI 20/7/75.

'There I was in Asbury Park on a dark, rainy night, a hurricane just came in, I'm walking down the street at three in the morning . . . had my jacket bundled up around me . . . Way down the end of the street walking through the monsoon, I seen this big figure . . . dressed in white, walking with a cane, a big guy, walking like there was no rain and the wind wasn't blowing, just walking like it was a beautiful summer day . . . So I duck into the doorway, I stood in the doorway like this and sure enough I hear them footsteps coming closer and closer . . . and right where I'm standing, he turns and faces off on me. So I did the normal thing: I was cool, I threw all my money on the ground, threw off my jacket . . . All he did was he reached out his arm.' – intro. to 'The E Street Shuffle', 20/07/75.

72. LINDA LET ME BE THE ONE
Known studio/demo recordings: Record Plant, New York 8+19/5/75; 29/6/75; 8/7/75. [TR]

Like 'Lonely In The Park', 'Linda Let Me Be The One' made it as far as the July 2 *Born To Run* sequence, before being removed to make way for the title track. However, the version on *Tracks* is not the one originally favoured (which was widely bootlegged). Credited to a June 28 session, it actually dates from the following day (there being no June 28 session logged), when Springsteen recorded two different versions of the song, a 'hard slow version' and a 'ballad version'. The familiar bootleg version has a lighter, more melodic feel, though it would have benefited from a vocal overdub (and may have got one. He returned to it ten days later).

73. NIGHT
Known studio/demo recordings: Record Plant, New York 10/5/75. [BTR]
First documented performance: The Bottom Line, New York 14/8/75.

Very much a lesser light on this star-studded album, the semi-realized status of 'Night' perhaps was a large part of its appeal to its author, who cut the song in a single session; a rare event that spring. Listed on a possible album sequence in the late fall of 1974, when almost nothing had been recorded, it was cut the following May in ten takes, of which take eight was marked 'Great – Hold'. Its slightly throwaway nature also made it a perfect set-opener, a position it held until May 1978, when far stronger songs from the pre-*Darkness* era were being cast to the wind.

74. MEETING ACROSS THE RIVER
Known studio/demo recordings: Record Plant, New York 28/5/75; 18/7/75. [BTR]
First documented performance: University of Iowa, Iowa City IA 26/9/75.

According to Appel, the song 'Meeting Across The River' (originally known as 'The Heist') was a hair's breadth away from not making the album. And yet, there it is on both the July 2 sequence and the final album. Whoever was unconvinced of the song's merits, he was right to feel this way. The idea is a strong one – a small-time hoodlum, offered the chance to take part in a heist, imagines telling his baby (and therefore the listener) how everything went to plan – but neither melody nor vocal wholly demand this listener's attention.

75. JANEY NEEDS A SHOOTER MK 2
Known studio/demo recordings: ?914 Studio, Blauvelt NY October 1974/ February 1975.

According to the *Backstreets* anthology, 'Studio records from *Born To Run* confirm that this song was again recorded by the band and seriously considered for this album. The production notes show that Springsteen's chord notations included a suggestion that the song adopt a "Spanish style" change after the first chorus.' The song was also listed on the earliest known sequence for Album #3, in spring 1974. If it was attempted – and there is no mention of it in the Sony logs – a 914 version from 1974 seems the likeliest scenario, especially given its thematic similarities to the later 'Linda Let Me Be The One'.

VIII) 76–85. Songs rehearsed and/or performed 1976-77:

76. FRANKIE
Known studio/demo recordings: Atlantic Studios, New York 3/6/77; 12/7/77.
First documented performance: Michigan State University, East Lansing MI 4/4/76.

One of Springsteen's most important works, and one of only two readily identifiable tracks in a handwritten March 1976 list for 'Album #4' – along with 'Darkness on the Edge of Town' – 'Frankie' would eventually be demoed at the first *Darkness* . . . sessions in June 1977. That bootlegged version suggests the band were a lot more engaged by the song at this juncture than Springsteen was, with him making no attempt to get the lyrics right. A second attempt at the song on July 12, at a time when Springsteen was applying himself to the best of the songs recorded over the past six weeks, may contain a more committed vocal and realized lyric. It remains uncirculated. [See discussion in main text p. 129]

77. SOMETHING IN THE NIGHT

Known studio/demo recordings: Atlantic Studios, New York 1, 14 + 16/6/77. [DA]

First documented performance: Monmouth Arts Center, Red Bank NJ 1/8/76.

Like 'Frankie', 'Something In The Night' was a song Springsteen seemed in an awful hurry to record when he finally entered the studio on 1 June 1977. But unlike 'Frankie' it had received a full lyrical workout at the fall 1976 and winter 1977 shows; and when he did demo the song, on the very first night of sessions, he nailed it. Though he returned to it a couple of times (one later take contains a lot of moaning, but merely confirms he caught it early), this was the basic track used on the album, albeit with a vocal overdub. Having already pruned any number of lines from the live version (as well as that eerily evocative horn part he used at the 1976-77 shows when the Miami Horns were in attendance), the 1 June lyric remained the template for the album. [See discussion in main text p. 131]

78. RENDEZVOUS

Known studio/demo recordings: Atlantic Studios, New York 1-3, 8, 17/6/77. [TP]*

First documented performance: Monmouth Arts Center, Red Bank NJ 1/8/76.

'Rendezvous' is the first of a number of great hook-filled pop songs Springsteen would record for *Darkness*, promptly reject, and finally give away to second parties (in this case, Greg Kihn and Gary US Bonds). But unlike most of its catchy kin it would enjoy a healthy life in the live set, extending all the way from August 1976 through December 1980, when an unexpected one-off *River*-period performance at the year-end Nassau show was captured on multitrack (and later included on *Tracks*).

79. THE PROMISE

Known studio/demo recordings: Atlantic Studios, New York 30/6/77; 1, 7–8, 13/7/77; 24+30/8/77 [TP]*; Record Plant, New York 28/9/77; 12/1/78; Boxwood, Rumson NJ 9+12/2/99 [18TR].

First documented performance: Monmouth Arts Center, Red Bank NJ 3/8/76.

If anybody ever wanted something that they couldn´t have, this is for you.. – intro to 'The Promise', Williamsburg MD 16/10/76.

The omission of 'The Promise' from the album it delineates and defines still stands as one of the great miscalculations of Springsteen's career. It certainly left a great gaping hole at the heart of the released *Darkness*. Maybe that was the point. Though no studio recording has yet emerged with the lines he rewrote mid-sessions – 'Well, my daddy taught me how to walk quiet and how to make my peace with the past/ I learned real good to tighten up inside and I don't say nothing unless I'm asked' – a full 'in studio' rehearsal featuring the change, allegedly from early 1978, appears on the *Thrill Hill Vault* DVD. This could be a live mix of the version he recorded on January 12 1978, which was included on the January 16 1978 'original' sequence for *Darkness* in the all-important last slot. Just eight days later, he was back recording the song solo at the piano, yet he was again dissatisfied with the results, and when the album was re-sequenced in March 'The Promise' was discarded. Nonetheless, for the first month of the *Darkness* tour he encored with a solo rendition of such infernoesque intensity it fanned the uproar to release the song. But not only did he hold back, he dropped the song from the set just before his first FM broadcast of the year, from LA's Roxy. [See discussion in main text pp. 130–1]

80. DON'T LOOK BACK

Known studio/demo recordings: Atlantic Studios, New York 1, 6–8, 17 + 24/6/77; 2+7/7/77 [TR]; Record Plant, New York 28/2/78; 2/3/78.

First documented performance: Sports Arena, Toledo OH 10/3/77.

The *Darkness* sessions' favourite pop song, 'Don't Look Back' ('Tonight we'll even the score and, honey, we won't look back') was debuted live in March 1977 with the lyrics still unfinished. Demoed at the first Atlantic session in June, and worked on for the next month, it slotted into the provisional album sequence on 16 January 1978, staying a part of the album even as he tinkered with it through March. Pressed onto an eleven-track final sequence, it was cut from the album when Springsteen decided something had to give if the album's sonic intensity wasn't going to be severely compromised by a forty-five minute length. Though not a feature of the 1978 live set, it was probably still a candidate for an 'album's worth of pop songs like "Rendezvous"' in the winter of 1979. Indeed, after offering the song to drummer (and Springsteen acolyte) Bruce Gary for his band The Knack's 1979 debut album, *Get The Knack*, it was pulled, in Gary's words, 'at the request of Springsteen's management in order to allow him to release the song first'. Or maybe not. The one track on *Tracks* not remixed in 1998.

81. (I WILL FOREVER BE) CANDY'S BOY
Known studio/demo recordings: Band rehearsal, Holmdel NJ Summer 1976 [THV]; Atlantic Studios, New York 3+6/6/77; 27/6/77; [24/8/77; 2/9/77]. [TP]

Another 'so near, so far' *Darkness* candidate, 'Candy's Boy' had a particularly long gestation period, being first rehearsed at the summer 1976 pre-Red Bank rehearsals (a video of this formative version appears on 2010's *Thrill Hill Vault*). Perhaps he intended to replace 'Frankie' with it, having taken two of her best lines: 'There's machines and there's fire on the outside of town/ Young boys for hire waiting to blow us all down'. If so, he decided it still needed work. Eighteen months' more work, only to donate its first verse and title to another song – 'The Fast Song (God's Angels)', when at the end of September he went with a reworked 'Fast Song' for the album, now called 'Candy's Room'. The June 1977 version finally appeared on 2010's *The Promise* almost entirely unscathed, suggesting Springsteen now thinks he missed a trick in casting Candy's original boy-toy aside.

82. SAVE MY LOVE
Known studio/demo recordings: Band rehearsal, Holmdel NJ Summer 1976 [THV]; Colt's Neck NJ 22/7/10. [TP]*
First documented performance: Carousel House, Casino, Asbury Park NJ 7/12/10.

The one song from 2010's *The Promise* which Springsteen openly admitted was a modern reconstruction of a lost *Darkness*-era composition, 'Save My Love' also crops up in the lavish boxed set as a 'bonus' track on the *Thrill Hill Vault* DVD, from a bare-chested summer 1976 rehearsal. Another simple song of affection, like the contemporaneous 'Because The Night', it was never considered for the album, presumably because, 'It was a love song, and I really felt that I didn't know how to write them at the time.'

83. ACTION IN THE STREETS
First documented performance: Auditorium Theatre, Rochester NY 8/2/77.

Another song he rehearsed, and in this case performed, in readiness for the Album #4 sessions, 'Action In The Streets' was a singular attempt to convince himself he could still write a song with all the good-times-roll zest of teenage years AM-radio favourites. In concert, with the Miami Horns lending a hand, admonishing his audience to 'just move your body side to side/ Raise your hand, shout until you're satisfied/ Oh tonight, there's action in the street all night', it works a charm. For such a dark record, it was a non-starter.

84. LOVE ON THE WRONG SIDE OF TOWN
85. LITTLE GIRL SO FINE

During the long break from the studio, sidekick Miami Steve threw some of his energies into making a second album with Southside Johnny, *This Time It's For Real*. Eschewing a plentiful supply of early lost Springsteen songs – with the exception of 'When You Dance' – Van Zandt wanted to stick to freshly minted originals, including two which bestow co-composition credits on Springsteen, presumably for lending a lyrical hand. Both titles have the ring of Springsteen, so maybe he came up with the basic ideas. As it is, the 'Spanish Harlem'-feel of 'Little Girl So Fine' skirts the borders of parody. 'Love On The Wrong Side of Town' suits the Southside shtick a whole lot better. With a stronger vocal, it might even have been a hit. The absence of either song from any 1976 show or 1977 session rather suggests this was a case of Brill Building Bruce punching in for a day of writing-to-order for a friend.

IX) 86–96. Songs ready to be recorded by June 1977:

86. OUTSIDE LOOKING IN
Known studio/demo recordings: Atlantic Studios, New York 1/6/77; Record Plant, New York 27/9/77. [TP]
First documented performance: Carousel House, Casino, Asbury Park NJ 7/12/10.

'Outside Looking In' would be one of twenty 'new songs' Springsteen was looking to demo in that first week at Atlantic Studios in June 1977. Listed as 'Outside Movin' In' in the song-list he brought to the sessions (reproduced in the 2010 *Darkness* boxed-set), it was recorded on that first evening in rough 'n' ready form and then put aside after producer and artist realized just how many songs they already had, from which they were expected to compile a ten-track album. However, it turns out the song was only awaiting an oil-change to its lyrics, which had altered quite dramatically by September. It is the latter version that serves as the basic track for the 2010 official release, an authentic but previously uncirculated 1977 recording.

87. BECAUSE THE NIGHT

Known studio/demo recordings: Atlantic Studios, New York 1/6/77; 1/7/77; Record Plant, New York 27/9/77. [TP]*

First documented performance: Music Hall, Boston MA 30/5/78.

According to latter-day Springsteen, 'I knew [all along] that I wasn't gonna finish ["Because The Night"] - because it was a[nother] love song.' It was really a song from the Album That Never Was, the one he came into the studio in early June 1977 to record, but by mid-July had abandoned in favour of an album he had barely begun to sketch out. Listed on one song-list as 'The Night Belongs To Lovers', and then as 'Because The Night (Belongs To Lovers)', it finally got there by the time he recorded a new version at the end of September (which was later broadcast on Sirius's E Street Radio). Whether this take was specifically a demo for Patti Smith is unclear. But from here on it became Patti's song.

88. BREAKAWAY

Known studio/demo recordings: Atlantic Studios, New York 1/6/77. [TP]*

'Breakaway', a song Springsteen cut on that auspicious first night and never returned to, ticks every box in the *Darkness* motif department. Actually, it covers the waterfront rather too well. Co-opting Sonny from 'The Promise', 'Janey' from her own song, and Bobby from 'Something In The Night', Springsteen gives them all a good reason to, as it were, break away. He even reveals the underlying moral to the whole shebang: 'Now the promises and the lies they demand it/ Let the hearts that have been broken stand as the price you pay'. The song did not circulate prior to its inclusion on *The Promise,* but he has clearly added a modern vocal, as well as (presumably) horns and backing singers. I guess that's the price you have to pay to break away.

89. I WANNA BE WITH YOU

Known studio/demo recordings: Atlantic Studios, New York 1/6/77; 1/7/77; Record Plant, New York 12/9/77; Power Station, New York 31/5/79; 21/6/79; 24/9/79. [TR]

First documented performance: Forum, Milan, Italy 20/4/99.

I had some lofty ideas about using my own music to give people something to think about. – Bruce Springsteen, 1997.

Those 'lofty ideas' undoubtedly did for 'I Wanna Be With You', one of those great throwaway songs too in the moment to make it through the quagmire of the Springsteen selection process. Yet it provided a magical moment the minute they rolled tape on 1 June, 1977, and two years of frustration poured on to tape, even if this joyous jaunt failed to figure in a single provisional *Darkness* sequence. By the time he got around to re-recording it in the summer of 1979, the intensity of that original 1977 version – a match for anything on *Darkness* – had set sail on its own sea-cruise. The 1979 version sounds like a Springsteen tribute band covering a lost classic. Weinberg, in particular, phoned in the kinda contribution that could give click tracks a bad name. Remarkably, twenty years later, it rediscovered its former frenetic self at a number of the *Tracks* tour gigs.

90. OUR LOVE'S GONNA LAST FOREVER
Known studio/demo recordings: Atlantic Studios, New York 1/6/77.

Widely assumed to be an early version of the Record Plant *Darkness* outtake, 'Someday (We'll Be Together)' (because of a single line of lyric, 'This love will last forever'), 'Our Love's Gonna Last Forever' was another song cut that first evening, only to be sidelined for good. A digital dub of the 'Atlantic Demo Tape' cassette reproduced in *The Promise* book would solve this minor mystery, but until then it gets its own number.
Note: This could a well be an otherwise-unrecorded song on a contemporary handwritten song-list, 'So Kiss Me Tonight'.

91. DARKNESS ON THE EDGE OF TOWN
Known studio/demo recordings: Atlantic Studios, New York 6, 8–9, 20+23/6/77; Record Plant, New York
8-10/3/78. [DA]
First documented performance: Shea's Buffalo Theatre, Buffalo NY 23/5/78.

Events often beat the humanity out of people until they just lose it all. 'Darkness On The Edge of Town' was about people holding on to that humanity. I started writing it right after *Born To Run*. – Bruce Springsteen, 1978.

Though the title track of Springsteen's fourth album is listed on that 'Atlantic Demo Tape', according to the Sony logs it was not cut until June 6. Documented evidence does, however, support his contention that he 'started writing it right after *Born To Run*'. It was listed on both the earliest known track-listing for Album #4, from February/March 1976 (see *Backstreets* #57), and another 15-track list from that spring, reproduced in *The Promise* set (where it is presciently listed first). Its inclusion so early in the process might lead one to think he intended to keep it from the outset. In fact, although he spent a great deal of time on it during that first month at Atlantic, it was not even *on* the eight-track album they mocked up in the fall (called *Badlands)*, or the 16 January 1978 sequence that almost got the green light. Only on March 8, with another deadline past and gone, did Springsteen begin work on the 'Sonny' version, cutting a number of takes over the next three days.

92. RACING IN THE STREET
Known studio/demo recordings: Atlantic Studios, New York 2/7/77; Atlantic or Record Plant, New York 1–4, 10, 12, 29–30/8/77; Record Plant, New York 28-30/11/77; 6+9/12/77; [21–23/3/78]. [DA]; [TP]*
First documented performance: Shea's Buffalo Theatre, Buffalo NY 23/5/78.

A circulating piano/vocal version (probably from July 2) represents a somewhat more distinct alternative than the one included on *The Promise*. This heartfelt performance omits the final verse, presumably because it has not yet been written. Instead, we get a lengthy coda which references one of the song's working titles, 'Dying In The Street': 'Yes, come on out now little one, and we'll go dying in the street [x2]/ Look at me, it's true, baby, what else can we do/ Racing in the street [x6]'. As for the version on *The Promise*, it was a tad optimistic to think the latter could be improved by a partial 2010 vocal overdub – especially with the 'correct' vocal in general circulation on the *Lost Masters* series of bootleg CDs.

93. INDEPENDENCE DAY
Known studio/demo recordings: Atlantic or Record Plant, NY 15/8/77; Record Plant, New York 26–27/9/77; Record Plant, New York 4+7/11/77; 9/12/77; Power Station, New York 29/5/79; 11/10/79; 24–25/4/80. [RI]
First documented performance: The Roxy, Los Angeles 7/7/78.

The fate of the 'finished' *Darkness* version of this song remains one of the great mysteries of Springsteen-collecting. Despite six bootleg CDs' worth of outtakes and three CDs of official takes out in the world, no such fish has ever come up for air. For a while it was even thought this might be the version on *The River*, but studio logs show he worked on the song as much in 1979-80. Collectors have had to be content with a 'guide vocal' version from *Darkness*, presumably recorded in August 1977, to convey a sense of how it sounded at this stage. Even that 'first' Atlantic August recording represented a belated entry for this important song, as if he were holding it back. He confirmed as much the night he first performed it, identifying it as part of a group of songs, along with 'Darkness On The Edge of Town' and 'The Promise', dating back to 1976.

94. HEARTS OF STONE
Known studio/demo recordings: Record Plant, New York 14/10/77. [TR]

One of just four tracks on *Tracks* from the *Darkness* sessions, 'Hearts of Stone' had initially been donated to the needy (Southside Johnny) back in 1977, appearing as the title track on the third of his r&b volumes. Rather than waste a perfectly decent E Street Band performance, Southside just dubbed a new vocal and some requisite horns onto the Record Plant backing track. A straightforward 'It Ain't Me Babe' rewrite (with one self-conscious nod, 'I'm not alone'), the song gave Clarence a rare chance to let rip at these sessions. But it was never gonna be a contender for such a heavyweight opus.

95. BRING ON THE NIGHT
Known studio/demo recordings: Atlantic Studios, New York ?June 1977.

A song for which there appears to be a circulating *Darkness* outtake – a muffled rehearsal take – yet no reference thereto in Sony's session-logs. As such, the attribution to Record Plant seems unlikely. The song *is* listed in the May 1977 list of 'New Songs', making it a pre-Atlantic composition, so if it *was* cut a June session seems likelier. Just to sprinkle more confusion, the recent Godfather boxed set of *Darkness* outtakes claims the song was included on a production tape dated 12 August, 1977. There *is* such a production tape, but again no mention of 'Bring On The Night' on the tape-box.

96. THE FAST SONG (GOD'S ANGELS)
Known studio/demo recordings: Atlantic Studios, New York 6, 9–10, 13–14, 20, 24/6/77; [24/8/77; 1–2/9/77].
as CANDY'S ROOM

Known studio/demo recordings: Record Plant, New York 27/9/77; 12/12/77; 3–5/3/78. [DA]
First documented performance: Shea's Buffalo Theatre, Buffalo NY 23/5/78.

I suspect 'The Fast Song's original title was probably 'God's Angels' (which was listed among the 'New Songs'). The reference to God's angels comes early – 'I wish God's angels would tear this town down/ And blow it into the sea, Man, that's alright with me'. Perhaps it was always intended as a companion piece to 'Candy's Boy'. It would be helpful to know when the cassette inlay card for the Atlantic Demo Tape in the *Darkness* notebook was written, because on there it was already called 'The Fast Song (Candy's Room)'. As to dating the great change into 'Candy's Room', it was on September 27 that the title 'New Fast Song' appeared for the first time. Over the next two days this song was worked on extensively, the results featuring in the January 16 sequence. However, he would spend a further three days in early March 1978 working through some seventy-nine 'takes' – surely a series of vocal overdubs – to remove any lingering vestige of'God's Angels'.

X) 97–107. Other songs recorded at Atlantic Studios, NY 1 June–13 July 1977:

97. CHEAP THRILLS
98. JON'S JAM (IT'S A SHAME)

Known studio/demo recordings [#98]: Atlantic Studios, New York 14/6/77. [TP]*

By June 14, Bruce and the boys had been hard at it for two weeks, having concentrated on songs rehearsed beforehand. Unfortunately, Springsteen's muse would not let him be, and every day he seemed to bring a new song he was more anxious to play than songs already tried, tested and true. Neither of the above songs appeared again at the sessions. Nor has any song bearing the titles 'Cheap Thrills' or 'Jon's Jam' ever seen the light of day. But one suspects that 'Jon's Jam' is 'It's A Shame', a previously undocumented *Darkness* outtake that popped up on *The Promise*, complete with 2010 horn section, because who should be playing drums on this AM-friendly little nipper but Jon Landau. If so, bass duties devolved to road manager Bob Chirmside, suggesting it was cut while they were waiting for the E Streeters to arrive; being something Springsteen wrote at the diner, after eyeing up the waitress and imagining 'I was born just to be your fool.'

'Cheap Thrills' is more of a mystery. The title tallies with no extant *Darkness* lyric or lost Springsteen song. However, as a summation of theme, it is a perfect description of 'Darlington County', a track which would not be properly recorded until 1982 (and not released until 1984). About two hopped-up hotheads who cross the county line in search of fun, only to end up with one of them hauled off to jail (presumably for transporting a minor across state lines with intent), it has long been known that 'Darlington County' dates from the *Darkness* era. Indeed, it is mentioned in the *Darkness* notebook on a 'work sheet' from the first Atlantic sessions, while a dissociated couplet from the same notebook provides a prototype for two lines in the 1982 incarnation: 'My eyes have seen the glory of the comin' of the Lord/ He was peelin' down the alley in a black and yellow Ford'. If 'Cheap Thrills' is not this devil in disguise, then we have a mystery to solve. And a tape to excavate.

99. DRIVE ALL NIGHT

Known studio/demo recordings: Atlantic Studios, New York 16/6/77; Atlantic or Record Plant, NY 24/8/77; Power Station, New York 24/2/80; 8, 16/3/80; 10/4/80. [RI]

First documented performance: Kiel Opera House, St Louis MO 18/10/80.

If, as the studio logs appear to indicate, Springsteen only worked on 'Drive All Night' at two *Darkness* sessions, one in mid-June, the other in late August, he was presumably happy with what he already had. He certainly should have been. The eight-minute Atlantic take, from June, is one of the great E Street Band studio performances – Bruce and Clarence particularly excelling in their respective roles. For once, Bruce lets it all hang out as need eats away at his very soul – 'Babe, I'd drive all night just to buy you some shoes, and to taste your tender charms'. Not since 'Fever' had he written such a song of naked yearning, infusing it with an almost gospel-like fervour by the simple expedient of allowing the band to strike a groove, while he mourned and moaned till the feeling passed. Another, shorter try-out (possibly from August), a simple piano/organ duet, also establishes its mood early. But when Springsteen revisited the song at the 1980 *River* sessions he was no longer singing (in line one) about losing his money, a possible reference to the lawsuit, but of losing his 'honey'. The hurt had faded away, and every extra take took it further away from inspiration's fleet foot.

100. ONE WAY STREET
101. FIRE
Known studio/demo recordings: Atlantic Studios, New York 17/6/77. [TP]*
First documented performance [#100]: Carousel House, Casino, Asbury Park NJ 7/12/10.
First documented performance [#101]: Shea's Buffalo Theatre, Buffalo NY 23/5/78.

One session, two lightweight pop songs, both of which would have to wait thirty-three years to see the light of day. 'One Way Street' condenses two pop classics – Hank Snow's 'Ninety Miles An Hour (Down A Dead-End Street)' and Lou Reed's 'Walk On The Wild Side' – to form a single clichéd hook, 'We were walking on the wild side/ Running down a one way street'. It should perhaps have stayed where it was, the opener on volume two of *Lost Masters,* issued as a labour of love by a European bootlegger. That 5:46 take was duly trimmed, given horns and a gravelly vocal by a sixty-year-old singer, before being presented in this spruced-up form on *The Promise*. But a lesser song it would remain.

The unforgettable 'Fire' was also treated to a wholly inferior 2010 vocal for its reincarnation. But this time fans had myriad live versions with which to compare it. Supposedly composed after he was one of 18,850 hardy souls who trekked to the Philadelphia Spectrum on 28 May 1977 to see the shadow man himself, Elvis, 'Fire' was recorded just once at these sessions, perhaps as a demo for Elvis (as has been suggested). More likely it was a rockabilly experiment from a man starting to get interested in the genre's possibilities. The heavy echo certainly suggests a conscious homage to the Sun studio sound; even as the lyric tips its hat to Little Willie John's 'Fever', an Elvis number one. When Elvis upped and died, Springsteen donated the song to Robert Gordon, who had come to local prominence fronting CBGBs favourites the Tuff Darts. His then-girlfriend Lynn Goldsmith suggested Bruce was less than happy with the Pointer Sisters' success at Gordon's expense.

102. SHERRY DARLING
Known studio/demo recordings: Atlantic Studios, New York 24+27/6/77; 1/7/77; Power Station, New York 25/5/79; 23/2/80; 8/3/80; 12/4/80. [RI]
First documented performance: Civic Center, Charleston WV 4/8/78.

A song he produced first on June 24, 'Sherry Darling' would be worked on for the next week, but as shadows lengthened it became just another lost summer night. And yet a terrific impromptu duet with Miami Steve at the piano, caught on film by Rebo, shows an abiding affection for the song. Its inclusion at summer 1978 shows also suggests he had started to realize joy and sorrow could be two sides of the same coin. Sure enough, once the decision was made to make *The River* a double, it was always a candidate for the side designed to represent 'this joy, this certain happiness that is, in its way, the most beautiful thing in life'.

103. STREETS OF FIRE

Known studio/demo recordings: Atlantic Studios, New York 24/6/77; Atlantic or Record Plant, New York 24+30/8/77; Record Plant, New York 6, 12, 29/12/77. [DA]

First documented performance: Shea's Buffalo Theatre, Buffalo NY 23/5/78.

According to Landau, '"Streets of Fire" was something that happened in the studio . . . That and "Badlands" are the two earliest on the record – late June or early July.' It is certainly the least fully-conceived song on the album. Which doesn't make the song a total failure. In fact, it sounds like the spark which ignited the process. A miniature noir movie, or indeed a noir trailer, 'Streets of Fire' is all sound and fury, thunder and lightning, as Springsteen shapes another rough draft on the spot. He did redub the vocal, though, changing, 'I'm lyin' flat out on my back, storm into the darkness,' into, 'I'm wandering, a loser down these tracks . . . 'Cause in the darkness . . .'; even if he stuck to that original backing track like a mountain-goat.

104. BADLANDS

Known studio/demo recordings: Atlantic Studios, New York 27+30/6/77; 11+13/7/77; Atlantic or Record Plant, New York 24+30/8/77; Record Plant, New York 12/12/77; 22–23+25/2/78. [DA]

First documented performance: Shea's Buffalo Theatre, Buffalo NY 23/5/78.

'Badlands', the second track to have 'happened in the studio' that last week of June, would also prove good enough to make the album, but it needed a lot more remedial care than 'Streets of Fire'. The first studio take, assuming it is the one on *Lost Masters Vol. 2*, is another Atlantic demo masquerading as a finished take. At some point, probably December 1977, the song finally became a rant against the dying of the light, sung to an unfeeling universe he wants to 'spit in the face of'.

105. SPANISH EYES
Known studio/demo recordings: Atlantic Studios, New York 30/6/77; ?13/7/77. [TP]*

One of the better ballads from these sessions, 'Spanish Eyes' provides a nice change of pace and a welcome return to the lovelorn lyricist of yore, imploring a resistant señorita to 'let your doubts slip away 'neath your sighs/ Let me kiss your Spanish eyes'. Displaying an elephantine memory (and a refusal to discard good couplets), Springsteen reused the opening couplet in 1982 when penning 'I'm On Fire'. The song was worked on a number of times on June 30. It is also presumably the track listed as 'New Spanish' a fortnight later, without latching onto its lyrical key – which is presumably why he grafted a new vocal to the 2010 version.

106. COME ON, COME ON (LET'S GO TONIGHT)
Known studio/demo recordings: Atlantic Studios, New York 2+13/7/77; Atlantic or Record Plant, New York 23–24, 30/8/77; Record Plant, New York 8/9/77; 2, 7–8/11/77; 9+29/12/77. [TP]
First documented performance: Carousel House, Casino, Asbury Park NJ 7/12/10.*
as FACTORY.
Known studio/demo recordings: Record Plant, New York 10+14/3/78. [DA]
First documented performance: Municipal Auditorium, Nashville TN 21/7/78.

We don't appear to have a version of 'Factory' which sets the 'Come On' lyric to the album backing-track, even though Landau told Paul Nelson: '"Factory" was just one of those things that happened in the studio . . . It was originally called 'Come On', and had . . . a different idea to it. We had a track for it, and he came in and he had this [new] set of words for it.' This is surprising, considering 'Come On, Come On' remained under consideration for the album throughout the whole process. Even the January 2 1978 take, logged as 'The Factory Song', seems to have been a version of 'Come On, Come On'. And yet, 'Come On, Come On' was absent from the January 16 sequence. On March 10 it reappeared, again listed as 'The Factory Song'. By the 14th, he was spending most of the day working on 'Factory', at one stage trying it 'slightly faster, [with] country piano'. But a dirge is what he wanted. And we got.

107. TALK TO ME

Known studio / demo recordings: Atlantic Studios, New York 8+13/7/77; Atlantic or Record Plant, New York 5, 9, 24, 26, 30/8/77; Record Plant, New York 14/10/77. [TP]

First documented performance: Carousel House, Casino, Asbury Park NJ 7/12/10.*

Another clear case of something which was just 'too pop' for the anti-hype album, 'Talk To Me' is hardly the usual 'try it and throw it away' Atlantic performance. Springsteen returned to the song time after time at these sessions (including another great impromptu version at the piano in the *Darkness* DVD documentary). The version on *The Promise,* previously only known as a backing track, appears to have retained its original 1977 vocal, though the horns sound like a later imposition. It had already received the full Jukes treatment on Southside Johnny's 1978 album, to which it was donated when it became apparent 'Talk To Me' was gonna be another silent partner in this one-man anti-pop process. A couple of live performances in 2012 have confirmed 'Talk To Me' as another innate crowd-pleaser he had pre-emptively cast aside.

XI) 108–113. Songs recorded at Atlantic or Record Plant, New York August 1977:

108. THE WAY

Known studio / demo recordings: Atlantic or Record Plant, New York 5+15/8/77; Record Plant, New York 12/9/77; 10–12/2/78. [TP]

After six weeks at Atlantic, Springsteen had some thirty songs, including in prototypical form the bulk of the album he would release the following year, plus another album of pop fare. A two and a half week break enabled everyone to return refocused, determined to complete the 'eagerly awaited' album. But when sessions resumed in early August, now alternating between Atlantic and Record Plant, Springsteen preferred bringing in new songs. Though few were the equal of ones already recorded and discarded, 'The Way' was very much the exception. Indeed, it made it all the way to the January 16 sequence, sandwiched between 'Adam Raised A Cain' and 'Prove It All Night'. Sung with real passion and purpose, the song has long been a favourite of Springsteen collectors. Springsteen gave the world the loveless 'Factory' instead. Having become ambivalent about the song's qualities – perhaps around take 66 on February 12 1978 – he even rejected it from

Tracks. And after initially putting it at the start of the bonus 'rarities' disc to a 2-CD *Essential Bruce Springsteen*, he rejected it a third time. Those outside said circle had to wait until 2010 to enjoy this torch ballad, when it made it to *The Promise* (albeit as a hidden track).

109. AFTER DINNER
Known studio/demo recordings: Atlantic or Record Plant, New York 5, 10–11/8/77.
110. I GOT MY EYE ON YOU
Known studio/demo recordings: Atlantic or Record Plant, New York 15/8/77; 14/9/77.

Further evidence that Springsteen could not keep his eye on the prize is provided by the recording history of these two songs – neither of which circulate. They may even be lost classics, though given the twenty-five outtakes released in the last fifteen years on assorted archival sets that seems improbable. Both songs were worked on extensively, in the former's case for a number of days, albeit as a diversion from the main fare. The latter track also racked up fourteen takes (a 'Tk14' is listed on one of the rough mix cassette inlay cards in the *Darkness* notebook). Recorded on a day when he was concentrating on other songs of known merit, like 'Independence Day' and 'The Way', back in the day 'I Got my Eye on You' was considered good enough to be placed on a comp. reel alongside finished takes of 'The Way' and 'Prove It All Night' (where it clocks in at 3:45). Twenty years later, a number of mixes were done for the *Tracks* project. As such, one of the stranger omissions from *The Promise*.

111. CRAZY ROCKER (IT'S ALRIGHT)
Known studio/demo recordings: Atlantic or Record Plant, New York ?9/8/77.

Even at this juncture Springsteen liked to spring a new song on the E Streeters, run it down for fun and then just as quickly put it aside. Emerging in the late nineties on the *Deep Down In The Vaults* 3-CD bootleg, 'Crazy Rocker' sounds a lot like it's the one and only take, as Springsteen calls out key changes and hollers dummy lyrics for all he's worth. Everyone is having a good time, someone else is paying the bills (for now), so they keep going beyond the five-minute mark. With a little tightening up, they could probably have got a song good enough to redo in 2010. As it is, the song was not even considered worth identifying in the logs, though it is probably the 'New Rocker' they attempted (twice!) at the August 9 session. Or the unlisted song on the following reel listed as 'New Song Rehearsal at Begin[ning] – Last Thing of the Night', which might explain how it ended up in the Lost and Found.

112. GOTTA GET THAT FEELING
Known studio/demo recordings: Atlantic or Record Plant, New York 9, 11–12, 30/8/77. [TP]*
First documented performance: Carousel House, Casino, Asbury Park NJ 7/12/10.
113. THE LITTLE THINGS (MY BABY DOES)
Known studio/demo recordings: Atlantic or Record Plant, New York 15/8/77. [TP]*

Of the half a dozen new songs which got try-outs the second week in August, only 'The Way' was worked on further at Record Plant. 'Gotta Get That Feeling' and 'The Little Things (My Baby Does)' represent the two extremes of effort E Streeters expended on essentially diversionary fare. 'The Little Thing (My Baby Does)' appears just once in the logs, as a single take. Listed as complete the same day they nailed 'Independence Day' and 'The Way', it was an attempt to put the sentiments of 'The Way' in a more sprightly setting – 'The way she kisses me tenderly/ The way she gives her love to me' . 'Gotta Get That Feeling', on the other hand, occupied multiple reels of tape over a four-day period and, on the evidence of the two bootlegged versions, one rough as Yogi's botty, the other in its Sunday best, received a thorough workout before Springsteen said hasta la vista, baby. Its transfer (in Sunday Best guise) to a 'comp.' reel at August's end, along with 'Racing In The Streets', led directly to its appearance on *The Lost Masters Vol. 2*, allowing one to discount another unnecessarily modernized reworking on *The Promise*.

XII) 114–136. Songs recorded at Record Plant, New York September 1977–March 1978:

114. KING'S BIG CHANCE AKA KING'S RANSOM
Known studio/demo recordings: Record Plant, New York 1, 8–9/9/77.

115. BLUE MOON
Known studio/demo recordings: Record Plant, New York 9/9/77; 14/10/77.

Another week's break at the start of September saw Springsteen transfer the *Darkness* sessions definitively to Record Plant, a place where he had worked himself into the ground before. But there was still no end in sight; not even a provisional album sequence. On the first coupla days back, he recorded these two songs, both clearly marked 'demos'. The first of these, logged under three different names, 'King's Rock (King's Big Chance)', 'King's Ransom' and 'The King's Revenge', was not heard of again. 'Blue Moon' could, of course, be a cover of The Marcels' doo-wop classic. But the E Street Band almost never warmed up with covers at these sessions (or if they did, tape wasn't rolling). And, in fact, this 'Blue Moon' cropped up again at an October session, along with the cryptic 'Sax Song', 'City At Night', 'English Sons' and the first 'Bo Do Rocker'.

116. PROVE IT ALL NIGHT
Known studio/demo recordings: Record Plant, New York 12, 14-16/9/77. [DA]
First documented performance: Shea's Buffalo Theatre, Buffalo NY 23/5/78.

After weeks of essentially unproductive sessions, Springsteen finally got back on track with this captured-on-tape corker. The first take, recorded on September 12, is presumably the extraordinary performance bootlegged on *Lost Masters 3*, in which he sings most of the lyrics of 'Something In The Night' to a full band arrangement of 'Prove It All Night'. It seems likely he worked on the lyric between sessions and brought the song to the session on the 14th, essentially finished. But only the first and last takes – both musically realized – are in general circulation, while even the early mixes of the album version have finished lyrics, suggesting that for all the various lyric drafts reproduced in *Songs*, once it got to the studio it was revved up and ready to go.

117. RAMROD
Known studio/demo recordings: Record Plant, New York 12/9/77.

At least four takes of 'Ramrod' were recorded at the September 12 session, one of which circulates, with what are clearly dummy lyrics set to a loose, frat-rock arrangement. None of the various double entendres drawn from the title itself and found in later versions are in evidence here, though it is clearly logged as

'Ramrod', pure and simple (along with the intriguing comment, 'Bullshit at Head'!). Like that other flirtation with frat-rock, 'Sherry Darling', it was a song he would return to on the 1978 tour, before spending many more hours at Power Station ramming it into gear (see #117a at the end of this section).

118. SOMEDAY (WE'LL BE TOGETHER)
Known studio/demo recordings: Record Plant, New York 26, 29–30/9/77. [TP]*

Listed on all the tape logs – and there are a fair few – as 'Someday (Tonight)', this was one of several uncirculated tracks meant to validate the decision to make *The Promise* a double CD. Without a circulating rough take it is impossible to say just how much work was done on this track in 2010, but the lead vocal and at-times-overpowering Alliance Singers are certainly latter-day incursions. It may well have some relation to the Atlantic demo 'Our Love Will Last Forever', but the focus of the released song is their night together, not the expiry date of their romance.

119. BREAK OUT
Known studio/demo recordings: Record Plant, New York 26-28/9/77; 4+7/11/77.
120. DOWN BY THE RIVER (SAY SONS)
Known studio/demo recordings: Record Plant, New York ?27/9/77.

Long known in collecting circles as 'All Night Long', 'Break Out' circulates in two forms, both pretty rough, neither hinting at latent greatness. So it is something of a shock to see just how much work was done on the track. And there evidently was a finished take because in November 1997 it was one of the tracks mixed for the *Tracks* project. 'Down By The River' supposedly had the working title 'Say Sons' (which may relate to the provisional title, 'Old Sons', also logged as 'New Old Song', from September 27). The vocals are so buried it is hard to figure out what is going on, but nothing about the track indicates it needs its own monograph. Both tracks first circulated on the 'Son You May Kiss The Bride' tape of 1977–79 outtakes, and may well be just rehearsal takes.

121. AIN'T GOOD ENOUGH FOR YOU
Known studio/demo recordings: Record Plant, New York ?26/9/77 [TP].
First documented performance: Carousel House, Casino, Asbury Park NJ 7/12/10.

Another track known under an entirely different name – 'What's The Matter, Little Darling?' – it appears on *The Promise* as 'Ain't Good Enough For You'. Another song lost in the mists of the tape logs, this one has a firmer audio history. Too firm a history. One cannot easily explain its omission from the logs when at least three versions are in circulation, all evidently finished. Indeed, the *Thrill Hill Vault* DVD shows him adding a vocal overdub at Record Plant, which rather suggests he thought he had something. The most likely location for the track is on September 26, where a 'First New Rocker' is listed. The song itself has a certain charm about it, with a groove enticing enough to be co-opted for 'This Little Girl' in 1980 and a sentiment later refined for 'My Best Was Never Quite Good Enough'. But the lyrics themselves are a disappointingly banal way of saying women nag (a theme found in English song in the early 15th century).

122. THE PROMISED LAND
Known studio/demo recordings: Record Plant, New York 30/9/77; 27/10/77; 1,27/12/77. [DA]
First documented performance: Shea's Buffalo Theatre, Buffalo NY 23/5/78.

No outtake version circulates of this song, just an alternate mix, but there are plenty in the vaults. The three takes from September 30 may well feature an early set of lyrics, because it is four weeks before work on the track started in earnest. Twenty takes would be attempted on the 27th October, with take 19 featuring a so-called 'long ending'. This probably refers to the harmonica coda that reintroduced some much needed tonal colour.

123. CITY OF NIGHT
Known studio/demo recordings: Record Plant, New York 14/10/77. [TP]

Another ten-day break leads to yet more new songs, Springsteen still failing to put a lid on this sustained jag of songwriting. When he returns, he has another song 'about' cars, but this one is a little different. Released in its original form as the 'closing' track on *The Promise*, it should have come directly after 'Candy's Boy'.

124. THE BALLAD (CASTAWAY)
Known studio/demo recordings: Record Plant 14/10/77.

Another song from the 'Son You May Kiss The Bride' tape which proves hard to nail down, this particular torch song was unhelpfully named 'The Ballad', though collectors have generally preferred 'Castaway'. 'Ballad' precedes 'City of Night' at the October 14 session, and what we have is an antecedent not only in proximity, but in tone. With a gorgeous church-organ intro, it soars musically even as the unfinished lyric endeavours to pull it back to earth. Again, we find ourselves on the same backstreet, beneath 'her' window: 'Baby's got on her new dress tonight/ With her hair piled high she looks so right/ And I will not be denied/ All I want is to be the one to try'.

125. ENGLISH SONS (WRONG SIDE OF THE STREET)
Known studio/demo recordings: Record Plant, New York 14/10/77. [TP]*

Bootlegged as 'Endless Night', and released as 'Wrong Side of the Street', this track is clearly marked 'English Sons' in the tape logs, one of a handful of new songs Springsteen sought to capture in a single day – October 14. It was quite a day. Springsteen started proceedings with more melancholic fare, 'The Ballad' and 'Taxi Cab', before giving full E Street workouts to 'English Sons' and 'I'm Going Back', both recorded with their guts hanging out. There may be more – two tracks at the session are identified simply as 'New Song'. 'English Sons' in its (modern vocal) *Promise* guise is curtailed just as the Big Man is threatening to cut loose (serving as a metaphor for this whole series of sessions), but the song retains a certain fire of unknown origin.

126. GIVE THE GIRL A KISS
Known studio/demo recordings: Record Plant, New York 11/10/77 *or* 11/11/77. [TR]
First documented performance: Convention Hall, Asbury Park NJ 19/3/99.

Like 'The Promised Land', 'Give The Girl A Kiss' nods vigorously in the general direction of its source, The Shangri-Las' 'Give Him A Great Big Kiss', not just in title, but in the whole sonic sheen; whilst taking much of its energy from the New York Dolls' reworking of that sixties staple (which he perhaps witnessed first-hand at Max's). Its inclusion on 1998's *Tracks*, though, seemed more about surprising collectors than capturing the essence of these marathon sessions. A song that went unlogged at the time, it became part of a 1993 'comp.' of 'lost' songs put together by a Sony engineer, many of which ended up on *Tracks*. The date given for the track on that comp. is 11/10/77. But there doesn't appear to be a session on November 10; whereas October 11 was Springsteen's second day back in the studio. He may then have returned to the track three days later, when an unidentified 'Sax Song' vied with 'Hearts of Stone', the precursor to 'Give The Girl A Kiss' on that 1993 'comp.' reel.

127. I'M GOING BACK
Known studio/demo recordings: Record Plant, New York 14 + ?27/10/77.
128. PREACHER'S DAUGHTER.
Known studio/demo recordings: Record Plant, New York 27/10/77.
First documented performance: Special Events Center, Austin TX 7/12/78.

Recorded two weeks apart, 'I'm Going Back' and 'Preacher's Daughter' were self-conscious attempts to craft songs around the same Bo Diddley beat that informed 'She's The One'. Indeed, both are logged as 'BoDo Rocker', i.e. Bo Diddley Rocker, with 'Preacher's Daughter' listed as 'New BoDo Rocker' on the October 27 reel (it is identified by both titles in an inlay card reproduced in the 2010 *Darkness* boxed set). However, in terms of importance there is no comparison. 'I'm Going Back' is one more 'break out' song. Literally. He's in prison dreaming of his gal and swearing, 'I'm movin' out, ah, so don't book me, Jack/ I'm goin' back'. Set on BoDo autopilot, for all its sense of fun it seems more suited to soundchecks.

'Preacher's Daughter', on the other hand, should have been released years ago. But, as he later admitted, 'On *Darkness* I just didn't make room for certain things.' One of those things was an irreverence bordering on blasphemy; another was the love of a good woman, who in this case 'gives me light and . . . brings me water'. A gloriously good-humoured rewrite of 'Rosalita', crossed with the daddy of all Diddley riffs, he gave the barest hint of what he sacrificed when he broke into the opening verse of this lost classic at December 1978 shows, before revisiting a more familiar heartbreaker and soul destroyer, 'She's The One'. [See discussion in main text pp. 156–57]

129. ICEMAN
Known studio/demo recordings: Record Plant, New York 27/10/77. [TR]
First documented performance: Tower Theater, Philadelphia PA 17/5/05 [solo show].

It is hardly surprising that 'when Bob Benjamin sent [him] a tape with about three songs on it' in the nineties, Springsteen had clean forgotten he'd 'even written ['Iceman'] and . . . had no idea what it was.' If he'd have been keeping up with his own bootlegs, rather than busting members of an industry which had done so much to engender a deserved reputation for discarding 24-carat classics, he would have known the track from the various vinyl and CD versions of the *Son You May Kiss The Bride* tape, where it appeared alongside 'Preacher's Daughter'. Indeed, one can't help but wonder if that three-song tape was from the October 27 session and comprised 'New Ballad', 'New Fast Song' and 'New BoDo Rocker'. (The 'New Fast Song' being his solution to the 'Candy's Boy' / 'Fast Song' imbroglio, while 'New BoDo Rocker' was 'Preacher's Daughter'. 'New Ballad' was the chilling 'Iceman', a song he cut just this one time.) [See discussion in main text p. 157]

130. ADAM RAISED A CAIN
Known studio/demo recordings: Record Plant, New York 9/11/77; 15/12/77; 15–17/2/78. [DA]
First documented performance: Shea's Buffalo Theatre, Buffalo NY 23/5/78.

'Adam Raised A Cain' was the second such attempt at these sessions to see his troubled youth through his father's eyes, as Springsteen starts to become more aware of the forces that brought his parent/s down. He was less aware of the forces that sometimes work against a song's strengths. 'Adam Raised A Cain' suffered at the hands of a Springsteen who, in pushing himself to break through the pain, ended up producing something defiant, but also definitely overwrought.

131. I WANNA BE WILD
Known studio/demo recordings: Record Plant, New York 11/11/77.

Long known to collectors as 'Don't Say No', this song was logged as 'I Want To Be Wild' (aka 'New Fast Rocker'). It would appear either is correct, as one take has the former chorus, another, the latter. The lyrics, designed to convince some chick how much he needs her – 'I'll get down on my knees . . . I'm your captive' – are so buried in the mix as to render them unimportant. A cassette inlay card in the *Darkness* notebook shows it was dubbed to a comp. tape of 'Ruffs', so it was presumably more than a demo. Just not an album candidate.

132. THE BROKENHEARTED
Known studio/demo recordings: Record Plant, New York 29/11/77. [TP]*
First documented performance: Carousel House, Casino, Asbury Park NJ 7/12/10.

The version of 'The Brokenhearted' on *The Promise* was entirely new to collectors. That the song was never a serious candidate for the album is clear from the notes attached to its original, November 29 reel: '1st Time Demo: Takes 1-3'. How much it was cleaned up in 2010 is less clear. The vocal certainly contains modern elements, with the horn section another obvious addition. Intriguingly, the song was attempted at an early tour rehearsal in May 1978, so maybe he started demoing album #5 before completing album #4.

134. TRIANGLE SONG
Known studio/demo recordings: Record Plant, New York 1/12/77.
135. (I LOVE) EVERYTHING ABOUT YOU
Known studio/demo recordings: Record Plant, New York 14/3/78.
136. TRAPPED AGAIN

#134 & 135 are both 'lost' songs recorded in the final days of *Darkness* . . ., in the latter's case the very last sessions. The former stands as another cryptic song-title, the latter sounds like a cover. Neither would be heard of again, though 'Triangle Song' would feature on a 1993 'comp.' that would form the starting point for *Tracks*. Meanwhile, 'Trapped Again' was another song donated to Southside Johnny to bulk up the third album he'd completed in the interregnum separating *Born to Run* from *Darkness*, though this time the main songsmith was Southside himself, with 'Bruce & Steve merely adding bits and pieces'. I'm prepared to wager one 'bit' Springsteen contributed was that opening couplet: 'Here I am, baby, right where you found me/ Trying to break these chains that surround me'.

XIII) 137–140, 117a. Songs performed, rehearsed or demoed May to December 1978:

137. POINT BLANK
Known studio/demo recordings: Home recording, Holmdel NJ January-May 1979; Power Station, New York 29-30/5/79; 23–25/8/79; 16/2/80. [RI]
First documented performance: The Roxy, Los Angeles 7/7/78.

On *Darkness* . . . I couldn't understand how you could feel so good and so bad at the same time . . . The song that I wrote right after *Darkness* . . . was 'Point Blank' – which takes that thing to its furthest. – Bruce Springsteen, 1981. [See discussion in main text pp.180–1]

138. THE TIES THAT BIND I
First documented performance: Capitol Theatre, Passaic NJ 20/9/78 soundcheck.
138A. THE TIES THAT BIND II
Known studio/demo recordings: 'Telegraph Hill Studio' 26/10/78; Telegraph Hill rehearsal, March 1979; Power Station, New York 10–11/4/79; 10/4/80. [RI]
First documented performance: Jadwin Gym, Princeton NJ 1/11/78.

By the end of November 1978, Springsteen was regularly performing the three songs that form the core of the double album he would release two years later – 'Point Blank', 'Independence Day' and 'The Ties That Bind'. All three songs were also previewed to a wider radio – and, inevitably, bootleg vinyl – audience during west coast live FM broadcasts from the Roxy in LA and The Winterland in San Francisco. He seemed to want people to know he had plenty of new songs ready to record, even if that wasn't the case. 'The Ties That Bind' – in its performance guise – would stay pretty much intact in its passage to Power Station, where a stomping version would be recorded at the second *River* session in April 1979. But, lyrically, he has entirely reversed the 'loner' sentiments of the version sound-checked in September 1978, making his loyal chick complicit in an 'us against the world' compact, that 'long dark highway and a thin white line connecting . . . your heart to mine'.

139. TONIGHT
140. I'M GONNA TREAT YOU RIGHT [AKA 'WILD KISSES']
Known studio/demo recordings: 'Telegraph Hill Studio' 26/10/78.

These two songs, rehearsed with the E Street Band the week before they resumed their assault on America's rock sensibilities in November 1978, were only minor additions to the oeuvre (though a live version of 'Wild Kisses' wouldn't have gone amiss). Another great little pop song, written fifteen years too late, it just needed someone to plug the lyrical gaps. If 'Tonight' was more of the same – with a hint of the honkytonk about it – Springsteen knew it wasn't quite ready for the road ahead.

117a. RAMROD

Known studio/demo recordings: Power Station, New York 12/6/79; 27/8/79; 5/9/79; 4+19/4/80. [RI]

First documented performance: Stanley Theatre, Pittsburgh PA 28/12/78.

When we left 'Ramrod' at the Record Plant sessions, it was still searching for a lyric. And though it was not one of the songs known to have been rehearsed before the last leg of the 1978 tour, it had evidently acquired a set of words by the time it made its live debut in Pittsburgh at the end of December. He chose to make very little of the double-entendre potential of the title phrase, save for a single line in the first *River* take, 'Come out little girl and let my ramrod rock'. By the time he has redubbed his vocal, even this has become banality itself, 'Come Saturday night I let my ramrod rock'. So much for emulating the unselfconscious charm of frat-rock 45s like 'Double Shot of My Baby's Love'.

Part Two: 1979–84

[Note: Between January 1979 and June 1984, Springsteen & The E Street Band would tour just once, albeit on the year-long *River* Tour (October 1980 to September 1981). He would also change his working methods as a songwriter dramatically, demoing much of the material at home, initially on cassette, and then on the TEAC Portastudio (still on cassette but in four-track, at 3 ¾ ips), and finally, from January 1983, using an eight-track home studio. One particular set of 1981–2 home demos would become the critically acclaimed *Nebraska*. But such an approach would also mean many songs were never recorded in the studio with his trusty band, but nonetheless circulate as demos (thanks to Springsteen's decision to rely on guitar-tech Mike Batlan to set up and operate the rudimentary home recording equipment). Batlan kept reference copies of much of this material, which eventually (partially) fell into the public domain after he left Springsteen's employment at the end of the *Born In The USA* tour. Not surprisingly, the songs on these demo-tapes exist in various states of (dis)repair and so, though they confirm the prolific nature of Springsteen's songwriting, the reader must be prepared to go from the sublime to the scarcely constituted in the twinkling of a piano.]

XIV) 141, 95a, 142–149, 139a, 250–160. Songs demoed January-May 1979:

141. JANEY NEEDS A SHOOTER MK.3

Known studio/demo recordings: Home recording, Holmdel NJ January-May 1979; 'Telegraph Hill Studio' band rehearsal March 1979 [x2].

as JEANNIE NEEDS A SHOOTER

Known studio/demo recordings: None.

Another gem from the 'Son You May Kiss The Bride' tape, 'Janey Needs a Shooter' has been a source of contention ever since. Most commonly assigned to the *Darkness* sessions, with a few dissenters preferring those for *The River*, it is found nowhere in Sony's studio logs, save in its 914 incarnation of 1973. There is probably a good reason – the song was never officially recorded with the E Street Band. The 6:42 'studio' version on the above tape sounds like a rehearsal. Corroboration, and a solid indication of a likely recording date, is provided by the recent, discreet circulation of a full spring 1979 band rehearsal featuring (among others) 'The Man Who Got Away' and this seven-minute 'Janey Needs A Shooter'. (An enticing acoustic fragment, recorded at home that March, had previously appeared on *Lost Masters VIII,* confirming its *River* status.) Virtually indistinguishable from the *SYMKTB* 'mix', the rehearsal in question was taped 'live' in the room – and contains a lead guitar-break that threatens to rip the roof from the rehearsal room and send it rolling down Telegraph Hill. The chorus seems to owe a certain debt to 'I'm Going Back' in the way it leans all over the title phrase, 'Janey needs a shooter, Jack'. To have not immediately taken this into the studio made no more sense than his decision to donate it to Warren Zevon to do his worse. [See discussion in main text pp. 193–4]

95a. Bring On The Night
Known studio/demo recordings: Home recording, Holmdel NJ January–May 1979; 'Telegraph Hill Studio' band rehearsal March 1979; 14/5/79; Power Station, New York ?13/6/79. [TR]

Given how much time Springsteen spent working on *Darkness* outtakes like 'I Wanna Be With You', 'Independence Day' and 'Sherry Darling' at the first sustained set of *River* sessions in May/early June, it should perhaps come as no surprise that he returned to 'Bring On The Night', another song attempted at the summer 1977 Atlantic sessions. This time the band was prepped, rehearsing the song in mid-May. But again, it is missing from the June 13 log, though it was a productive day, with 'White Town', 'Night Fire' and 'The Man Who Got Away' all recorded. (That date comes from the not-always-reliable *Tracks* booklet.) Its first appearance in the Sony logs comes as part of the 1993 'comp.' reel mentioned previously.

142. BABY COME BACK
143. LOVE WILL GET YOU DOWN
144. WALKING ON THE AVENUE
145. FIND IT WHERE YOU CAN
146. LOVE AND KISSES

Known studio/demo recordings: Home recording, Los Angeles January-February 1979; [#146:] 'Telegraph Hill Studio' band rehearsal March 1979.

All these tracks appeared in 1996 on the ninth instalment in the *Lost Masters* bootleg series, culled from the legendary Batlan tapes. The tape in question, a home cassette with decent sound but zero production values, also contains a few fragments whose existence I've not numbered. Only one of those now taped would make it to the pukka sessions ('Under The Gun' – #152) and none to the album itself. Which is perhaps the rub. The song he works on the hardest, 'Love Will Get You Down', illustrates a painstaking but unfocused working method, and an unshakeable belief that something inspired will come along just by giving every love cliché a repeat spin to the accompaniment of a few standard chord changes. The song has a single idea adhering to it, that no matter how one feels initially in a love affair, 'pretty soon, you'll find out a smile turns to a frown', a sentiment he will address with far greater resolve the following year, on 'Your Love (Is Gonna Let You Down)'.

The rest of the tape yields little juicy in the way of forbidden fruit. Soured by the same attitude to relationships as 'Love Will Get You Down', 'Love and Kisses' starts with a line straight from 1965 Dylan, 'If I wanted to, I'd be with you', but quickly runs out of steam. 'Walking On The Avenue' suggests some rough lyrics hinting at the underlying loneliness of the road scribbled out in advance, 'Girls come to my hotel room/ Well, they just want to sit and talk'; though by the second take we are treading familiar ground, waiting to find out when she's gonna decide to 'turn me out again/ I remember back when . . .'. All in all, I'm hard-pressed to agree with the bootlegger's claim that 'some true gems [are] included here, and several examples of Bruce at his melodic and rhythmic best'.

147. OUT ON THE RUN (LOOKING FOR LOVE)
148. BABY DON'T YOU GO
149. PROTECTION MK.1
139a. BREAK MY HEART [aka 'Tonight']

Known studio/demo recordings: [#147-49:] Home recording, Holmdel NJ

January–May 1979; [#139a & 147:] 'Telegraph Hill Studio' band rehearsal March 1979.

Resuming the demo process in New Jersey, Springsteen continued for a few more weeks to put song ideas onto cassette. 'Protection' and 'Baby Don't You Go' are two tracks he plays around with, but in both cases the idea fizzles out before inspiration dawns. ('Protection' has no connection to the track he later donated to Donna.) Other song ideas spanning the two relevant volumes of *Lost Masters* (IX and X) are so threadbare that to call them songs would be stretching the term to breaking-point. Generally speaking, Springsteen is chewing the carpet looking for love.

'Out On The Run' would be the one snippet that warranted a series of band rehearsals at the end of March (three of these are on *Lost Masters XIV*); and though the lyrics are impossible to glean when submerged 'neath the full E Street roar, it has a decent pop hook and its own frenetic energy. Also back for a second beating is 'Tonight', rehearsed the previous October, which retains its beat sensibility but amped up to amphetamine speed. That sense of living on the edge of a mad, mad world would probably have counted against it. As it did for a number of spring 1979 songs.

150. I DON'T WANNA BE
Known studio/demo recordings: 'Telegraph Hill Studio' band rehearsal ?May 1979.

The curio 'I Don't Wanna Be', where Clarence's backing vocals at times drown out the boss, represents one of the odder oddities from the weeks which prefaced the resumption of studio work, this time in earnest, in late May 1979. Like other songs that spring, it seems to have been all but worked out structurally and melodically by the time of band rehearsals (from which the misdated 16/9/79 version on *Lost Masters IV* originates), but Springsteen only has dummy lyrics.

151. IN THE CITY TONIGHT
Known studio/demo recordings: 'Telegraph Hill Studio' band rehearsal 25/3/79.
as NIGHT FIRE
Known studio/demo recordings: 'Telegraph Hill Studio' band rehearsal 30/3/79; Power Station, New York 13/6/79.

152. UNDER THE GUN

Known studio/demo recordings: Home recording, Holmdel, NJ January-March 1979; 'Telegraph Hill Studio' band rehearsal 30/3/79; Power Station, New York 14/6/79.

153. THE MAN WHO GOT AWAY

Known studio/demo recordings: Home recording, Holmdel, NJ January-May 1979; 'Telegraph Hill Studio' band rehearsal 30/3/79 & March 1979; Power Station, New York 13/6/79; 5/7/79.

All four of these songs would be rehearsed with the E Street Band, the last three on March 30, probably intended as the final band rehearsal before sessions started in earnest. 'Night Fire' had already appropriated the tune of a song called 'In The City Tonight' which Springsteen and the band had spent a whole day working on five days previously. The other two tracks, which had already occupied Springsteen at his Holmdel homestead, were clearly always intended to be put on duty, though he took his time getting to them. All three were cut at the June 13–14 sessions as Springsteen finally focused on the new songs he needed to fill out forty minutes of vinyl. However, only 'The Man Who Got Away' would be revisited; featuring on an initial sequence for *The Ties That Bind*. All three tracks would also be pulled to the aforementioned 1993 'rarities' reels, though none made it to *Tracks* or circulate in studio guise.

154. CHAIN LIGHTNING

Known studio/demo recordings: Home recording, Holmdel, NJ January–March 1979; 'Telegraph Hill Studio' band rehearsal 30/3/79; Power Station, New York 17/2/80.

Like the above trio of try-outs, the only versions of 'Chain Lightning' in circulation precede the Power Station sessions. Thankfully, these include a terrific grease-lightning rendition from that final March rehearsal. Something prompted him to remember it the following February, when it finally got an actual studio slot, with perhaps his decision to dispense with the rockabilly 'You Can Look' a factor. Yet not only didn't it make *The River*, it didn't make the *Tracks* short-list either. So much for that professed 'passion for chain lightning'.

155. ROULETTE

Known studio/demo recordings: Home recording, Holmdel, NJ March 1979; Power Station, New York 3/4/79; [11-12/4/80]. [TR]

First documented performance: The Centrum, Worcester MA 25/2/88.

At the time he wrote 'Roulette', Springsteen thought it was one of the best things he had ever done. And he was right. But by the time he had signed up for the No Nukes concert in September – a commitment he made on the back of his new-found awareness of man as a political animal – he was already looking to drop the song from the shows (it was replaced at the last minute by the recently-penned 'The River') and the ill-fated *The Ties That Bind*. Asked what had happened to it the following year, he went all defensive: 'I just didn't like the way it sounded . . . We might redo it and put it out later.' [See discussion in main text pp. 191–2]

Note: The original April 3 vocal has significantly different lyrics. The 'final' vocal, probably cut the following week, appears to have been remixed in April 1980.

156. TAKE 'EM AS THEY COME

Known studio/demo recordings: Home recording, Los Angeles, winter 1979; Home recording, Holmdel NJ January–May 1979; Power Station, New York 5/12/79; [10/4/80]. [TR]

First documented performance: Stadion Bieberer Berg, Offenbach, Germany 15/6/99.

If Springsteen was in a hurry to record 'Roulette', he was positively lackadaisical when it came to 'Take 'Em As The Come', one of the best melodies he pulled from *The River* and dumped on *Tracks*. First found as the merest snatch on the first LA home demo in the winter of 1979, it crops up again a month or so later with the same trusty tape recorder. Already he has the germ of a good ol' pop song. Yet it never figures in computations around the initial 'pop' album, *The Ties That Bind*, and it is December before the E Streeters get to embrace this rousing call. It was finally made official on *Tracks*, and from there moved to its rightful berth, rockin' around the world rousing the rabble on the E Street reunion tour.

Note: The version on *Tracks* is credited to 10 April 1980, when Springsteen was making last-minute changes to the album shortlist. That is probably the date of the vocal but not the backing track.

157. YOU CAN LOOK (BUT YOU BETTER NOT TOUCH)
Known studio/demo recordings: Home recording, Holmdel, NJ January–May 1979; Power Station, New York 24–25/8/79; 'Telegraph Hill Studio' band rehearsal 11/1/80; Power Station, New York 17+23/2/80; 1, 9+21/4/80. [RI]
First documented performance: Coliseum, Richfield OH 7/10/80.

The first song at these sessions to really go with the new sideburns, 'You Can Look' began life as a dose of irreverent humour, the punch line of each put-upon verse being . . . you guessed it. In this guise, it became the buffer between 'The River' and 'The Price You Pay' on *The Ties That Bind*. But this homespun homage was rethought, restrung and rehung; and when sessions resumed in February 1980, he decided to kill two birds with one rolling stone – grafting the music from 'Held Up Without A Gun' to 'You Can Look'. Mistake.

158. DOLLHOUSE
Known studio/demo recordings: Home recording, Holmdel, NJ January-May 1979; Power Station, New York 20–21/8/79. [TR]
First documented performance: Stadthalle, Vienna, Austria 24/4/99.

Another slightly formulaic piece, 'Dollhouse' suggested Springsteen quietly yearned to join one of those chintzy new wave, skinny-tie bands. Unfortunately, this vocal don't drip with the requisite 'Joe Jackson meets the Jags' misogyny. Perhaps he secretly envied The Knack, on the brink of multi-platinum success; as they in turn envied his effortless ability to synthesize the very best in sixties radio sounds. He certainly seems to have it in for some woman, or indeed womankind, berating her for an inability to grow up/move on.

159. JACKSON CAGE
Known studio/demo recordings: Home recording, Holmdel, NJ ?May 1979; Power Station, New York 22/5/79; 'Telegraph Hill Studio' band rehearsal 5/2/80; Power Station, New York 17/2/80; 10/4/80. [RI]
First documented performance: Chrysler Arena, Ann Arbor MI 3/10/80.

A fascinating snatch (or two) of 'Jackson Cage' on *Lost Masters VII*, a disc of 1979 home demos, hints at a very different approach than that of its released guise. This undated demo, generally credited to the fall of the year, probably dates from the weeks leading up to the resumption of studio work in May 1979, because almost the whole of the 'first' session, on May 22, was spent working on a song logged as 'Jackson Cage'. However, he would not return to the track again until an E Street Band rehearsal the following February, the arrangement having received a full set of booster shots and the lyrics their own overhaul. In keeping with many songs from this period, the rough edges it had in rehearsal would be smoothed away by the recording process.

160. PARTY LIGHTS
Known studio/demo recordings: Home recording, Holmdel NJ 1979; Power Station, New York 8/10/79; Colt's Neck NJ April 1981.

Found on the same four-song home demo as 'Jackson Cage', 'Party Lights' focuses on another wasted life. Recorded just four days after he delivered *The Ties That Bind*, it seems an unlikely starting-point for the next set of sessions, but so it proved. He returned to the idea again in the spring of 1981, demoing another fragment with the same basic idea, before quietly turning out this particular lovelight.

XV) 161–172. Other songs recorded for *The Ties That Bind* May–September 1979:

161. MARY LOU
Known studio/demo recordings: Home recording, Holmdel, NJ January–May 1979; 'Telegraph Hill Studio' band rehearsals 14/5/79; 'Telegraph Hill Studio' band rehearsal ?16/5/79; Power Station, New York 30/5–1/6/79; 13/7/79. [TR]
as LITTLE WHITE LIES
Known studio/demo recordings: Power Station, New York 1+13/6/79.
162. BE TRUE
Known studio/demo recordings: Power Station, New York 18/7/79; [22/4/80]. [TR]
First documented performance: Capital Centre, Largo MD 26/8/84.

Almost as central to the whole *The River* project as the title track, 'Be True' would go through transformations galore before it finally 'linked together in a certain way'. When Springsteen did find the right setting, in mid-July 1979, he was content to let it be, earmarking it for all three known sequences for *The Ties That Bind*. But for most of its early life, 'Mary Lou' was her name. Thanks to the availability of home demos, pre-session band rehearsals, as well as the (officially available) outtake from May 30, the evolution from 'Mary Lou' to 'Be True' is thoroughly documented. Also in circulation, and in many ways better, is an intermediate incarnation from June 1, generally known as 'Don't Do It To Me' or 'White Lies', but clearly logged as 'Little White Lies'. 'Little White Lies' explodes the moment the drums kick in (which is presumably why Weinberg always considered it one of his favourite E Street songs), stripping 'the falseness of some of those things' layer by layer.

Note: The so-called September 1979 rehearsal version of 'Mary Lou' – which appears on *Lost Masters IV* – is certainly misdated.

163. HUNGRY HEART
Known studio/demo recordings: Power Station, New York 14,21/6/79; 5/9/79; [24/3/80; 10/4/80]. [RI]
First documented performance: Kiel Opera House, St Louis MO 18/10/80.

'Hungry Heart' was the moment Springsteen surrendered to the process of crafting, not creating, music in a state-of-the-art 24-track studio, sacrificing at the altar of commercial success a song with a ravenously real heart. The song certainly came quickly enough, being completed the same day he recorded the definitive 'Stolen Car' (though Flo and Eddie's overdubbed 'la-la-las' were a later addition; as was the decision to fade the song before things got too 'Hey Jude'-ish).

164. DO YOU WANT ME TO SAY ALRIGHT
Known studio/demo recordings: Power Station, New York 14/6/79.

An uncirculated outtake from a highly productive coupla days at the Power Station, 'Do You Want Me To Say Alright' musta had something going for it, because it was one of the tracks pulled to the 1993 'rarities' compilation reels.

165. THE PRICE YOU PAY
Known studio/demo recordings: Power Station, New York 15, 18, 19 + 21/6/79; [4/4/80]. [RI]
First documented performance: Memorial Sports Arena, Los Angeles 31/10/80.

First recorded the day after 'Hungry Heart', 'The Price You Pay' finds the same lost soul in a more contemplative mood, reflecting on all he has loved and lost. In its *Ties That Bind* incarnation, the song's message was made clearer by the inclusion of a bridge which gave the listener the real pay-off: 'Some say forget the past, some say don't look back/ But for every breath you take, you leave a track/ And though it just don't seem fair/ For every smile that breaks, a tear must fall somewhere/ Oh, the price you pay'. This verse would remain an integral part of 1980–81 shows, leading fans to assume it had been added after the fact. Actually, he had simply cut these lines from the album take, an inferior alternate take cut at the same time as the one previously assigned to *The Ties That Bind*.

166. STOLEN CAR

Known studio/demo recordings: Power Station, New York 20–21/6/79; 24/9/79 [TR]; Home recording, Holmdel, NJ January 1980; Telegraph Hill Studio' band rehearsal 16/1/80; Power Station, New York 21/1/80; 20/2/80; [1+9/4/80; 9/5/80]. [RI]

First documented performance: Chrysler Arena, Ann Arbor MI 3/10/80.

Finally, two months into these sessions, Springsteen felt the tendrils of a familiar but tardy inspiration. With 'Stolen Car', Springsteen chanced upon a way to tie together all the elements he looked to address on *Darkness On The Edge of Town*'s successor, some of which he'd already explored in single-idea songs. ('From these banks I can see those party lights shine', self-consciously references 'Party Lights'). What took him half an hour to evoke would take him nine months to dismantle, as the Tinker Man again set about deconstructing a song he – and the E Street band – captured in all its ineffable essence those first two days in the studio (*Tracks* says this version was recorded on July 26, but there is no record of the original version being attempted after July 21). The thematic centrepiece of *The Ties That Bind* LP, it would become a shadow of its ghostly self when Springsteen returned it to rehearsals in the new year with a different arrangement and truncated lyric. [See discussion in main text pp. 196–7]

167. TIME THAT NEVER WAS

Known studio/demo recordings: Power Station, New York 27/6/79; 16/3/80.

A lost song in every sense of the word, 'Time That Never Was' has never circulated. Nor was it shortlisted for *Tracks*. And yet the fact that he returned to it in mid-March 1980 when starting to sequence the double album suggests Springsteen felt it merited further consideration.

168. I WANNA MARRY YOU
Known studio/demo recordings: Power Station, New York 5, 11–12/7/79; 12/4/80; 6–7/5/80. [RI]
First documented performance: Chrysler Arena, Ann Arbor MI 3/10/80.

A wedding song for Marc Brickman. [See discussion in main text p. 198]

169. RICKI WANTS A MAN
Known studio/demo recordings: Power Station, New York 16/7/79; 10/4/80. [TR]
First documented performance: Sprint Center, Kansas City MO 24/8/08.

Having got the picture-postcard version of marriage out of his system, Springsteen returned to putting a New Jersey spin on a version of *This Year's Girl* jointly recorded by Manfred Mann and The Animals. 'Ricki Wants A Man' would be the first recorded proof that the author of 'Fire' and 'Because The Night' had not entirely lost his touch. But Ricki would share the fates of Mary Lou and Cindy, sisters in wilful spirit, sidelined by a Springsteen no longer sure what kind of album he was making.

170. CINDY
Known studio/demo recordings: Power Station, New York 16–17/7/79; 11–12/4/80.

The songs cut at the sessions on July 16–18 suggested Springsteen was back on track. The one track on *The Ties That Bind* October 4 1979 'safety' that remains unreleased – even after three non-album B-sides, the 4-CD *Tracks* and *The Essential Bruce Springsteen* bonus 'rarities' disc – 'Cindy' is one of the great lost Springsteen songs . It is also perhaps the perfect representation of what the 1979 album would have been had it remained a bunch of 'early English-style stuff'. 'Cindy', placed second on *The Ties That Bind*, effortlessly achieves that rare balance between pop sensibility and fractured reality he was reaching for.

171. LOOSE ENDS
Known studio/demo recordings: Power Station, New York 18/7/79. [TR]
First documented performance: Palais Omnisports de Paris-Bercy, Paris, France 3/6/99.

Though it would take Springsteen another month to reach 'The River', he had already reached that edge of desperation on this song. Originally the closer of *The Ties That Bind*, these loose ends were left dangling free, though he would return to 'Loose Ends' at a later date, replacing the homicidal fury of the original with the world-weary resignation of 'Baby I'm So Cold', a *Born In The USA* outtake.

172. OH ANGELYNE

Known studio/demo recordings: Home recording, Holmdel, NJ January–May 1979.

as THE RIVER

Known studio/demo recordings: Power Station, New York 26+29/8/79; 21/1/80; 12+24/4/80. [RI]

First documented performance: Madison Square Garden, New York 21/9/79. [NN]

An instant classic, 'The River' – a reworking of an earlier home demo – was quickly recorded at the end of August, with no background vocals, in a sparser arrangement than the released version and slotted onto *The Ties That Bind* as opening track on side two. Coming after 'Stolen Car', its inclusion necessitated a wholesale rethink for the album, which resulted in Springsteen substituting 'Cindy' for 'Ricki Wants A Man of Her Own', 'You Can Look' for 'Ramrod' and 'The River' for 'The Man Who Got Away'. [See discussion in main text p. 199]

XVI) 173–187. Songs demoed September 1979–January 1980:

173. FROM SMALL THINGS, BIG THINGS COME

Known studio/demo recordings: Power Station, New York 2/9/79. [TE]

First documented performance: Big Man's West, Red Bank NJ 7/8/82 [w/ Beaver Brown].

With *The Ties That Bind* still being sequenced, Springsteen turned up at a session in early September with one of those great rockabilly throwaways he used to bring to the *Darkness* sessions just to keep the band on its toes. As he puts it in *The Essential* notes, he ran the song down for the other musicians 'and the band drove the hell out of it in a take or two'. Was the version cut on the 2nd always intended as a demo, or was Springsteen making an early start on the rockabilly album he felt he had in him? Either way, it never figured again in the recording process for *The River*. The following year he palmed it off on Dave Edmunds, who knew a rocker when he heard one and made a fine job of heaping the Rockpile sound on top.

174. WHERE THE BANDS ARE
Known studio/demo recordings: Power Station, New York 9/10/79. [TR]
First documented performance: Forum, Milan, Italy 19/4/99.
175. CRUSH ON YOU
Known studio/demo recordings: Power Station, New York 11–12/10/79. [RI]
First documented performance: Chrysler Arena, Ann Arbor MI 3/10/80.

Whatever doubts he had about *The Ties That Bind* as an advance on *Darkness*, they didn't take long to manifest themselves. Just four days after the master was made (and presumably delivered to CBS) he was back in the studio working on these two freshly minted songs. He later claimed the songs chosen for *TTTB*, 'lacked the kind of unity and conceptual intensity I liked my music to have', but what these two makeweights brought in the way of 'conceptual intensity' is anybody's guess.

176. CHEVROLET DELUXE
Known studio/demo recordings: Home recording, Holmdel, NJ, Fall 1979; 'Telegraph Hill Studio' band rehearsal 15/11/79.

Brushing aside criticisms that he was starting to repeat himself, Springsteen spent a great deal of time and effort trying to whip this song into shape. It concerned a Chevrolet Deluxe which had become a substitute for the (ubiquitous) estranged wife: 'I had a wife and kid, and I tried to settle down/ I just wanted to live an honest life on the edge of an honest town/ But in the end they left me dangling in the night'. By the sixth home demo we discover he 'can't keep those payments up'. Though not exactly a refashioned 'Street Queen', the band arrangement, rehearsed in mid-November, was surprisingly complex and the six-minute song itself quietly ambitious. Taken at a stately pace with ornate fills from guitar/ organ, it does suggest 'a separate thing happening' but the subject matter meant it was quietly returned to the garage.

177. LIVING ON THE EDGE OF THE WORLD
Known studio/demo recordings: 'Telegraph Hill Studio' band rehearsal 15/11/79; Power Station, New York 7/12/79. [TR]
First documented performance: Madison Square Garden, New York 28/11/80.*

If 'From Small Things . . .' was the first tiny step on the highway to *Nebraska*, 'Living On The Edge of the World' is more of a long stride. Rehearsed alongside 'Chevrolet Deluxe' and recorded at the December sessions, this bop-away-the-blues B-side would be given the musical makeover to end all such makeovers, re-emerging as 'Open All Night'. Meanwhile, two lines giving the raspberry to the radio preacher's promise of salvation, 'Hey mister deejay gotta hear my last prayer/ It's a hey ho rock and roll, deliver me from nowhere,' would reappear in 'State Trooper', an altogether more fitting home.
*Note: Springsteen inserted a verse from this song into 'Ramrod' at this 1980 New York show.

178. SOMEBODY WANTS MY BABY
179. I WANT TO START A NEW LIFE
180. BABY I DON'T KNOW
181. MR OUTSIDE
182. YOU GOTTA FIGHT (FOR WHAT YOU WANT)
183. STOCKTON BOYS

Known studio/demo recordings: Home recording, Holmdel, NJ, Fall 1979.

All of the above songs can be found on another Batlan cassette, this one undated. Undoubtedly from the fall of 1979, it featured just three songs later recorded at Power Station: 'Held Up Without A Gun', 'You Can Look' and 'Mr Outside' (as 'Down In White Town', see below). Having got the hang of how to record himself in private moments, these demos are sonically superior to those recorded the previous winter, and the songs themselves seem to have more of a preordained structure. If other ideas from the same tape/s – 'Everybody's Looking For Somebody', 'The Time In Between' and 'Love's Gonna Be Tonight' – are quickly discarded, the likes of 'You Gotta Fight' ('Every day is a battle within/ The state of the future looks so dim . . . Well, you just got to fight for what you want') and 'Baby I Don't Know' have attractive constructs. The former was set to a light calypso beat, while the latter resembles the kinda thing often found on E Street. However, 'Mr Outside' would be the only idea deemed worthy of studio reconfiguration.

184. I'M A ROCKER

Known studio/demo recordings: Power Station, New York 4/12/79; 10/4/80. [RI]

First documented performance: Kiel Opera House, St Louis MO 18/10/80.

With *The Ties That Bind* definitely off the Xmas schedule, Springsteen continued recording what new material he worked up in short bursts of studio time. Six more songs occupied him from the third to the seventh of December, with one song (listed only as 'No Title Yet') occupying most of the first two days. Of these, only 'I'm A Rocker' would make the final record, albeit with a change of person, from third to first (on takes 4 and 6 from December 4 he sings 'She's A Rocker', though it is listed as 'I'm A Rocker'). Along with the already-recorded 'Where The Bands Are' and 'Crush On You', this high-octane rocker suggested he was looking to include more crowd pleasers to take around the arenas of America.

185. DEDICATION
Known studio/demo recordings: Power Station, New York 4+6/12/79.

'Dedication', the title track of Gary US Bonds' comeback album when it appeared in 1981, began life as a candidate for *The River*, being recorded with the E Street Band across two days in December 1979. However, it probably had a little too much irreverence for Springsteen's own now-sprawling statement. Whether Bonds re-recorded the whole song or simply used the 1979 backing track (as he did on 'Jole Blon', a song recorded at Power Station the following month) is not clear from the album credits; but the Gary US Bonds 'version' could be a vocal-overdubbed *River* outtake.

186. YOUR LOVE
187. THIS LITTLE GIRL

When exactly Springsteen wrote these two slices of pop ephemera for his early idol, Gary US Bonds, is undocumented, but if it was during the sessions for *The River*, as seems likely, he should have saved 'Your Love' for himself. But it was 'This Little Girl', a song which came straight from the discard pile, that was a respectable hit for Bonds, the bouncy arrangement and novelty value of a Bonds/Springsteen collaboration probably doing more for the song's chances than any romantic insights on offer.

XVII) 188–200, Other songs recorded February–April 1980:

188. I'M GONNA BE THERE TONIGHT
Known studio/demo recordings: Home recording, Holmdel NJ January 11/1/80.
as OUT IN THE STREET

Known studio/demo recordings: Power Station, New York 21/3/80. [RI]
First documented performance: Chrysler Arena, Ann Arbor MI 3/10/80.

By 1980 the lyrics have begun to play a subsidiary role in a number of songs, revisiting familiar aspects of an increasingly narrow worldview (the world is tough, really tough, or really, really tough and/or baby, little girl so young and so fine, get your red dress on, you're mine, all mine). 'Out In The Street' was one that began life at January band rehearsals musically complete, but with only dummy lyrics (and a dummy song-title). It would have to wait until March to get a first look at its lyrics, a 'Friday on my mind – walk it, talk it' piece of blue-collar bravado.

189. YOU GOTTA BE KIND
as DOWN IN WHITE TOWN
Known studio/demo recordings: Home recording, Holmdel NJ Fall 1979; home recording, Holmdel NJ January 11, 1980; Power Station, New York 16/3/80.

'Down In White Town' was another composite effort, combining elements of 'You Gotta Be Kind' – a reggae song he demoed at home in the fall – and 'Mr Outside', another song demoed at the same time (see above). This one he persevered with, recording it for *The River* in March as final selections were being made. [See discussion in main text p. 209]

190. SLOW FADE
Known studio/demo recordings: 'Telegraph Hill Studio', Holmdel NJ 5/2/80.

A source of great confusion, and much frustration, this explosive song exists only as a series of band rehearsals, set up presumably to hone arrangements without Power Station's pricey clock ticking. That said, given the six known attempts made at this song on February 5, each an E Street tour de forceful, it would be somewhat surprising if the song went unrecorded at Power Station. (Actually, they spent most of January 31 and February 1 working on an untitled song. But if I had to put my money on a likely contender, it would be 'I Will Be The One' [#198], one of three songs recorded on February 16.) As with a number of songs done in band rehearsal that winter, the vocals are buried deeper than the devil and 'Slow Fade' is merely the title on the tape-card, offering no clue as to its subject-matter or line of attack. The musical evidence, though, suggests something potentially remarkable.

191. FADE AWAY
Known studio/demo recordings: Home recording, Holmdel NJ ?December 1979; Power Station, New York 9, 15–17/3/80; 9, 29/4/80. [RI]
First documented performance: Memorial Sports Arena, Los Angeles 1/11/80.

The compilers of the *Lost Masters* series did no one any favours by including a solo demo of 'Fade Away' as a 'bonus' track on one of two 'best of' sets culled from the 19-CD series, and giving it the same title as the song above, 'Slow Fade'. They bear no resemblance to each other. The demo in question is actually a terrific, fully-conceived prototype for 'Fade Away', probably dating from the nether end of 1979, though Springsteen did not bring the song to a pukka Power Station session until mid-March. But he knew right away he had a good strong ballad to hand. All he needed to do was decide where it fit. As a prelude to 'Stolen Car'?

192. HELD UP WITHOUT A GUN
Known studio/demo recordings: 'Telegraph Hill Studio' band rehearsal 22/2/80; Power Station, New York 23/2/80; 1,9+20-21/4/80. [45]
First documented performance: Nassau Coliseum, Uniondale NY 31/12/80. [TE]

Determined to prove his band had the chops to out-punk The Ramones, Springsteen decided to put all the fury of this angry lil' song into the arrangement, if one can call it that. A two-minute sprint to the finishing line, one barely has time to catch one's breath, let alone catch the clearest reference yet to the price of this particular kinda fame: 'Some damn fool with a guitar walks in off the street/ Ain't got nowhere to go, ain't got nothing to eat/ Man with a cigar says, "sign here son"/ Whoa! Held up without a gun'. The 'man with a cigar' smacks more of Colonel Tom Parker than Mike Appel, being presumably a conscious nod to Bobby Bare's classic Elvis send-up, 'All-American Boy', even if the maniacal delivery makes the whole thing sound personal.

193. RESTLESS NIGHTS
Known studio/demo recordings: 'Telegraph Hill Studio' band rehearsal 10–11/1/80; Power Station, New York 14/1/80; 12/4/80; [2/5/80]. [TR]
First documented performance: HSBC Arena, Buffalo NY 22/11/2009.

By January 1980, Springsteen knew he was coming up short on songs to top those already sidelined from *The Ties That Bind*. 'Restless Nights', though, was a welcome exception and, not surprisingly, it was one he was anxious to run down when work resumed at Power Station. In fact, he seems to have set aside a session on January 14 to record 'Restless Nights' (and 'Jole Blon', rehearsed the same day), having spent the past few days at Telegraph Hill whipping it into shape. Once again, the rehearsal versions allowed Springsteen to give this up-tempo rocker the full 'Prove It All Night' treatment, before trimming it down to pop single length. Even in its truncated Power Station form (faded prematurely for *Tracks*), the song has muscle to spare. And yet, despite receiving a 'final' mix for inclusion on *The River* in early May, it was one more casualty of the kinda 'conceptual intensity' that rated 'Ramrod' and 'I'm A Rocker' over such substantial fare.

194. TWO HEARTS

Known studio/demo recordings: 'Telegraph Hill Studio' band rehearsal 22/2/80; Power Station, New York 23–24/2/80; 17/3/80; 9+26/4/80. [RI]
First documented performance: Coliseum, Richfield OH 6/10/80.

Along with 'Out In The Street' and 'Cadillac Ranch', 'Two Hearts' seemed to confirm that Springsteen had firmly lost the plot sometime in February 1980, recording songs for recording's sake; and that any ol' cliché would suffice for a lyric if the arrangement was radio-friendly enough to make a mnemonic imprint.

195. WRECK ON THE HIGHWAY

Known studio/demo recordings: 'Telegraph Hill Studio' band rehearsal 11/1/80; Power Station, New York 10–12/4/80. [RI]
First documented performance: Chrysler Arena, Ann Arbor MI 3/10/80.

The last song recorded for the album, 'Wreck On The Highway' still occupied three days of studio time. He presumably already knew it would serve as a coda to 'Drive All Night'. The third downer in a row, its intimations of mortality would serve as both an album closer and a (presumably intentional) semi-ironic farewell to albums about cars and girls.

196. ANGELYNE

Known studio recordings: Power Station, New York 1/2/80.

One of two Springsteen originals recorded for *The River* which ended up being donated to Gary US Bonds to engineer his own commercial comeback, 'Angelyne' would not appear until 1982's *On The Line*. However, it could well be a 1980 outtake, given that resounding Big Man sax solo. The Bruce and the E Streets take had enough merits to be included on those intriguing 1993 'rarities' reels.

197. A THOUSAND TEARS (WILLIAM DAVIS)
Known studio/demo recordings: Power Station, New York 31/1–1/2/80.
198. I WILL BE THE ONE
Known studio/demo recordings: Power Station, New York 16+26/2/80.
199. STRAY BULLET
Known studio/demo recordings: Power Station, New York 24/2/80; 9/3/80; 10/4/80.

Just as *The Ties That Bind* sessions produced a surprising number of songs that have managed to bypass both official archival releases and the more unofficial variety, the February 1980 sessions produced three more mysteries-in-song – all worked on for more than a single session; though only 'I Will Be The One' seems to have ever been under consideration for *Tracks* (see 'Slow Fade'). However, a song called 'William Davis' [#247] would be recorded at the May 1982 *Born In The USA* sessions, suggesting 'A Thousand Tears (William Davis)' may well have received a treatment similar to 'Loose Ends', another *River* reject he recast at the self-same sessions.

200. CADILLAC RANCH
Known studio/demo recordings: Power Station, New York 16/2/80; 9,15+17/3/80; 9+26/4/80. [RI]
First documented performance: Chrysler Arena, Ann Arbor MI 3/10/80.

I guess if it took The Beatles eighty-six takes to get the risible 'Ob-La-Di, Ob-La-Da', the effort expended on this 'homage' to the graveyard of America's car industry can't be considered any more misguided. But when one realizes that Springsteen had already recorded enough strong songs for his own version of *Sandanista!*, one has to wonder what he was thinkin'. And that was before it became a live embarrassment.

XVIII) 201–211. Songs demoed, soundchecked and/or performed October 1980–December 1981:

201. ROBERT FORD

Known studio/demo recordings: Colt's Neck NJ Spring 1981; Colt's Neck NJ January–April 1982; Power Station, New York 27/4/82.

A seventy-five-second fragment on the spring 1981 home demo (bootlegged as *Fistfull of Dollars*) suggests the start of a western ballad: 'Robert Ford and Jesse James were like brothers/ Together they would loot the [mail] trains.' A year later, post-*Nebraska*, he fleshed this earlier notion out to make it about Ford's betrayal of his friend, and the price he paid: 'Robert Ford shot Jesse in the back/ He ran to Maria, but the freedom he gained for his sins/ She said Bobby, oh Bobby what have you done/ And she would not marry him . . . [And] everywhere across the land people came/ To meet the man who shot Jesse James'. The song was presumably inspired by Woody Guthrie's 'Jesse James', which branded Robert Ford 'that dirty little coward' and wondered aloud 'how he feels/ For he ate of Jesse's bread and he slept in Jesse's bed'. Recorded at the *Electric Nebraska* sessions.

202. DANGER ZONE
203. LION'S DEN

Known studio/demo recordings: Colt's Neck NJ April 1981; [#202:] Band rehearsal, Colt's Neck NJ April 1982; [#203:] Hit Factory, New York 25/1/82.
First documented performance [#203]: Palais Omnisport de Paris-Bercy, Paris, France 3/6/99.

The relationship between another tough-guy song demoed in the spring of 1981 ('Man, you're messin' in a danger zone/ Let the girl go home'), and an otherwise undocumented full-blooded gaol song rehearsed with the band in the lead-up to the *Electric Nebraska* sessions is tenuous, but both warn about entering the 'Danger Zone'. Never one to throw away a good song title, he also reused another from the same cassette. 'Lion's Den' then consisted solely of the line, 'Daniel's in the lion's den.' (He presumably already knew (of) the traditional ballad of the same name.) Nine months later it became a riposte to a lioness of his acquaintance: 'At night I hear you out prowling around/ Tearing guys up, scaring 'em down/ Now all that growling's gotta come to an end'. One of the better songs Springsteen gave to Gary US Bonds for the follow-up to *Dedication*, 'Lion's Den' went unused and uncirculated until *Tracks*.

204. FIST FULL OF DOLLARS
205. MY HEART IS AN OPEN BOOK
206. RIDING HORSE
Known studio/demo recordings: Colt's Neck NJ Spring 1981.

Of the songs on the spring 1981 home tape, 'My Heart Is An Open Book' is the most interesting idea left wholly unused. It directly anticipates Elvis Costello's 1982 song, 'Every Day I Write The Book', Springsteen dividing a budding relationship into a series of chapters: 'chapter 1, we're going out, we're having fun . . . chapter 2, there's a story of my love for you . . . chapter 3, it tells you how good our love could be'. 'Riding Horse' also has an interesting premise, a girlfriend 'so tall and fair/ I need a stepladder to run my fingers through her hair/ I'm gonna kill the next guy who asks, how's the weather up there?' – but little else to set the pulses racing.

207. JOHNNY BYE BYE
Known studio/demo recordings: Colt's Neck NJ spring 1981; Power Station, New York 27/4/82; 'Thrill Hill West', Los Angeles ?4/1/83; 9,24/3/83. [TR]
First documented performance: Apollo, Manchester, England 13/5/81.

The legendary *Nebraska* version of 'Johnny Bye Bye' does not exist – the version on the tape he sent Landau was almost certainly a live 1981 take. (When the *Nebraska* tape was backed up in June 1982 in its entirety, alternate takes and all, there was still no 'Johnny Bye Bye'.) For all its significance to the man himself, the song – originally included on the July 1983 sequence for *Born In The USA* – had to be content with being B-side to 'I'm On Fire'; and even then not in its most complete form. The released version omits one verse, recorded in the winter of 1983 – [see discussion in main text pp. 222 and 262].

208. ALL I NEED
Known studio/demo recordings: Colt's Neck NJ Early July 1981.
First documented performance: Brendan Byrne Arena, East Rutherford NJ soundcheck 8/7/81.

Aside from his two 'Elvis' tributes, Springsteen refrained from playing any new songs on the year-long *River* tour; perhaps because he was undecided as to his next step forward. Even the few documented soundchecks show little evidence of a next stage in the songwriting. The one time he did break the trend was during a record-breaking stint at the recently-opened Brendan Byrne Arena, when he turned up with a song he'd just demoed on his home recorder, and ran it down for the band. At his insistence, this soundcheck version was taped by Batlan, presumably as an *aide de memoire*. The song itself, 'All I Need', is a simple testament to the gal he loves, receiving the kind of r&b arrangement he long ago left behind on his own artefacts. This would be no exception, being donated to Gary US Bonds at the earliest opportunity.

209. VIETNAM BLUES
210. LOVE IS A DANGEROUS THING
211. CLUB SOUL CITY

Known studio/demo recordings: Colt's Neck NJ September–December 1981.

The story of Springsteen championing the Vietnam Veterans' cause in the summer of 1981 is well known. As always, he was looking to find a way to put these feelings into song. But the transition from advocate to proselytizer was not a straightforward one. The song he began immediately on his return east, 'Vietnam Blues', merely provided spare parts for 'Shut Out The Light' and 'Born In The USA'. Both 'Club Soul City' and 'Love Is A Dangerous Thing' inhabit more familiar Bruce territory. The fall 1981 demo of 'Club Soul City' is the merest snatch, but by January 1982 it would be a hostage to Bruce's Bondsman, Gary US. Set in the nightclub next door to the Heartbreak Hotel, this is another torch ballad for the losin' kind. 'Love Is A Dangerous Thing' would become one of those potentially-promising songs that instead donated a single line to a Bruce classic (in this case, 'Pink Cadillac').

XIX) 212–226. Songs demoed and recorded for *Nebraska* or Electric *Nebraska*:

212. FADE TO BLACK

Known studio/demo recordings: Colt's Neck NJ July & September–December 1981; January–April 1982; Power Station, New York 11/5/82.

According to Brucebase, the first ruminative elements of 'Fade To Black' were demoed at the same time as 'All I Need' (this version appears on *Lost Masters VII*). A finished version was cut during the May 1982 *Born In The USA* sessions. Quite a journey, raising its own issues, one being how the E Street Band could add a great deal to a song the tenor of which was very much the same emotively bleak landscape as the coeval *Nebraska*. [See discussion in main text p. 233]

213. JOHNNY 99
Known studio/demo recordings: Colt's Neck NJ September–December 1981; Portastudio Sessions, Colt's Neck NJ 17/12/81–3/1/82 [NE]; Power Station, New York 27–28/4/82; 3/5/82.
First documented performance: Civic Arena, St Paul MN 29/6/84.

The first of the 'desperado' songs written for *Nebraska*, predating even the title track, 'Johnny 99' is sung entirely as if Springsteen really *was* walking in a murderer's shoes (the murderer in question being a fictionalized Gary Gilmore – see discussion in main text pp. 237–8).

214. ATLANTIC CITY
Known studio/demo recordings: Colt's Neck NJ September–December 1981; Portastudio Sessions, Colt's Neck NJ 17/12/81–3/1/82 [NE]; Power Station, New York 26-28/4/82.
First documented performance: Civic Arena, St Paul MN 29/6/84.

In the notes to *Nebraska* he sent to Landau, Springsteen wrote, 'This song should probably be done with whole band + really rockin' out.' But, according to Landau, when it came time to record the song electric, 'No way was it as good as what he had goin' on that demo tape.' On the other hand, Clarence Clemons in his autobiography described the band version as 'good . . . more heat'. The fact that they spent three days working on the song in the studio does suggest a determination to render it right.

215. BORN IN THE USA
Known studio/demo recordings: Colt's Neck NJ September–December 1981; Portastudio Sessions, Colt's Neck NJ 17/12/81–3/1/82 [TR]; Power Station, New York 27–28/4/82; 3/5/82. [BITUSA]
First documented performance: The Stone Pony, Asbury Park NJ 8/6/84.

When Springsteen sent the completed 'BITUSA' demo to Landau, he denigrated the initial result (now released on *Tracks*) – 'this song is in very rough shape but is as good as I can get it at the moment' – and envisaged something that 'should be done very hard rockin''. On 27 April 1982 he did indeed rerecord the song in a new electric arrangement which by any criteria qualified as 'very hard rockin'. 'Born In The USA' was the third song recorded for the *Electric Nebraska* (after five takes of 'Johnny Bye Bye'), and was captured in just four takes, two of which were complete (take 4 being marked 'Great!' on a rough-mix reel the following day), before becoming the title track of a wholly independent artefact hewn from more commercial rock.

216. USED CARS

Known studio/demo recordings: Colt's Neck NJ September–December 1981; Portastudio Sessions, Colt's Neck NJ 17/12/81–3/1/82 [NE]; Power Station, New York 30/4/82.

First documented performance: Civic Arena, St Paul MN 29/6/84.

Always conflicted about wealth, Springsteen now wrote an entire song from the vantage point of 'a rich man [who] felt like a poor man inside'. The whole idea of a rock star imagining 'the day the lottery I win' (a horrible circumlocution to retain the rhyme) is an amusing conceit, as are some of the spoken intros in concert: 'When I was a kid, there was only two things I wanted, a pony and a convertible . . . [Me and my sister,] we'd be out in the backyard going "Please, daddy, please." He said, "Well, come on, we'll go down to the car lot." . . . We went down to this car lot, that was called like Big Al's Used Cars, and he had a sign up front that said, "I'd give 'em away, but my wife won't let me.' . . . We'd be looking around and we'd end up coming home in a Rambler – that would break down about three months later.'

217. DOWNBOUND TRAIN

Known studio/demo recordings: Colt's Neck NJ September–December 1981; Portastudio Sessions, Colt's Neck NJ 17/12/81–3/1/82; Power Station, New York 27–28/4/82; 3, 5–6/5/82 [BITUSA]; ?'Thrill Hill West', Los Angeles 3/2/83.

First documented performance: Civic Arena, St Paul MN 2/7/84.

One of the highlights of the original 14-track *Nebraska* demo tape. Also one of just three songs from the *Electric Nebraska* sessions that worked well enough in its electric guise to be bumped from the acoustic album. The electric version affirmed how such remorseless, downbound songs could still benefit from the full-on E Street Band heat treatment.

218. THE LOSIN' KIND
Known studio/demo recordings: Colt's Neck NJ September–December 1981; Portastudio Sessions, Colt's Neck NJ 17/12/81–3/1/82; Power Station, New York 30/4/82; 'Thrill Hill West', LA 12/3/83.

The omission of 'Losin' Kind' from both *Nebraska* and *Tracks* makes it the one song from that original demo-tape still unreleased *in any form*. The fact that he returned to it in March 1983 suggests he hadn't entirely decided to discard it, but its absence from any of the *Tracks* compilation reels is baffling. A notable loser in the *Nebraska/BITUSA* lottery.

219. NEBRASKA
Known studio/demo recordings: Portastudio Sessions, Colt's Neck NJ 17/12/81–3/1/82 [NE]; Power Station, New York 27–28, 30/4/82.
First documented performance: Civic Arena, St Paul MN 1/7/84.

"There was something about ['Nebraska'] that was the centre of the record, but I couldn't really say specifically what it was, outside of the fact that I'd read something that moved me . . . I think in my own life I had reached where it felt like I was teetering on this void. I felt a deep sense of isolation, and that led me to those characters and to those stories . . . I was at a place where I could start to really feel that price . . . for not sorting through the issues that make up your emotional life." – Bruce Springsteen, 1999. [See discussion in main text pp. 235–36]

220. OPEN ALL NIGHT
Known studio/demo recordings: Colt's Neck NJ spring 1981; Portastudio Sessions, Colt's Neck NJ 17/12/81–3/1/82 [NE]; Power Station, New York 27/4/82.
First documented performance: Stone Pony, Asbury Park NJ 3/10/82.

An update of 'Drive All Night', the narrator of 'Open All Night' remains sure 'she' will be waiting, no matter how long it takes him to negotiate the New Jersey Turnpike: 'Sit tight, little mama, I'm comin' 'round/ I got three more hours but I'm coverin' ground'. The idea of recrafting 'Living on the Edge of the World' as 'Wanda' (the working title for 'Open All Night') dated to April 1981, when it first appeared on some home demos.

221. MANSION ON THE HILL

Known studio / demo recordings: Portastudio Sessions, Colt's Neck NJ 17/12/81–3/1/82 [NE]; Power Station, New York 27, 28+30/4/82.

First documented performance: Civic Arena, St Paul MN 29/6/84.

The subtext throughout this sprightly song remains, 'First the limousine, then the big mansions on the hill – I've always been suspicious of the whole [fame] package deal'. Suspicious mind or not, the song refuses to resolve whether the narrator watching the cars rushing 'home from the mill' is standing outside that mansion on the hill. One of the *Nebraska* songs that worked especially well live, hence presumably why he felt like playing it at The Apollo in 2012.

222. PINK CADILLAC

Known studio / demo recordings: Portastudio Sessions, Colt's Neck NJ 17/12/81–3/1/82; The Hit Factory, New York 31/5/83. [TR]

First documented performance: Civic Arena, St Paul MN 1/7/84.

The only song from the acoustic *Nebraska* ignored at the electric sessions three months later, 'Pink Cadillac' would nonetheless effortlessly achieve the transition few of its kith and kin could, Springsteen reviving this deft slice of rockabilly heaven during the summer 1983 E Street sessions.

223. STATE TROOPER

Known studio / demo recordings: Portastudio Sessions, Colt's Neck NJ 17/12/81–3/1/82. [NE]

First documented performance: Civic Center, Hartford CT 8/9/84.

'I dreamed this one up comin' back from New York one night. I don't know if it's even really a song or not . . . It's kinda weird.' – Springsteen's description of 'State Trooper' in his notes to *Nebraska*, January 1982.

224. HIGHWAY PATROLMAN

Known studio / demo recordings: Portastudio Sessions, Colt's Neck NJ 17/12/81–3/1/82 [NE]; Power Station, New York 30/4/82.

First documented performance: Civic Arena, St Paul MN 29/6/84.

Prefacing 'State Trooper' on *Nebraska*, 'Highway Patrolman' was written from the perspective of a cop who lets a fugitive get away because the man in question is his brother, Frankie. Though not someone who had an older brother to 'catch him when he's strayin'', Springsteen's vantage point is very much that of someone with a strong family bond. Not surprisingly, it also appealed to Johnny Cash, who the following year covered it in his trademark gravel as a way of announcing *Johnny 99*.

225. REASON TO BELIEVE
Known studio/demo recordings: Portastudio Sessions, Colt's Neck NJ 17/12/81–3/1/82 [NE]; Band rehearsal, Colt's Neck NJ April 1982; Power Station, New York 27–28/4/82.
First documented performance: Civic Arena, St Paul MN 1/7/84.

A recently emerged band rehearsal preceding the *Electric Nebraska* sessions suggests Springsteen intended to give 'Reason To Believe' a more rockabilly arrangement, complete with flickering guitar licks. Which is not the arrangement it received on the *Born In The USA* tour. The 1984 live arrangement did little more than superimpose the E Street Band on the acoustic arrangement (a complaint which could be made for a few *Nebraska* tracks). In fact, one might argue the first really successful full-band arrangement was not until the 2008 *Magic* shows, when a wacky hillbilly hoedown showed faith and reason really could be bedfellows. [See discussion in main text p. 244]
Note: In his note to Landau, Springsteen refers to two versions of this song, the second of which has an extra verse. The version on the album is a first take, so presumably a whole verse was cut.

226. CHILD BRIDE
Known studio/demo recordings: Portastudio Sessions, Colt's Neck NJ 17/12/81–3/1/82.
as WORKING ON THE HIGHWAY
Known studio/demo recordings: Band rehearsal, Colt's Neck NJ April 1982; Power Station, New York 30/4/82; 6/5/82. [BITUSA]
First documented performance: Civic Arena, St Paul MN 29/6/84.

The four months separating the last of the *Nebraska* sessions from its stillborn electric equivalent were productive ones for Springsteen. He wrote and recorded a number of songs for Gary US Bonds and Donna Summer, and continued to demo new material at his home studio (the thirteen tracks on *Lost Masters X* possibly represent the tip of an audio iceberg). But the fifteen songs he had just demoed in January went largely untouched – save for 'Child Bride', the last track recorded, a song 'in which the protagonist violates the Mann act and is left to ponder his fate'. He soon set to work shifting gear, lopping off the entire original ending of the song and giving it a quite different sensibility, before returning it to the side of the road – working on a chain-gang (see discussion in main text p. 243).

XX) 227–243. Other songs demoed January–April 1982:

227. COVER ME

Known studio/demo recordings: Hit Factory, New York 25/1/82; Power Station, New York 12/5/82. [BITUSA]

First documented performance: Civic Arena, St Paul MN 2/7/84.

Three weeks to the day after sequencing the original 14-track *Nebraska* cassette, Springsteen returned to making rock music. Still producing a bewildering number of songs that were surplus to current requirements, he had written this groovy pop song specifically for Donna Summer. But when Jon Landau heard the finished track, it was 'Hungry Heart' all over again. He insisted his employer give the lady something else, this one was a keeper. Springsteen thought not. It would take Landau some two years to convince him otherwise. During this time 'Cover Me' would be reworked at the May 1982 *Born In The USA* sessions (over nine takes), but still did not make the 'final' 1982 *BITUSA* sequence. Nor would it make 1983's equivalent. But Landau got his way in the end.

228. WORKIN' ON IT

Known studio/demo recordings: Hit Factory, New York 25/1/82.

229. OUT OF WORK

230. HOLD ON

231. LOVE'S ON THE LINE

232. SAVIN' UP

Known studio/demo recordings: Hit Factory, New York ?25[-??]/1/82 and/or Hit Factory, NY 23/2/82 .

Leaving aside 'Cover Me' and 'Lion's Den', the one other song definitely recorded on that January day, logged as 'Workin' On It', remains uncirculated. But at least four more songs were recorded at this time for the use of Gary US Bonds, each probably recorded with a Springsteen guide vocal and overdubbed by Bonds later. The resultant album, *On The Line*, may have been top-heavy with Springsteen originals, seven in all, but two were older songs ('Angelyne' and 'Rendezvous'). 'Lion's Den' and 'Savin' Up' would be deemed surplus to requirements, the latter cropping up instead on Clarence Clemons' 1983 debut LP.

233. PROTECTION
Known studio/demo recordings: The Hit Factory, New York 23/2/82.

This one was written to order – a replacement order – after 'Cover Me' never left the office. Given its recipient, disco queen Donna Summer, and the premise (he needs protection from her love although she is his obsession), the resultant song shouldn't be as good as it is. According to Summer, he even 'came to my house in Los Angeles for several days to get it done'. He also contributed backing vocals and guitar to her perfectly respectable rendition. Overlooked for *Tracks*, it was almost a surprise inclusion on *The Essential Bruce Springsteen* bonus 'rarities' disc, but as of now it's just one more lost master from a period when two years of studio time equated to a single album.

234. TRUE LOVE IS HARD TO COME BY
Known studio/demo recordings: Colt's Neck NJ January–April 1982; Hit Factory, New York 2/6/83.

Of the thirteen songs on the *Lost Masters X* demo tape, recorded sometime in early 1982 (suggesting the Portastudio used on *Nebraska* was continuing to earn its keep), over half would be attempted at E Street Band sessions that spring. But 'True Love Is Hard To Come By', which he made three attempts to whip into shape at home, would not receive the full E Street treatment until June 1983. Even then, it merely served as a precursor to 'Janey Don't You Lose Heart', to which it would donate the clichéd couplet, 'Till the sun is torn from the sky / Till every river, baby, it runs dry'. Shortlisted for *Tracks*.

235. JAMES LINCOLN DEER
Known studio/demo recordings: Colt's Neck NJ January–April 1982; 'Thrill Hill West', Los Angeles 20/1/83; 15, 17/2/83; 12/3/83.

Another song demoed in the winter of 1982, only to be left out in the rain for a full year. Like 'True Love Is Hard To Come By', 'James Lincoln Deer' was then reworked, becoming 'Richfield Whistle' (save for one couplet, 'Man said, "These jobs are goin' boys/ And they ain't comin' back"', he reapplied to 'My Hometown'). Given its thematic proximity and empathic similarity to much of *Nebraska*, it is perhaps surprising he returned to the self-same song in the winter of 1983, when hard at work on a set of eight-track demos that threatened to become something grander. None of those versions recorded shortly before its transition into 'Richfield Whistle' circulate, but he clearly rated the song, working on it for at least four sessions.

236. I NEED YOU
237. RULED BY THE GUN
Known studio/demo recordings: Colt's Neck NJ January–April 1982.

Of the songs on *Lost Masters X* that did *not* make it to band rehearsals, let alone pukka sessions, 'I Need You' takes a familiar Springsteen idea and spins it out to two minutes: 'I don't need no money, I don't need you to drive me around/ I don't need no pretty face cause that just gets me down/ I need you'. Elsewhere, he extends his repertoire to songs about cars, girls *and* guns; even if those who wield them seem determined to live down Raymond Chandler's observation, 'So many guns, so few brains'. 'Ruled By The Gun', a distant cousin of 'Under The Gun', may conceivably have evolved into 'Gun In Every Home', an uncirculated track cut that May, though it contains no such line.

238. YOUR LOVE IS ALL AROUND ME
Known studio/demo recordings: Colt's Neck NJ January–April 1982; Band rehearsal, Colt's Neck NJ April 1982; Power Station, New York ?10/5/82.

Such a cracking song was bound to benefit from some E Street magic, but until recently no such beast had emerged. Thankfully, the April rehearsal tape includes a full band version, and the song has clearly been worked on since it was home-demoed. A middle eight has been acquired, for starters. As such, it always seemed unlikely the song wasn't at least run through at the band sessions in May. Sure enough, a two-inch tape of the song, undated but on the same reel as 'Wages of Sin' (so probably recorded the same day – May 10), was logged by Sony and, frankly, requires immediate excavation for the *Born In Nebraska* boxed-set. [See discussion in main text p. 246]

239. WAGES OF SIN

Known studio/demo recordings: Colt's Neck NJ January–April 1982; Power Station, New York 10/5/82. [TR]

The refrain remains, 'Wages of sin, we keep paying for the sins we've done,' from the first demo to its May studio debut, even if initially the man in the song doesn't 'know what it is I've done'. What is absent from the demo is the memory dredged up from some therapy session, providing the song's summation when recorded in May: 'I remember when I was a little boy out where the cottonwoods grow tall/ Trying to make it home through the forest before the darkness falls/ Baby, all the sounds I heard, even if they weren't real/I was running down that broken path with the devil snapping at my heels.' These lines convinced him he should address those feelings in a more personal song. The glorious result was 'My Father's House'.

240. FOLLOW THAT DREAM

First documented performance: Palais des Sports, Paris, France 19/4/81.

241. BABY I'M SO COLD

Known studio/demo recordings: Colt's Neck NJ January-April 1982; Band rehearsal, Colt's Neck NJ April 1982; Power Station, New York 11/5/82.

as FOLLOW THAT DREAM MK.2

Known studio/demo recordings: 'Thrill Hill West', Los Angeles 29–30/1/83; 7-8, 17/2/83.

Conceived before he had decided what shape 'Johnny Bye Bye' might take, 'Follow That Dream' held its own throughout the spring/summer 1981 shows. But rather than being demoed in the months either side of *Nebraska*, it became – with a little help from 'Loose Ends' – 'Baby I'm So Cold', a superior all-original. So what then prompted him to demo 'Follow That Dream' in the winter of 1983, when he spent five whole days working on the song in his new Los Angeles home? Maybe he had arrived at a more positive place. He even added a more positive middle verse: 'Now I've been searching for a heart that's free/ Searching for someone to search with me/ I need a love, a love I can trust/ Together we'll search for the things that come to us'. That version was positioned mid-point on side two of the July 1983 *BITUSA* sequence.

242. THE BIG PAYBACK

Known studio/demo recordings: ?Colt's Neck NJ January–April 1982. [TE]

According to Springsteen's 2003 *Essential* notes, 'The Big Payback' was 'cut at home shortly after the *Nebraska* album'. Presumably it therefore shares a berth with the winter 1982 demos, also absent from the Sony logs. But 'shortly after' could cover a multitude of sins, especially as the song did not appear until 1983.

243. GLORY DAYS

Known studio/demo recordings: Colt's Neck NJ January–April 1982; Band rehearsal, Colt's Neck NJ April 1982; Power Station, New York 5/5/82. [BITUSA]
First documented performance: The Stone Pony, Asbury Park NJ 8/6/84.

The downbeat message of 'Glory Days' was partly ameliorated by the judicious removal of a verse from the released version, recalling when his father 'was working at the Metuchen Ford plant assembly line/ Now he just sits on a stool down at the Legion Hall, but I can tell what's on his mind'. The song would go on to become almost vaudevillian in concert, and a long way removed from its genesis, whether that was at a roadside bar or in a cinema seat. [See discussion in main text p. 253]

XXII) 244–255, 98a, 80a, 256. Other songs recorded during *Electric Nebraska* sessions April 1982 & *Born In The USA* May 1982 sessions:

244. TV MOVIE

Known studio/demo recordings: Band rehearsal, Colt's Neck NJ April 1982; The Hit Factory, New York 13/6/83. [TR]

More light-hearted than 'Johnny Bye Bye' or 'Follow That Dream', 'TV Movie' was presumably Bruce's response to John Carpenter's 1979 biopic of Elvis, with Kurt Russell playing the young firebrand. Another song he rehearsed in April 1982 but did not record for another fourteen months, this rapier-thrust at reality TV has the fictional wife of the rock star turning over in bed to tell him 'my life would be immortalized/ not in some major motion picture/ or great American novel ... / No, they're gonna make a TV movie out of me.' Once again, a song which pricked his own ego would be deemed too lightweight even for B-side status. But not *Tracks*.

245. ON THE PROWL
Known studio/demo recordings: Power Station, New York 30/4/82.
First documented performance: The Stone Pony, Asbury Park NJ 8/8/82 [3/10/82].

Because of the timing of the two live performances, it has long been assumed that this song dated from summer 1982, when he was hanging out with all those Jersey girls. But it had already been recorded the previous spring, at the last of the *Electric Nebraska* sessions; a first-person narrative where I, for once, was not another. [See discussion in main text pp. 249–50]

246. WILLIAM DAVIS
Known studio/demo recordings: Power Station, New York 27–28/4/82.
247. GUN IN EVERY HOME
Known studio/demo recordings: Power Station, New York 30/4/82; 6/5/82.
248. COMMON GROUND (STAY HUNGRY)
Known studio/demo recordings: Power Station, New York 11/5/82.

Three songs from those April/May 1982 sessions which remain uncirculated, though both 'William Davis' and 'Gun In Every Home' were evidently songs Springsteen took seriously enough to record at least twice. 'Common Ground' was ultimately replaced by 'This Hard Land' (the 'stay hungry' motif, 'Stay hard, stay hungry, stay alive if you can', would re-emerge there). #246 is probably related to an earlier *River* outtake, 'A Thousand Tears (William Davis)' – see #197; while 'A Gun In Every Home' may be a synthesis of 'gun'-song ideas demoed in the past year. It warranted both an *Electric Nebraska* and a *BITUSA* outing. 'Common Ground' was cut alongside 'Johnny Bye Bye' and 'Baby I'm So Cold' on what sounds like a dark day at the Power Station. But he gave it up when compiling *Tracks*, for which it was shortlisted.

249. MURDER INCORPORATED
Known studio/demo recordings: Power Station, New York 3–4/5/82. [GH]
First documented performance: Tramps, New York 21/2/95.

With 'Born In The USA' already in the can, he recorded this snarling spit at the home of the brave next. But when that 5 July 1982 sequence became another 'lost' album, it would be left to the bootleggers to reclaim the song as the title track of their own alternate *BITUSA*, dubbed *Murder Incorporated*. The 1999 reunion finally gave him – and a reinvigorated E Street Band – the opportunity to make it an integral part of the live set, where it had belonged all along; and where it nightly proved 'you can't compete with murder incorporated'.

250. MY LOVE WILL NOT LET YOU DOWN

Known studio/demo recordings: Power Station, New York 5–7/5/82. [TR]
First documented performance: Convention Hall, Asbury Park NJ 18/3/99.

'When we first got [back] together [in 1999], the first thing we did was play a lot of unfamiliar material, a lot of things from *Tracks* ... We picked things off Tracks that weren't particularly familiar, like a song like 'My Love Will Not Let You Down'. That should have been on the *Born In The USA* record; I don't know why it got left off. It was one of those things we pulled out in the first rehearsal and went, "Whoa!"' Bruce Springsteen, 2001.

251. STOP THE WAR

Known studio/demo recordings: Band rehearsal, Colt's Neck NJ April 1982; Power Station, New York 5–6/5/82.

One imagines that the man who in 1985 covered Edwin Starr's 'War' also knew his 1970 follow-up single, 'Stop The War Now', a minor hit in its own right. But Springsteen's 'Stop The War', the studio version of which remains uncirculated, turns out to be about marital war, as evidenced by the April band rehearsal. In fact, he begs her to 'tell me what we're fighting for, I don't care anymore/ I just wanna stop the war.' A replacement of sorts for 'Cover Me', it allowed every element of the E Street Band to return fire.

252. A GOOD MAN IS HARD TO FIND (PITTSBURGH)

Known studio/demo recordings: Band rehearsal, Colt's Neck NJ April 1982; Power Station, New York 5–6/5/82. [TR]

Rehearsed in the days/week leading up to the *Electric Nebraska* sessions, this plaintive ballad would certainly have fit on the same album as 'Fade To Black' and 'Baby I'm So Cold', provided every copy included a free set of razor blades. Instead, the song was attempted at the *BITUSA* sessions in May, where its country-rock arrangement struck a slightly discordant note. Although it was eventually included on

Tracks, placed between two *River* outtakes, it never quite fits. Only ever recorded with full band backing, this always seemed more suited to an acoustic guise. Much to fans' delight, it finally got one on the night in May 2005 when Springsteen delivered a gripping solo rendition at a show in St Paul, Minnesota.

253. I'M ON FIRE
Known studio/demo recordings: ? Hit Factory, New York January 1982; Power Station, New York 11/5/82. [BITUSA]
First documented performance: Civic Arena, St Paul MN 29/6/84.

This song is rumoured to have been cut at the Hit Factory in January 1982, at the same session as 'Cover Me'. But if so, it was the May Power Station take which got the vote for the 1982 *BITUSA* sequence. Voted off in 1983, it was back on in 1984, when it also received a promo video that proved Springsteen was not so much a method actor as an actor with no method. He wisely stuck to the day job.

254. I'M GOING DOWN
Known studio/demo recordings: Power Station, New York 12–13/5/82. [BITUSA]
First documented performance: Rosemont Horizon, Rosemont IL 17/8/84.

An end-of-tether discourse, its original title 'Down, Down, Down' said it best. Recorded in a hurry (over ten takes) on the 13th with its own punch-drunk arrangement, this was another song on which Springsteen allowed the band to vamp away, only to curtail them in the final mix. Side-one closer on the original 1982 sequence, it was only a last-minute addition to the 1984 album.

255. THIS HARD LAND
Known studio/demo recordings: Power Station, New York 11, 13 –14/5/82; 'Thrill Hill West', Los Angeles 3+15/2/83. [TR]
First documented performance: Tramps, New York 21/2/95.
While 'This Hard Land' still has its champions among fans, it proved beyond any shadow of doubt that the world had no need for a second (or third) Woody in 1982. If he wisely gave the song a hearty shove sideways after the 1983 *BITUSA* sessions – though only after trying it solo at the winter 1983 home sessions – he returned to it in 1995, as he again fell under the spell of the creator of 'Tom Joad'. This time he re-recorded it in a faithful but inferior arrangement and released it alongside 'Murder Incorporated' (and two minor new songs) on a bogus *Greatest*

Hits. In the album notes, Springsteen claimed the song contained one of his favourite final verses. A little too *Brokeback Mountain* for my taste, I'm afraid.

98a. DARLINGTON COUNTY MK.2
Known studio/demo recordings: Band rehearsal, Colt's Neck NJ April 1982; Power Station, New York 13/5/82. [BITUSA]
First documented performance: The Stone Pony, Asbury Park NJ 8/6/84.
80a. FRANKIE MK.2.
Known studio/demo recordings: Power Station, New York 14/5/82. [TR]
First documented performance: Continental Arena, East Rutherford NJ 9/8/99.

Though there is no circulating 1977 take of 'Darlington County' with which to compare the 1982 retake, all indications are that the song survived pretty much intact. It may even have been cut in a single take. What appears to be a slightly longer, slower take on *Lost Masters XIX* is actually the released version before vocal overdubs, fixed-up intro, and the use of varispeed to speed the track up. The April rehearsal confirms they had already given the song a full service before it left garageland. As for the protagonists in the song, they remained as revved up and randy, reckless and brain-dead as five years earlier. Though both the 1982 'Frankie' and 'Darlington County' would make the 1982 sequence for *BITUSA*, only the latter would make the 'final' version . 'Frankie' would finally see the light of day on *Tracks*, where it was the *BITUSA* version that was served up. Which was also the case when it was restored to live duties the year of the E Street reunion tour. [see discussion in the main text p. 256]

256. MY FATHER'S HOUSE
Known studio/demo recordings: Colt's Neck NJ 25/5/82. [NE]
First documented performance: CNE Grandstand, Toronto ON 26/7/84.

Eleven days after Springsteen finished work on an E Street Band album, he again pulled out the Portastudio and cut two versions of 'My Father's House' on separate cassettes. A week later, he devised the final *Nebraska* sequence, with 'My Father's House' as a prelude to 'Reason To Believe'. A synthesizer overdub, its one concession to production values, was an unnecessary embellishment; though it was less of an intrusion than that made by the E Streeters on the five occasions 'My Father's House' graced the live *BITUSA* set. All it needed was an honest man, an attentive audience and an investment in the song's meaning for this starkly personal song to shine. [See discussion in main text pp. 257–8]

XXIII) 257 –264. Songs demoed January –April 1983:

257. THE KLANSMAN

Known studio/demo recordings: 'Thrill Hill West', Los Angeles ?4/1/83; 10/3/83.

258. SEVEN TEARS

Known studio/demo recordings: 'Thrill Hill West', Los Angeles ?4/1/83; 15/2/83.

According to the Sony logs, Springsteen resumed recording solo material for an as-yet-undefined successor to *Nebraska* on January 18, 1983. However, *Lost Masters XVI* includes a four-song tape from these sessions – featuring 'The Klansman', 'Seven Tears', 'Don't Back Down' and 'Johnny Bye Bye' – dated January 4. If correct, all four songs would feature again at the sessions. But an error in dating seems likelier. As it is, the only circulating versions of 'The Klansman' and 'Seven Tears' are on said bootleg CD. Together they provide an apposite indication of the type of song he was looking to record. If 'The Klansman' is Bruce channelling Woody (see discussion in main text pp. 263–64), 'Seven Tears' tells the strange story of a man whose wife left after seven years, so he had seven tears tattooed on his face. Nicely executed, it has some delightful double-tracked vocals that suggest someone getting the hang of this home-studio lark.

259. DELIVERY MAN

Known studio/demo recordings: 'Thrill Hill West', Los Angeles January 1983.

An interesting little number. And the only song on the two volumes of *Lost Masters* culled from these 1983 solo sessions that is absent from the Sony logs. In fact, the sound is quite distinct from that of the other songs demoed, with the bass/drum track more integrated, suggesting it may come from a stand-alone session. The track itself, another movie-short-in-song, is really quite enjoyable. Set to a rough-hewn rockabilly riff and cut in two takes, it tells the story of a delivery man transporting some chickens from his Pa's farm to market/slaughterhouse.

260. BETTY JEAN

Known studio/demo recordings: 'Thrill Hill West', Los Angeles 20/1/83.

A close cousin of 'Delivery Man', 'Betty Jean' lists the various reasons the singer has reached the conclusion, 'Honey, you're cute, but you sure are mean'. Unfortunately, Alan Vega had already released his own rockabilly album and Bruce could think of no one else to whom he could donate this song.

261. ONE LOVE
Known studio/demo recordings: 'Thrill Hill West', Los Angeles 19/1/83.
262. LITTLE GIRL (LIKE YOU)
Known studio/demo recordings: 'Thrill Hill West', Los Angeles 20/1/83.

These two tracks – strictly B-side fare – were recorded at three consecutive days of home sessions in January, which produced nine tracks. A list made that winter does indeed suggest he intended to use some of the better tracks as potential single B-sides. The album they were intended to 'promote' was still the 1982 *BITUSA* – with a single winter 1983 addition, 'Johnny Bye Bye'.

263. I DON'T CARE
264. THE MONEY WE DIDN'T MAKE
Known studio/demo recordings: 'Thrill Hill West', Los Angeles 15/2/83.
265. JOHNNY GO DOWN
Known studio/demo recordings: 'Thrill Hill West', Los Angeles 9,12/3/83.

As already stated, not all of Batlan's tapes passed to the pair who issued the *Lost Masters* series. A reclusive New York collector purchased most of the paper goods and a healthy portion of the tapes (including, apparently, elements of the *Electric Nebraska*). He almost certainly has more from these solo sessions. Certainly, the Sony logs indicate at least three songs recorded that have not passed into circulation. 'I Don't Care' and 'The Money We Didn't Make' appear on a February 24-track 'mix' tape that also includes a solo version of 'This Hard Land' and an (alternate?) take of 'Seven Tears'. 'Johnny Go Down' provides a prelude to the 'cricket' version of 'Johnny Bye Bye' found on *Lost Masters XVI*. Initially entitled 'Johnny Cool Down', it is marked 'new idea' on the March 9 reel, and is clearly *not* 'Johnny Bye Bye'. It ended up on a 24-track 'mix' tape with three other songs, 'Don't Back Down', 'Jim Deer' (i.e. 'James Lincoln Deer') and 'Losin' Kind' (presumably a 1983 reworking), and in 1993 was copied to the pre-*Tracks* rarities reels.

XXIV) 266–275 Songs demoed acoustically, then recorded w/ band January–June 1983:

266. SUGARLAND
Known studio/demo recordings: 'Thrill Hill West', Los Angeles 18–19, 30/1/83; 7–8,14,17/2/83; The Hit Factory, New York [25/5/83; ?1/12/83.]
First documented performance: Hilton Coliseum, Ames, Ia. 16/11/84.

According to the Sony logs, the 'Thrill Hill West' (i.e. Springsteen's LA home) solo sessions ran from January to late April 1983 and, aside from the nine songs above (#257 –265) and a handful of songs written earlier which he re-recorded, he would tape ten more songs that received E Street embellishment later in the spring. Of these ten, four would feature on the 26–27 July 1983 *BITUSA* sequence in their Thrill Hill West guise, two others would appear gussied up by the boys, and four would remain under wraps. 'Sugarland', the track he worked on hardest, was assigned opening slot on side two of that 'album'. That version clocked in at 2:55, so it could be any of the five versions in circulation, all solo. The fourteen takes supposedly recorded the same day as 'Light of Day' (May 25) probably merely applied E Street embellishment to one of these. After all, the song had already gone through enough style changes to fill an album – from Cajun to country to rockabilly – but the almost bebop version on *Lost Masters XVII* would for now get my vote.

267. MY HOMETOWN
Known studio/demo recordings: 'Thrill Hill West', Los Angeles 29–30/1/83; 9, 17/2/83; The Hit Factory, New York 29/6/83. [BITUSA]
First documented performance: The Stone Pony, Asbury Park NJ 8/6/84.

The recording of 'My Hometown' that made Springsteen's 1984 multi-platinum platter seems to have been a last-minute decision, the result of spending one final session in late June 1983 seeing if the E Street Band could embellish his latest hometown vision. They could, and did, cutting the song in four takes. The third was preferred, after they trimmed some of the fat off the arrangement (according to the log, each of the first two takes ran over six minutes). An obvious album-closer, it was initially sandwiched between 'Follow That Dream' and 'Glory Days'.

268. BODY AND SOUL

Known studio/demo recordings: 'Thrill Hill West', Los Angeles 20/1/83; The Hit Factory, New York 25/5/83; 2/6/83; 29/11/83.

A song which repeatedly crops up during the 1983 session logs, both solo and with the full E Street band, 'Body and Soul' has yet to see the light of day, even in the solo guise in which it was first recorded.

269. DON'T BACK DOWN (ON OUR LOVE)

Known studio/demo recordings: 'Thrill Hill West', Los Angeles 4,18,20/1/83; 8–10,14–15/2/83; 10,12/3/83; The Hit Factory, New York 15/6/83.

'Don't Back Down' may not be the best song demoed that winter, but Springsteen refused to back down or give up on the song, which features on *Lost Masters* in no fewer than eleven distinct incarnations, only one of which (take 5) is a false start. The version recorded the same day as 'The Klansman', March 10, slower than most of the others and with a synthesizer washing gently over it, would perhaps have been best equipped to be a B-side. But he didn't linger long with it at the Hit Factory sessions, cutting a single take at the 'Cynthia' session.

270. COUNTY FAIR

Known studio/demo recordings: 'Thrill Hill West', Los Angeles 24/3/83; The Hit Factory, New York 23/5/83. [TE]

First documented performance: Performing Arts Center, Buffalo NY 20/9/03.

'County Fair' was one memory he carried with him from March, cutting it at the Hit Factory the first session in May, its brooding arrangement anticipating a number of live *Nebraska* arrangements. But when he decided it warranted being included on a 'rarities' disc accompanying the otherwise-pointless *Essential Bruce Springsteen*, it was the acoustic version cut in California he chose. On its live debut on the 2003 tour he got a little help from the one E Streeter who seemed truly comfortable busking at this familiar fairground, Danny Federici.

271. FUGITIVE'S DREAM

Known studio/demo recordings: 'Thrill Hill West', Los Angeles 20/1/83; 24/3/83.

as.........

272. UNSATISFIED HEART.

Known studio/demo recordings: 'Thrill Hill West', Los Angeles 24/3/83; 16/4/83; The Hit Factory, New York 13/6/83.

Without knowing which of the above versions are on *Lost Masters XVI* and *XVII*, there is a distinct possibility that the transition from 'Fugitive's Dream' to 'Unsatisfied Heart' occurred *between takes* on March 24. It is some change – even if the gut-wrenching version of 'Fugitive's Dream' on *Lost Masters XVI* (sequenced after the January 19 'Shut Out The Light') does come from the January 20 session. Whereas 'Fugitive's Dream' tells its straightforward narrative at a funereal pace, reflecting the heavy burden the fugitive is carrying, 'Unsatisfied Heart' interjects a nagging chorus, 'Can you live with an unsatisfied heart?'. He was convinced enough of the latter's merits to look at it again at the Hit Factory sessions, when a single 5.38 take served to suffice.

273. CYNTHIA

Known studio/demo recordings: 'Thrill Hill West;, Los Angeles 20–21/4/83; The Hit Factory, New York 15/6/83. [TR]

First documented performance: Giants Stadium, East Rutherford NJ 31/8/03.

The E Street Band performance finally nailed this song's sorry ass five months after Springsteen recorded it rockabilly-style on a set of homesick demos. If the band wondered what they were bringing to the majority of these countryesque, character-driven songs their boss brought back from the land of plenty, 'Cynthia' temporarily released them from such cares. Cut the same day as 'Stand On It', in three takes of which two were complete, the song seemed a cert for the next album, appearing after the title track on the 1983 *BITUSA* sequence. But by 1984 it was another afterthought. However, Springsteen recorded a song of the same name the day he cut 'The Ghost of Tom Joad' (May 23, 1995).. Finally, the E Street Band got to take her out on the road in 2003, where she surely belonged.

274. RICHFIELD WHISTLE

Known studio/demo recordings: 'Thrill Hill West', Los Angeles 23/4/83; The Hit Factory, New York [27/5/83; 10/6/83.]

The only circulating version of 'Richfield Whistle' is an eight-track demo from April. Introducing himself as James Lucas, he is James Lincoln Deer in disguise. And as such, an album too late. The song also seems to have been subsequently tackled with the E Street Band, unless it was merely subjected to overdubs on the two Hit Factory dates.

275. SHUT OUT THE LIGHTS
Known studio/demo recordings: 'Thrill Hill West', Los Angeles 19/1/83 [TR]; The Hit Factory, New York [23+27/5/83.]
First documented performance: Coliseum Arena, Oakland CA 22/10/84.

Nothing quite like 'Shut Out The Lights' had been attempted to date by Springsteen, who missed a trick when he removed this one from *BITUSA*, a decision he thought he'd partly rectified when he placed it on the rear of the 'Born In The USA' 45. But this was not the sixties – there were no double A-sides. Sharing the same album, the message would have been unambiguous: Viet-Vets need more peace, love and understanding. [See discussion in main text p. 264]
Note: Though the song was worked on at the first and third Hit Factory sessions in May, this was probably the violin overdub by Soozie Tyrell used on the released version.

XXV) 276 –286 Other songs recorded w/ E Street Band May–June 1983:

276. GONE GONE GONE
Known studio/demo recordings: The Hit Factory, New York 25/5/83; 31/5/83. as SEEDS
First documented performance: Wembley Stadium, London, England 3/7/85.

'Gone Gone Gone' was one song tackled a couple of times at the summer 1983 Hit Factory sessions. Assuming – as I think we can – that Bruce hadn't developed a proclivity for Everly Bros. covers, the title surely came from the final line of said song, 'Movin' on, movin' on, it's gone, gone, it's all gone'. If so, it confirms that one of the stand-out songs on the *BITUSA* tour *was* recorded in the studio. Surprisingly – given that the song was still being performed in 2009 – Springsteen never okayed the studio take's release. It appears he actually rated the overwrought version from the October 1985 LA Coliseum shows; by which time the true spirit of the song was, well, gone, gone, gone.

277. KING'S HIGHWAY
Known studio/demo recordings: The Hit Factory, New York 23–24/5/83.

278. INVITATION TO YOUR PARTY
Known studio/demo recordings: The Hit Factory, New York 31/5/83.
279. BAD BOY
Known studio/demo recordings: The Hit Factory, New York 2/6/83.

Of these three uncirculated outtakes from the summer 1983 sessions, 'King's Highway' is probably the one which would excite fans the most. A feature of two separate nineties 'rarities' compilations, from which most of *Tracks* would be compiled – one from 1993, the other November 1997 – the song probably takes its title from the traditional robber's song, 'Wild and Wicked Youth'. It required seven takes on days one and two at the Hit Factory. 'Invitation To Your Party' received at least two takes of its own, one logged as 'fast'. 'Bad Boy' remains for now merely a title on a tape box.

280. JUST AROUND THE CORNER TO THE LIGHT OF DAY
Known studio/demo recordings: The Hit Factory, New York 25/5/83.
First documented performance: The Stone Pony, Asbury Park NJ 12/4/87.

'['Light of Day'] is just a pretty generic rock song, but it ends up being a little more than that because of the context. It's ended up ending the show. Partly because it gives itself over to shtick very easily! [Laughs] It's so basic that you can do anything with it. Start it. Stop it. Do all kinds of routines inside it. It's one of those all-purpose pieces of material' – Bruce Springsteen, 2001.

281. DROP ON DOWN & COVER ME
Known studio/demo recordings: The Hit Factory, New York 31/5–2/6/83.

There are still people who think this oft-bootlegged classic was the prototype for the Donna demo of 'Cover Me', when it is obviously an advance on that song's conceit. The final version, recorded on June 2 1983, originally ran for seven minutes but was pruned to a lean, mean 4:35 then slotted between 'None But The Brave' and 'Shut Out The Light' (a great piece of sequencing) on the July 27 1983 *BITUSA* sequence. But still he thought he heard whispering from the other side of the console; finally sacrificing one of his great songs to self-doubt. The song was even omitted from *Tracks*, despite pulling takes 6, 7, 9, 10 and 11 in June 1998 as final selections were being made. Nor did it slip onto *The Essential*, along with 'None But The Brave'. All of which means a generational cassette of the rough mix still has to suffice whenever fans wish to hear what happened when Springsteen dismissed 'Cover Me' and came up with something better.

282. CAR WASH (SMALL TOWN GIRL)
Known studio/demo recordings: The Hit Factory, New York 31/5/83; 30/11/83. [TR]
First documented performance: Bruno-Plache-Stadion, Leipzig, Germany 13/6/99.

Cut the same day they started 'Drop On Down & Cover Me', 'Car Wash' was logged throughout under its original title, 'Small Town Girl'. Although Springsteen returned to it in the fall of 1983, it was never part of the July album-sequence. Pleasant pop fare from the perspective of a Jersey girl dreaming on her job at the car wash, it has its moments; notably, 'Someday I'll sing in a night club/ I'll get a million-dollar break/ A handsome man will come here with a contract in his hand/ And say, "Catherine, this has all been some mistake."'

283. NONE BUT THE BRAVE
Known studio/demo recordings: The Hit Factory, New York 6, 13+27/6/83. [TE]
First documented E Street performance: GM Place, Vancouver BC 31/3/08.

A song which has something of the flavour of Springsteen's 1976 liner-notes to the Southside Johnny LP, *I Don't Wanna Go Home*. And there's a touch of Southside Johnny about the arrangement, too; an uplifting roar of affirmation in which the E Street Band go higher and higher. . He was still working on the song as the sessions closed down, and mixing began. As good as these sessions get.

284. STAND ON IT
Known studio/demo recordings: The Hit Factory, New York 16/6/83. [TR]*
First documented performance: Giants Stadium, East Rutherford NJ 31/8/85.

A can-they-still-cut-it workout, 'Stand On It' became a B-side, a cut on the *Ruthless People* film soundtrack, and in its original, fuller guise (with the extra observation 'Well if you've lost control of the situation at hand/ Go grab a girl; go see a rock and roll band'), one of sixty-six *Tracks*. It also got a handful of belated outings at the scrag-end of the *BITUSA* tour, where stadium crowds were mostly too busy whooping and buying hot dogs to notice some little doses of humour in there like: 'Well now, Columbus he discovered America even though he hadn't planned on it/ He got lost and woke up one morning when he's about to land on it.'

285. JANEY DON'T YOU LOSE HEART

Known studio/demo recordings: The Hit Factory, New York 16/6/83. [TR]

First documented performance: Memorial Coliseum, Los Angeles 27/9/85.

If, as Max Weinberg has suggested, the June 16 session was the occasion when they finally cut an E Street 'Pink Cadillac' – though the logs say it was captured a fortnight earlier – then this really was The Night of The Lost B-Sides. 'Janey Don't You Lose Heart', like 'Stand On It', would not be attempted again at the remaining *BITUSA* sessions (though a session in summer 1985 allowed Nils Lofgren to dub new backing vocals on there). Originally the closing track on the 1983 *BITUSA*, it took a couple of lines apiece from 'Baby I'm So Cold' and 'True Love Is Hard To Come By', and added a spirit of affirmation those tracks denied.

286. BOBBY JEAN

Known studio/demo recordings: The Hit Factory, New York 28/7/83; 10/10/83. [BITUSA]

First documented performance: Civic Arena, St Paul MN 29/6/84.

On 26 and 27 July 1983 Springsteen, Landau and Plotkin made a 'rough mix' assembly of the next E Street Band album, which clocked in at a hefty fifty minutes. The following day, Springsteen brought the band in and cut eight takes of a new song, 'Bobby Jean'; which they probably knew was Brucespeak for the album's on the backburner again. The point at which he stopped saying anything new at these sessions.

XXVI) 287–300. Songs recorded for *Born In The USA* September 1983–February 1984:

287. BROTHERS UNDER THE BRIDGES

Known studio/demo recordings: The Hit Factory, New York 14–16/9/83; 10/10/83. [TR]

On its official release in 1998, what took everyone hearing this oft-rumoured song by surprise was the pugnacious performance it received, notably a sassy sax solo from the Big Man. All somewhat at odds with the song's sentiments, which would not have been out of place on *Nebraska*.

288. NO SURRENDER

Known studio/demo recordings: The Hit Factory, New York 25–27/10/83;

29/11/83. [BITUSA]

First documented performance: Civic Arena, St Paul MN 29/6/84.

Recorded in late October in the form later released, Springsteen looked at the song again on November 29 and, according to the tape notes, made 'an acoustic remake with Chuck Plotkin'. Though he ultimately reverted to the more bellicose original, it took Little Steven to all-but-demand its inclusion on an eleven-track *BITUSA*. Still undecided, Bruce took both arrangements on the road with him.

289. GLORY OF LOVE

Known studio/demo recordings: The Hit Factory, New York 16/9/83.

290. SHUT DOWN

291. 100 MILES FROM JACKSON

Known studio/demo recordings: The Hit Factory, New York 26/10/83.

292. ROLL AWAY THE STONE

293. SWOOP MAN

294. UNDER THE BIG SKY

Known studio/demo recordings: The Hit Factory, New York 30/11/83.

295. REFRIGERATOR BLUES

Known studio/demo recordings: The Hit Factory, New York 16/2/84.

296. IDA ROSE (NO ONE KNOWS)

Known studio/demo recordings: The Hit Factory, New York 20/2/84.

Ever the optimist, Springsteen thought that when he resumed recording in September 1983 he'd be done in a matter of days. Five months later, when doing final mixes on the eleven or twelve tracks that constituted the latest version of the album, he was still bringing new things to the party. The February day he brought some last-minute tweaks to 'Dancing in the Dark', he also produced 'Refrigerator Blues'. Four days later, mixing 'My Love Will Not Let You Down', he produced 'Ida Rose (No One Knows)'. Born too late to make *BITUSA*, 'Ida Rose' was deemed worthy of inclusion on the 1993 'rarities' reels, as was 'Glory of Love', a song recorded the previous September.

In fact, in the months that separate these two wholly forgotten songs, Springsteen recorded enough tracks for *another* E Street album, had he not already got two albums' worth in the can. At least this time he kept a lid on these songs. Not one of the eleven songs recorded at these sessions but omitted from

BITUSA have passed into the world of collectors. Three of them would, however, be slotted onto *Tracks*. None of the others would be heard of again, although 'Under The Big Sky', a song he seemingly rediscovered in the process of compiling *Tracks,* was apparently recorded afresh in April 1998 (as 'Under A Big Sky').

297. MAN AT THE TOP
298. ROCK AWAY THE DAYS
Known studio/demo recordings: The Hit Factory, New York 12/1/84. [TR]
First documented performance [#297]: Alpine Valley, East Troy WI 12/7/84.

Not sure how he wanted 'Man At The Top' to sound, Springsteen tried it 'fast acoustic' and 'slow acoustic' on January 12. The former, which almost qualifies as country-rock, is presumably the one on *Tracks*. The slow version provided the template for the couple of times he gave such feelings rein on the *BITUSA* tour, two of his best acoustic performances of the era. A pro-shot video of the 1985 Washington performance circulates and is worthy enough, but it is the first live performance at Alpine Valley in July 1984 which really suggests someone fully cognisant with the dangers of brandishing that double-edged sword. 'Rockaway The Days', a more affirmative song, cut the same day, also seems to have come surprisingly easily (the February 3 date attributed to it on *Tracks* was presumably a mixing session). [See discussion in main text pp. 272–73]

299. DANCING IN THE DARK
Known studio/demo recordings: The Hit Factory, New York 14/2/84. [BITUSA]
First documented performance: Civic Arena, St Paul MN 29/6/84.

Guy gets up in the evening. Got nuthin' to say. But says it anyway. His manager, the schmuck, can't hear a single hit single on an album that will generate seven of 'em, every one Top Ten. So he gets to work. Turns on the radio – a Classic Rock station. They're playing last year's model – The Police, 'Every Breath You Take'. Hey, I can do that. Clipped lines, repetitious riff, synth wash, go schmoozing in the dark, Cyd and me. The next day, back in the studio, time to spring it on the band, and his co-producers. Whaddya think? Well, it ain't gonna make no dove cry, but what the hell! They try it six times, extended intro, extended outro, are we done? Fifty-eight mixes later, they are. It's March 8 now, and the album needs to be put to bed. Oh, you know what, we need a promo video, 'cause with the right MTV coverage, y'know, sky's the limit....

300. BENEATH THE FLOODLINE

First documented performance: The Spectrum, Philadelphia PA Soundcheck 17/9/84.

According to Brucebase, 'Beneath The Floodline' was 'one of the final tracks recorded at the [*BITUSA*] sessions.' Not according to the Sony logs, it wasn't. The first time the song popped up was at a coupla soundchecks in the summer of 1984, one of which, at the Philadelphia Spectrum, some enterprising taper caught. But, aside from the title phrase and a strong melody line, it is almost impossible to discern what the song is actually about. Nor was the song attempted at the *Tunnel of Love* sessions, as also rumoured. However, just like 'Cynthia' and 'Under The Big Sky', it was considered ripe for resurrection in the mid-nineties, a song of the same name being recorded at several solo sessions between November 1997 and January 1998, before the E Street Band were reconstructed and the song was quietly sidelined, along with the album he was then working on.

[Note: Since mention is made a few times of a 1993 compilation for an archival project (which presumably became *Tracks*), the (mouth-watering) track-listing is as follows:

A Love so Fine, Sha La La (live from C.W. Post). New Spanish. Hearts of Stone. Give The Girl A Kiss. Dollhouse. Night Fire. The Man Who Got Away. King's Highway. Triangle Song. Do (You) Want Me To Say All Right. Arnie. I Will Be The One. [From Small Things,] Big Things [One Day Come]. Take 'Em As They Come. Johnny Go Down. The Glory of Love. Ida Rose (No One Knows). Bring On The Night. Under The Gun. Where The Bands Are. Loose Ends. Living On The Edge of the World. Angelyne. That's Okay.]

Acknowledgments

This book – though it comes relatively quickly on the heels of my *All the Madmen* (Constable, 2011) – has been a long time coming. I have always wanted to do a history of the E Street Band era, but in the immediate aftermath of their 1989 disbandment the climate did not seem right; and after catching the first rays of reunion, I have to admit I listened to Bruce's music – old and new – less and less. What first set me thinking along these lines again were the performances Springsteen & the E Street Band gave of the albums they had made between 1972 and 1984 in their sequential entireties at the end of the 2009 tour – performances so fresh and committed that they made me look again at those songs. Hard on the heels of the general circulation of these shows (in what I like to call their 'hearing aid' versions) came Springsteen's own 2010 recasting of the *Darkness* sessions, the 2-CD *Promise* and – altogether more enticing and authoritative – the *Darkness On The Edge of Town* boxed-set, a triple-DVD, triple-CD extravaganza housed in a remarkably well-executed facsimile of one of Bruce's 1977 notebooks. I dived in.

Immediately, I wanted to know more about the sessions, and in particular whatever happened to some of the things he still saw fit to omit from his official oeuvre – could he really have decided 'Preacher's Daughter' was less deserving of release than 'Outside Looking In'? What about all those songs he demoed the first night at Atlantic (1 June 1977)? My good friend Glenn Korman, archivist extraordinaire, showed me just how much *Darkness* material was catalogued in the Sony database. And a book-idea was born. So my first and most fulsome thanks go to Glenn, who once again couldn't have been more generous with his time and expertise, helping me to construct – for the first time, I believe – an authoritative studio chronology of the E Street era using Sony's own documentation.

The next candidate I wish to put forward for Saint in New York City status is Mike Appel. I had always thought that Appel's role in the rise of Bruce Springsteen had been somewhat muddied by the Marsh-man. With no love lost between Springsteen's ex-manager and rock scribe Dave Marsh, the latter's two-pronged bios, *Born To Run* and *Glory Days*, were bound to minimize the Appel contribution to Springsteen's climb to the top. And with the field of Brucebiography to himself until the nineties, Marsh lore became rocklore. Marc Elliott's *Down Thunder Road* (1992) gave Appel's side of the story for the first time, but Elliott was himself hamstrung by a poor sense of Springsteen's musical graph and the seventies music industry's own workings (despite once writing a book called *Rockanomics*). Thankfully, Appel graciously agreed to sit down and answer all the questions I couldn't find the answers to in previous tomes. And when, after three hours, the hubbub of the Roosevelt Hotel bar got too much, he allowed me to persevere with my queries via email and even unto the diners of Brooklyn. I found a man as generous with his opinions as he was with his time. Thank you, Mike.

If Mike Appel's role in the formulation of the E Street sound and live reputation has gone under-recognized, so has the contribution of Vini 'Mad Dog' Lopez. Though he had been interviewed a number of times previously, again the one man who had been an integral part of Child, Steel Mill, Dr Zoom, the Bruce Springsteen Band and the first two incarnations of the E Street Band gave up an afternoon to answer my questions and allow me to pry into his painful removal from the band that had been his life. He remains, for me, the most sympathetic stickman Springsteen ever had.

Another aspect of the E Street history that I felt had been lacking in previous accounts was the whys and wherefores of his relationship with label and management, i.e. the general 'branding of Bruce' in the aftermath of the dissolution of the Appel management set-up. Tying the strands together required the unstinting help of the redoubtable Debbie Gold, the urbane Dick Wingate and the garrulous Paul Rappaport, all of them mainstays of Springsteen's transformation from *Newsweek* cover to bona fide rock star between 1975 and 1980, and none of them interviewed in depth before. Between them, they gave me my own golden triangle.

God bless y'all. Leo Hollis, Andreas Campomar and Kevin Doughten were my estimable E Street editors. Fanx ta-ra.

Others who talked to tape included Lenny Kaye, wearing both his rock scribe hat and PSG guitarist, as he regaled me with his own Bruceian anecdotes; Joel Bernstein, wearing his sometime-rock photographer hat, and equally forthcoming about his brief sojourn in Springsteen's inner circle in 1979–80; and Alan Vega, who recalled his experiences at Power Station in the year he and Springsteen were each engaged on making their first statement of the eighties. *Muchas gracias*.

Of others who helped, directly and indirectly, connect the dots, one has been this book's unstinting cheerleader, Erik Flannigan, keeper of a number of keys and general good guy and solid friend. Been a long time since we risked the slings and arrows of a panel at the *Badlands* Springsteen Convention, huh, Erik? Another old-time Springsteen stalwart, Dan French, agreed to renew our acquaintance and answered many an impertinent query. And Steve Jump at Badlands was, as ever, his irascibly helpful self. Especial thanks for putting me in touch with Stan Goldstein and Jean Mikle, who gave me their own private guided tour of Asbury Park complete with local colouring.

Scott Curran and Nick Carruthers have allowed me to raid their Bruce archives over the years and kept me up-to-date in all things grey. Music librarian extraordinaire Steve Shepherd, as ever, responded to book requests and used his ILL skills on my behalf. Mitch Blank dug into the David Gahr collection at Getty on my solicitous behalf. Kevin Avery kindly provided me with a transcript of his own 2007 interview with Bruce in memoriam of the late, great Paul Nelson, and put me in touch with Paul's son, Mark, who agreed to allow me access to his father's audio archives. Brian Magid gave me useful background on the so-called Mike Batlan tapes and the early days. Also, much thanks are due to those who helped me accumulate a Springsteen paper archive of sorts over the years, especially Simon Gee and Craig Wood, whose industrious work in the eighties has gone unacknowledged till now. Pete Russell responded promptly and courteously to queries about information on Brucebase, the online resource which he oversees with remarkable enthusiasm and energy. Finally, thanks to Ed Kazinski, Jeremy Tepper, Robert Duncan, Dan Levy and Chris Phillips for letting me bug you about the tiniest matter. Guys, it's been a blast . . .

– Clinton Heylin, June 2012

Selected Bibliography

(i) Unpublished sources

Avery, Kevin – Transcript of interview w/ Bruce Springsteen, August 21, 2007. © Kevin Avery. Used with permission.

Landau, Jon – Memo to Fred Humphrey, 26/10/78.

Nelson, Paul – Interview w/ Bruce Springsteen, December 1972. [audio] © Mark Nelson. Used with permission.

Nelson, Paul – Interview w/ Jon Landau, 1978. [audio] © Mark Nelson. Used with permission.

Sony database of Bruce Springsteen tapes held, as of 2010.

Tannen, Michael – Letter to Dick Wingate, 26/1/77, relaying Springsteen's instructions re forthcoming tour.

Wingate, Dick – internal CBS memos circa 1977–78 & sales projections for Darkness LP.

(ii) Books

There is no shortage of books on Springsteen, though a bewildering number of these address his apparent blue-collar credentials, the American-ness of his work and 'the phenomenon' of his success, carefully circumventing the man and his actual music. Below are the books that I have referred to and referenced (those I have quoted on more than a couple of occasions herein have been given a square bracket 'code', to delineate when I have done so):

Coles, Robert – *Bruce Springsteen's America* (Random House, 2003).

Cross, Charles R. & editors of Backstreets – *Springsteen: The Man and his Music* (Harmony Books, 1989).

Cusic, Don (ed.) – *Hank Williams: The Complete Lyrics* (St Martin's Press, 1993).

Dannen, Fredric – *Hit Men: Power Brokers & Fast Money Inside the Music Business* (Muller, 1990).

Davis, Clive w/ James Willwerth – *Clive: Inside the Record Business* (Ballantine Books, 1976).

Elder, Lynn – *You Better Not Touch: The Complete Bruce Springsteen Bootleg CD Guide* (pp, nd).

Eliot, Marc, w/ Mike Appel – *Down Thunder Road: The Making of Bruce Springsteen* (Plexus, 1992). [DTR]

Flanagan, Bill – *Written In My Soul* (Contemporary Books, 1986).

French, Dan – *Songs To Orphans* (pp, nd).

Gee, Simon – *Looking For That Million Dollar Sound* (pp, 1986).

George-Warren, Holly & editors of *Rolling Stone* – *Bruce Springsteen: The Rolling Stone Files* (Hyperion, 1996). [see section iv for itemized features of note – all of which are contained herein.]

Gilmore, Mikal – *Night Beat: A Shadow History of Rock & Roll* (Doubleday, 1998).

Gold & Appel (ed.) – *Follow That Dream: The Unreleased Lyrics of Bruce Springsteen 1972–1985* (pp, 1987).

Goldsmith, Lynn – *PhotoDiary* (Rizzoli, 1995).

Goodman, Fred – Mansion on the Hill: Dylan, Young, Geffen, Springsteen . . . (Times Books, 1997). [MOTH]

Hammond, John Snr. w/ Irving Townsend – *John Hammond on Record: An Autobiography* (The Ridge Press, 1977).

Heylin, Clinton & Gee, Simon – *The E Street Shuffle: Springsteen & The E Street Band In Performance 1972–1988* (pp, 1989).

Heylin, Clinton – *Dylan Behind the Shades: The 20th Anniversary Edition* (Faber, 2011).

Heylin, Clinton (ed.) – *The Penguin Book of Rock & Roll Writing* (Penguin, 1992).

Hilburn, Robert – *Bruce Springsteen: Born In The USA* (Sidgwick & Jackson, 1985).

Himes, Geoffrey – *Born In The USA* (Continuum Books, 2005).

Humphries, Patrick & Hunt, Chris – *Springsteen: Blinded by the Light* (Plexus, 1985).

Jones, Allan (ed.) – *Springsteen: The Ultimate Music Guide* (Uncut, 2010).

Lynch, Kate – *Springsteen: No Surrender* (Proteus, 1984).

Marsh, Dave – *Born To Run: The Bruce Springsteen Story* (Dell, 1981). [BTR]

Marsh, Dave – *Glory Days: Bruce Springsteen in the 1980s* (Pantheon Books, 1987). [GD]

Meyer, Marianne – *Bruce Springsteen* (Ballantine Books, 1984).

Nobakht, David – *Suicide: No Compromise* (SAF, 2005).

O'Connor, Flannery – *Collected Works* (The Library of America, 1988).

Prial, Dunstan – *The Producer: John Hammond & the Soul of American Music* (Farrar-Strauss, 2006).

Rodenrijs, Jan – *Wanted: The Bruce Springsteen Bootleg Guide* (pp, 1994).

Rodenrijs, Jan – *Wanted: The Bruce Springsteen Bootleg Guide Vol. 2* (pp, 1995).

Sandford, Christopher – *Springsteen Point Blank* (Warner Books, 1999). [PB]

Sawyer, June Skinner (ed.) – *Racing In The Street: The Bruce Springsteen Reader* (Penguin, 2004). [see also section (iv) for itemized features of note – marked RITS]

Scaduto, Anthony – *Bob Dylan: An Intimate Biography* (Grosset & Dunlap, 1971).

Shelton, Robert – *No Direction Home* (NEL, 1986).

Smith, Larry David – *Bob Dylan, Bruce Springsteen & American Song* (Praeger, 2002).

Springsteen, Bruce – *Songs* (Avon Books, 1998).

Stewart, Michael – *Bruce Springsteen* (Star Books, 1985).

Sweeting, Adam – *Springsteen: Visions of America* (Holborn Group, 1985).

Whitburn, Joel (ed.) – *The Billboard Book of Top Forty Albums* (Billboard Books, 1995).

Yetnikoff, Walter w/ David Ritz – *Howling at the Moon: Confessions of a Music Mogul in an Age of Excess* (Abacus, 2004).

(iii) Fanzines (in chronological order)

Thunder Road [US] – 5 issues, February 1978–1980.

Candy's Room [UK] – 7 issues, Summer 1980–1985.

Point Blank [UK] - 11 issues, 1980–1988.

Backstreets [US] – 90 issues to date, 198[2]–present.

Wanted [Holland] – 5 issues, December 1997–December 1999.

For True Rockers Only [UK] – 20 issues, 1989–1996.

The Ties That Bind [UK] – 14 issues, 1996–1999.

(iv) Magazine articles

For a full magazine bibliography, I would refer readers to the online listings for the Bruce Springsteen collection previously housed at the Asbury Park Library, and recently removed to Monmouth College [www.brucespringsteenspecialcollection.net] Items in bold highlight interviews with Springsteen himself:

??? – Interview w/ Southside Johnny, MM 15/8/81.

Anon. – 'The Lost Interviews Part One', Swedish interview w/ Bruce Springsteen, 11/75, *Backstreets* #57 [Winter 1997].

Anon. – 1986 Folk/Rock interview w/ Jon Landau [translation by Chantal Constant], *Backstreets* #21. [Summer 1987].

Ahrens, Susan – Interview w/ Bruce Springsteen, *Good Times*, February 1975.

Allan, Steven – Interview w/ Suki Lahav, *Backstreets* #16 [Winter/Spring 1986].

Altman, Billy – Review of *The River*, *Creem* 1/81.

Backstreets (eds.) – 'Rockin' All Over the World', Report on overseas leg of BITUSA tour, *Backstreets* #14. [Summer 1985].

Backstreets (eds.) – 'Superbruce', Report on final US leg of BITUSA tour, *Backstreets* #15 [Fall 1985].

Backstreets (eds.) – 'This Is Not a Dark Ride', Tunnel of Love Express report, *Backstreets* #25 [Summer 1988].

Backstreets (eds.) – 'Walk Like a Man', Tunnel of Love Express report II, *Backstreets* #26 [Fall 1988].

Bangs, Lester – Review of *Greetings*, *Rolling Stone* 5/7/73.

Bangs, Lester – Review of Born To Run, *Creem* 11/75.

Berman, Marshall – 'Blowin' Away The Lies', *Village Voice* 9/12/86.

Bohn, Chris – Review of *Nebraska*, *NME* 25/9/82.

Bream, Jon – Interview w/ Bruce Springsteen, *Creem* 1/85.

Bull, Debby – Review of *BITUSA*, *Rolling Stone* 19/7/84.

Bull, Debby – 'Bruce In The Heartland', *Rolling Stone* 18/6/84.

Burchill, Julie – Review of *The River*, *NME* 11/10/80.

Cain, Barry – Interview w/ Bruce Springsteen, *Record Mirror* 25/11/78.

Carr, Roy – Review of *Born To Run*, *NME* 6/9/75.

Carr, Roy – 'The Album You Won't Hear', *NME* 22/12/79.

Carr, Roy – 'Jimmy Iovine & the Gentle Art of Production', *NME* 24/11/79.

Carr, Roy – Interview w/ Steve Van Zandt, *NME* 20/11/82.

Cocks, Jay – 'The Backstreet Phantom of Rock', interview w/ Bruce Springsteen, *Time* 27/10/75.

Cohen, Mitch – Review of *Darkness*, *Creem* 9/78.

Coleman, Ray – Interview w/ Bruce Springsteen, *Melody Maker* 15/11/75.

Connelly, Christopher – Preview of *Nebraska*, *Rolling Stone* 14/10/82.

Cook, Richard – 'A Love Supreme', *Sounds* 2/7/88.

Cross, Charles R. – Interview w/ Southside Johnny, *Backstreets* #12 [Winter 1985].

Cross, Charles R. & Flannigan, Erik – 'Get Up Stand Up', *Backstreets* #27 [Winter 1989].

Cross, Charles R. – 'Hiding on the Back of the Sheet', *Backstreets* #57 [Winter 1997].

Dadomo, Giovanni – 'Bruce in Boots', review of *Fire on the Fingertips*, *Sounds* 1979.

Dawson, Walter – Interview w/ Bruce Springsteen, *Memphis Commercial Appeal* 16/7/78.

Deevoy, Adrian, Transcript of St. Paul press conference 1/7/84, [???].

DiMartino, Dave – Interview w/ Bruce Springsteen, *Creem* 1/81.

Du Noyer, Paul – Review of Wembley Arena show, *NME* 6/6/81.

Duncan, Robert – Interview w/ Bruce Springsteen, *Creem* 1/76.

Duncan, Robert – 'Bruce Springsteen's Longest Season', Creem 4/77.

Duncan, Robert – Interview w/ Bruce Springsteen, *Creem* 10/78.

Emerson, Ken – Review of *The Wild, The Innocent*, *Rolling Stone* 31/1/74.

Fielder, Hugh – Review of Wembley Arena show, *Sounds* 6/6/81.

Flanagan, Bill – Interview w/ Bruce Springsteen, *Musician* November 1984.

Flippo, Chet – Interview w/ Bruce Springsteen 8/84. *Time Out* 9–15/5/85.

Franklin, Linda – 'So How Does It Feel to Marry The Boss?', ???

Fricke, David – Review of Live 75—85, *Rolling Stone* 15/1/87.

'Genie, Eugene' – 'Funky Punk Bruce Slays L.A.', *NME* 25/10/75.

Gilbert, Jerry – Interview w/ Bruce Springsteen, *Sounds* 16/3/74.

Gilbert, Jerry – Interview w/ Bruce Springsteen, *Zigzag* #45 [September 1974].

Gilbert, Jerry – Review of *Born To Run*, *Sounds* 13/9/75.

Gilmore, Mikal – Interview w/ Bruce Springsteen, *Rolling Stone* 5/11/87.

Gilmore, Mikal – 'Voice of the Decade', *Rolling Stone* 15/11/90.

Grabel, Richard – Review of Meadowlands gig, *Sounds* 1/9/84.

Hagen, Mark – Interview w/ Bruce Springsteen, *Mojo* #62 [January 1999].

Henke, James – Interview w/ Bruce Springsteen, *Rolling Stone* 6/8/92.

Henke, Jim – Interview w/ Bruce Springsteen, *Backstreets* #89 [Summer 2010].

Hepworth, David – Interview w/ Bruce Springsteen, *Q* #71 [August 1992].

Hewitt, Paolo – Review of *The River, Melody Maker* [11/10/80].

Hewitt, Paolo – Interview w/ Bruce Springsteen, **Melody Maker** 9/5/81.

Hewitt, Paolo – Review of Wembley Arena show, *MM* [6]/6/81.

Hewitt, Paolo – Review of Nebraska, Melody Maker [25/9/82].

Hilburn, Robert – Interview w/ Bruce Springsteen, *Melody Maker* 24/8/74 & *Thunder Road* #1.

Hilburn, Robert – Interview w/ Bruce Springsteen, *LA Times* 2/7/78.

Hilburn, Robert – Review of Nebraska, LA Times 19/9/82.

Hogan, Peter – 'Tunnel Vision', *MM* 2/7/88.

Humphries, Patrick – Review of Manchester Apollo show, *MM* 23/5/81.

Humphries, Patrick – Review of *Nebraska, World Music* 21/9/82.

Irwin, Colin – Interview w/ Warren Zevon, *MM* 1980.

Katz, Robin – Interview w/ Bruce Springsteen, *Street Life* 1–14/11/75.

Kent, Nick – Review of *No Nukes, NME* 22/12/79.

Kirkup, Martin – Interview w/ Bruce Springsteen, *Sounds* 31/8/74.

Kent, Nick – 'Springsteen: Forged Passports To A Promised Land', *NME* 4/7/81.

Knobler, Peter – 'Who Is Bruce Springsteen . . . ?', interview w/ Bruce Springsteen, *Crawdaddy* 3/73. [RITS]

Knobler, Peter – 'Running On The Backstreets', Crawdaddy 10/75.

Knobler, Peter – 'Wounded in the Badlands', *review of Darkness, Crawdaddy* 8/78.

Knobler, Peter – Interview w/ Bruce Springsteen, *Crawdaddy* 10/78.

Kubernik, Harvey – 'Springsteen: re-born & running again', *MM* 27/5/78.

Leyland, Don – Interview w/ Bruce Springsteen, *Sounds* 18/10/75.

Loder, Kurt – Interview w/ Bruce Springsteen, *Rolling Stone* 6/12/84.

Lombardi, John – 'Saint Boss', *Esquire* December 1988.

Mann, Billy – 'The Final Screw?', review of *Live 75–85*, *Sounds* 15/11/86.

Marcus, Greil – 'Between Rock and A Hard Place', *New West* 2/7/79.

Marcus, Greil – Review of *Born To Run*, *Rolling Stone* 9/10/75.

Marcus, Greil – 'The Man Who Would Save Rock & Roll', *NME* 28/2/81.

Marsh, Dave – Review of *Greetings*, *Creem* 5/73.

Marsh, Dave – 'Walk Tall . . . Or Don't Walk At All', *Creem* 10/74.

Marsh, Dave – Review of the Bottom Line residency, *Rolling Stone* 25/9/75.

Marsh, Dave – 'Little Egypt from Asbury Park', *Creem* 10/75.

Marsh, Dave – Review of *Darkness*, *Rolling Stone* 27/7/78.

Marsh, Dave – 'Bruce Raises Cain', ***Rolling Stone*** **24/8/78.**

Marsh, Dave – Interview w/ Bruce Springsteen, ***Musician*** **2/81.**

Martin, Gavin – Review of *Live 75–85*, *NME* 15/11/86.

Martin, Gavin – Interview w/ Bruce Springsteen, ***NME*** **9/3/96.**

McGee, David – 'Springsteen at New School', *Record World* 25/12/76.

McGee, David – 'Bruce Springsteen reclaims the future', Rolling Stone 11/8/77.

McGee, David – 'Little Steven on Main Street, USA', *Record* September 1984.

McGee, David – 'Blinded By The Hype', *NME* 18/7/87.

McLeese, Don – Interview w/ Bruce Springsteen, ***Record World*** **October 1984.**

Meltzer, Richard – 'The Meaning of Bruce', in *Penguin Book of Rock and Roll Writing*.

Meola, Eric – In Conversation with Mike Appel, *Backstreets* #90 [Winter 2011/12].

Mitchell, Greg – Interview w/ Bruce Springsteen, ***Sounds*** **6/9/75.**

Morley, Paul – 'The Springsteen Syndrome', NME 6/10/79.

Murray, Charles Shaar – Review of *Greetings From Asbury Park & The Wild, The Innocent*, *NME* 1/2/75.

Murray, Charles Shaar – 'The Sprucing of the Springbean', *NME* 11/10/75.

Nelson, Paul – 'Is Springsteen Worth The Hype?', *Village Voice* 25/8/75.

Nelson, Paul – 'Springsteen Fever', *Rolling Stone* **13/7/78.**

Nelson, Paul – Review of *The River*, Rolling Stone 12/11/80.

Nesin, Jeff – Review of *Born In The USA*, *Creem* 9/84.

O'Grady, Lorraine – 'A Critic's Look at Bruce Springsteen', *Playback* 2/74.

Orth, Maureen – 'Making of a Rock Star', *Newsweek* 27/10/75.

Parsons, Tony – 'Blinded By the Hype', *NME* 9/10/76.

Parsons, Tony – 'Bruce Is the Word', *NME* 14/10/78.

Percy, Will – Interview w/ Bruce Springsteen, ***Double Take*** **Spring 1998. [RITS]**

Phillips, Christopher – 'Guitar Man: The Nils Lofgren Interview', *Backstreets* #74 [Spring/Summer 2002].

Phillips, Christopher – Interview w/ Bruce Springsteen, *Backstreets* #80 [Summer/Fall 2004].

Phillips, Christopher – Interview w/ Bruce Springsteen, *Backstreets* #87 [Spring 2008].

Pond, Steve – Review of *Nebraska*, *Rolling Stone* 28/10/82.

Pond, Steve – Review of *Tunnel of Love*, *Rolling Stone* 3/12/87.

Rambali, Paul – Review of *Darkness*, *NME* [10/6/78].

Rath, Fred – Interview w/ Bruce Springsteen, *Record Mirror* 22/7/78.

Robertson, Sandy – Preview of *BITUSA*, *Sounds* 9/6/84.

Robinson, Lisa – review of Bottom Line gig, *NME* 30/8/75.

Robinson, Lisa – Interview w/ Bruce Springsteen, *NME* 26/3/77.

Rockwell, John – 'Springsteen's Rock Poetry at its Best', *New York Times* 29/8/75. [RITS]

Rockwell, John – 'New Dylan from New Jersey?', *Rolling Stone* 9/10/75.

Rockwell, John – Review of Buffalo gig, *New York Times* 25/5/78.

Rockwell, John – Interview w/ Bruce Springsteen, *New York Times* 26/5/78.

Rolling Stone [eds.] – 100 Best Singles [inc. 'Born To Run'], *Rolling Stone* 8/9/88.

Rolling Stone [eds.] – 100 Greatest Albums of the Eighties [inc. BITUSA], Rolling Stone 16/11/89.

Rose, Cynthia – 'Old Glory Days', *NME* 5/10/85.

Sacks, Leo – 'Springsteen Speaks', ??? June 1978.

Santinelli, Robert – Interview w/ Vini Lopez, *Backstreets* #15 [Fall 1985].

Santinelli, Robert – Interview w/ Boom Carter, *Backstreets* #17 [Summer 1986].

Santinelli, Robert – Interview w/ Vini Roslin, *Backstreets* #19 [Winter 1987].

Santinelli, Robert – Interview w/ George Theiss, B*ackstreets* #20 [Spring 1987].

Santinelli, Robert – 'Exit Off E Street', *Backstreets* #42 [Spring 1993].

Schruers, Fred – 'Bruce Springsteen & The Secret of the World', *Rolling Stone* 5/2/81.

Schwartz, Tony – 'Springsteen Resprung', *Newsweek* 5/6/78.

Sciaky, Ed – Transcript of interview w/ Bruce Springsteen on WIOQ 8/78, *Thunder Road* #3 [Spring 1979].

Silverton, Pete – Review of *Darkness, Sounds* 10/6/78.

Simmons, Sylvie – Interview w/ Bruce Springsteen, Sounds 29/7/78.

Springsteen, Bruce – Transcript of induction speech for Bob Dylan at R'n'R Hall of Fame 1/88, *Backstreets* #24.

Springsteen, Bruce – sleeve-notes to *Greatest Hits* (Sony, 1995).

– sleeve-notes to *The Essential Bruce Springsteen*, 3-CD edition (Sony, 2003).

–sleeve-notes to *Hammersmith Odeon, London '75* (Sony, 2006).

– 2010 sleeve-notes, lyric drafts and related ephemera, circa 1976–77, in *The Promise:The Darkness On The Edge of Town story* (Sony, 2010).

– letter to Jon Landau, circa January 1982, reproduced in *Songs* (Avon Books, 1998).

– transcript of key-note speech @ South By South West, Austin, TX, March 15, 2012 on rollingstone.com.

Springsteen, Bruce – sleeve-notes to *Greatest Hits* (Sony, 1995).

Springsteen, Bruce – sleeve-notes to *The Essential Bruce Springsteen*, 3-CD edition (Sony, 2003).

Springsteen, Bruce – sleeve-notes to *Hammersmith Odeon, London '75* (Sony, 2006).

Springsteen, Bruce – sleeve-notes, lyric drafts A releated ephemera, circa 1976–77, in *The Promise: The Darkness On The Edge of Town Story* (Sony, 2010).

Springsteen, Bruce – letter to Jon Landau, circa January 1982, reproduced in *Songs*. (Avon Books, 1998) pp 137, 140–41.

Springsteen, Bruce – transcript of key-note speech @ South by South West Austin, TX, 15/3/2012 on rollingstone.com.

Sutcliffe, Phil – Interview w/ Bruce Springsteen, *Mojo* #146 [January 2006].

Sutherland, Steve – Review of *Tunnel of Love, MM* 10/10/87.

Swartley, Ariel – '*The Wild, the Innocent & the E Street Shuffle*', in *Stranded*, ed. Greil Marcus (Knopf, 1979).

Sweeting, Adam – Review of *Born In The USA, MM* 28/7/84.

Sweeting, Adam – 'Springsteen: The Boss Is Back', *MM* 8/6/85.

Sweeting, Adam – Interview w/ Bruce Springsteen, *Uncut* #64 [September 2002].

Taylor, Neil – Review of *Tunnel of Love, NME* 10/10/87.

Thrills, Adrian – 'What The Boss Does After Work', *NME* 20/6/81.

Turner, Steve – 'Was Bob Dylan the previous Bruce Springsteen?', *NME* 6/10/73.

Tyler, Andrew – Interview w/ Bruce Springsteen, *NME* 15/11/75.

Tyler, Tony – 'The Buck Stops on E Street', review of Hammersmith gig, *NME* 29/11/75.

Viola, Ken & Cohan, Lou – Interview w/ John Hammond, *Thunder Road* #5 [Winter 1979/80].

[Viola, Ken] – Interview w/ David Sancious, *Thunder Road* #5 [Winter 1979/80].

Waller, Johnny – Review of *Nebraska, Sounds*, 25/9/82.

Waller, Johnny – 'Boss A Nova!', *Sounds* 6/7/85.

Walls, Richard C. – Review of *Nebraska, Creem* 1/83.

Ward, Ed – Review of *The Wild, The Innocent, Creem* 4/74.

Washburn, Jim – 'I Owe Bruce Springsteen $63,536.50: A History of Orange County's Illicit Recording Industry', *O.C. Weekly* 4/4/96.

Watts, Michael – Interview w/ Bruce Springsteen, *Melody Maker* 30/11/74.

Watts, Michael – Interview w/ Bruce Springsteen, *Melody Maker* 22/7/78 [includes quotes from Mike Appel and Jon Landau].

Watts, Michael – Interview w/ Bruce Springsteen, *Guardian* []/5/81.

Werbin, Stuart – 'Bruce Springsteen: It's Sign Up a Genius Month', *Rolling Stone* 26/4/73.

Wheelock, Jim – 'Growin' Up Part 1: Early Asbury Park', Thunder Road #4 [Summer 1979].

Williams, Paul – The Lost Bruce Springsteen Interview 13/10/74, *Backstreets* #24 [Spring 1988]. [RITS]

Williams, Richard – 'A Responsible Rocker', *Sunday Times* 31/5/81.

Wolcott, James – 'The Hagiography of Bruce Springsteen', *Vanity Fair* December 1985. [RITS]

Zeff, Sharisse – Interview w/ Bruce Springsteen, *Upbeat* December 1980.

(v) Websites

Backstreets.com
brucebase.wikispaces.com
Killing Floor database [brucespringsteen.it]
Springsteenlyrics.com
brucespringsteenspecialcollection.net

A Selective Bootleg CD Discography

The official discography of the E Street era – the seven studio albums and a ghastly 3-CD live anthology – has been significantly expanded since 1998, with the release of *Tracks*, *The Essential Bruce Springsteen* (with a bonus disc of rarities), a complete Hammersmith 1975 show, and the 2-CD set of *Darkness* outtakes, *The Promise*. But there remains a substantial body of live and studio recordings from the years 1972–85 available only on bootleg CD (and, as an inevitable by-product, download). Since I remain a fan of the artifact, and since a bootleg CD is likely to exist somewhat longer than some of the website links which afford fans the opportunity to download these precious, unauthorized moments, I have provided a subjectively selective list of recordings that will help fill in the blanks, affirming to anyone with ears the E Street Band's incontestable status as the most consistently great live American rock band of the seventies!

Studio CDs:

Note: Of the four classic vinyl bootlegs of Springsteen studio outtakes – *The Demo Tapes*, *Fire On* the *Fingertips*, *E Ticket* and *Son You May Kiss the Bride* – all save *E Ticket* have been issued on CD (in *Fire On the Fingertips'* case, as the equally splendid *Forgotten Songs*). However, the *Son You May Kiss the Bride* CD should be avoided at all costs, being simply a very poor transfer of the vinyl version. The release of *Tracks* and the unauthorized *Prodigal Son* has rendered *Fire On the Fingertips* largely redundant. As for *E Ticket*, all the tracks can be found on the 2-CD Godfather set, *Running Out of Innocence*. Of the nineteen volumes of *Lost Masters* issued from the Mike Batlan tapes in 1996, a significant number were taken from band rehearsals, recorded with a condenser mike on a ghetto blaster, and probably qualify as 'for completists only'. The few highlights of these rehearsal tapes do, however, appear on the second of the two 2-CD *Essential Lost Masters* anthologies, issued at the same time by Labour of Love. As for the recent 6-CD set of *Darkness* outtakes issued by Godfather – *The Unbroken Promise* – it probably represents overkill, and I have preferred an earlier collection on the inestimable E Street label. In the anthology department, for all its failings in presentation, *The Genuine Tracks* remains the best one-stop shop of Springsteen rarities – live and studio – available in the netherworld of boots. Suffice to say, equally essential is some version of the 1979 single-album he aborted, *The Ties That Bind*; if not the bootleg CD, then the recent upgrade available online.

Prodigal Son (bootleg version) – 2 CDs, Demos & studio o/ts 1972-73 + Berkeley 3/73.

The Demo Tapes – 1972–73 publishing demos.

The Unsurpassed Springsteen Vol. 3: CBS Audition (Yellow Dog) – The John Hammond demos 3/5/72.

Running Out of Innocence (Godfather) – 2 CDs, Studio o/ts 1973–75.

The Definitive Darkness Outtakes Collection (E St. Records) – 2 CDs, Darkness o/ts 1977.

The Ties That Bind – Unreleased 1979 LP.

The Lost Masters Vol. I (Labour of Love) – The 'original' Nebraska tape 1/82.

The Lost Masters Vol. II (Labour of Love) – Darkness o/ts 1977.

The Lost Masters Vol. III (Labour of Love) – Darkness o/ts 1977.

The Lost Masters Vol. IV (Labour of Love) – Rehearsals & demos 1979.

The Lost Masters Vol. X (Labour of Love) – Solo demos 1–4/82.

The Lost Masters Vol. XIII (Labour of Love) – Band rehearsals 1/80.

The Lost Masters Vol. XVI (Labour of Love) – Solo demos 1–4/82.

The Lost Masters Vol. XVII (Labour of Love) – Solo demos 1–4/83.

The Lost Masters Vol. XVIII (Labour of Love) – Solo demos 1–4/83.

The Lost Masters Vol. XIX (Labour of Love) – Born In The USA o/ts 1982–83.

The Lost Masters (Labour of Love) – Essential Collection I. 2 CDs, Demos & studios o/ts 1977–83.

The Lost Masters (Labour of Love) – Essential Collection II. 2 Cds, Studio o/ts, demos & rehearsals 1977–83.

Murder Incorporated: The Lost Masterpiece – Born In The USA o/ts 1982–83.
The Genuine Tracks (Scorpio) – 4 CDs. Misc. studio/live 1972–96.
Deep Down In the Vaults (E St. Records) – 3 CDs. Misc. studio/live 1966–96.

Live CDs:

Note: Remarkably, the twenty-odd-year-old 5-CD boxed-set, *All Those Years*, from the first of the pro-Springsteen bootleg CD labels, Great Dane, remains a terrific collection of great performances from the halcyon days and, save for marginal upgrades in the sonic department, could hardly be bettered, even now. Though Godfather have recently been responsible for a fine series of classic seventies performances of the E Street Band (and beyond), the benchmark for most live Springsteen bootleg CDs was set many years ago by three Springsteen-specialist labels, Crystal Cat, E Street Records and the –R label, Doberman. The first of these continues to match presentation to quality source material in a way that puts most official record labels – and certainly Sony – to shame. Both Godfather and Crystal Cat also maintain a surprising willingness to keep their perennial sellers in print, so many of the following titles should still be available from your local bootleg emporium, should such a thing still exist.

All Those Years (Great Dane) – 5 CDs. Misc live 1971–82.
Max's Kansas City Night (Crystal Cat) – Max's Kansas, NY 31/1/73.
My Father's Place (Great Dane) – My Father's Place, Rosslyn, NY, 31/7/73.
Live From Joe's Place (Godfather) – Joe's Place, Boston, 6/1/74.
The Lost Radio Show (Whoopy Cat) – KLOL, Houston, Tx. 9/3/74.
Rock & Roll Punk (E St. Records) – Harvard Sq. Theatre, Cambridge, Ma. 9/5/74.
Flesh & Fantasy (Doberman) – 2 CDs. Music Hall, Boston, Ma. 29/10/74.
You Can Trust Your Car to the Man With the Star (Labour of Love) – 2 CDs. Main Point, Bryn Mawr, Pa. 5/2/75.
A Star Is Born (Godfather) – 2 CDs. Palace Theater, Providence, RI 20/7/75.
The Roxy Theatre Night (Crystal Cat) – 2 CDs. Roxy, Hollywood, LA 17/10/75.
London Calling – 2 CDs. Hammersmith Odeon, London. 24/11/75.
Mountain of Love (Godfather) – Tower Theatre, Upper Darby, Pa. 31/12/75.
Hidden Worlds That Shine (E St. Records) – 2 CDs. Michigan State Uni., East Lansing, Mi. 4/4/76.

A Selective Bootleg Cd Discography

Runners in the Night (Doberman) – 2 CDs. Allen Theatre, Cleveland, Oh. 7/4/76.

We Gotta Get Out of This Place (Great Dane) – 2 CDs. Palladium, New York 4/11/76.

Higher and Higher (Doberman) – 3 CDs. Music Hall, Boston, Ma. 22–25/3/77.

Roxy Night (Crystal Cat) – 3 CDs. Roxy, Hollywood, LA 7/7/78.

Passaic Night (Crystal Cat) – 3 CDs. Capitol Theater, Passaic, NJ 19/9/78.

Second Night at the Capitol Theater (Godfather) – 3 CDs. Capitol Theater, Passaic, NJ 20/9/78.

Last Night at the Capitol Theater (Godfather) – 3 CDs. Capitol Theater, Passaic, NJ 21/9/78.

Winterland Night (Crystal Cat) – 3 CDs. Winterland, San Francisco. 15/12/78.

Coliseum Night (Crystal Cat) – 3 CDs. Nassau Coliseum, Uniondale, NY 29/12/80.

Follow That Dream (Godfather) – 3 CDs. Isstadion, Stockholm. 7/5/81.

A Night for the Vietnam Veteran (Scorpio) – 3 CDs. Sports Arena, LA 20/8/81.

Alpine Valley Night (Crystal Cat) – 3 CDs. Alpine Valley, East Troy, Wi., 12/7/84.

Where The Rivers Meet (E St. Records) – 3 CDs. Civic Arena, Pittsburgh, PA 22/9/84.

Broken Dreams & Reasons to Believe (Godfather) – 3 CDs. Live versions of Nebraska songs: 1984, 1990, 1996 & 2005.

Greetings From Buffalo, Dream Night (Crystal Cat) – 3 CDs. HSBC Arena, Buffalo, NY 22/11/09.

Index

Page numbers followed by 'fn' indicate a footnote

Index

Index